Lecture Notes in Economics and Mathematical Systems

599

Founding Editors:

M. Beckmann
H.P. Künzi

Managing Editors:

Prof. Dr. G. Fandel
Fachbereich Wirtschaftswissenschaften
Fernuniversität Hagen
Feithstr. 140/AVZ II, 58084 Hagen, Germany

Prof. Dr. W. Trockel
Institut für Mathematische Wirtschaftsforschung (IMW)
Universität Bielefeld
Universitätsstr. 25, 33615 Bielefeld, Germany

Editorial Board:

A. Basile, A. Drexl, H. Dawid, K. Inderfurth, W. Kürsten, U. Schittko

Andrea Consiglio
(Editors)

Artificial Markets Modeling

Methods and Applications

With 84 Figures and 28 Tables

Springer

Professor Andrea Consiglio
Department of Statistics and Mathematics 'Silvio Vianelli'
University of Palermo
Viale delle Scienze - Ed. 13
90128 Palermo
Italy

Library of Congress Control Number: 2007932226

ISSN 0075-8442

ISBN 978-3-540-73134-4 Springer Berlin Heidelberg New York

Springer is a part of Springer Science+Business Media

springer.com

© Springer-Verlag Berlin Heidelberg 2007

Production: LE-TEX Jelonek, Schmidt & Vöckler GbR, Leipzig
Cover-design: WMX Design GmbH, Heidelberg

SPIN 12078806   88/3180YL - 5 4 3 2 1 0   Printed on acid-free paper

Preface

Agent-based computational models, generally named "Artificial economics" (AE), represent a new methodological approach where economies, and more generally social structures, are modeled as evolving systems consisting of heterogeneous interacting agents with some degree of cognitive skills. Assuming a precise mechanism that regulates the interaction among different agents, this approach allows through simulation to compute numerically the aggregate behavior of the economy and to discover the regularities emerging from the micro-behavior of the agents. The AE approach has provoked a great deal of academic interest among social scientists because it represents an alternative to both the fully flexible but not computable and testable descriptive models, and the logical consistent but highly simplified analytical models. With AE the researcher retains much of the flexibility of pure descriptive models in the specification of the interaction structure and the individual behavior, while having the precision and consistency imposed by the computer language. The methodology opens up new avenues for analyzing decentralized, adaptive, emergent systems. The use of computer simulations provides an experimental format allowing free exploration of system dynamics, and, at the same time, the opportunity to check the various unfolding behaviors for plausibility. An early use of agent-based models was by R.M. Axelrod in his research on the evolution of cooperation. He employed extensive computational simulations to study individual strategic behavior in the iterated prisoner's dilemma. This work has stimulated a new approach to game theory based on computational ideas. The research on complex adaptive systems has received a great impulse starting from the mid-eighties with the foundation of the Santa Fe Institute, a non-profit institution specifically devoted to understand the basic principles of human and natural systems, following a multidisciplinary approach and using computer-based modeling. A new field of scientific inquiry, called Artificial Life (AL), has emerged with the aim to study biology by attempting to synthesize biological phenomena such as life, evolution, and ecological dynamics within computers. This approach has led to wider ideas such as complexity, evolution, auto-organization, and emergence that have influenced social scientists. The initial attempts to mix computational methods and social sciences include pioneering AE work in finance, specifically the "Santa Fe Artificial Stock Market Model" of W.B. Arthur, J.H. Holland, B. LeBaron, R.G. Palmer, and P. Taylor. This model, based on bounded rationality and inductive reasoning, has led to a new generation of agent-based computational models aimed to reproduce stock market dynamics and to explain financial market puzzles. Recently, there has been a surge of interest in studying social interaction, the process by which people form and transmit ideas and information. The emergence of this new topic has been driven by the recognition that understanding the formation and dynamics of social networks may represent the missing element to uncover the functioning of complex systems such as asset markets. Agent-Based Computational Economics, with its intrinsic multidisciplinary approach, is gaining increasing recognition in the social sciences. The methodology is now widely used both to compute numerically analytical models and to test them for departures from theoretical assumptions, and to provide stand-alone simulation models for problems that are analytically intractable.

This book collects a selected range of refereed papers that have been gathered in five sections, each of them devoted to one the following topics:

- Macroeconomic Issues
- Market Mechanisms and Agents Behavior
- Market Dynamics and Efficiency
- Analysis of Economic and Social Networks
- Methodological Issues and Applications

The first section includes papers using an agent-based approach to give micro-foundations to macro-economic analyses. The second section is dedicated to papers developing agent-based computational models aimed to investigate the dynamics of financial markets in order to understand their properties. In this section relevant issues such as the fairness of different trading mechanisms and the evaluation of the performance of technical trading are analyzed. The third section is devoted to models simulating the process of market adjustment towards equilibrium. The section covers different interesting applications spanning from the introduction of an option market, to a model with endogenous costly information acquisition. The fourth section is devoted to papers investigating networks formation and evolution with applications to the labor market and to the R&D industry. Finally, the last section includes more methodological contributions and some applications such as a model of the venture capital market where the quality of the investment projects is only imperfectly available and venture capitalists play the function of screening high-quality investments.

I would like to thank all the members of the Scientific Committee for their invaluable effort in refereeing more than 60 papers:

- Frédéric AMBLARD - Université de Toulouse 1, France
- Gérard BALLOT - ERMES, Université de Paris 2, France
- Bruno BEAUFILS - LIFL, USTL, France
- Olivier BRANDOUY - CLAREE, USTL, France
- Charlotte BRUUN, Aalborg University, Denmark
- José Maria CASTRO CALDAS - ISCTE, DINAMIA, Portugal
- Silvano CINCOTTI - University of Genova, Italy
- Christophe DEISSENBERG - GREQAM, France
- Jean-Paul DELAHAYE - LIFL, USTL, France
- Wander JAGER - University of Groningen, The Netherlands
- Marco JANSSEN - Arizona State University, USA
- Philippe LAMARRE - LINA, Université de Nantes, France
- Marco LI CALZI - University of Venice, Italy
- Michele MARCHESI - University of Cagliari, Italy
- Luigi MARENGO - St. Anna School of Advanced Studies, Pisa, Italy
- Philippe MATHIEU - LIFL, USTL, France
- Nicolas MAUDET - Université Paris 9 Dauphine, France
- Akira NAMATAME - National Defense Academy, Japan
- Paolo PELLIZZARI - University of Venice, Italy
- Denis PHAN - Université de Rennes I, France
- Juliette ROUCHIER - GREQAM, France
- Elpida TZAFESTAS - National Technical University of Athens, Greece
- Murat YIDILZOGLU - IFREDE-E3i, Université Montesquieu Bordeaux IV, France
- Stefano ZAMBELLI - Aalborg University, Denmark

A special thank goes to Valerio Lacagnina and Annalisa Russino who helped me for the preparation of this volume.

A final acknowledgment goes to the Ministero dell'Università e della Ricerca that, under the PRIN04 project *"Models for the price dynamics of financial securities: institutional aspects and behavioral assumptions in a agent-based framework"*, contributed to the publishing expenses.

Palermo, August 2007   *Andrea Consiglio*

Contents

Part I Macroeconomic Issues

1 Beyond the Static Money Multiplier: In Search of a Dynamic Theory of Money
Michele Berardi 3

2 Macroeconomic Effects of the Interest Rate Level: Growth and Fluctuations in an Economy with Bank Capital Adequacy Standards
Gianfranco Giulioni 17

3 Monetary Policy Experiments in an Artificial Multi-Market Economy with Reservation Wages
Marco Raberto, Andrea Teglio, Silvano Cincotti 33

Part II Market Mechanisms and Agents Behavior

4 Testing Double Auction as a Component Within a Generic Market Model Architecture
Julien Derveeuw, Bruno Beaufils, Philippe Mathieu, Olivier Brandouy 47

5 A Conceptual Framework for the Evaluation of Agent-Based Trading and Technical Analysis
Olivier Brandouy, Philippe Mathieu 63

6 Which Market Protocols Facilitate Fair Trading?
Marco LiCalzi, Paolo Pellizzari 81

Part III Market Dynamics and Efficiency

7 An Artificial Economics View of the Walrasian and Marshallian Stability
Marta Posada, Cesáreo Hernández, Adolfo López-Paredes 101

8 The Performance of Option–Trading Software Agents: Initial Results
Omar Baqueiro, Wiebe Van der Hoek, Peter McBurney 113

9 Studies on the Impact of the Option Market on the Underlying Stock Market
Sabrina Ecca, Mario Locci, Michele Marchesi 127

10 On Rational Noise Trading and Market Impact
Florian Hauser 141

Part IV Analysis of Economic and Social Networks

11 A Note on Symmetry in Job Contact Networks
Andrea Mario Lavezzi, Nicola Meccheri 157

12 Innovation and Knowledge Spillovers in a Networked Industry
Jose I. Santos, Ricardo del Olmo, Javier Pajares 171

13 Heterogeneous Agents with Local Social Influence Networks: Path Dependence and Plurality of Equilibria in the ACE Noiseless Case
Denis Phan 181

14 Economy-Driven Shaping of Social Networks and Emerging Class Behaviors
Philippe Caillou, Frederic Dubut, Michele Sebag 195

15 Group Effect, Productivity and Segregation Optimality
Raúl Conejeros, Miguel Vargas 209

16 The Grass is Always Greener on the Other Side of the Fence: The Effect of Misperceived Signalling in a Network Formation Process
Simone Giansante, Alan Kirman, Sheri Markose, Paolo Pin 223

Part V Methodological Issues and Applications

17 Market Selection of Competent Venture Capitalists
David Mas 237

**18 A Binary Particle Swarm Optimization Algorithm
for a Double Auction Market**
Calogero Vetro, Domenico Tegolo 249

19 Better-Reply Strategies with Bounded Recall
Andriy Zapechelnyuk 259

List of Contributors

Baqueiro Omar
Department of Computer Science
University of Liverpool, UK
omar@csc.liv.ac.uk

Beaufils Bruno
Laboratoire dInformatique
Fondamentale de Lille
USTL,France
beaufils@lifl.fr

Berardi Michele
School of Social Sciences
University of Manchester, UK
Michele.Berardi@manchester.ac.uk

Brandouy Olivier
Lille Economie et Management
USTL, France
olivier.brandouy@univ-lille1.fr

Caillou Philippe
LRI
Université Paris Sud, France
caillou@lri.fr

Cincotti Silvano
DIBE-CINEF
University of Genova, Italy
cincotti@dibe.unige.it

Del Olmo Ricardo
University of Burgos, Spain
rdelolmo@ubu.es

Conejeros Rául
Department of Biochemical
Engineering
Catholic University of Valparaíso,
Chile
rconejer@ucv.cl

Derveeuw Julien
Laboratoire dInformatique
Fondamentale de Lille
USTL, France
derveeuw@lifl.fr

Dubut Frederic
LRI
Université Paris Sud, France
dubut@lri.fr

Ecca Sabrina
DIEE
University of Cagliari, Italy
sabrina.ecca@diee.unica.it

Giansante Simone
CCFEA
University of Essex, UK
sgians@essex.ac.uk

Giulioni Gianfranco
Department of Quantitative
Methods and Economic Theory
University of Chieti-Pescara,
Italy
g.giulioni@unich.it

Hauser Florian
Department of Banking and
Finance
University School of Management,
Innsbruck, Austria
florian.hauser@uibk.ac.at

Hernández Cesáreo
INSISOC
University of Valladolid, Spain
cesareo@insisoc.org

Kirman Alan
GREQAM
Université dAix Marseille, France
kirman@ehess.univ-mrs.fr

Lavezzi Andrea Mario
Department of Studies on Politics,
Law and Society
University of Palermo, Italy
lavezzi@unipa.it

LiCalzi Marco
Dept. Applied Mathematics and
SSAV
University of Venice, Italy
licalzi@unive.it

Locci Mario
DIEE
University of Cagliari, Italy
mario.locci@diee.unica.it

López-Paredes Adolfo
INSISOC
University of Valladolid, Spain
adolfo@insisoc.org

Marchesi Michele
DIEE
University of Cagliari, Italy
michele@diee.unica.it

Markose Sheri
CCFEA
University of Essex, UK
scher@essex.ac.uk

Mas David
ERMES-CNRS
Université Panthéon-Assas Paris
II, France
David.Mas@u-paris2.fr

Mathieu Philippe
Laboratoire dInformatique
Fondamentale de Lille
USTL, France
mathieu@lifl.fr

McBurney Peter
Department of Computer Science
University of Liverpool, UK
peter@csc.liv.ac.uk

Meccheri Nicola
Department of Economics,
University of Pisa, Italy
meccheri@ec.unipi.it

Pajares Javier
University of Valladolid
pajares@eis.uva.es

Pellizzari Paolo
Dept. Applied Mathematics and
SSAV
University of Venice, Italy
paolop@unive.it

Phan Denis
GEMAS UMR, 8598 CNRS &
University of Paris IV
Sorbonne CREM UMR, 6211
CNRS & University of Rennes 1,
France
dphan@msh-paris.fr

Pin Paolo
Economics Department University of Venice,
and ICTP, Trieste, Italy
pin@unive.it

Posada Marta
INSISOC
University of Valladolid, Spain
posada@insisoc.org

Raberto Marco
DIBE-CINEF
University of Genova, Italy
raberto@dibe.unige.it

Santos Jose I.
University of Burgos, Spain
jisantos@ubu.es

Sebag Michele
LRI
Université Paris Sud, France
sebag@lri.fr

Teglio Andrea
DIBE-CINEF
University of Genova, Italy
teglio@dibe.unige.it

Tegolo Domenico
Department of Mathematics and
Applications
University of Palermo, Italy
tegolo@math.unipa.it

Van der Hoek Wiebe
Department of Computer Science
University of Liverpool, UK
wiebe@csc.liv.ac.uk

Vargas Miguel
Diego Portales
University School of Business,
Chile
miguel.vargas@udp.cl

Vetro Calogero
Department of Mathematics and
Applications
University of Palermo, Italy
vetro@math.unipa.it

Zapechelnyuk Andriy
Center for Rationality
the Hebrew University, Israel
andriy@vms.huji.ac.il

Part I

Macroeconomic Issues

Beyond the Static Money Multiplier: In Search of a Dynamic Theory of Money

Michele Berardi

University of Manchester
School of Social Sciences
Michele.Berardi@manchester.ac.uk

1.1 Introduction

Though we all live in a monetary economy where credit money plays a fundamental role, the process through which money is created in the economy is largely neglected by modern macroeconomic theory. A common approach maintains that the process starts with an exogenous increase in the monetary base made by the central bank, and that this, through a fixed multiplier, gives rise to a proportional increase in the amount of money in the economy. The multiplier is usually taken as constant in this process, at least on short time scales, and most importantly, independent from the money creation process itself. The result is essentially a static, aggregate theory, with very poor behavioral micro-foundations, that completely neglects the *process* through which money is generated in an economy.

As a consequence of this representation, money is taken to be exogenously determined and its quantity explained through changes in the monetary base magnified proportionally by the fixed multiplier. Unfortunately, this theory is not able to provide any insights about the process that generates money in a credit economy, apart from assuming that changes in the monetary stock are originated by central bank interventions, and proportional to them. It misses completely the idea that money is created and destroyed endogenously, through the interactions of the many actors (mainly banks, households and firms) participating in the monetary and credit markets.

An important drawback of the traditional theory, as represented by the static multiplier,[1] is that it does not allow for a proper theory

---

[1] We dub the traditional multiplier as static, to emphasize its lack of attention to the dynamics involved in the process of money creation.

of endogenous money creation that many economists think would be necessary.[2] Presenting the whole process of money creation as a pure deterministic response of the monetary stock to an exogenous change in the monetary base is deeply misleading. In the words of Goodhart (1984), the standard multiplier theory of money creation is " ... such an incomplete way of describing the process of the determination of the stock of money that it amounts to misinstruction".

In modern economies, where the central bank wants to control the interest rate, money is necessarily endogenous to the system as the policymaker must provide enough monetary base so that the equilibrium interest rate on the market is the desired one. Though this fact is often recognized even in standard macroeconomic textbooks, then an exogenous and fixed multiplier is still considered to be the link between the monetary base and the amount of money available in the economy. It is completely neglected the fact that the ratio between these two aggregates can vary according to the behavior of the system and must not be assumed fixed *a priori*.[3]

In this work we take a narrow perspective regarding the creation of money in a credit economy and focus our attention only on its *process*. In particular, our analysis should help explain the short term variability in the amount of money, for the part that can be imputed to the volatility in the multiplier.[4] Our work does not try to analyze the determinants of the behavior of banks and households but puts emphasis on the heterogeneity of the actors involved in the monetary and credit market and tries to provide a better understanding of the dynamics of the process of money creation, stripped down to its mechanics and deprived of any behavioral content. Still, we believe that this approach can provide useful insights and help build a more comprehensive theory of money in a credit economy.

---

[2] Post-Keynesian economists, in particular, have long argued about the need of an endogenous theory of money, one that recognizes the fact that the financial system is able to generate monetary liabilities in response to real sector's needs. But also on the other side of the macroeconomics spectrum (see, e.g., Kydland and Prescott, 1990) there is support for the view of endogenous money.

[3] These issues are somewhat related to the debate between verticalists and horizontalists that was popular in the 1970s. For a detailed exposition and analysis of the two positions, see Moore (1988).

[4] Moore (1988) shows that variations in the monetary base can explain only about 40% of the variability in the M1 aggregate on a monthly base, while this proportion raises to about 65% with quarterly data and to 90% over horizons of one year. Over short time horizons, therefore, a lot of variability in M1 is left unexplained by the standard theory.

1.2 Models of money creation

1.2.1 The static multiplier

Standard macroeconomic theory explains the amount of money available in an economy starting from the monetary base (H), which is composed of currency held by the public (CU) and reserves held by the banking sector (R).[5] The money multiplier is simply derived as the ratio between the monetary base provided by the central bank and a monetary aggregate (M), composed of currency (CU) and deposits (D):[6]

$$H = CU + R \qquad (1.1)$$
$$M = CU + D, \qquad (1.2)$$

from which, dividing everything by D and defining $cu = CU/D$, $re = R/D$, it follows that

$$m = \frac{M}{H} = \frac{1 + cu}{cu + re}. \qquad (1.3)$$

The standard money multiplier represents therefore an aggregate characteristic of the economy, with essentially no behavioral content. Nevertheless, the ratios re and cu are often taken to represent agents' individual preferences, assumed constant and homogeneous. The whole approach is essentially static and neglects completely the process through which money is created.

1.2.2 A dynamic version of the multiplier

We present here a different way to obtain the multiplier: instead of using ratios of aggregate quantities, we consider the dynamic process that unfolds through monetary and credit transactions. We start with an increase in monetary base, in the form of an increase in funds available to the public. Suppose we are in a situation where households have exactly the proportion of cash/deposits (cu) that they wish, and banks have the proportion of reserve/deposit (re) that they want to hold. Therefore households will split the additional funds they receive

---

[5] It is customary not to distinguish between households and firms, and consider them as an aggregate entity (the public). We will follow here this simplification as well.

[6] In this work we will refer to a generic monetary aggregate M, which could be understood as M1 in US or Europe.

between deposits and cash, in the proportion cu. Banks in turn will keep a fraction (re) of the additional deposits they receive as reserves and use the rest to extend new loans (L) to the public, who will split them again into cash and deposits, and the process continues.[7]

From the definitions above, we get that at each step i of the process:[8]

$$CU_i = \frac{cu}{1 + cu} L_i \tag{1.4}$$

$$D_i = \frac{1}{1 + cu} L_i \tag{1.5}$$

$$L_{i+1} = (1 - re) D_i \tag{1.6}$$

which lead to

$$M_i = \left(\frac{1 - re}{1 + cu}\right)^i M_0 \tag{1.7}$$

and therefore

$$m = \frac{\sum_{i=0}^{\infty} M_i}{M_0} = \sum_{i=0}^{\infty} \left(\frac{1 - re}{1 + cu}\right)^i = \frac{1}{1 - \frac{1-re}{1+cu}} = \frac{1 + cu}{cu + re}, \tag{1.8}$$

where M_0 is the original increase in monetary base, in the currency component. This alternative derivation of the static multiplier shows its micro-foundations when the behavioral parameters cu and re are constant and homogeneous. But once we introduce heterogeneity in those individual parameters, the system changes significantly its behavior.

To better analyze the importance of heterogeneity, the aggregate description for the process (1.4)-(1.8) must be replaced with a distributed one, where each single bank and household are represented and explicitly considered. This implies that in general a closed form solution for the multiplier will not exist, and computer simulations will be used to gain insights into the behavior of the system.

---

[7] The following restrictions apply: $0 \leq re \leq 1$, $cu \geq 0$.

[8] Here CU_i is the additional amount of cash available at time i with respect to time $i - 1$, not the total cash available at time i. The same for the other variables here used.

1.2.3 Introducing heterogeneity

In a heterogeneous setting, each bank has its own reserve/deposit ratio and each household its own currency/deposit ratio. If we assume that each agent (bank or household) in linked to only one agent of the other type, so that the flow of money is never split into different streams, it is then possible to express the multiplier (for a unitary increase in the monetary base) as

$$m_d = 1 + \sum_{i=0}^{\infty} \left(\prod_{j=1}^{i} \frac{1 - re_j}{1 + cu_j} \right), \tag{1.9}$$

where the index i refers to a " round" in the process (i.e., household i deposits money in bank i; bank i extends a loan to household $i + 1$, who will deposit money into bank i+1). A bank or household can be activated in more than one round during the process, as the index does not identify an agent uniquely, only the action of an agent.

We can see that if $re_z = 1$, or $cu_z = \infty$, for some generic z, then the terms in (1.9) for $i \geq z$ are all zero, because agent z acts as an absorbing state in the system and interrupts the multiplicative process of money creation. This implies that heterogeneity is important, and can not be simply averaged out. In fact, the value of the multiplier computed with (1.9) is different from the one we would obtain by using averages of all the reserve/deposit and currency/deposit ratios:

$$m_a = \frac{1 + \frac{1}{n} \sum_{h=1}^{n} cu_h}{\frac{1}{n} \sum_{h=1}^{n} cu_h + \frac{1}{k} \sum_{b=1}^{k} re_b}, \tag{1.10}$$

where k is the number of banks and n the number of households in the economy. Here indexes represent individual banks and households. Under homogeneity ($\forall b$, $re_b = re$; $\forall h$, $cu_h = cu$), (1.8) = (1.9) = (1.10). But with heterogeneous agents, this is not in general true, as it can be seen from a simple experiment. We create 100 different economies, each characterized by 1000 banks and 1000 households with randomly drawn individual ratios and derive the empirical cumulative distribution function (cdf) for the dynamic multiplier computed using (1.9) and for the one computed using averages as in (1.10). As can be seen in Figure 1.1, the average multiplier m_a varies over a restricted range of values, as much of the variability is washed out by the averaging.

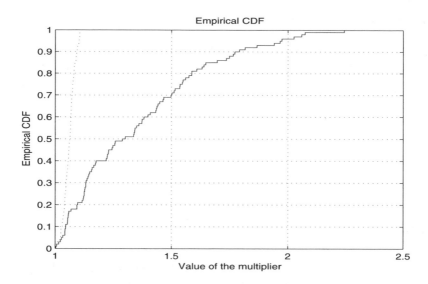

Fig. 1.1. Empirical CDF of average (dotted line) and dynamic (solid line) multipliers.

When the behavioral parameters are heterogeneous, the value of the dynamic multiplier depends, among other things, on the position where the process starts (for an exogenous intervention, where the CB "drops" the monetary base). The system is in fact path dependent and the order by which agents take part in the process becomes relevant. This is confirmed by our simulations when we compute the dynamic multiplier 1000 times for the same economy, each time changing the order by which agents are activated. Results show that the multiplier can vary over a wide range of values, *for the same economy*, depending on the order by which agents take part in the process.[9]

The standard way to represent the multiplier is therefore misleading, as in that representation the coefficients re and cu are not really behavioral parameters, as it may appear by their definitions, but simply ratios of aggregate quantities.

Note then that equation (1.9) is valid only when all the money remains in a unique stream and never gets split into different branches. If we allow each agent (bank or household) to be connected with more than one counterpart, we then need to keep track of all the streams

---

[9] In one of the experiments that we ran, the dynamic multiplier showed a distribution of values in the interval 1-2.5. Of course m_a was instead constant (and equal to 1.06).

of money that get generated, and the analytic formula becomes intractable.

1.2.4 Monetary network

We therefore build an artificial economy and try to gain some insights into the process of money creation by means of simulations. We abstract from any considerations involving the real side of the economy and only model the structure of monetary and credit transactions, considering different possible network topologies at the base of the system and their impact on the multiplicative process.

The network composed of banks and households is a bipartite network, where edges exist only between nodes belonging to different classes. In the process that we describe, each node (bank or household) receives some money from its incoming links, keeps part of it (as reserves or cash holdings) and passes along the rest through the outgoing edges. We can uniquely define each node by its ratio of reserve/deposit or currency/deposit, and build two matrices, one for the links from banks to households (where the edges of this network represent the flow of credit that banks extend to households), and one for the links from households to banks (where the edges represent the flow of deposits from households to banks).

We will consider three different network topologies and try to understand how they impact on the size distribution of the multiplier: a random graph, a regular graph and star graph. Other topologies of course could be considered (e.g., small-world á la Watts and Strogatz (1998) or scale-free á la Albert and Barabasi (2002)), but we restrict for now to these more common structures.

We start by considering a random network, where banks and households are assigned random behavioral ratios (cu_h and re_b)[10] and are randomly linked to each other. The system is composed of 5 banks and 100 households, with each bank receiving money from and extending loans to a random number of households. We simulate 100 economies and compute for each the average and the dynamic multiplier. In Figure 1.2 we show the distributions (as histograms) of the two measures. We can see that the variability in the dynamic multiplier is much higher than in the average one, where the part due to heterogeneity gets washed out.

We then consider one single economy with a fixed set of parameters (thus fixing the average multiplier) and simulate 1000 different pro-

---

[10] With re_b and $\frac{cu_h}{1+cu_h}$ uniformly distributed between 0 and 1.

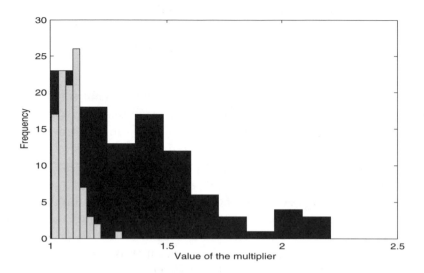

Fig. 1.2. Histograms of average (grey) and dynamic (black) multiplier with a random network of monetary transactions.

cesses of money creation by randomly inject money on different sites. Figure 1.3 shows the empirical cdf of the resulting dynamic multiplier: as it can be seen, the monetary system is path dependent and the final size of the money multiplier depends, among other things, on the position where money is injected into the economy. This means that the multiplier could change even when behavioral ratios for banks' reserves and households' currency remain fixed, an aspect that is completely neglected by the standard theory.

The next topology that we consider is a regular structure, where banks and households are laid down on a bi-dimensional lattice. Each bank is linked to four households, and each household to four banks. Each link is bi-directional, for deposits and loans (though some can have zero weight). We simulate the process of money creation on a lattice composed by 18 banks and 18 households, and show the distribution (histograms) for the average and the dynamic multipliers in Figure 1.4. Compared with the case of a random graph, the variability in the dynamic multiplier is now reduced, as the presence of absorbing states does not disconnect entire regions of the system.

To conclude, we look at the extreme case of a star topology, where all households are linked to one single bank which receives deposits and extends loans to them. We simulate the process of money creation on a structure of this type with 100 households and one bank, and show

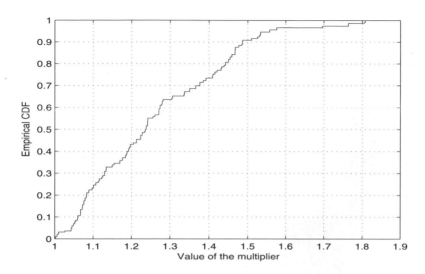

Fig. 1.3. Empirical cdf of the dynamic multiplier in a random economy with different paths of propagation.

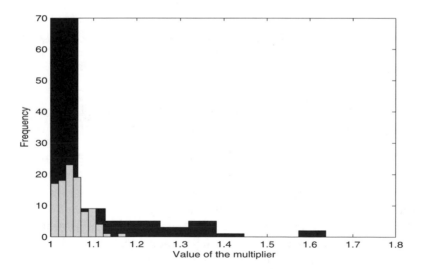

Fig. 1.4. Histograms of average (grey) and dynamic (black) multiplier with a regular network of monetary transactions.

the results in Figure 1.5. As we can see, the variability in the dynamic multiplier increases again now, because the presence of only one bank makes the whole system dependent on the behavior of that bank.

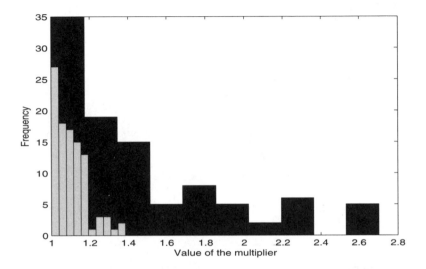

Fig. 1.5. Histograms of average (grey) and dynamic (black) multiplier with a star network of monetary transactions.

1.2.5 Monetary cascades and the sandpile model: an attempt at perspective

We try to suggest here an alternative but somewhat complementary interpretation of the process through which money is created in a credit economy, viewing it as an avalanche that propagates across the economy through monetary and credit transactions.

An interesting phenomenon that has been studied in physics is that of self-organized criticality (SOC), where a system drives itself on the edge of a critical state, right between stability and instability.[11] The classical example is that of the sandpile model developed by Bak et al. (1987).

We think that this interpretation could provide useful insights for the explanation of the process of money creation in a credit economy. If the system operates right on the edge of a critical state, the introduction of new monetary base could have a final effect on the monetary

---

[11] For a review of the concept, see Turcotte (1999).

aggregate that is unpredictable and can vary across a wide range of values.

Suppose that banks try to keep an average reserve/deposit ratio in line with legislation requirements, but take actions and extend new loans only when their individual reserve/deposit ratio reaches a fixed threshold; and that households try to keep an average currency/deposit ratio according to their individual needs/preferences, but take actions and deposit funds into a bank only when their ratio reaches a certain upper bound. So that when banks extend new loans and households make new deposits, they will do it for an amount that exceeds the marginal availability of funds beyond their own threshold.[12] In this way, as time passes, the system could drive itself towards a critical state, on the edge between stability and instability.

Once in this critical state, for each increase in monetary base we could see a final increase in the monetary aggregate M of any size. At times, the process of money creation would end soon, when money reaches an agent that is below its threshold and therefore hoards the additional money he receives; but at times the process could spread out and generate an avalanche, if many nodes involved reach their own threshold and pass along money to others.

This interpretation could provide a good explanation of the variability observed in the multiplier, and if the analogy with the sandpile model is correct, the size of monetary cascades should be distributed according to a power-law.[13] [14]

We now turn to data to see if a power law characterizes the size of the multiplier. In this respect, there are a number of issues to keep in mind. First, the central bank does not "drop" monetary base constantly and regularly in fixed amounts in the economy; secondly, the temporal scale is such that different avalanches may overlap, as there is no guarantee that the time between one central bank intervention and the next is enough for the system to fully respond and adjust to the

---

[12] Technically, these behaviors prevent the system from reaching a stationary state of equilibrium, where all agents have just the desired reserve and currency ratios and simply pass along any additional funds they receive.

[13] A feature that is crucial in the sandpile model is the dispersion of the sand involved in the avalanche. In the monetary system, of course, there is no dispersion of money, so that the "pile" of money keeps growing in absolute size, but the relative size with respect to deposits, that is what matters here, remains constant.

[14] While earlier studies of the sandpile model were done using a regular lattice to represent the interactions among sand grains, Goh et al. (2003) study the avalanche dynamics of the sandpile model on a scale-free network with heterogeneous thresholds and find that the avalanche size distribution still follows a power law.

first intervention; third, we have data available at regularly intervals (bi-weekly or monthly), but an avalanche of money may take different lengths of time to reach its full extent at different times; finally, we detrend the multiplier, as its trend is likely to derive from long-run changes in behaviors that we do not try to explain here and want to abstract from.[15] Having all these limitations in mind, we test for the presence of a power law in the size distribution of the multiplier.[16] Figure 1.6 (in a log-log scale) shows the best fit of the estimated Pareto distribution for the right tail (dashed-dotted line) with the vertical dotted line showing the point from which the Pareto distribution has been identified. Out of the 568 observations available (bi-weekly data for US, February 1984–November 2005),[17] only 157 were identified to be distributed according to a power-law, and the estimated coefficient is 2.55.

According to this test, the evidence for a Pareto distribution in the data for the multiplier seems rather weak so far, though we believe that a more careful analysis is required. In particular, it has to be identified the measure that better captures the avalanche style behavior of the system, since the multiplier, suffering from the limitations described above, might be a poor indicator of such a behavior.

1.3 Conclusions

This paper is a tentative contribution in the field of monetary economics and offers a representation of the money creation process in a credit economy that is alternative to the standard one provided by the static multiplier. We have focused our attention on the mechanics of the process, and we have shown the importance of the role played by the heterogeneity of the actors involved and their interactions. An important feature that has been shown here is the path dependence of

---

[15] The series is detrended using the Hodrick-Prescott filter.

[16] We apply a procedure that first tests for the presence of a Pareto distribution in the data, identifies a region that with a 95% confidence interval follows such a distribution and then applies bootstrapping techniques to find the Hill estimator for the coefficient of the distribution.

[17] We also applied the same procedure to a constructed series for the multiplier, obtained as the ratio between the monetary aggregate M1 and the monetary base, using US monthly data for the period 01/1959-08/2006, with the resulting multiplier then detrended using the HP filter. We obtained similar results in terms of the proportion of data appearing to be Pareto distributed, though the estimate for the coefficient was lower, about 2.25.

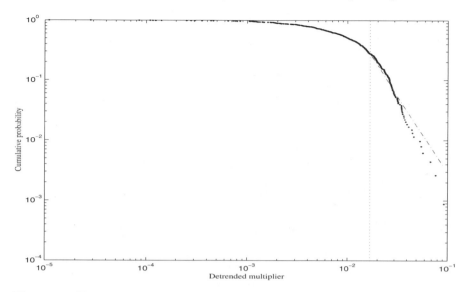

Fig. 1.6. Empirical distribution of the detrended money multiplier. The dashed-dotted line indicates the best fit for a power-law.

the system, which implies that position and timing of CB's interventions on the money market will have an impact on their effectiveness. Finally, the structure of the monetary system has been shown to affect the variability of the multiplier and therefore the process of money creation. It is therefore important that some effort be devoted in order to understand the empirical structure of monetary and credit transactions.

The approach we have adopted in this work, we believe, is well suited for supporting a theory of endogenous money, as it does not imply a deterministic and causal relationship between the monetary base and the quantity of money. Emphasis is placed on the monetary and credit transactions, and though we did not try to link these transactions to the economic activity, the two aspects are clearly interrelated.

Our analysis is just an initial step and much road has still to be covered in order to develop a theory that can properly account for the process of money creation, but we hope that our work will stimulate others to join the ride.

References

R. Albert and A.L. Barabasi. Statistical mechanics of complex networks. *Review of Modern Physics*, 74:47, 2002.

P. Bak, C. Tang, and K. Wiesenfeld. Self-organized criticality: an explanation of 1 / f noise. *Physical Review Letters*, 59(4):381–384, 1987.

K.-I. Goh, D.-S. Lee, B. Kahng, and D. Kim. Sandpile on scale-free networks. *Physical Review Letters*, 91(14):148701, Oct 2003.

C.A.E. Goodhart. *Monetary theory and practice*. Macmillan, London, 1984.

F.E. Kydland and E.C. Prescott. Business cycles: real facts and a monetary myth. *Federal Reserve Bank of Minneapolis Quarterly Review*, pages 3–18, Spring 1990.

B.J. Moore. *Horizontalists and verticalists: The macroeconomics of credit money*. Cambridge University Press, New York, 1988.

D.L. Turcotte. Self-organized criticality. *Reports on Progress in Physics*, 62:1377–1429, 1999.

D.J. Watts and S.H. Strogatz. Collective dynamics of "small world" networks. *Nature*, 393:440–442, 1998.

2

Macroeconomic Effects of the Interest Rate Level: Growth and Fluctuations in an Economy with Bank Capital Adequacy Standards

Gianfranco Giulioni

Department of Quantitative Methods and Economic Theory, University of Chieti-Pescara, Italy
g.giulioni@unich.it

2.1 Introduction

A large part of the macroeconomic literature is dedicated to identifying the determinants of two phenomena: the growth and fluctuations of the aggregate output. Among the proposed explanations, the one concerning financial factors (see Gertler, 1988, for a survey) is that adopted in this study.

Our goal is to investigate how the interest rate affects the growth rate and fluctuations (represented by the growth volatility) of the economy when the banking sector matters. [1] Intermediaries and especially the banking sector have been the object of increasing interest in recent years, because it could be the cause of serious crisis due to the interactions on the interbank market and the consequent contagion effect of an eventual bank failure. In real life, the importance of bank's financial soundness was recognized by the Basel accords (Basel Committee, 2003, 1998) that impose a minimum capitalization level on banks.[2] As we'll see shortly this is a basic ingredient of the model presented in this paper.

The paper is organized as follows. After this introduction, the agents and their behavior are presented and discussed in section 2.2. In sec-

---

[1] The literature on this topic is wide. As examples one can see Levine (1997) for a survey on financial development and growth; Greenwald and Stiglitz (1993) for a theoretical model on financial markets imperfections and business cycles, and Beck et al. (2006) for an empirical paper on financial intermediary development and growth volatility.

[2] The relationship between adequate capital ratios and bank failure is analyzed by Estrella et al. (2000).

tion 2.3 the microeconomic equations obtained in section 2.2 are turned into macroeconomic ones. This allows us to derive our main theoretical result: the growth rate of the economy and to analyze its determinants. The aggregation in this section employs the commonly used device of the representative agent. Although it is a very convenient makeshift, this way of obtaining macroeconomic results hides several drawbacks (see Kirman, 1992, for example). In section 2.4 we show and discuss the results of an agent based implementation of the model. Simulating the model using a bottom up approach is useful for at least two reasons. The first one is that it is a way to check the reliability of the theoretical results that may have been biased by the representative agent hypothesis. In the simulations the agents are heterogeneous, but we have no problem of aggregation having the possibility to compute the variable we are interested in (bottom-up approach). Secondly, and more importantly, agent based models allow a very detailed analysis of the results of a model. The analysis of simulated data gives us the possibility to study how the growth volatility (basically the fluctuations of the economy) varies with the interest rate. Section 2.5 concludes the study.

2.2 Microfoundations

In this model we have two types of agents (firms and banks) and a policy maker. The behavior of firms and banks is similar to that presented by Delli Gatti et al. (2005). In the following subsections we describe the behavior of these agents.

2.2.1 Firms

Firms obtain the production (Y_{it}) implementing a linear production function using only capital (K_{it}) (we assume for simplicity that $Y_{it} = \phi K_{it}$ where ϕ is the capital productivity), they sell the output and realize the economic result (π_{it}) (profit or loss). After having observed the economic result, a firm adjusts its capital stock before starting a new cycle of production, deciding the investment level (I_{it+1}). Investment is financed first by profit and, if that is not enough, changing the debt stock (ΔL_{it+1}). The firm's stock variables are tied by the balance sheet identity $K_{it} = L_{it} + A_{it}$ where A_{it} is the equity base. For future reference it is useful to define the equity ratio $a_{it} = A_{it}/K_{it}$ and the debt ratio $l_{it} = L_{it}/K_{it}$. From the balance sheet equation we have $a_{it} + l_{it} = 1$. The dynamics of capital and equity base are $K_{it+1} = K_{it} + I_{it+1}$ and

$A_{it+1} = A_{it} + \pi_{it+1}$ respectively. Looking at the last equality, it is worth noting that a loss ($\pi_{it+1} < 0$) decreases the firm's equity base and when it becomes negative (due to a sequence of losses) the firm goes bankrupt.

Our main interest is in deriving the production of the firm. According to the description above, it depends on the investment that, in turn, depends on credit. In the following we describe in a detailed way the investment decision and the consequent change in the demand for credit.

Investment

Firms use the following rule to decide the investment level:

$$I_{it}^d = \gamma \pi_{it-1} \qquad \text{with} \qquad \gamma > 1, \tag{2.1}$$

where the d superscript stands for demanded.

This behavior can be justified in two different ways. The first one is based on the empirical evidence (Hubbard, 1998). The second one is that a similar rule can be obtained from the profit maximization (Giulioni et al., 2002).

The $\gamma > 1$ assumption ensures that investment decisions involve credit so that investments are financed by past profits and debt. A natural way to express this is

$$I_{it}^d = \pi_{it-1} + \Delta L_{it}^d. \tag{2.2}$$

This equation tells us also that investment depends on credit. In fact, if the firm obtains all the credit it wants it can attain its desired investment, but nothing ensures that this will happen: the realized investment I_{it} is different from the desired one if the firm is credit constrained ($\Delta L_{it} < \Delta L_{it}^d$). We present here an alternative way to express the dependence of the investment on credit. This alternative presentation will be useful later on.

Let's start with the investment rule (equation (2.1)). Using this it is possible to verify that the debt ratio converges to its steady state value $l^* = \frac{\gamma-1}{\gamma}$ (see the appendix). [3]

---

[3] The existence of an optimal financial structure in firms' balance sheets is in line with the view adopted in this work. Here banks exist and are important. Economic theory tells us that banks gain importance in a world where market imperfections are present. But, if these phenomena exist, the Modigliani-Miller theorem does not hold true so that an optimal financial structure for firms exists.

A convenient way to define investment is using the steady state debt ratio instead of equation (2.1). Indeed from

$$\frac{L_{it}}{K_{it}} = \frac{L_{it-1}}{K_{it-1}} = l^* \qquad \text{we have} \qquad \frac{L_{it-1} + \Delta L_{it}}{K_{it-1} + I_{it}} = \frac{L_{it-1}}{K_{it-1}}$$

and rearranging [4]

$$I_{it} = \frac{\gamma}{\gamma - 1} \Delta L_{it}. \tag{2.3}$$

So, the change in debt is the only determinant of the investment.

The desired change of credit demand

Plugging equation (2.1) into (2.2) one obtains:[5]

$$\Delta L_{it}^d = (\gamma - 1)\pi_{it-1}. \tag{2.4}$$

In equation (2.4) the economic result is involved. Let's give its definition:

$$\pi_{it} = u_{it}Y_{it} - (rL_{it} + r^A A_{it}) - \beta K_{it} \tag{2.5}$$

where u_{it} is the selling price, $rL_{it} + r^A A_{it}$ are financing costs and βK_{it} are production costs. Assuming that the remuneration of the equity base is equal to that of debt[6] ($r^A = r$) we can write equation (2.5) as $\pi_{it-1} = u_{it-1}\phi K_{it-1} - r(L_{it-1} + A_{it-1}) - \beta K_{it-1}$ and using the balance sheet identity we get

$$\pi_{it-1} = u_{it-1}\phi K_{it-1} - rK_{it-1} - \beta K_{it-1}. \tag{2.6}$$

Substituting (2.6) into (2.4) one obtains

$$\Delta L_{it}^d = (\gamma - 1)(u_{it-1}\phi - r - \beta)K_{it-1}. \tag{2.7}$$

---

[4] Developing on the last written formula one can go through the following passages $(L_{it-1} + \Delta L_{it})K_{it-1} = L_{it-1}(K_{it-1} + I_{it}) \Rightarrow I_{it} = (K/L)\Delta L_{it} = (l^*)^{-1}\Delta L_{it} = [\gamma/(\gamma - 1)]\Delta L_{it}$.

[5] Note that, if firms are not rationed so that $\Delta L = \Delta L_{it}^d$, inserting (2.4) into (2.3) one recovers equation (2.1).

[6] In Delli Gatti et al. (2005) this simplifying assumption is also present.

2.2.2 Banks

Banks extend loans to firms being limited by a Basel like rule. Bank's j balance sheet is $L_{jt} = D_{jt} + E_{jt}$ where $L_{jt} = \sum_{i \in \omega} L_{it}$ is the total loan of the bank (ω is the bank's set of costumers), and D_{jt} and E_{jt} are the bank's deposits and equity base respectively. The bank realizes an economic result π_{jt}^B given by the difference between the interest earned on loans (rL_{jt}) and the one paid on deposits ($r^D D_{jt}$) and to shareholders ($r^E E_{jt}$). It has further losses if any of its costumers goes bankrupt. We'll refer to these losses as "bad debt" (B_{jt}). We mentioned before that a firm goes bankrupt when $A_{it} < 0$. Using the firms' balance sheet identity ($K_{it} = L_{it} + A_{it}$) this implies $K_{it} < L_{it}$, that is, the bank lent L_{it} but can only receive K_{it} so that the bad debt due to firm's i bankrupt is $L_{it} - K_{it}$.

In this part of the paper, our goal is to determine the desired change in the credit supply. It will be used in section 2.3 together with the desired change in credit demand to derive the growth rate of the economy.

The desired change in credit supply can easily be derived using the Basel rule

$$L_{jt}^s \leq \alpha E_{jt} \qquad \text{with} \qquad \alpha \gg 1.$$

It is sufficient to express it in terms of variations and, assuming further that lending is preferred by banks to other activities, we can use the equality sign

$$\Delta L_{jt}^s = \alpha \Delta E_{jt}. \tag{2.8}$$

The sole determinant of the desired change in credit supply is the change of the bank's equity base. As mentioned before, this change is given by the sum of the bank's economic result (π_{jt-1}^B) and bad debt (B_{jt-1}):

$$\Delta E_{jt} = \pi_{jt-1}^B - B_{jt-1}. \tag{2.9}$$

π_{jt-1}^B and B_{jt-1} are defined hereafter.

Economic result

The bank's economic result is:

$$\pi_{jt-1}^B = rL_{jt-1} - r^D D_{jt-1} - r^E E_{jt-1}.$$

For the sake of simplicity we assume that $r^D = 0$ and, like above as we did for firms, that $r^E = r$ so that we can write

$$\pi_{jt-1}^B = r(L_{jt-1} - E_{jt-1}).$$

According to the Basel rule $E_{jt-1} = \alpha^{-1}L_{jt-1}$ so that the bank's economic result can be written as

$$\pi^{B}_{jt-1} = r\eta L_{jt-1} \qquad \text{with} \qquad 0 < \eta = \left(1 - \frac{1}{\alpha}\right) < 1. \qquad (2.10)$$

Bad debt

The total bad debt for a bank can be modeled as a share (σ) of loans:

$$B_{jt-1} = \sigma_{jt-1}L_{jt-1}. \qquad (2.11)$$

Such a share is positively related to the probability of a firm's loss. This probability can be endogenously derived. Imposing the condition $\pi_{it-1} < 0$ and assuming that u_{it-1} has a uniform distribution with bounds $1 - \nu$ and $1 + \nu$ (where $0 < \nu \leq 1$) it is given by

$$Pr(u_{it-1} < \bar{u}_{it-1}) = \frac{1}{2\nu}\frac{r + \beta}{\phi}.$$

We put σ_{jt-1} proportional to the calculated probability ($\sigma_{jt-1} = \vartheta Pr(u_{it-1} < \bar{u}_{it-1})$ where $0 < \vartheta \ll 1$ is a constant):

$$\sigma_{jt-1} = \xi\left(\frac{r}{\phi} + \frac{\beta}{\phi}\right) \qquad \text{where} \qquad \xi = \frac{\vartheta}{2\nu}. \qquad (2.12)$$

Substituting equation (2.12) in (2.11), the total bad debt is

$$B_{jt-1} = \left[\xi\left(\frac{r}{\phi} + \frac{\beta}{\phi}\right)\right]L_{jt-1}. \qquad (2.13)$$

The desired change in credit supply

Substituting profits and bad debt (equations (2.13) and (2.10)) into (2.9) and the result of this substitution into (2.8) we get:

$$\Delta L^{s}_{jt} = \alpha\left[r\eta - \frac{\xi}{\phi}(r + \beta)\right]L_{jt-1}. \qquad (2.14)$$

2.2.3 The Policy maker

The role of the policy maker is limited to setting the interest rate r. To avoid complications we assume that banks apply this interest rate to all their customers.

2.3 The macroeconomic model

2.3.1 From micro to macro

Our aim in this section is to derive the growth rate of the economy. The aggregation here is made by the commonly used device of the representative agent. The representative agent's variables are obtained using the average versions of the equations presented in the previous section. The variables we need are: the investment, the desired change in credit demand and the desired change in credit supply (equations (2.3), (2.7) and (2.14)): [7]

$$I_t = \frac{\gamma}{\gamma - 1} \Delta L_t. \tag{2.15}$$

$$\Delta L_t^d = (\gamma - 1)(\phi - r - \beta) K_{t-1}. \tag{2.16}$$

$$\Delta L_t^s = \alpha \left[r\eta - \frac{\xi}{\phi}(r + \beta) \right] l^* K_{t-1}. \tag{2.17}$$

2.3.2 The growth rate of the economy

Our main point is that the effective level of the change of credit (ΔL_t) is the minimum between the desired change in credit demand (in this case banks' lending activity is limited by the low level of credit demand) and the desired change in credit supply (in this case banks are not able to satisfy firms' requests and as a result credit rationing appears):

$$\Delta L_t = \min(\Delta L_t^d, \Delta L_t^s).$$

Plugging this into investment (equation(2.15)) we get:

$$I_t = \min \begin{cases} \gamma(\phi - r - \beta) K_{t-1} \\ \frac{\gamma}{\gamma-1} \alpha \left[r\eta - \frac{\xi}{\phi}(r + \beta) \right] l^* K_{t-1} \end{cases}.$$

Dividing by K_{t-1}, using the result on l^* in the appendix and remembering that $\eta = \frac{\alpha-1}{\alpha}$ it is possible to express the growth rate of capital in terms of the parameters. With a linear production function the growth rate of capital is equal to the growth rate of the aggregate output:

---

[7] In averaging (2.7) remember that $E[u_{it-1}] = 1$. To obtain (2.17) we use the fact that $L_{t-1} = l_{t-1} K_{t-1}$ and that l converges to l^*.

$$g^Y = g^K = \frac{I_t}{K_{t-1}} = \min \begin{cases} \gamma(\phi - \beta) - \gamma r \\ \left(\alpha - 1 - \frac{\alpha\xi}{\phi}\right) r - \alpha\frac{\xi\beta}{\phi} \end{cases} \cdot \qquad (2.18)$$

The two relationships are linear; the second one is upward sloping (being $\alpha \gg 1$) and the other one is downward sloping so that when equating them it is possible to determine the interest rate that maximizes the growth rate:

$$r^*(\alpha, \gamma, \phi, \xi, \beta) = \frac{\gamma\phi^2 - \gamma\phi\beta + \alpha\xi\beta}{(\alpha - 1)\phi - \alpha\xi + \gamma\phi}. \qquad (2.19)$$

Figure 2.1 is the graphical representation of these results.

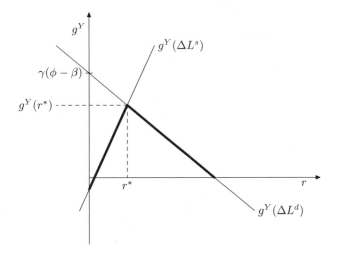

Fig. 2.1. The graphical representation.

It is evident from the figure that if $r > r^*$ the growth rate is a decreasing function of the interest rate. For $0 \le r < r^*$ the relationship is positive. A very important task for the policy makers comes out: they should set the interest rate to the level that maximizes the growth rate. The above results have a very clear explanation. For high interest rates banks make profits and increase their lending capacity, but firms are penalized and the investment decreases. Decreasing the interest rate in this situation is good because the investment increases and can be funded by banks. For $0 \le r < r^*$ firms want to increase investments but banks cannot satisfy their demand for credit.

2.4 The agent based implementation

In this section we simulate the model using an agent based approach. Our implementation is easily understandable by looking at figure 2.2.

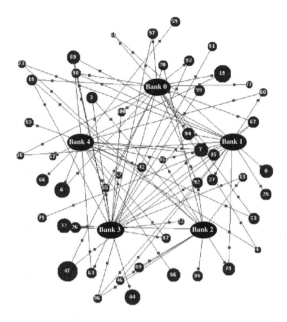

Fig. 2.2. The simulated model.

At the beginning of the simulation a certain number of firms and banks are created (in figure 2.2 we have 50 firms (circles) and 5 banks (ovals)). A link between a firm and a bank means that the firm is a customer of that bank. In the case of the figure, the number of links a firm has is an integer randomly chosen number between 1 and 3. The network here is static in the sense that the links remain the same for the entire life of the firm. When a firm goes bankrupt it disappears and the links are canceled, a new firm enters the market (replacement of exiting firms is one to one), but in this case the links may be different to those of the replaced firm. The size of the circle representing a firm reflects the firm's size.

Firms and banks behavior basically follow the equations showed in section 2.2, but there are two differences.

First of all, differently from the representative agent case, firms have to decide how much credit they want from each bank they are linked with. In our simulations we use a simple rule: the firm asks each bank for the same amount.[8] So if n_i is the number of banks firm i is tied to, the amount of debt firm i demands to bank j (denoted with $L_{it}^d(j)$) is $L_{it}^d(j) = L_{it}^d/n_i$.

Secondly, the banks' equity base dynamics can be computed precisely as the amount of bad debt can be calculated. As explained earlier, a firm's bankrupt causes a bad debt to the banks for a total amount equal to $(L_{it} - K_{it})$. This is shared proportionally among the banks that the firm is linked with, so that the bad debt for bank j is: [9]

$$B_{it}(j) = \begin{cases} L_{it}(j) \left(1 - \frac{K_{it}}{L_{it}}\right) & \text{if} \quad A_{it} < 0 \\ 0 & \text{if} \quad A_{it} \geq 0 \end{cases}.$$

As a consequence the bank's equity base dynamic is

$$\Delta E_{jt} = r(L_{jt-1} - E_{jt-1}) - \sum_{i \in \omega} B_{it-1}(j).$$

The other equations are the same as in section 2.2.

2.4.1 Growth

The output from the simulations confirm the theoretical results and are shown in figures 2.3 and 2.4.

Simulations relate to a scenario with 5 banks and 500 firms.

Figure 2.3 reports the time series of the logarithm of the aggregate production for 5 different levels of the interest rate. The figure shows how the growth rate is not monotonic in the interest rate.

The results of a more detailed experiment are reported in figure 2.4. Here the average growth rate (μ) of the time series is plotted against the interest rate used to obtain the series. Each line is obtained running 100 simulations raising the interest rate from 0 to 10% by a factor of 0.001. The shape of the lines is basically what we expected from the theoretical investigation (compare figure 2.4 to figure 2.1). The results of two comparative static exercises are also reported. Starting with the case $\gamma = 2$ and $\beta = 0.5$, an increase in γ increases both the "optimal" interest rate and the "optimal" growth rate, while an increase in the firms' variable costs (an increase in β) leads to a reduction of both the variables.

---

[8] This seems to be a good rule in this context, because all the banks have the same interest rate.

[9] Due to the presence of the Basel rule, the amount of obtained credit from bank j, $L_{it}(j)$, can be less than the demanded one: $L_{it}(j) \leq L_{it}^d(j)$.

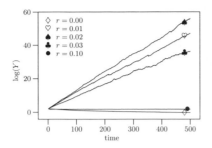

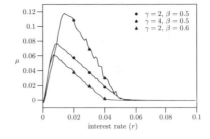

Fig. 2.3. Time series of aggregate production from the simulations ($\phi = 0.1$, $\gamma = 2$, $\beta = 0.5$, $\alpha = 12.5$).

Fig. 2.4. Growth rate of the economy from the simulations ($\phi = 0.1$, $\alpha = 12.5$).

The peculiarity of these results is the upward sloping part of the lines showed in figure 2.4. An explanation of this phenomenon based on the microeconomic principles illustrated earlier is as follows. When the interest rate is low, firms have high profits and this increases the credit demand. Investments are limited by the low level of credit supply, but limiting investment means limiting the size of the firm and therefore the next period's profit (remember that the firm's profit is proportional to its dimension). The reduced level of profit lowers the desired investment.

The voluntary reduction in investment produced by the model urges us to look for parallel mechanisms in the real world. The economic theory attributes to banks the goal of selecting the most productive projects and helping firms to realize them. The key issue here is that these mechanisms, improving the growth rate of the economy, work well if the lending activity is profitable for banks. Indeed, if the revenues from lending to firms are low, banks have no incentive to bear the costs of the selection activities and they could decide to dedicate the available funds to financial investments or lending to families. On the other hand it can be argued that the firms don't know the exact productivity of their investment projects. The banks evaluation could in this case be a signal for the entrepreneur of the validity of the project. Now if, due to a low interest rate, banks reject firms applications for financing new investment, the entrepreneurs could think that the proposed investment was bad even though it was good.

These are possible explanations why a low interest rate reduces the growth rate of the economy.

2.4.2 Fluctuations

From a simulated time series of the aggregate production it is easy to recover the distribution of the growth rates relative to that series. In the previous sections we took a first step in the investigation of this distribution: figure 2.4 reports how the average value of this distribution changes with the interest rate. The second step is to analyze how the dispersion of the distribution changes with the interest rate and the parameters.

But, before taking this step we have to answer a crucial question: does the distribution of the growth rate generated by the simulations possess moments? Indeed recent scientific investigations show how systems with a large number of heterogeneous and interacting components (the so called complex systems) give rise to a particular kind of distribution (see Bak, 1997, for instance). These distributions are usually characterized by the fact that some or all their moments don't exist. If this is the case one can compute the moments from the simulated data, but they are completely meaningless. Fortunately the output of our model suggests that the distribution we are interested in has moments.[10]

Once checked that figures obtained from simulated data are meaningful, we verify how the standard deviation of the growth rate changes with the interest rate. The result of the exercise is reported in figure 2.5 where one can see that in this model the relationship between the growth volatility (σ) and the interest rate is not linear. Moving the interest rate affects the volatility and the policy maker should also take this into consideration.

Figure 2.5 prompts two more questions. The first one is whether there is a relationship between the interest rate that maximizes the growth rate and the one that minimizes the aggregate output volatility. The second is if this property exists in the real data. We have left both these issues for future investigation; however, a hint to the answer of the first question is briefly addressed hereinafter.

We ran simulations for two different values of the capital requirement parameter ($\alpha = 10$ and 15). Figure 2.6 reports the averages and the standard deviations of the growth rate distribution in the two cases. The interest rate that minimizes the growth volatility changes with the parametrization and it seems to move together with the interest rate

---

[10] In Delli Gatti et al. (2007) it is also shown how the growth rate distribution conforms to the empirical one and is of the Laplace type (see also Canning et al., 1998). This kind of distribution possesses moments.

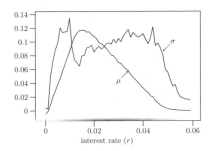

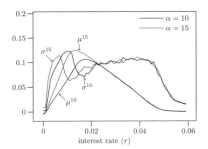

Fig. 2.5. Mean (μ) and standard deviation (σ) of growth rate. The reported values are means over 10 runs (for each level of the interest rate) of the simulation with the same parameters ($\gamma = 4$, $\alpha = 12.5$, $\phi = 0.1$, $\beta = 0.05$) and different seeds.

Fig. 2.6. Changing the capital requirements. The reported values are means over 50 runs for each level of the interest rate obtained with different seeds.

that maximizes the growth rate. If this is confirmed by future empirical investigations, it could be very good news for the policy maker: setting the "optimal" interest rate the policy maker could achieve the maximum growth rate with the minimum level of fluctuations.

2.5 Conclusions

Economists think that lowering the interest rate is a good way to positively affect the aggregate economic activity. The basic principle is, of course, that a low level of the interest rate increases firms' investments. In this paper we highlight that this is an incomplete reasoning, the firms being only one of the economic actors. The previous principle is true if entrepreneurs have no difficulties in funding their projects, or putting it another way if banks are viewed as cash dispensers where entrepreneurs obtain the money whenever they need to fund investments. In this paper banks have a crucial role in the supply of funds. In this context it is of course true that a low level of the interest rate fosters firms' investment, but it also penalizes banks' by reducing their profit. The low level of profits slows down the banks' equity base accumulation and, if a Basel rule on capital adequacy is considered, their lending activity. Of course when this reasoning is considered, the level of investment may decrease when the interest rate is lowered because of funds shortage. Abstracting from the model and thinking in the real world, a low level of growth rate accompanied by a low interest rate level has a different explanation. It is widely accepted that banks improve resource allocation because they are able to select the best investment projects. But these activities are costly. Our results suggest that banks undertake monitoring and screening activities if they are profitable: if the interest rate is not too low! In this case banks put effort into inducing firms to undertake investments. On the contrary, if the interest rate is low banks have no incentive in financing even good investments making no effort to induce firms to invest. In recent years some countries have experienced long periods where low growth rates have been associated with low interest rates (Japan and the Euro Area are two relevant examples). The effect outlined in this work may have had a role in these facts.

The second and more fruitful thing we have done in this paper is to build an agent based implementation of the theoretical model. We concentrate our attention on the aggregate output series provided by simulations and in particular on the distribution of the growth rate one can obtain from each time series. After checking for the existence of the moments of this distribution we analyze how average and standard deviation varies with the interest rate. The behavior of the average confirms the theoretical results. Analyzing the behavior of the standard deviation means getting insight into the fluctuations of the economy. Our results show how the growth volatility depends on a non linear path of the interest rate (it reaches two local maximum and of course one minimum in the relevant range of the interest rate).

These considerations could be useful for the policy maker in setting the interest rate. In fact, knowing how the average and standard deviation of the growth rate varies with the interest rate represents one of the pillars that economic policy should be based on.

References

P. Bak. *How Nature Works. The science of Self-Organized Criticality.* Oxford University Press, Oxford, 1997.

Basel Committee. The new basel capital accord. consultative document. Technical report, Bank for International Settlements, April 2003.

Basel Committee. International convergence of capital measurement and capital standards. Technical report, Bank for International Settlements, July 1998.

T. Beck, M. Lundberg, and G. Majnoni. Financial intermediary development and growth volatility. *Journal of International Money and Finance*, 25:1146–1167, 2006.

D. Canning, L.A.N. Amaral, Y. Lee, M. Meyer, and H.E. Stanley. Scaling the volatility of gdp growth rates. *Economic Letters*, 60:335–341, 1998.

D. Delli Gatti, C. Di Guilmi, E. Gaffeo, M. Gallegati, G. Giulioni, and A. Palestrini. A new approach to business fluctuations: heterogeneous interacting agents, scaling laws and financial fragility. *Journal of Economic Behavior and Organization*, 56:489–512, 2005.

D. Delli Gatti, E. Gaffeo, M. Gallegati, G. Giulioni, A. Kirman, A. Palestrini, and A. Russo. Complex dynamics and empirical evidence. *Information Sciences*, 177:1204–1221, 2007.

A. Estrella, S. Park, and S. Peristiani. Capital ratios as predictors of bank failure. *FRBNY Economic Policy Review*, July:33–52, 2000.

M. Gertler. Financial structure and aggregate economic activity: an overview. *Journal of Money, Credit and Banking*, 20:559–88, 1988.

G. Giulioni, D. Delli Gatti, and M. Gallegati. Financial fragility, heterogeneous agents' interaction, and aggregate dynamics. In R. Cowan and N. Jonard, editors, *Heterogenous Agents, Interactions and Economic Performance*. Springer Verlag, 2002.

B.C. Greenwald and J.E. Stiglitz. Financial market imperfections and business cycles. *Quarterly Journal of Economics*, 108:77–114, 1993.

R.G. Hubbard. Capital market imperfections and investment. *Journal of Economic Literature*, 36:193–225, 1998.

A.P. Kirman. Whom or what does the representative individual represent. *Journal of Economic Perspective*, 6:117–36, 1992.

R. Levine. Financial development and economic growth: Views and agenda. *Journal of Economic Literature*, 35(2):688–726, 1997.

Appendix

From the definition of equity ratio and the dynamics of A and K we can write:

$$a_t = \frac{A_0 + \sum_t \pi_t}{K_0 + \sum_t \gamma \pi_t} = \frac{A_0 + t\pi}{K_0 + t\gamma\pi} \quad \text{where } \pi = \frac{\sum_t \pi_t}{t}.$$

The derivative with respect to t is

$$\frac{da_t}{dt} = \pi(K_0 + t\gamma\pi)^{-1} - (A_0 + t\pi)(K_0 + t\gamma\pi)^{-2}\gamma\pi.$$

The analysis of the sign goes as follows

$$\frac{da_t}{dt} \gtreqless 0 \;\Rightarrow\; 1 - \frac{A_0 + t\pi}{K_0 + t\gamma\pi}\gamma \gtreqless 0 \;\Rightarrow\; \frac{A_0 + t\pi}{K_0 + t\gamma\pi} \lesseqgtr \frac{1}{\gamma},$$

but the left hand side of the last inequality is the definition of a_t we started from, so that we can conclude that

$$\frac{da_t}{dt} \gtreqless 0 \Leftrightarrow a_t \lesseqgtr \frac{1}{\gamma}.$$

Summing up, the steady state values of the equity and debt ratios are

$$a^* = \frac{1}{\gamma} \qquad \text{and} \qquad l^* = \frac{\gamma - 1}{\gamma}.$$

Monetary Policy Experiments in an Artificial Multi-Market Economy with Reservation Wages

Marco Raberto, Andrea Teglio, and Silvano Cincotti

DIBE-CINEF, University of Genova, Italy
{cincotti, raberto, teglio}@dibe.unige.it

3.1 Introduction

The agent-based framework provides an useful computational facility for economics, where performing experiments on policy design issues in a realistic environment, characterized by non-clearing markets and bounded rational agents (see Tesfatsion and Judd, 2006, for a recent survey). Under this respect, this study addresses the issue of monetary policy design by investigating an appropriate rule for the central bank interest rate. Our work consists in pursuing a general equilibrium approach to the problem by considering a multi-market economy characterized by a goods, a labor and a credit market, where agents are price makers on the supply side and act according to sensible rules of thumb. A previous paper (Raberto et al., 2006) by the authors showed the absence of real effects of monetary policy in an agent-based model characterized by price-taking agents. However, if agents are price makers, prices may be set far away from their market clearing values, thereby allowing potential real effects of monetary policy.

The concept of price stickiness as a source of monetary non-neutrality is central in the new-Keynesian literature (Clarida et al., 1999; Mankiw and Romer, 1991; McCallum and Nelson, 2004), where models are usually characterized by a limited number of dynamic forward-looking equations, derived from a log-linear approximation of a general equilibrium model with optimizing, representative and homogenous agents, e.g., a representative consumer and a continuum of homogeneous firms. While recent developments regarded the introduction of learning within the usual new-Keynesian framework (see e.g. Casaccia et al., 2006; Evans and Honkapohja, 2003), this paper may offer a new contribution to the study of monetary policy from the perspective of the economics of heterogenous and interacting agents. In particular, we study the effects of a nominal interest rate as the operational instrument of monetary policy, according to the current approach within monetary economics (see e.g. Walsh, 2003; Woodford, 2003) we investigate an interest rate rule which depends on the gap between the current output of the economy and the full-employment output (i.e., all households that apply for a job are hired). Being labor the only factor of production, when a full employment state is reached, the output can not be further increased, causing the price-setting productive sector to strongly increase prices if it faces a higher demand with respect to its productive capacity, thus generating an price inflation. This may give rise to instability and undermine the economy. In order to keep the inflation monitored and to guarantee stability, a monetary policy that keeps the output somewhat below the maximum potential output may be effective. It is worth noting that, in the optimizing sticky price model of the new-Keynesian literature (Clarida et al., 1999), a concept of output gap, defined as the deviation of output from its level under flexible prices, plays a central role both as a source of fluctuations in inflation (represented by the new-Keynesian Phillips curve), and as a policy target (e.g., the well-known Taylor's rule Taylor (1993)). It is worth noting that, irrespective of the different definition provided in our model, the output gap has a similar role here both as a determinant of inflation dynamics and as key policy variable. Furthermore, the maximum potential output is not fixed in the model but it is an endogenous variable, because the productive capacity of the firm is bounded by the households' labor supply, and this in turn depends on the current real wage. Indeed, the principal driver of the labor supply dynamics resides in the heterogeneity of the reservation wages, i.e., each household is characterized by a reservation real wage that indicates the wage that makes households indifferent between taking a job or remaining unemployed. These features gives rise to a very rich economic behavior which poses challenging issues to the monetary policy maker.

The paper is organized as follows. The model is outlined in Section 2. Computational experiments and results are discussed in Section 3. Section 4 provides some concluding remarks.

3.2 The model

The model is composed by a labor, a goods and a credit market. Households supply the labor force in the labor market and are organized in a trade union that sets the nominal wage. Each worker is characterized by a reservation wage, i.e., a minimum real wage in order to apply for a job. A monopolistic firm hires workers to produce the scheduled quantity of output. The firm acts in the goods market as a price setter, and supplies the output according to a profit maximizing behavior. The aggregate demand is given by the sum of each household's demand, which is modeled according to a rule of thumb proposed by Deaton (1991a,b), based on the assumption that households, if liquidity constrained, save in order to smooth consumption over time. The individual consumption rule has been adapted here to our framework. The firm borrows money from the central bank in the credit market in order to pay wages, the bank sets an the interest rate according to the policy rule.

3.2.1 Households

Households take two key decisions in the model, determining the labor supply, according to their heterogeneous reservation wages, and how much to save or to consume in order to smooth consumption over time. Furthermore, a trade union sets the nominal wage w in order to increase the aggregate real labor income U, given by $(w/p)N$, henceforth workers' utility, where N is the number of workers (with $N \leq M$, M being the total number of households) and w/p is the real wage (being p the price level). The wage policy of the trade union is based on a backward looking behavior. If the correlation $\rho(dU, dw)$ between nominal wage variations dw and variations of workers' utility dU, computed in a backward time window T^U, is positive, i.e., nominal wage increments dw led in the past to an increase of workers' utility, the trade union raises the nominal wage. If the correlation is negative, the trade union keeps the nominal wage unchanged. In the former case, the wage bill is increased according to a fixed rate π^* set by the central bank, corresponding to a fixed planned rate of inflation. The trade union's decision rule can be summarized as:

$$w_t = \begin{cases} w_{t-1}(1 + \pi^*) & \text{if } \rho(dU, dw) \geq 0, \\ w_{t-1} & \text{if } \rho(dU, dw) < 0. \end{cases} \tag{3.1}$$

This wage indexation rule has been selected in accordance with the current practice in some European countries, e.g., Germany and Italy.

Reservation wages

Households' labor supply depends on the comparison between the current real wage and the reservation wage of each household. If the current real wage exceeds its reservation wage, then household i-th applies for a job, if not, the household does not apply for a job unless its financial condition does not allow it to buy the essential goods for survival. Formally, the i-th household applies for a job according to the following rule,

$$
\begin{cases}
(\frac{w_t^i}{p_t} \geq w_i^R) \cup (\frac{X_{t-1}^i}{p_t} \leq S^C) & \longrightarrow \text{ job application}, \\
(\frac{w_t^i}{p_t} < w_i^R) \cap (\frac{X_{t-1}^i}{p_t} > S^C) & \longrightarrow \text{ no job application},
\end{cases}
\tag{3.2}
$$

where w_i^R is the i-th household real reservation wage, X_{t-1}^i is its available cash at the end of the previous period and S^C, expressed in real terms, represents the indispensable quantity of goods to consume, that we call survival real cash, taken as homogeneous among agents and constant in the model. This is due to the fact that we consider S^C as a parameter that characterizes the whole population of households with a cultural attitude towards spending. S^C has therefore to be interpreted as a minimal arbitrary quantity of goods for a decent living rather than as a survival level *tout court*. Reservation wages w_i^R, defined as the wage that makes households indifferent between taking a job or remaining unemployed, are heterogeneous but constant. They represent a sort of social stratification for households that is kept constant along time. It is worth noting that in this model reservation wages are not, at least directly, a determinant of the actual wage, that is fixed by the trade union in order to increase workers'utility, but they have an essential part in determining the unemployment rate (see Hogan, 2004, for empirical evidence on these topics). Each household is endowed with a specific reservation wage according to a uniform distribution that varies form a minimum level $w_{\min}^R$ (generally set to zero) to a maximum level $w_{\max}^R$ that is used as a varying parameter for computational experiments.

Consumption rule

Household consumption choice is based on the theory of buffer-stock saving pioneered by Deaton (1991a,b), which states that households, if restricted in their ability to borrow to finance consumption, have a precautionary demand for saving in order to smooth consumption in case of bad draws of income, e.g., unemployment. The theory proposes accordingly a rule-of thumb as an approximation of the usual intertemporal maximization problem for the determination of the consumption path. The rule-of-thumb has been modified in order to take into account price inflation and is based on the comparison between the current income and past income stream realized in the last time window T^i. Let us define as X_{t-1}^i the quantity of cash at the i-th household disposal before its consumption choice c_t^i at period t. The households's disposable income for consumption I_t^i is composed by the previous period wage, w_{t-1}, and the dividends from profits that the firm made in the previous period, i.e., $I_t^i = \delta_{t-1}^i w_{t-1} + m_{t-1}^i d_{t-1}$, where δ_{t-1}^i is equal to 0 or 1, depending on the employment status of the household at time $t-1$ and the integer m_{t-1}^i is the number of shares in the portfolio of household i at the end of previous period. Dividends d_{t-1} are given by $p_{t-1}\Pi_{t-1}/K$, where Π_{t-1} are the real profits realized by the firm in the previous period and K is the total number of shares of the monopolistic firm. The households' target is to maintain a stable rate of consumption, i.e., saving when income is high in order to accumulate cash for periods of low income. Deaton assumes that individuals consume cash as long as current nominal income I_t^i is less, in real terms, than the average past real income $\bar{I}_t^i$, while, if the income exceeds $\bar{I}_t^i$, households save a constant fraction $(1-v)$ of the excess income. Thus, given the price p_t set by the firm in the current period, Deaton's decision rule can be formalized as:

$$c_t^i = \begin{cases} \min\left(\bar{I}_t^i, (I_t^i + X_{t-1}^i)/p_t\right) & \text{if } I_t^i/p_t \leq \bar{I}_t^i, \\ \bar{I}_t^i + v(I_t^i/p_t - \bar{I}_t^i) & \text{if } I_t^i/p_t > \bar{I}_t^i. \end{cases} \qquad (3.3)$$

Aggregate goods demand Y_t^d is then given by $Y_t^d = \sum_i c_t^i$.

3.2.2 The monopolistic firm

The model includes a single monopolistic firm whose role is:

- to set the price and the quantity of the goods to be produced, according to a profit maximizing behavior,
- to hire workers, to produce and sell the goods,
- to distribute profits to households.

The firm produces an homogeneous perishable good according to a production function whose only input is labor:

$$Y_t = \zeta N_t^\alpha. \qquad (3.4)$$

The parameters $\zeta > 0$ and $\alpha > 0$ are determined by the current technology and are kept constant in our computational experiments. The firm knows the nominal wage w_t that has been already set by the trade union, and acts as a price setter, facing the problem to decide the price p_t of the good and the quantity Y_t of goods to be produced. The firm also knows the labor supply N_t^s and has a perfect knowledge of the demand elasticity. In order to set the price, the firm takes into consideration a set of hypothetical prices p_t^h, that lie in a neighborhood of the last market price p_{t-1}. The prices p_t^h are chosen inside a grid parameterized by $(1 + j\epsilon)p_{t-1}$, with $j = -n, -n+1, \ldots, n-1, n$, where ϵ represents the minimum relative variation of the price and $n\epsilon$ is the higher bound for variation. Consequently, the firm calculates the exact goods' demand relative to each price, i.e., $Y_t^d(p_t^h)$. Therefore, the firm computes, for each pair $(p_t^h, Y_t^d(p_t^h))$, the value of real profits, considering nominal costs given by:

$$C_t = (1 + r_t^L)w_t N_t , \tag{3.5}$$

where r_t^L is the interest that has to be paid on the loan $w_t N_t$, and $N_t = (Y_t/\zeta)^{1/\alpha}$, with the constraint $N_t \leq N_t^s$. The price and quantity couple $(p, Y)_t$ is therefore chosen as the one that corresponds to the higher real profits, i.e.,

$$(p, Y)_t = \mathrm{argmax}_{(p,Y)_t} \Pi_t , \tag{3.6}$$

where

$$\Pi_t = Y_t - C_t/p_t . \tag{3.7}$$

Finally, the firm distributes profits to households. Each household will receive dividends at the beginning of the next period, proportionally to the number of stocks it owns.

3.2.3 The central bank

The model incorporates a bank, which fulfills the functions of both a commercial bank and a central bank. The bank performs the following actions:

- to set an inflation target π^*,
- to remunerate the household's cash account at a fixed rate r^D,
- to provide credit to firms at a lending rate r_t^L,
- to set r_t^L according to a monetary policy rule.

The rate on deposit r^D is set by the bank at the target level of inflation π^*, in order to let the money aggregate of the households grow at the same rate of inflation. A policy rule, that uses the nominal interest rate r^L as the operational instrument, has been designed. It is based on the control of the output gap, and sets the lending rate r_t^L as:

$$r_t^L = r^{L_{\min}} + \phi \exp\left(-\beta \frac{Y_t^p - Y_t}{Y_t^p} \right) , \tag{3.8}$$

where β is a policy tuning parameter, ϕ represents the policy strength, varied to compare different monetary policies in the computational experiments, and Y_t^p is the potential output, given by the quantity of goods that would have been produced if all the available labor force had been employed, i.e., $Y_t^p = \zeta(N_t^s)^\alpha$. The effect of the rule on the economy is discussed in Section 3.3.

3.2.4 Rationing and accounting

As described in Section 3.2.2, the firm knows in advance the aggregate demand curve. Accordingly, it sets the price and chooses the goods supply in order to match the goods demand at that price. Therefore, the firm is never rationed in the goods market. The firms also knows in advance the labor supply. Consequently, while taking price and quantity decisions, it considers its possible rationing in the labor market. If there is not enough labor supply to produce the desired quantity, the firm hires all the households applying for a job and produces a quantity of goods lower than the demand level, implying that households will be rationed in the goods market. Furthermore, households are often rationed in the labor market. In both cases, households are rationed according to a random priority list, drawn from a uniform distribution.

After transactions in the goods and in the labor markets, households cash is reallocated for the next period, i.e., for the i-th agent:

$$ X_t^i = X_{t-1}^i + \delta_{t-1}^i w_{t-1} + m_{t-1}^i d_{t-1} - p_t c_t^i + r^D X_{t-1}^i , \qquad (3.9) $$

where r^D is the fixed rate on deposit of the bank, δ_{t-1}^i indicates the employment state of agent i at time $t-1$ (i.e., $\delta_{t-1}^i = 1$ or $\delta_{t-1}^i = 0$ denote employment or unemployment state at $t-1$ respectively), and $m_{t-1}^i d_{t-1}$ denotes the capital income due to m_{t-1}^i stocks paying dividend d_{t-1}. The term $p_t c_t^i$ takes into account the nominal expenses for consumption and $r^D X_{t-1}^i$ is the remuneration of the saving account.

3.3 Computational results and discussion

We present a study on the effects of using a nominal interest rate as the operational instrument of monetary policy. The interest rate r^L has an influence on the economy through the decision making of the firm, which borrows money to pay wages. Given the nominal wage set by the trade union, nominal labor costs incurred by the firm depend directly on the interest rate level, as shown by Eq. 3.5. As an example, a rise of

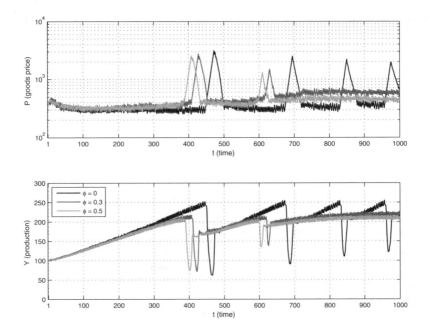

Fig. 3.1. The dynamics of price and output for three different values of the monetary policy strength parameter ϕ.

the interest rate at time t implies an increase of costs, and determines at the same time step an upward shift of the firm's supply curve in the (Y,p) plane. Due to the fact that the aggregate demand curve at time t is not yet affected by this interest rise, the goods market clears at a higher price and at a lower quantity. However, a rise of the interest rate, if negative in the short run, may have positive effects in the long run by keeping the economy below its full capacity.

The computational experiment presented here have been realized considering the following parameters values: $M = 1000$, $T^U = 20$, $\pi^* = 0.5\%$, $\zeta = 1$, $\alpha = 0.9$, $\delta = 0.1$, $n = 50$ (implying a maximum price variation of $\pm 5\%$, $r^D = 0.005$, $r^L_{\min} = 0.1$, and $w^R_{\min} = 0$. No stock trading is considered, and each household has been endowed with the same amount of stock holdings $m^i = K/M$ which is keep constant over time. Different values for the maximum reservation wage $w^R_{\max}$ and for the monetary policy strength parameter ϕ have been considered. Figure 1 shows the dynamics of price and output for three different values of the monetary policy strength parameter ϕ. Figure 1 points out the presence of price spikes and simultaneous falls of production; they occur when the economy reaches its full capacity. In that case, the firm can not hire more workers to increase production and profits. Thus, obeying to its profits maximizing behavior, it has to rise the price. Consequently, consumers' demand is depressed and this reduces the market clearing output of the economy. Furthermore, the price rise reduces the real wage and therefore the labor supply, which is a binding production factor when the economy is running at its full capacity. The objective of the monetary policy rule, outlined in Eq. 3.8, is to prevent, by rising the interest rate, the firm from scheduling a production level that could not be sustained by the labor supply, i.e., to prevent the economy from reaching its full capacity. The policy strength parameter ϕ weights the importance of the output gap in the interest rate setting. The monetary policy experiments showed in Figure 1 point out that a monetary policy which takes into account the output gap, i.e., $\phi > 0$, gives rise to an higher inflation rate and lower output growth in the short run, but it is able to contain output negative fluctuations and to significatively reduces the volatility of prices and output in the long run. Furthermore, it is worth remarking that caution has to be payed in tightening the monetary policy, and a tradeoff is necessary between a lower inflation rate ($\phi = 0.5$) and an higher output growth rate ($\phi = 0.3$). Figure 3.2 shows how reservation wages affect the labor market dynamics and therefore the output level of the economy. Simulation shown in Figure 3.2 has been performed with the usual monetary policy rule with ϕ set at 0.1. The reservation wages are heterogeneous among households and uniformly distributed between zero and a maximum value w_{max}^R. Raising w_{max}^R, the reservation wages range becomes larger and there are more households that require a higher salary to work. Figure 3.2 allows one to observe that a higher lever of the maximum reservation wage w_{max}^R has a clear depressive effect on the labor supply, e.g,. for $w_{max}^R = 0.35$, there is a few number of households that are disposable to work (around 250). Thereby, this contraction on the labor supply has a depressive effect on the long-term level of production in the economy. An effective monetary policy should then take into account this feature in order to address the usual trade-off between long-run output level and inflation control. Figure 3 shows the mean value of the relative output gap, i.e., $(Y_p - Y)/Y_p$, relative to the last 500 time steps. Each bin represents an output gap value calculated for a couple (w_{max}^R, ϕ) where w_{max}^R varies from 0.1 to 0.5 with a step interval of 0.025 and ϕ varies from 0.1 to 0.5 with a step interval of 0.1. As expected, the value of relative output gap diminishes with the increasing monetary policy strength. Furthermore, it is worth noting that the relative output gap

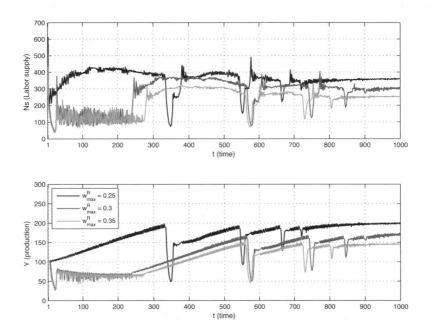

Fig. 3.2. The dynamics of labor supply and output for three different values of the maximum reservation wage $w_{\max}^{R}$.

shows a clear dependence on the maximum reservation wage. Indeed, according to our model, the maximum value of the reservation wage, setting the labor supply, determines the potential output of the economy, i.e., higher $w_{\max}^{R}$ correspond to lower Y_p. Besides, Figure 3 points out that also the relative value of the output gap decreases for rising values of $w_{\max}^{R}$. This results suggests that a milder monetary policy, i.e., lower values of ϕ, should be considered as more appropriate in the case of lower $w_{\max}^{R}$.

3.4 Concluding remarks

The model presented should contribute to the agent-based approach for monetary policy design along two main different perspectives. First, it provides a sensible micro-foundation to a monetary policy rule based on output gap control, with a complementary approach to the new-Keynesian Phillips curve literature. Under this respect, it shows that the optimizing behavior of a price setting monopolistic firm is sufficient

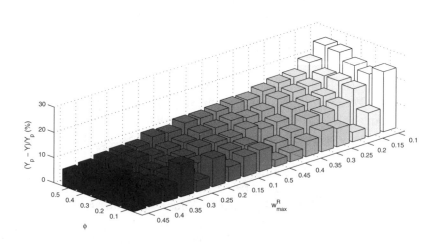

Fig. 3.3. Average relative output gap for different values of ϕ and $w_{\max}^R$.

to produce inflation when the economy reaches full employment. Second, the model shows how an effective monetary policy design should to take into account the distributional property of reservation wages among agents, i.e, an individual heterogeneous feature which determine aggregate labor supply, and, thus, the potential output of the economy at full employment.

Acknowledgement. This work has been partially supported by the University of Genoa, and by the Italian Ministry of Education, University and Research (MIUR) under grants FIRB 2001 and COFIN 2004, and by the European Union under IST-FET STREP Project EURACE.

References

S. Casaccia, S. Cincotti, M. Raberto, and A. Teglio. Monetary policy subject to measurement errors of private sector adaptive expectations. In G. Setti and T. Ushio, editors, *Proceedings of the 2006 International Symposium on Nonlinear Theory and its Applications,* pages 335–338. Research Society of Nonlinear Theory and its Applications, 2006.

R. Clarida, J. Gali, and M. Gertler. The science of monetary policy: A new keynesian perspective. *Journal of Economic Literature*, 37(4): 1661–1707, December 1999.

A. Deaton. Savings and liquidity constraints. *Econometrica*, 59(5): 1221–1248, September 1991a.

A. Deaton. Household saving in ldcs: credit markets, insurance and welfare. *The Scand. J. of Economics*, 94(2):253–273, 1991b.

G.W. Evans and S. Honkapohja. Adaptive learning and monetary policy design. *Journal of money credit and banking*, 35(6):1045–1072, December 2003.

V. Hogan. Wage aspirations and unemployment persistence. *Journal of Monetary Economics*, 51(8):1623–1643, November 2004.

N.G. Mankiw and D. Romer, editors. *New Keynesian Economics*. MIT Press, 1991.

B.T. McCallum and E. Nelson. Timeless perspective vs. discretionary monetary policy in forward looking models. Technical report, The Federal Reserve Bank of St. Louis, 2004.

M. Raberto, A. Teglio, and S. Cincotti. A general equilibrium model of a production economy with asset markets. *Physica A*, 370(1):75–80, 2006.

J.B. Taylor. Discretion versus policy rule in practice. In *Carnegie-Rochester Conference Series on Public Policy*, volume 39, pages 195–214, 1993.

L. Tesfatsion and K. Judd. *Agent-Based Computational Economics*, volume 2 of *Handbook of Computational Economics*. North Holland, 2006.

C.E. Walsh. *Monetary theory and policy*. The MIT Press, 2003.

M. Woodford. *Interest & Prices*. Princeton University Press, 2003.

Part II

Market Mechanisms and Agents Behavior

4

Testing Double Auction as a Component Within a Generic Market Model Architecture

Julien Derveeuw[1], Bruno Beaufils[1], Philippe Mathieu[1], and Olivier Brandouy[2]

[1] Laboratoire d'Informatique Fondamentale de Lille, USTL,France
  {derveeuw,beaufils,mathieu}@lifl.fr
[2] Lille Economie et Management, USTL, France
  olivier.brandouy@univ-lille1.fr

4.1 Introduction

Artificial stock markets are models designed to capture essential properties of real stock markets in order to reproduce, analyze or understand market dynamics with computational experiments. Despite research advances in modern finance many questions remain unsolved: market dynamics exhibit, for instance, particular statistical properties, called *stylized facts*, which origins are not clear. As real markets are complex systems, it is really hard to study them directly because too many parameters stay out of control. Hence, multi-agents simulations of these markets seem to be a key for a better understanding of their properties.

Building such models implies to simplify reality as most as it can be in order to keep markets most representative and characteristic features. In the literature (see for example LeBaron et al. (1999), Cincotti et al. (2006) or Ghoulmie et al. (2005)) real markets structure complexity is often circumvented by the use of an equation weighting the balance between bids and offers as a price formation model. This simplification is in complete contradiction with the reality of stock markets where prices *emerge* from agents interactions through an order book which do not act as a central weighting entity but as a peer-to-peer meeting point used by agents to exchange stocks. However, such studies manage to reproduce realistic price series, which seems odd regarding market models used. We can then wonder if some of these models are more suited than others to capture market dynamics.

To answer this question, it seems that a comparison between these models needs to be realized in order to put them to the proof and investigate their robustness. Hence, we propose in this article a generic market model architecture based on four independent entities, each of which can be modeled in different ways. We show that existing models found in literature fit well in this architecture. We then propose an artificial stock market model which takes into account real markets characteristics: trading activity takes place *continuously* through an *asynchronous* mechanism. Agents interact through the market by posting *orders* in an *order book*, as it happens on real market places. We show that without making any strong assumption on agents behaviors, this model exhibits many statistical properties of real stock markets.

4.2 Quick review of different ASMs architectures

Since the first artificial stock market was developed in the early nineties at the Santa-Fe Institute Palmer et al. (1994), many market models have been developed. Though almost all of them aim to reproduce the same market properties (the so-called stylized facts) with the same multi-agents simulation methods, they all exhibit different properties: some are synchronous, while others are asynchronous. Some of them require agents to emit realistic orders (direction/price/quantity) while others only require a direction (buy/sell) to compute the new stock price. Without pretending to be completely exhaustive, we investigate in this section some of these models in order to identify the most represented microstructures and trading rules in artificial stock markets.

The Santa-Fe artificial stock market

Historically, the first model to be developed was the *Santa-Fe Artificial Stock Market*. This model is mainly characterized by the use of a macroscopic equation based on demand and supply law to compute the new traded stock price. Hence, agents take their decisions synchronously and emit their desires as a direction $a_{i,t}$ (buy $a_{i,t} = 1$ or sell $a_{i,t} = -1$) to the market, which calculates the imbalance between demand and supply ($I_t = \sum_i a_{i,t}$), to finally compute the price according to equation 4.1.

$$p_{t+1} = p_t(1 + \beta \times I_t) \qquad (4.1)$$

Though this model may seem attractive due to its relative simplicity, its lack of realism regarding real market microstructure is obvious:

agents take their decisions synchronously without being able to reason about others beliefs; moreover, agents are not even aware of the quantity of stocks they will trade due to the clearing process used to realize exchanges between agents once the price is calculated.

The $-game

To solve the question of market clearing, a possible solution is to add a market maker to the model, so agents are always satisfied with the quantity they want to trade. This feature was incorporated in the $-game ASM Andersen and Sornette (2003). As the market maker provides liquidity to the market (e.g. he buys excess stocks and provides supplementary stocks when needed), his position needs to be covered to avoid bankruptcy. Hence, Andersen et al. use in their model a slightly modified version of the previous price calculation equation. Instead of only considering the current imbalance between demand and supply, they also take into account the global imbalance since the beginning of the simulation, which is the market maker current position. Using the same naming as above, the price update equation is then given by 4.2.

$$(\ln(p_t) - \ln(p_{t-1})) = \frac{I_t + \sum_{i=0}^{i=t-1} I_i}{\lambda} \tag{4.2}$$

Though this model correctly addresses the problem of stock liquidity and market clearing, it can't be considered as a realistic one: agents still interact synchronously with the market and only emit a desired quantity to trade, without having the ability to associate it with a desired price for the transaction.

The Genoa artificial stock market

To bring more realism to synchronous models, researchers from Genoa proposed a model called the *Genoa artificial stock market* in which agents are allowed to emit classical limit orders to the market (see Raberto et al. (2001), Cincotti et al. (2003) or Raberto et al. (2003)). In this model, agents still take their decisions synchronously, but as they associate a limit price to the desire they pass to the market, a different clearing mechanism needs to be used to ensure that agents do not buy or sell stocks for a different price than the limit they asked for. This is achieved by computing a clearing price, which is defined as the crossing of the demand quantity curve function of price and of the supply quantity curve function of price (see equations 4.4 and 4.3 for a definition of these two series).

$$f_{t+1}(p) = \sum_{u|p_u \geq p} q_u^b \tag{4.3}$$

$$g_{t+1}(p) = \sum_{v|p_v \geq p} q_v^s \tag{4.4}$$

Though this model is more realistic than the previous ones, it still lacks an essential feature of real markets microstructure: the asynchronism of transactions.

Toy model of an asynchronous double auction

In order to get a more realistic time handling process in artificial markets, some researchers proposed models in which transactions take place asynchronously. This is the case of the toy model proposed in Bak et al. (1996). In this model, there are only $\frac{N}{2}$ stocks on the market, where N is the number of agents. Agents do not have the right to own more than one share at a time. They can therefore be sellers if they own a share, or buyers if they own nothing.

At each time step, an agent is given speak randomly and has the possibility to emit a desire according to the pre-cited rules. This desire is a composed of a price and a direction. If this agent finds an other one who is willing to make the opposite transaction with a compatible price, they immediately exchange one share. If no counterparts are available, the agent's order is saved in a list until a counterpart is found.

Even if it is a toy model, this model is one of the first to take into account the asynchronism of exchanges on real market places. Agents act in a random order and a simplified order book is used to save agents desires. A criticism which can be made is that the market rules used (an agent can at most own one share) tend to make the market illiquid and prevent from testing realistic investment strategies.

We have seen in this section that many different market models are used to reproduce high frequency dynamics from real stock markets. Despite of their heterogeneity, they are used to reproduce the same three main stylized facts: the shape of the return distribution (which is fat-tailed and leptokurtic), the autocorrelation of absolute returns and clustered volatility. We can notice strong differences in the way agents express their desires, in the set of information they are able to get from the market, and in the way they are given speak by the market. This a major problem regarding our main goal, which is to be able to compare heterogeneous market models in similar experimental environment.

4.3 A generic market model architecture

In the previous section, we have presented some of the most representative market models microstructures and trading rules found in the
literature. Their diversity is so great that it seems difficult to correctly
identify which of these models parts are responsible for the statistical
properties of computed price dynamics: are they due to the microstructure of the market ? to the way time is handled ? to the agent investment strategies ? In order to address these open questions, we expose in
this part a generic model of market architecture which allows to unify
these different models. We also show that this formalization allowed
us to develop a concrete implementation of this generic architecture,
which will make us able to compare artificial stock markets.

4.3.1 The abstract generic model

Fig. 4.1. General market model architecture.

If we look at how markets operate, we can decompose them in three
parts: the *market*, which allows agents to exchange stocks, *agents*, who
trade through this market, and the *external world*, which can for example influence agents with information. This situation is summed up
in figure 4.1: agents communicate their desires to the market, being
influenced by their peers or exogenous information. They can also be
influenced by public information available from the market. If we make
a parallel between this abstract model and multi-agents models of markets, we can see from the previous section that each of these three
components can be modeled in different ways: the market can be an
averaging equation or a complex microstructure; agents can be either
cognitive, reactive or replaced by equations.

4.3.2 The concrete generic model

In order to experiment the influence of each of these modules on price
dynamics, we need to be able to compose heterogeneous modules coming from the literature. For example, to investigate the influence of

market microstructure on prices, it seems interesting to study some of their different implementations for a given set of agents behaviors. Unfortunately, as we have seen in section 4.2, most of market models require agents to emit their desires in many different ways: there are sometimes expressed as a direction, sometimes as a quantity or even as limit orders. Hence, it seems obvious that to make our generic architecture practical, we need to propose some concrete details on its implementation.

Information

In our formalism (see figure 4.1), we showed that agents were able to use some information coming from the market in order to take a decision. As we saw in the first section, information required by agents or published by market models are heterogeneous: some market models only publish the last transaction price, while others make all of the agents current positions public. Hence, to be able to compose any agents model with any market model, it is necessary to define the maximum set of information needed by agents models and to define how all of these information can be approximated when they are not present in a given market model.

According to our literature review, agents use *at most* the following information from the market:

- the last transaction price, which is an information available on every market model
- other agents desires (which represent the order book in asynchronous models).
- current demand and supply disequilibrium, which is available in most synchronous models. In asynchronous model, it is easy to deduce this information from the current order book state by summing quantities available in both sides of the order book.

To be able to compose any market model with any agent model, we have to define a set of translators able to fill missing information from some market models if it is required by the agents. An example of such a translator (or wrapper) is described in table 4.1. Though we provide in our framework a full set of information translators which allow to translate any type of emitted information in any type of required information, the effect of these translators on experimental results still has to be investigated.

emitted by market	required by agent	translator description
(price, agents positions)	(price, disequilibrium)	translator sums up quantity associated to agents positions in order to compute the global demand/supply imbalance

Table 4.1. An example of information translator.

Agents desires

In figure 4.1, we identified that agents emit trading desires to the market, which are then interpreted according to market model trading rules. These desires, in artificial markets as well as on real ones, are defined by a composition of the three following characteristics: a direction, a price and a quantity. Obviously, the direction is the minimal requirement in order to get a valid desire (emitting a desire to a market without saying if one wants to buy or sell makes no sense). The two others desires properties (price and quantity) are optional according to the agent or market model. As we would like to compose any agents and markets models which emit or require different types of desires, we need to define a translation system to make this composition possible.

Assuming that a direction is the minimum required to express an economic desire and that the maximum is a direction, a price and a quantity (which was deduced from our intensive literature investigation), it is possible to propose a first set of translators (which are called wrappers in computer science) that are required to allow communication between any agent model and any market model. The effect of these wrappers on agents and market behaviors still has to be investigated. An example of such a translator is described in table 4.2.

emitted by agent	required by market	translator description
(d, , q)	(d, p, q)	interpret order as a market order, and fill the missing price with the best offer in opposite direction

Table 4.2. An example of desire wrapper.

Time handling

In addition to the differences between information required or emitted by the different modules of a market, time handling is managed in very different ways regarding the market model used: some are synchronous while others are asynchronous. Moreover, each of this time handling philosophy can be implemented in several different ways. These differences are a major problem to solve while trying to compose heterogeneous modules: if an agent strategy is built to operate in an asynchronous context, is it possible to make its strategy make sense in a synchronous one ?

To address this problem, we have split time handling from the market module and separated it in what we call a *simulation engine*. This additional module is responsible for giving the ability to talk to the agents and for making the market treat agent desires when it is time to do so. For example, a synchronous simulation engine will give to all of the agents the ability to talk, and will then ask the market to compute the new stock price, whereas an asynchronous one will perhaps pick randomly an agent and then immediately ask the market to take his desire in account.

Global framework layout

Due to lack of space, we can not explain further all of the implementation details that are needed to allow free market modules composition. Figure 4.2 sums up the general layout of our simulation framework, which we detail step by step:

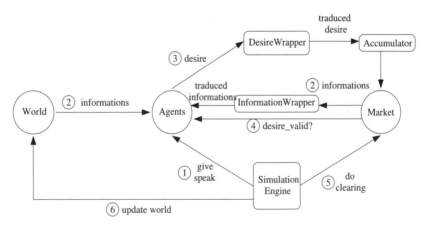

Fig. 4.2. Framework functioning.

- *step 1*: The simulation engine gives speak to the agent(s) who are allowed to speak at current time according to the time policy in use.

- *step 2*: Before taking a decision, agents are able to ask the market some information about its current state (best offers, current stock price, demand/supply imbalance, etc). As each market model can exhibit different public information, they need to be treated by a wrapper which traduce them so they can be used by any agent model. Agents can also ask external world about its current state if their decision making process requires such an exogenous information.

- *step 3*: Once agents have sufficient information to take their decisions, they can emit a desire to the market. As we have seen before, this desire can be expressed in many different ways, so it needs to be traduced by a wrapper to be understood by any market model. These desires are then stored in an accumulator, which is useful to keep track of agents desires, in particular if the simulation engine is synchronous.

- *step 4*: Each time the market receives an agent desire, it immediately informs the emitter about its validity. This is required as some market models require agents to meet specific conditions to be able to emit desires.

- *step 5*: Once the simulation engine has given speak to the agents allowed to do so, it notifies the market that it is time to take the agents desires into account. If the market is order book based, this means "insert new desires in the book", whereas in equation-based models, this means "enter in a clearing phase and compute a new price".

- *step 6*: The simulation engine finally gives the possibility to the world model to update itself.

Limitations

Even if our generic architecture is implemented and practical, it still has some limitations inherent to the major differences between models we try to compose one with another.

For example, some information translators need to be able to translate an information expressed as a single price in an information expressed as other agents positions. Even if other agents positions may be assimilated to the current stock price, impact of such translations on agent trading strategy have still to be investigated. The same observation can be made about the composition of agents designed to work in an asynchronous context with market models designed to work in a synchronous one.

Hence, our generic architecture still has to be improved and validated with intensive experiments, in order to make sure that translators do not bias simulations results. Even at this early stage, this generic architecture can however be merely considered as a formalism able to describe any artificial stock market model through their components.

4.3.3 An example of application: the market component as double auction

We have seen in section 4.2 that most of existing market models lack realism: some do not respect real markets asynchronism while others over simplify the way agents emit desires to the market. In consequence, we choose to illustrate the use of our generic market simulation framework by implementing a simple asynchronous double auction model following our formalism. This model can be linked up to the one used in Raberto et al. (2005). We will detail in this section how each module is defined according to the formalism we presented before.

The market component

The market component is a classical order book similar to the one used on market places such as EURONEXT. This order book requires agents desires to be expressed as a *direction*, a *price* and a *quantity*, which defines an order. These orders are all *limit prices orders*, which means that the price associated to the order is the maximum (respectively minimum) price the agent is willing to buy (sell) stocks. When an order is received by the market, it is stored in the order book according to price and time priorities if it has no counter part. When a counterpart is found, a transaction occurs immediately and the price of this transaction is published.

The simulation engine component

In order book based markets, time handling does not follow the same logic as in equation-based ones: central quotation system does not aggregate agents decisions at particular time steps and market participants are free to talk when they want. Hence, we need to implement the simulation engine component as a process which asks agents to speak asynchronously and which asks the market to update its current state each time an agent has spoken.

Our choice is to give randomly an agent the opportunity to talk regardless to the fact he has already spoken or not. The major inconvenient of this method is that some agents can be out of the market (have never the opportunity to speak) because of the random generator used in the scheduler. However, on real markets, some agents are very active (speak a lot) whereas others rarely interact with the market. For these reasons, this is the scheduling principle we choose.

The agent component

Following the works of Gode and Sunder (1993), our agents are designed as purely reactive ones (as simple as possible), which implies that we do not make any strong hypothesis about the agents reasoning capabilities, nor on the information set they use to take their decisions, as it is done in most of other studies. The choice of using simple agents behaviors in this article is hence deliberate: our goal, here, is not to design realistic agents but to validate our microstructure model separately from the two other components of the market architecture.

These agents can be assimilated to *zero intelligence traders* who post orders with a random direction, a random price for a random quantity of stocks. When an agent emits a new order, he stops emitting new ones until his order is fulfilled or until the order reached his *timeout*. This *timeout* is randomly assigned to each agent at the beginning of the simulation and stays constant over time. This mainly guarantees that an order with a price too far from the current limits of the order book won't stay in it for an endless time.

4.4 Experiments

We present in this section some experiments we have designed to test our generic framework. Only a part of the statistical tests we made are reproduced here due to lack of space. Full experimental tools and results used to produced data presented in this paper may be downloaded at `http://cisco.univ-lille1.fr/papers/ae2007`. This experiments are realized using the market model, agents and scheduler exposed in previous section. All of our experiments are run on 20 000 time steps with 100 agents.

First, we interested ourselves to the returns distribution as its shape is one of the major characteristic of real price dynamics. This distribution, on real markets, is leptokurtic and exhibits fat tails. Table 4.3 shows some statistical results: the excess kurtosis measured oscillates around 4.5 which is similar to what can be observed with real markets data (see right column for a comparison). To further illustrate this property, figure 4.3 shows one of our experimental returns distribution compared to a theoretical normal distribution.

Description	Value (experimental)	Value (real data)
Excess kurtosis	4.52	4.158
Aug. Dickey-Fuller	-20.47	-18.47
ARCH	100%	100%

Table 4.3. Statistical results obtained with our interaction-based model, compared to the one obtained on real data (BMW daily stock returns coming from DAX30).

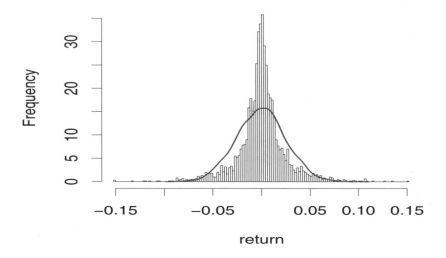

Fig. 4.3. Experimental returns distribution compared to a theoretical normal distribution with same mean and variance.

Another major characteristic of returns is that they do not exhibit significant autocorrelation but that a short-range autocorrelation decaying over time exists when looking at their absolute value. Figure 4.4 presents the ACF plot for both returns and absolute returns. Comparing them to the ones obtained with real market data, we can see that returns properties similar to reality can be obtained with our interaction-based model. These properties are further verified by the use of the Augmented Dickey-Fuller test which tests for the null hypothesis *"The serie has a unit root"*. Table 4.3 shows its result on our time series: the presence of a unit-root is rejected at a high confidence level as with real data (right column).

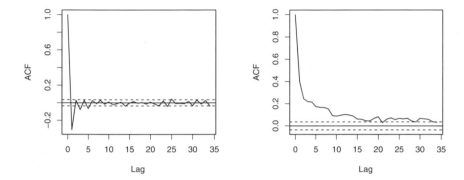

Fig. 4.4. ACF of returns and squared returns obtained in our experiments.

We have seen in this section that time series obtained with our model exhibit the same statistical properties as real data sets. This results improve the preliminary ones obtained by Raberto et al. (2005). This shows that our asynchronous and continuous auction model is able to reproduce most of markets characteristics without making any assumption on agents behaviors or on an external world model.

4.5 Conclusion

In this article, we introduced a generic architecture of artificial market models. This architecture is composed of four independent parts: a model for the external world, another for agents behaviors, one for the market structure and a last for time handling. We have shown that most of existing market models can fit in this architecture, so it can therefore be considered as a description formalism of artificial stock markets. Moreover, our generic architecture allows to compose existing market and agent models, which is a major benefit if one plans to compare market models between them: it is now possible to do such comparisons in identical environments (e.g. with the same agents) and to draw strong conclusions from these experiments, which was not the case before. However, some of the effects of our generic model still needs to be investigated in order to make sure that translators do not bias simulation results.

We have also presented and tested an artificial stock market component based on an order book, which implies that quotation is *asynchronous* and *continuous* as on real markets. This is opposed to classical approaches, which aggregates agents decisions synchronously with an equation as a substitute for market interaction mechanism. First results show that it is possible to reproduce most of the *stylized facts* observable on real markets with a pure multi-agents model based on local interactions. This may confirm recent statements implying that most market features are due to the exchange process more than to agents behaviors.

We argue that such continuous and asynchronous models should be used in stock markets simulations. The order book model is so close to reality that no validation problems subsist about the mechanism used to make the agents exchange stocks. Moreover, developing agents behaviors is simplified: real traders investment strategies could be implemented "as is", without having to modify their output to match the model requirements.

Concerning technical issues, we can notice that the order book does not require specific parameters: this ensures that no hazardous tweaking is necessary to make the market model work in a proper way. Moreover, our model is carefully designed with respect to multi-agents modeling paradigms: by adapting blackboard mechanism and well-known techniques of scheduling to the field of market simulation, we reduce the probability to get unwanted side effects due to technical issues in our simulations.

Now that we both have a realistic market model and a generic market architecture, we are going to be able to compare our model with other ones from the literature. By doing such intensive experiments, we hope to bring some more elements to the theories which impute most of the stylized facts to the market structure. We will also be able to test new investment strategies coming from classical economic literature such as the self referential agents proposed in Orlean (1999).

Acknowledgement. This work is supported by European funds of FEDER and the CPER TAC of Nord-Pas-de-Calais region.

References

J. Andersen and D. Sornette. The $-game. *European Physics Journal*, 31:141–145, 2003.

P. Bak, M. Paczuski, and M. Shubik. Price variations in a stock market with many agents. *Physica A*, 246:430–453, 1996.

S. Cincotti, M. Raberto, S.M. Focardi, and M. Marchesi. Who wins ? study of long-run trader survival in an artificial stock market. *Physica A*, 324:227–233, 2003.

S. Cincotti, L. Ponta, and S. Pastore. Information-based multi-assets artificial stock market with heterogeneous agents. In *WEHIA06*, 2006.

F. Ghoulmie, R. Cont, and J.P. Nadal. Heterogeneity and feedback in an agent-based market model. *Journal of Physics: Condensed Matter*, 17:1259–1268, 2005.

D.K. Gode and S. Sunder. Allocative efficiency of markets with zero-intelligence traders: Market as a partial substitute for individual rationality. *Journal of Political Economy*, 101:119–137, 1993.

B. LeBaron, W.B. Arthur, and R. Palmer. Time series properties of an artificial stock market. *Journal of Economic Dynamics and Control*, 23:1487–1516, 1999.

A. Orlean. *Le pouvoir de la finance*. Odile Jacobs, 1999.

R.G. Palmer, W.B. Arthur, J.H. Holland, B. LeBaron, and P. Tayler. Artificial economic life: A simple model of a stockmarket. *Physica D*, 75:264–274, 1994.

M. Raberto, S. Cincotti, S.M. Focardi, and M. Marchesi. Agent-based simulation of a financial market. *Physica A*, 299:320–328, 2001.

M. Raberto, S. Cincotti, S.M. Focardi, and M. Marchesi. Traders' long-run wealth in an artificial financial market. *Computational Economics*, 22:255–272, 2003.

M. Raberto, S. Cincotti, C. Dose, S.M. Focardi, and M. Marchesi. Price formation in an artificial market: limit order book versus matching of supply and demand. *Nonlinear Dynamics and Heterogenous Interacting Agents*, 2005.

A Conceptual Framework for the Evaluation of Agent-Based Trading and Technical Analysis

Olivier Brandouy[1] and Philippe Mathieu[2]

[1] Lille Economie et Management, USTL, France
olivier.brandouy@univ-lille1.fr
[2] Laboratoire d'Informatique Fondamentale de Lille, USTL,France
philippe.mathieu@lifl.fr

5.1 Introduction

The major part of research dedicated to technical analysis and active trading (*i.e.*, the management of financial portfolios using chartism or moving average indicators for instance) generally focuses on single "signals" giving the opportunity to buy or sell a financial commodity *frequently a well diversified portfolio* (see the extensive survey of Park and Irwin, 2004). In this context, it has been extensively argued that technical analysis is useless in order to outperform the market (Jensen and Benington, 1969). The reason for that is, assuming informational efficiency (Fama, 1970), all relevant piece of information is instantaneously aggregated in prices. Therefore, there is nothing to extract from previous quotations relevant for one willing to trade on this basis. Since information is, by definition, unpredictable, next price fluctuations will be driven by innovation and the price motion will fluctuate randomly as a result. Nevertheless, empirical investigations tackling this question of "technical trading" exhibit heterogeneous results. On the one hand, a large part of these researches shows that, once risk taken into account, no-one can seriously expect any rate of return over what can be earned with a simple *Buy and Hold* strategy (henceforth B&H). On the other hand, some intriguing results seem to attest that technical analysis is useful to a certain extent (Brock et al., 1992; Dempster and Jone, 2005; Detry and Gregoire, 2001). More generally speaking, this idea is trusted and shared by many practitioners.

We argue here that this confusion depicted by this heterogeneous set of results comes from ill-defined concepts, confusing measures and fuzzy evaluation procedures. We propose in this paper some elements to correct these imprecision and to elaborate a conceptual framework for technical analysis evaluation.

We consider these elements using an Agent-Based approach because we ultimately would like to investigate large sets of technical trading strategies, to encompass automatic trading issues and to generalize as much as possible our investigations. Thus, in this research, an *agent* is systematically an *artificial agent*, that is, a virtual entity endowed with *Artificial Intelligence*, mimicking a *real investor*, and able to deal with information, learning, and adaptation procedures.

Therefore, our propositions are a contribution to organize as rigorously as possible the large set of problems linked to the evaluation of automatic trading, technical analysis and related topics including those where *Artificial Intelligence* is used to investigate large sets of investment strategies.

This paper is organized as follows. In section 1, we discuss the basis upon which technical analysis is usually analyzed. We show why it must be distinguished between *signals*, *strategies* and *behaviors* although this distinction is seldom done in other researches. Section 2 focuses on the problematic link between technical indicators received by the traders and their ability to benefit from them when they try to implement them in "winning" strategies. Section 3 deals with the value added by increasing cognitive capabilities of the agents in plugging sets of technical signals rather than a single signal in their rationality. Section 4 enlarges the discussion to several strategies and addresses several questions around the design of tests for weak-form Market efficiency and automatic trading. It also serves as a conclusion.

5.2 Why confusing elements have lead to a controversy

If one considers the basic elements in most researches dealing wit technical analysis or weak-form market efficiency, it is often the case that one specific "strategy" (or a limited set of strategies) is systematically replicated over various time windows, using real stock market data. Performance is computed comparing this active-investment strategy to a specific benchmark, like a simple B&H behavior. Some refinements concerning the statistical properties of the performance distribution is also usually proposed, such as Monte-Carlo simulations or Bootstrap Reality Checks (see for instance White, 2000).

However, no one can seriously sustain that these tests directly assess what a real technical trader would do. This practitioner would certainly mix a large number of *"receipts"* to strategize his behavior. His performance is supposed to be grounded on various "signals", "special skills" allowing him to have a correct diagnosis, and a professional "know-how" : this mix makes any evaluation complex because the origin of performance (or lack of performance) is not easily observable. To make this point clearer, let's consider briefly figure 5.1. A large part of the evaluation complexity arises from the interaction between:

- elements constituting investors' intelligence (and consequently, virtual agents' artificial intelligence) : their cognition is a structured mix of information – extracted from market observation – and knowledge coming from the organization of these information *plus* the result of their past behavior,
- and external constraints : what kind of commodity are they allowed to trade? Are they subject to budget or credit constraints? Can they go *short* or not?

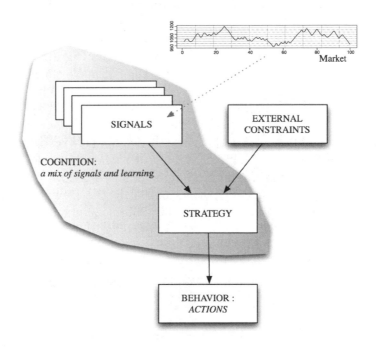

Fig. 5.1. Elements of complexity in performance evaluation

Every evaluation problem has to take into account these elements to be satisfying. The most difficult of them, and clearly the less treated in the literature, tackles the ability of technical traders to evolve and to mix various elements to achieve good performance in the market. We will present this point at the end of the following example : to introduce the discussion, we propose first a basic situation, a very direct evaluation problem where trader's intelligence is limited since she applies systematically a strategy based on a "Mixed Moving Average 90-10 signal" (MMA_{90-10}). A "moving average" of range K (K being equal, in our example, to 10 and 90 since we mix these indicators) and a "mixed moving average (n, p)" are respectively proposed in the following expressions 5.1 and 5.2 :

$$MA_{K,t} = \frac{1}{K} \sum_{t-K+1}^{t} p_t \tag{5.1}$$

$$MMA_{n,p} = \{MA_{n,t}, MA_{n,t}\} \tag{5.2}$$

Chartists consider the situation in which the short-term moving average crosses the long term one from the bottom to the top as a "buy" signal (*resp.* from the top to the bottom as a "sell" signal). We use the daily closing value of the Dow-Jones from 26/05/1896 to 22/11/2005 (27424 quotation days) to generate a series of 478 signals (figure 5.2 shows a subset of this signals from 21/05/1996 till the end). We consider that it is always possible to trade a tracker based on this index. The allocation rule for the trader is simply maximum investment (that is, to buy as much trackers as possible or to sell them massively).

On the basis of the signals, the agent trades the DJ-tracker 477 times (the first signal being a "sell" signal). Do these chartist signals actually signal something useful for trading or not *(question 1)*? Would a portfolio, solely composed of trackers based on the Dow-Jones Industrial, have benefited from such a trading rule if one considers various performance indexes *(question 2)*? Especially, do these signals allow smart traders to elaborate strategies that outperform the market *(question 3)*? Is it possible to improve dramatically this Limited Intelligence Trader's performance in endowing her with higher cognitive skills *(question 4)*?

question 1:

The idea behind this question is the actual power of chartist signals to predict correctly, regularly and with a sufficient reliability, the next moves of one specific market. We can quantify this power with a very simple indicator called "Hit Rate":

$$HR_{MMA_{90-10}} = \frac{\text{correct signals}}{\text{total number of signals}} \tag{5.3}$$

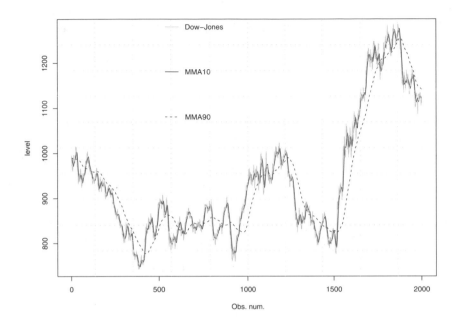

Fig. 5.2. Moving Averages 10 and 90 over 10 years of DJI

Others definitions of such indicator can be found in the literature (Hellström and Holmström, 1998).The average score of our chartist signal, in terms of Hit Rate is here of 52%. This score may vary significantly over sub samples of time, and to some extent, it is hard to say that this 52% score is better than what a pure random rule would do. Nevertheless, we can still hypothesize that a subset of rules (whatever these rules are) in the infinite space of possible rules actually performs well.

question 2:

Assuming the MMA_{90-10} signal has been selected by a trader, would she be able to obtain a good performance implementing it in a basic strategy [3]? Graphs 5.2 shows the evolution of a trader's portfolio composed of one tracker (at date 26/05/1896) and managing her portfolio with a basic strategy using MMA_{90-10} signals against a passive trader receiving at the same date the same tracker, and playing a B&H strategy. Rules for managing the portfolio are as follows: when a trader

---

[3] in other terms, following what the signals suggest: to buy when the market is supposed to rise, to sell when it is supposed to decrease

decides to sell her portfolio, all the trackers she holds are sold. When she decides to buy, she invests all her cash in trackers (considering she will have to pay in both cases transaction costs at $x\%$). One can easily observe that when transactions costs are zero (graph 5.3), the basic MMA_{90-10} seems to perform well whereas it is a good road to ruin when transaction costs are non-zero, even if they are extremely low (graph 5.4).

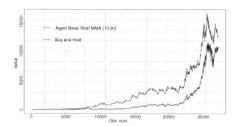

Fig. 5.3. Without trans. costs   **Fig. 5.4.** With 0.5% trans. costs

question 3:

The previous graphical analysis is obviously not sufficient. When applying standard performance indexes, especially those including a risk/return analysis (a Sharpe ratios as instance), one can clearly see that all supposed advantages for a MMA_{90-10} vanish as soon as transaction costs are considered (see Table 5.2).

Transaction Costs		0%	0.5%
Buy&Hold	Mean return	2.0344 E-4	
	σ	0.01145	
	Sharpe Ratio	0.0177	
	Portfolio	10871.43	
Basic Strat.	Mean return	2.0964 E-4	1.2267 E-4
	σ	0.00724	0.0073
	Sharpe Ratio	0.02893	0.01679
	Portfolio	12852.61	1183.57

Table 5.1. Performance evaluation based on a MMA90-10

question 4:

Do increasing cognitive abilities for the agents lead to better results in terms of risk/return performance? In other terms, assuming that *"perceiving good signals"* necessarily leads to *"achieving a good strategy"* – and this assertion will be extensively discussed – can we design agents sufficiently smart to adapt their behavior to many signals and many external constraints to outperform the market? Would this kind of agents *prove* really any ability in this game? How should we design an evaluation framework taking these elements into account if we want to design automatic trading platforms and/or tests of market efficiency with agents duplicating as well as possible the behavior and the cognition of true technical traders? What kind of implications, both theoretical and practical, these considerations can highlight?

5.3 On the link between *good market signals* and the capacity for building up simple good strategies

In this section, empirical investigations use daily data from the Euronext Paris Stock Exchange between 1988 and 2005. The traded tracker is now based on the CAC40 index. Agents have access only to past values of this index. We first present some technical/theoretical arguments and propose a series of illustrations afterwards.
We first propose to distinguish two fundamental concepts that must be considered separately previously to be articulated. Technical trading is always based on "signals" indicating either that the market is about to increase or to decrease, and "strategies" based on these signals as well.

1. As evoked previously, a "signal" is generally grounded on the (controversial) idea that profitable persistence or inertia characterize the price motion in stock markets. One difficulty here is to detect which "signal" is actually able to reveal such persistency. We consider in this paper a large number of instances of signals; these instances are based on several generally accepted technical rules (moving averages, rectangle, triangle, RSI, momentum ...), each of them being modeled as a parametric function. These signals will be active or not, depending on the existence of "patterns" in prices provoking their activation. Once activated, the signal sends a recommendation to the trader expressed like: *"according to my own logic"*, *"the market should increase"* or *"should decrease"*.
2. A "strategy" is the way agents use these signals to build a trading behavior.

a) Some agents will only observe one signal (some being endowed with multiple signals), and will follow it systematically (we call this behavior "Basic Strategy").

b) Others will be "contrarians" (i.e. will follow an "Inverse Strategy")

c) Others will choose sometimes to follow the signals, sometimes to ignore them. We call them "Lunatic" traders.

d) ...

Extracting best candidates from a large soup of signals

In this section, a limited sample of results from a series of massive empirical investigations is reported. We select, among many thousands of chartist/technical signals, some of them exhibiting good "Hit Rates" (HR, see equation 5.3) and a minimum activity (that is, signals frequently activated and useful to manage a portfolio – at least one signal per week –). Table 5.3 shows a limited subset of this "good signals" (a "signature" is simply the name and the parameters used to compute this signal).

Num. of signals	with HR $\geq$ 50%	with min activity
110288	6640	97
	(6.02%)	(0.08%)
Signature		
MMA-1-4 ; MMA-1-6 ; MMA-1-7		
Momentum-2-1 ; Momentum-5-0		
Variation-1-1-4 ; Variation-1-5-1		
Variation-1-7-1 ; Variation-1-8-1 ; Variation-1-9-1		

Table 5.2. Subsets of "good signals"

Executing these best candidates with a simple strategy

We show how we can use the signals selected in section 5.3 to design "pseudo-good" strategies.

An agent decides, at each time step and according to the set of information it accesses, to manage the portfolio, selling, buying or letting the number of held trackers unchanged. This set of information is as follows:

- $S_1, S_2, ..., S_n$, the set of signals exploited by her strategy.
- $HR_1, HR_2, ..., HR_n$, the corresponding set of Hit Rates.

One can notice here that we did not design a very complex set of information, including performance evaluation in terms of risks-returns, rate of activity, memory etc... This is obviously possible but leads to an increasing computing time and a huge amount of data to analyze.

We focus here on the simplest imaginable strategy: one signal, one Hit Rate, no evolution, and a strict application of what the signal suggests : if the market is identified as a rising market, *"Buy"*, if identified as a decreasing one, *"Sell"*. In all other circumstances, *"stay unchanged"*. Table 5.3 presents the results for 10 strategies based on the signals in Table 5.3, for two transaction costs levels. It is illustrated that no strategy is able to outperform the market when transaction costs are fixed at 0.5%.

Signature	0% rate				0.5% rate			
	Mean (10^{-4})	σ (10^{-2})	Sharpe Ratio	Rank /97	Mean (10^{-4})	σ	Sharpe Ratio	Rank /97
B&H	3.0879	1.09	0.0283	–	3.0879	0.0109	0.0283	–
MMA-1-4	3.9428	0.74	0.0529 *	13	-0.010	0.00870	-0.1151	88
MMA-1-6	4.4715	0.74	0.0599 *	2	-6.006	0.00852	-0.07043	69
MMA-1-7	4.1877	0.74	0.0562 *	7	-5.6647	0.00845	-0.06701	67
Mom.-2-1	3.2710	0.81	0.0402 *	51	-9.3296	0.00915	-0.10194	83
Mom.-5-0	4.1035	0.74	0.0552 *	8	-6.3746	0.00835	-0.07630	70
Var.-1-1-4	3.9915	0.74	0.0535 *	12	-6.5312	0.0083	-0.0778	72
Var.-1-5-1	3.1547	1.07	0.0294 *	67	1.5685	0.01081	0.01450	23
Var.-1-7-1	3.0960	1.08	0.0285 *	70	2.8503	0.01087	0.02622	5
Var.-1-8-1	3.0403	1.08	0.0279	71	2.8839	0.01088	0.02650	4
Var.-1-9-1	2.9761	1.08	0.0273	73	2.9091	0.01088	0.0267	3

MMA: mixed moving average, Mom.: momentum, Var.: Variation
* stands for "actually outperform the Market"

Table 5.3. Performance evaluation of 10 strategies based on "good signals"

In figure 5.5 we show that a good signal (MMA 1-4) can lead to disastrous results when transaction-costs are non-zero, while it can be profitable when transaction costs are not paid. This is linked to the fact that a good Hit Rate can produce a lot of activity that will not be profitable because the costs for transacting exceed the benefits one can obtain with small upwards or downwards in prices.

In figures 5.6 and 5.7 and we have extended this analysis including the entire set of agents endowed with signals presenting a HR > 50% (6640 signals, see section 5.3). They are plotted in a risk/return space.

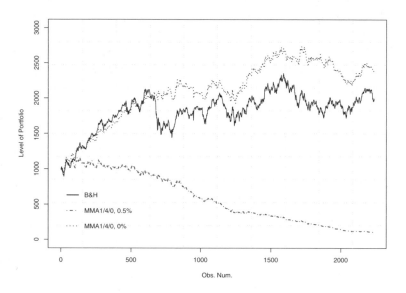

Fig. 5.5. Agents using MMA(1,4) signals

Agents under the market line (black plain line) underperform the B&H strategy.

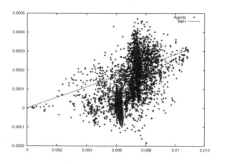 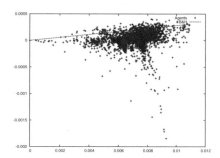

Fig. 5.6. Without trans. costs   **Fig. 5.7.** With 0.5% trans. costs

It appears that once transaction costs are implemented, the number of agents being able to exploit their signals in order to "outperform" the market decreases extremely rapidly with limited increments for these costs. It is noticeable that the agents seemingly well-performing are not those endowed with best signals.

5.4 Do intelligent agents outperform ZIT?

In this section, we want to address the following question: do agents endowed with a set of signals of size N behave systematically better than agents endowed with a set of signals of size $N - i, i \in [1, N - 1]$? Do "smart" agents behave better than Zero Intelligence Traders (ZIT)? In other terms, does increasing cognitive skills, that is, the ability to detect potential opportunities to trade, actually lead to a better performance? This is a recurrent question in economics and finance that has provoked many intriguing results (see for instance Gode and Sunder, 1993; Greenwald and Stone, 2001). As stated previously, a first obstacle is the profitable implementation of good signals in the agent. One potential solution could be to allow the agents to select the signals upon which they trade on the basis of their individual Hit-Rate (or some indicator based on this measure).

Technical elements

The first step here consists in allowing each agent to let her rationality evolve along time. To a certain extent, we must consider agents endowed with learning capabilities or adaptive reasoning. This is a specific topic in Agent Based literature (see for example Weiss, 1996), which is not developed here. We just exhibit a limited treatment for this problem:

1. Agents are endowed with N signals (in the following examples $N \in [1, 11]$), previously selected on a large set of signals in order to ensure some (arbitrary) level of "effectiveness" [4].
2. At each time-step, agents compute for each signal the corresponding Hit-Rate.
3. Every P time steps, agents observe which signal has performed well in terms of HR and select this predictor to trade over the next P time steps. In the following developments, and for the sake of simplicity, $P = 100$.

It is relatively easy to imagine various learning and adaptive procedure that may lead to better results, and it could be argued here that the results shown might be dramatically improved. This is presumably true, although this should be done with a correlative increased complexity of agents' design, solution which has not been retained in this article.

---

[4] We mix three indicators: individual Hit-Rate, number of emitted signals, balance between "buy" and "sell" signals.

Basic strategies based on sets of best signals

We present now one typical answer to an instance of the generic question proposed at the beginning of this section: *"On the basis of the 10 best signals proposed in Table 5.3, is it possible to create basic strategies using many signals (2, 3, ..., 10) in order to outperform the market?"*
It is particularly contra-intuitive to imagine that adding cognitive skills to the agents should lead to a decrease in performance. One should expect to observe a rise in performance for agents accessing a larger set of decision rules when evolving in the market. This is not actually the case.

To answer these questions we create a series of agents endowed with an increasing number of signals, from 1 to 10, $Agent_i$ being endowed with the $i - th$ first signals in terms of Hit-Rate. We then investigate their relative performance when transaction costs are respectively fixed at a 0% rate and 0.5% using the adaptive procedure proposed in the technical discussion above. Figure 5.8 and 5.9 clearly show that increasing the number of signals in the agents do not systematically allow for obtaining a higher level of performance in terms of Sharpe Ratio. This

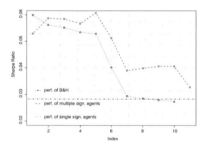
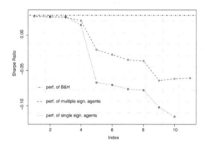

Fig. 5.8. With 0% trans. costs   **Fig. 5.9.** With 0.5% trans. costs

is obvious when transaction costs affect the agents'global performance, but it is also generally true with no transaction costs. We have tested all possible values for P between 10 to 500 days, and obtained similar results. These considerations suggest that either the complexity of agents is not appropriate to increase their performance, either an other kind of rule should be implemented to select "good signals" (like their average profitability in terms of return, which is especially complex), or that the market being efficient, technical trading is definitively useless.

5.5 On the validity of technical trading arguments

A last point must be explicitly evoked now: technical trading, and more generally speaking the weak-form market efficiency have been studied using sophisticated statistical tests[5] to verify if *simple* technical rules can convincingly outperform the market. Nevertheless, a research tackling the question of the relative performance for *complex* technical trading rules, including artificial intelligence agents, able to evolve in a wide decision-rules universe, has still to be done.

This would be the ultimate stage to obtain a strong test for market efficiency. As it has been shown in a previous communication Brandouy and Mathieu (2006), even if one explores an enormous number of signals individually "plugged" in artificial traders playing a "Basic" strategy, it seems to be impossible to obtain risk-adjusted rates of return in excess to a simple Buy and Hold strategy. This is an empirical evidence that strongly support the weak-form EMH.

The following illustrations suggest that if one does not accept to increase significantly the complexity of the agent-based architecture used in this kind of research, it will certainly not be possible to obtain strong evidence of an abnormal over-performance.

Four strategies and the Tale of Technical trading efficiency

In this last empirical investigation, we report results that clearly illustrate the previous discussion. We consider here four strategies using various sets of "good signals". These four strategies are:

1. Basic strategy, that will serve as a benchmark.
2. Inverse Strategy
3. Deterministic Lunatic Strategy
4. Stochastic Lunatic Strategy

Firstly, we focus on agents endowed with multiple signals[6] applying them on the daily closing price of the Dow-Jones (see section 5.2). These signals have been selected considering their Hit-Rate over a subsample of observations. Agents try to exploit these signals using various strategies, as proposed previously. Their relative performance are compared to a simple Buy and Hold behavior on the same sample. In this example there is no transaction costs.

---

[5] Including risk/return measures, in-sample selection and out-of sample tests, data-snooping control procedures see Lo and MacKinlay (1990) for a technical point and Park and Irwin (2004) for a general survey about these topics.

[6] RSI_{42-20}, RSI_{15-34}, $Momentum_{17-6}$, $Momentum_{13-10}$.

Strategy	Mean return	Standard deviation of returns	Sharpe Ratio
BH	$2.0152 \ 10^{-4}$	0.0113	0.0177
Basic	$1.6459 \ 10^{-4}$	0.0072	0.0227 *
Inverse	$1.9481 \ 10^{-4}$	0.007466	0.02608 *
Lunatic D.	$1.8826 \ 10^{-4}$	0.0080	0.0234 *
Lunatic S.	$1.0989 \ 10^{-4}$	0.008160	0.01346 *

stands for "actually outperform the Market"

Table 5.4. Performance of 4 strategies based on "(pseudo)good signals"

Considering this simple illustration, one can see that the best strategy here consists in doing exactly *the opposite* of what the signals suggest (*i.e.* to follow an Inverse Strategy, see table 5.5) . One can also achieve a better Sharpe Ratio with the "Deterministic-Lunatic" strategy than with the "Basic" strategy. One has to keep in mind that this result does not prove any inefficiency in the market because it might well be due to data-snooping, because its stability and robustness has not been checked, and last but not least, because it has been obtained without transaction costs. It is proposed for the sake of illustration and we therefore do not argue that it *proves* any dominance in performance. We only highlight the fact that whatever the "strategy" we consider, one can achieve a similar result with any other kind of strategy (apart "Stochastic-Lunatic", which basically is similar to a coin toss).

Some other amazing results

We now briefly propose some results of massive investigation on French data (see section 5.3) leading to similar conclusion.

Cheating is not playing: The following "strategy" is only given to fix some kind of boundaries. We call it the "cheating strategy". It has been designed to allow the agents to know at date t what will happen at date $t + 1$. They can therefore directly benefit from this information to (easily) outperform the market. The result of this behavior (Sharpe Ratio = 0.46349) is presented in figure 5.10. Our best non-cheating agent using a single signal is only able to produce 14.35% of this performance.

Good performance on bad basis: It is perfectly possible to design good agents (obtaining a Sharpe Ratio over the B&H one). As instance, signals "Variation-2-7-14" and "MA-85" obtain very bad Hit-Rates.

When these signals are "plugged" in an agent playing a Basic strategy and switching from one to the other every 500 dates (with respect to their relative Hit-Rate at these dates) we obtain a very satisfying performance with a Sharpe Ratio of 0.0288, while B&H Sharpe Ratio is 0.0283.

Signals do not signal anything: As quoted previously, it is frequently better to do exactly the opposite of what the signals suggest: if one wants to trade using a signal "indic-7-18-5" with an "Inverse Strategy" one should obtain a Sharpe Ratio of 0.0666 while following this signal would lead to a Sharpe equal to -0.0292 with a "Basic Strategy".

On the nature of the best strategies: Our set of signals is composed of 360.288 elements, 250.000 of them being "periodic signals": they propose to go long after "n" days and to go short after "m" other days. They cannot really be called "technical" signals but they can catch some special patterns such as the so-called "Monday Effect". Nevertheless, many of them can simply be analyzed as stochastic signals or zero-intelligence signals. Nevertheless, each of the 200 first agents ranked by Sharpe Ratio use these kind of signals. The best agent is therefore plugged with a "periodic signal 21-56" (obtaining a Sharpe Ratio equal to 0.0467). It is easy to find a similar agent using an "Inverse" strategy based on periodic signals, and behaving nearly as well as this pseudo-champion.

Thus, if one only scratches the surface of weak-form market efficiency, there is nothing to expect from technical trading. In other words, little evidence in terms of superior performance should arise from a cautious analysis of simple active trading rules. Nevertheless one cannot seriously affirm that these last tests completely answer the question.

This set of results as well of the elements we have discussed in this paper strongly suggest that:

1. Automatic trading based on technical analysis depends upon external factors such as leverage, transaction costs. There is an enormous variability in performance linked to these parameters.
2. It appears necessary to separate at least "signals" and "strategies". Naïve increases in agents cognitive skills are also useless to achieve satisfactory levels of performance(once incorporating risk). A fine-tuning aiming to balance the complexity of agents' capabilities and information resources is necessary.
3. To go deeper in this analysis would imply the definition of generic strategies describing learning procedures, adaptation and decision making processes.

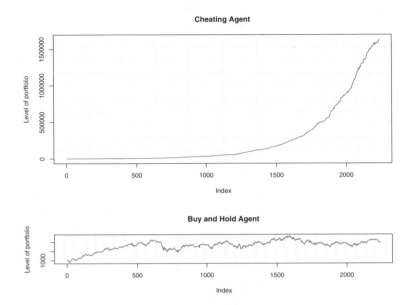

Fig. 5.10. With 0% trans. costs

Therefore, from a conceptual point of view, a robust framework for the evaluation of Agent-Based trading and technical analysis should systematically answer each of these 3 points at least, which obviously constitute a first step before rigorous statistical examinations.

Acknowledgement. This work has received a grant from European Community – FEDER – and *"Region Nord-Pas de Calais"* – CPER TAC – and from ACI *"Systèmes Complexes en SHS"*

References

O. Brandouy and P. Mathieu. Large-scale agent-based simulations and the efficient markets hypothesis. In C. Bruun, editor, *Advances in Artificial Economics*, volume 584 of *Lecture Notes in Economics and Mathematical Systems*, pages 15–27. Springer, 2006. 3-540-37247-4.

W. Brock, J. Lakonishock, and B. LeBaron. Simple technical trading rules and the stochastic properties of stock returns. *Journal of Finance*, 47:1731–1764, 1992.

M. Dempster and C. Jone. Can technical pattern trading be profitably automated ? 1. channels. Working paper, Center for Financial Research Working paper, udge Institute,University of Cambridge, 2005.

P.J. Detry and P. Gregoire. Other evidences of the predictive power of technical analysis: the moving-average rules on european indices. In *Proceedings of the Lugano European Financial Management Association Conference*, 2001.

E. Fama. Efficient capital markets: A review of theory and empirical work. *Journal of Finance*, 25:383–417, 1970.

D. K. Gode and S. Sunder. Allocative efficiency of markets with zero-intelligence traders: Market as a partial substitute for individual rationality. *Journal of Political Economy*, 101(1):119–137, February 1993.

A.R. Greenwald and P. Stone. Autonomous bidding agents in the trading agent competition. *IEEE Internet Computing*, 5(2), 2001.

T. Hellström and K. Holmström. Predicting the stock market. Technical Report IMa-TOM-1997-07, Center for Mathematical Modeling, Department of Mathematics and Physics, Märdalen University, Sweden, August 1998.

M.C. Jensen and G.A. Benington. Random walks and technical theories: Some additional evidence. *Journal of Finance*, 25:469–482, 1969.

A.W. Lo and A.C. MacKinlay. Data-snooping biases in tests of financial asset pricing models. *Review of Financial Studies*, 3(3):431–467, 1990.

C.H. Park and S.H. Irwin. The profitability of technical analysis. *AgMAS project Research Report 2004-4*, October 2004.

G. Weiss. Adaptation and learning in multi-agent systems: some remarks and a bibliography. In G. Weiss and S. Sen, editors, *Adaptation and Learning in Multi-Agent Systems*, volume 1042 of *Lecture Notes in Artificial Intelligence*, pages 1–21. Springer-Verlag, 1996.

H. White. A reality check for data snooping. *Econometrica*, 68(5): 1097–1126, September 2000.

Which Market Protocols Facilitate Fair Trading?

Marco LiCalzi and Paolo Pellizzari

Dept. Applied Mathematics and SSAV, U. of Venice, Italy
[licalzi,paolop]@unive.it

6.1 Introduction

The evaluation of an exchange market is a multi-faceted problem. An important criterion is the ability to achieve allocative efficiency. Gode and Sunder (1993) shows that a continuous double auction for single-unit trades leads to an efficient allocation even when the traders exhibit "zero-intelligence"; in other words, market protocols are active contributors in the search for a better outcome. Under reasonable circumstances, most of the commonly used market protocols share the ability to help traders discover an efficient allocation.

As suggested in Hurwicz (1994), however, the attainment of allocative efficiency is only a necessary condition for the effectiveness of a trading protocol and one should take into account other dimensions. Assuming zero intelligence, LiCalzi and Pellizzari (2007) compares the performance of different market protocols with regard both to allocative efficiency and other criteria such as excess volume or price dispersion. Their study considers agents with decreasing marginal utility that can repeatedly make single-unit trades and examines four common protocols: batch auction, continuous double auction, nondiscretionary dealership, and a hybrid of these latter two. All protocols exhibit a remarkable capacity to achieve allocative efficiency. However, stark differences in performance emerge over the other dimensions. These differences persist even when the assumption of zero intelligence is removed; LiCalzi and Pellizzari (see 2006).

The general conclusion is that although common market protocols may be close substitutes in helping (even zero-intelligent) traders to attain efficiency, they behave quite differently in many respects. This paper expands this line of research moving from the evaluation of allocative effectiveness to the assessment of allocative fairness. See Fehr et al. (1993) for a different line of attack on this theme.

Any trading protocol that attains allocative efficiency has two effects. From a static point of view, it moves the traders from their initial endowment to a final (efficient) position where no further paretian improvements are possible and all gains from trade are realized. This ability to help traders discover and exploit all gains from trade pertains to the allocative effectiveness of a market protocol. From a dynamic point of view, on the other hand, the denouement of a trading session decides how these gains are distributed among the traders. The performance of a trading protocol in this respect pertains to its allocative fairness.

A protocol that is allocatively efficient never leaves unrealized gains from trade. A protocol that is allocatively fair makes sure that these gains are equitably distributed among the traders. While many definitions of equitability are possible, there is a general sense that each traders should be entitled to a share of the gains from trade that his being in the market creates. In this paper, we consider the same four common protocols that we have shown to be allocatively efficient (even under zero intelligence) and we ask the following question. Suppose that the market is populated with only two families of agents. Both families are using trading strategies that are individually rational, but the second family enjoys a potential trading advantage on the first one. Which of these market protocols is more effective in making sure that the first family of agents overall loses the least on his "fair share" of gains from trade?

The organization of the paper is the following. Section 6.2 describes the model tested in our computational experiments and formalizes our research question. Section 6.3 details the experimental design and provides detailed instructions for its replication. Section 6.4 reports on the results obtained and Section 6.5 offers our conclusions.

6.2 The model

We use the same setup as in LiCalzi and Pellizzari (2007), where a simple exchange economy admits a unique efficient allocation for the single good to be traded. Given that the market protocols attain allocative efficiency, this implies convergence to the same final allocation of the good and facilitates comparisons.

6.2.1 The environment

We consider an economy with n traders. There is cash and one good, which we call "stock". Each trader i has an initial endowment of cash $c_i \geq 0$ and shares $s_i \geq 0$. Each trader i has CARA preferences over his final wealth, with a coefficient of risk tolerance $k_i > 0$. Therefore, trader i's excess demand function for stock (net of his endowment s_i) is the linear function

$$q_i(p) = \tau k_i(\mu - p) - s_i. \tag{6.1}$$

where μ is the mean and $\tau = 1/\sigma^2$ is the reciprocal of the variance (a.k.a. as the "precision") of the distribution of the final value of the stock. Each trader knows μ and τ as well as his endowment and his demand function, but otherwise has no information on the other agents.

Let $K = \sum_i k_i$ be the sum of traders' coefficients of risk tolerance, while $S = \sum_i s_i$ and $C = \sum_i c_i$ are the total stock and cash endowments. The unique efficient allocation of shares in this economy requires that trader i holds $s_i^* = (S/K)k_i$ shares of the stock. This is also achieved in the (unique) competitive equilibrium at price $p^* = \mu - S/(\tau K)$; see Wilson (1968). Clearly, the unique efficient allocation of shares is associated with a continuum of feasible allocations for cash; each of these determines a different apportionment of the gains from trade. Therefore, allocative efficiency corresponds to handing out stock in a unique way; allocative fairness has to do with how cash is redistributed during the trading that takes place before the efficient stock allocation is attained.

We emphasize that our setup is not meant to replicate the structure of a stock market; in particular, informational effects are ruled out. The underlying economy can be described as an exchange market for one good, where traders have strictly decreasing linear demands and heterogeneous preferences that are driven by a particularly simple parameterizations.

6.2.2 The market protocols

We compare the performances of four market protocols: a batch auction, a continuous double auction, a nondiscretionary dealership, and a hybrid of these last two. The first protocol is simultaneous, while the other three are sequential. The following features are common to all protocols. See LiCalzi and Pellizzari (2006, 2007) for a complete description of the protocols and details on their implementation.

A protocol is organized in trading sessions (or days). Agents participate in every trading session, but each of them can exchange at most one share per session. Reaching an efficient allocation requires multiple rounds of trading. If the protocol is sequential, the order in which agents place their orders is randomly chosen for each trading session. If the protocol is simultaneous, all order are made known and processed simultaneously so the time of their submission is irrelevant. The books are completely cleared at the end of each trading session. Prices are ticked and, for convenience, the tick is set equal to 1; in other words, prices must be integers.

6.2.3 Behavioral assumptions and fair shares

The following behavioral assumptions hold for each trader. An agent is restricted to trade one unit at a time. Budget constraints must be satisfied. Given the demand function (6.1), trader i has decreasing marginal utility for additional units. If the current endowment of a trader is s, his valuation for the next unit to trade is

$$v_i(\pm 1) = \mu - \frac{s \pm 1}{\tau k_i} \qquad (6.2)$$

where the $\pm$ sign depends on whether the attempted trade is a purchase or a sale. Hence, his reservation price depends on the side of the transaction he is entering and on his current endowment s_i. Moreover, his certainty equivalent for holding quantities c and s of cash and stock is

$$m_i(c, s) = c + \left(\mu - \frac{s}{2\tau k_i}\right) s \qquad (6.3)$$

It is worth noting that the certainty equivalent m_i accounts for c at face value but evaluates s using an individual "price of risk" $\mu - [s/(2\tau k_i)]$.

The initial endowment (c_i^0, s_i^0) of a trader i provides him with a certainty equivalent $m_i^0 = m_i(c_i^0, s_i^0)$. We define his "fair share" m_i^* of gains from trade as the certainty equivalent he would attain under the fictitious protocol of Walrasian tâtonnement, where a centralized market maker iteratively elicit traders' excess demand functions and keeps adjusting prices to equilibrate them *before* trade takes actually place. Under standard conditions, this protocol is a natural benchmark because it attains allocative efficiency in one giant step, while simultaneously minimizing both the volume of transactions and price dispersion. For later use please note that, under this protocol, a trader with *ex ante* knowledge of the equilibrium price p^* would attain exactly the same final certainty equivalent and thus would not be able to increase his fair share.

Under the Walrasian protocol, a trader i ends up with cash $c_i^* = c_i^0 - p_i^*(s_i^* - s_i^0)$ and stock $s_i^* = (S/K)k_i$. After substitution, the certainty equivalent of his fair share is

$$m_i^* = c_i^0 - p^*(s_i^* - s_i^0) + s_i^*\left(\mu - \frac{s_i^*}{2\tau k_i}\right) =$$
$$c_i^0 + \left(\mu - \frac{S}{2\tau K}\right)s_i^0 + \frac{S}{2\tau K}\left(\frac{S}{K}k_i - s_i^0\right)$$

which nicely decomposes into the sum of three terms. The first one is the initial cash endowment of trader i; the second is the "value" of his initial stock endowment at the market price of risk; the third one is a positive correction term that is increasing in the difference between the efficient and the initial stock endowment for i. Since trading is voluntary, individual rationality implies that the difference between the fair share and the initial certainty equivalent for each i is positive:

$$m_i^* - m_i^0 = \frac{(Ks_i^0 - k_iS)^2}{2\tau k_i K^2} \geq 0$$

We expect that market protocols affect how much of their fair share different families of agents manage to obtain in the end. This requires to aggregate social welfare over groups of agents. We measure the social welfare of a group G by the sum of the certainty equivalents across the traders in G. Given the initial endowments (c_i^0, s_i^0) of each trader i, the (initial) social welfare of the entire traders' population is $M^0 = \sum_i m_i(c_i^0, s_i^0)$. After reaching an efficient allocation, the social welfare increases to

$$M^* = \sum_i m_i^* = C + \left(\mu - \frac{S}{2\tau K}\right)S \qquad (6.4)$$

which is the analog of Equation (6.3) at the market level. We slightly abuse notation here, because M^* is achieved by any efficient allocation including (but not limited to) the one induced by the Walrasian procedure. Looking at the left-hand side of Figure 6.1, efficient trading expands the pie from M^0 to M^*.

Consider now a strict subset G of traders. They start with an initial endowment that corresponds to a social welfare $M_G^0 = \sum_{i \in G} m_i^0$ for the group G. The fair share of this group is $M_G^* = \sum_{i \in G} m_i^* \geq M_G^0$. In the right-hand side of Figure 6.1, we represent M_G^0 as the circular sector from the inside circle and M_G^* as the union of M_G^0 and the annular sector

Fig. 6.1. Gains from trade and fairness.

topping it. In general, M_G^* expands but need not be proportional to M_G^0. Suppose now that at the end of a trading protocol, the social welfare of a group G is $M_G^* \cup A_G$ so that the group G is extracting higher gains from trade than its fair share. Then we say that the protocol has been too favorable to the traders in G or, equivalently, that it has been unfair to the traders in the complementary set G^c. Hence, allocative fairness is about how the larger pie created by trading is redistributed among different groups of traders. Similarly to a zero-sum game, a trader gets more than his fair share by taking away a piece of someone's else fair share.

Our approach to study allocative fairness is to split the traders' population into two families and compare the ability of market protocols to prevent one group from exploiting the other one. For realism, we assume that all agents are individually rational: regardless of which family he belongs to, each agent accepts a trade only if this cannot decrease his current certainty equivalent. An agent who undertakes a sequence of trades over time increases (possibly, weakly) his own certainty equivalent in each transaction. This assumption, for instance, is consistent with zero-intelligence.

Our two families of interacting traders are chosen to emphasize differences in the ability to appropriate gains from trade. Notably, individual rationality alone cannot prevent a purchase from an inframarginal seller even if this reduces the potential gains from a specific trade. Put differently, individual rationality protects a buyer from making a personal loss on a trade but does not imply that he is trading with the "right" counterpart. This stronger guarantee requires knowledge of the equilibrium price p^* in order to spot and refuse inframarginal trades. We assume that some traders satisfy only individual rationality while others can do better because they know p^* as well.[1]

The first group is formed by the truth-telling (from now on, TT) traders described in LiCalzi and Pellizzari (2007). At the start of a

---

[1]   An alternative assumption is that only the second type of traders are able to compute or deduce p^* from the available information.

trading session, a TT trader chooses with equal probability on which side of the market (buy or sell) he attempts to trade one unit. Suppose he goes for a purchase; the case of a sale is analogous. Given his current endowment, the agent knows that his valuation for the next unit to buy is $v_i(+1)$ from Equation (6.2). In a batch auction, he truthfully bids $v_i(+1)$. In a sequential protocol, he checks first if the best current ask price is $p \leq v_i(+1)$; if so, he buys one unit at p. Otherwise, he places a bid equal to $v_i(+1)$. In other words, when no better deal is available, a TT buyer posts a bid equal to his current valuation for the next unit to buy and thus "truthfully" reveals his reservation value. Compared to zero-intelligence trading, a TT agent is less greedy because he posts the largest bid that is individually rational given his own valuation. When a TT agent buys one unit at a price p higher than the equilibrium price p^*, he increases his certainty equivalent but eats up a piece $(p - p^*)$ of his fair share.

The second group of agents consists of traders that know the correct equilibrium price; we call them price-informed (from now on, PI). This extreme assumption is a very parsimonious way to endow these agents with the ability to cut down on inframarginal trades and make sure that they never lose on their fair share. Given his current endowment, a PI agent knows that he should be a buyer if $v_i(+1) \geq p^*$ and a seller if $v_i(-1) \leq p^*$. Therefore, he never needs to guess which side he should take.

Suppose that the PI agent should be a buyer; the opposite case is analogous. In a batch auction, he simply bids p^*. In a sequential protocol, a PI trader must take action when he is called out and cannot wait for better terms. When it is his turn, he first looks for "sure deals" by checking whether the best current ask price is $p_a \leq p^*$ or the best bid price is $p_b \geq p^*$; if so, he buys or sell one unit, respectively. Otherwise, and limitedly to the two book-based protocols, a PI agent places a bid that improves the current best bid p_b by one tick and achieves time-price priority at a buying price never greater than p^*. In general, the trading strategy of a PI agent has three characteristics: first, he never fails to exploit opportunities for trading off the equilibrium price; second, he never trades at a price worse than p^* (and hence never loses on his fair share); third, conditional on these two constraints, he maximizes the probability of trading in the right direction. This last restriction is chosen to emphasize the ability of PI traders to take advantage of TT agents.

Depending on the protocols and the random sequence of trades, the attainment of full allocative efficiency may sometimes fail. For instance, in the nondiscretionary dealership, the existence of a fixed bid-ask spread may prevent two or more TT agents from completing their few last trades. This may (albeit marginally) reduce the overall gains from trade and lower allocative efficiency, confusing our study of allocative fairness. To rule out this spurious effect, after all trading opportunities within the protocol are exhausted, we force agents to carry out all residual efficient trades at price p^*. We emphasize that this has the only purpose of actually realizing the full pie M^* so that we can concentrate on its redistribution; in particular, none of these final trades eats up on the fair share of a trader.

Let M_G^T be the final fair share of a group G when trading takes place using a trading protocol T. Given their information and trading strategies, only PI agents can "exploit" TT traders. Therefore, whenever allocative efficiency is attained, $M_G^T \geq M_G^*$ for $G = PI$ and any protocol T among the four we consider. We can thus test the ability of a trading protocol T to foster a fair allocation by comparing $M_G^T - M_G^*$ for $G = PI$.

Clearly, the ability of the PI group to exploit TT traders depends also on the proportion π of PI traders in the market. The more the exploiters, the harder becomes the competition for trades at prices different from p^*. Therefore, we study how allocative fairness is affected by the proportion π in $(0, 1)$. Endpoints of the interval are ruled out to avoid trivialities.

6.3 Experimental design

6.3.1 Identification

The global parameters are the number n of traders, the mean μ and the variance σ^2 of the realization value of the asset, the number t of trading sessions, and the number λ of PI traders. (The proportion of PI agents is $\pi = \lambda/n$.) Individually, a trader i is characterized by his coefficient k_i of risk tolerance and by his endowment of cash c_i and asset shares s_i. Finally, for protocols involving the dealer, we need to select her initial quotes and a (fixed) spread.

The exemplar for our simulations is similar to that one used in LiCalzi and Pellizzari (2006). The basic parametric configuration is reported in Table 6.1. The ratio $S/K = 2$ implies that the competitive equilibrium price is $p^* = \mu - \sigma^2(S/K) = 760$. The initial dealer's quotes in the nondiscretionary dealership are a bid of 755 and an ask of 765, with a fixed bid-ask spread of 10. In the hybrid protocol, where

	Parameters		Initialization
Global	n	$=$	$1,000$
	μ	$=$	$1,000$
	σ^2	$=$	120
	t	$=$	500
	λ	$=$	integer in $(0,n)$
Trader	k_i	$=$	divisors of σ^2 in $\{10,\ldots,40\}$
	c_i	$=$	$50,000$
	s_i	$=$	permutation of $2k_i$

Table 6.1. Exemplar for identification.

the dealer's presence restricts the ability of PI traders to steal better deals, the initial bid and ask prices of 745 and 775 exactly straddle the equilibrium price of 760, with a fixed spread of 30.

The robustness tests reported in Section 6.4.1 change one parameter at a time with respect to this exemplar. We have worked out simulations where the ratio S/K is 1 (or 3), making the equilibrium price higher (lower); where the dealer's fixed spread in the nondiscretionary dealership is 6 (or 30), making the market more (less) liquid; and where the fixed spread in the hybrid protocol takes different values between 4 and 300, making the dealer's presence more or less influential.

6.3.2 Simulations and data representation

A round of testing simulates traders' behavior in 4 different protocols for different values of λ. A typical cycle is run as follows. We fix an integer value of λ in the range $\{1,\ldots,n-1\}$ and then we randomly choose different queues of traders for each trading session. These choices are kept fixed across the four protocols, so that each of them is tested using the same fraction of PI traders and the same orderings in each trading sessions. All other parameters are instantiated as per the exemplar in Table 6.1. The number of agents is $n = 1000$; we run 999 trials per cycle and test each value of λ from 1 to 999. At the end of each simulation, we compute and record all relevant statistics. The simulations are run using a package of routines written in Pascal. The statistical and graphical analysis of the data are made using R, an open-source environment for statistical computing available at http://www.r-project.org/.

We use two (normalized) measures to assess the allocative fairness of a protocol. Let M_G^T be the final share of the group G when trading takes place using a trading protocol T and M_G^* their fair share (using the Walrasian protocol). As discussed above, only PI agents can "exploit" TT traders; hence, we fix $G = PI$ for the rest of the paper. The first measure is the absolute *excess gain* $(M_G^T - M_G^*)/M^0$ for the group G. The division by the size M^0 of the initial pie is a normalization introduced to make the index scale–free and allow direct comparisons; however, for simplicity, in the rest of the paper we write the absolute excess gain as $M_G^T - M_G^*$ and leave the normalization implicit. The second measure is the relative *excess gain* $(M_G^T - M_G^*)/M_G^*$. The absolute excess gain reports how much welfare PI traders collectively take away from TT traders with respect to the initial pie. The relative excess gain measures how much (on average) a PI trader is expected to improve his final welfare by trading within a given protocol.

A graphical representation of each set of data is obtained as follows. Given a protocol T, we plot the 999 data points produced in a simulation. We then fit a smoothing function generated by applying a Friedman smoother to all the data points associated with the same protocol; see Venables and Ripley (2002). Reading Figure 6.2 from left to right exemplifies this procedure for the case of a continuous double auction.

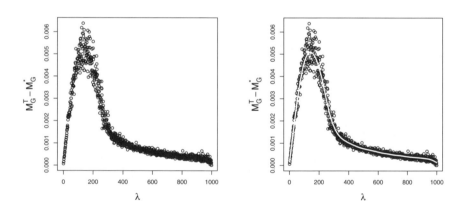

Fig. 6.2. Realizations (left) and a superimposed Friedman smoother (right).

6.4 Results

Figure 6.3 shows two representative pictures based on our exemplar. The figure on the left reports the (normalized) absolute excess gain

$M_G^T - M_G^*$ collectively achieved by the PI traders as a function of their cardinality λ for four protocols: batch auction, continuous double auction, nondiscretionary dealership, and the hybridization of these two latter protocols. Note that dividing λ by $n = 1000$ gives the proportion π of PI agents active in the market.

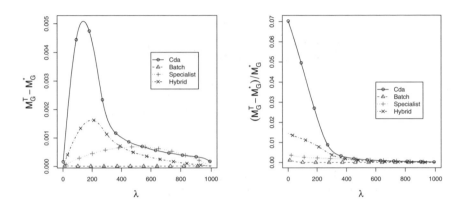

Fig. 6.3. Absolute (left) and relative (right) excess gain for PI traders.

The first comment is that the batch auction protects the TT traders much more effectively than any other protocol for both measures and for any number of PI traders. This is not surprising: the batch auction protocol requires simultaneous submission of trading orders and is therefore much more difficult for PI agents to exploit. By posting an order at p^*, each PI trader maximizes the probability of trading under the constraint of never losing on his fair share. Whenever the trading price issued in a session of the batch auction is different from p^*, he cuts away a piece of a TT trader's fair share. However, because the batch auction aggregates all the orders received in a trading session, it is very unlikely to issue a trading price different from p^*. We can thus shift our focus of interest to the three sequential protocols. For completeness, however, we report also the data relative to the batch auction.

The second comment is that in general the absolute excess gain for sequential protocols is a unimodal function of λ. Therefore, the collective ability of PI to exploit TT traders peaks at some intermediate value of λ. In this respect, there is a *natural ordering* of protocols from dealership to hybrid protocol to continuous double auction that appears twice. First, the maximum excess gain for PI traders is increasing in the natural ordering of protocols. Simultaneously, the value of λ that maximizes the PI excess gain is decreasing. In other words, PI traders can achieve a greater excess gain in a continuous double auction, but their most effective proportion in such protocol is lower.

The result that the excess gain is increasing in the natural ordering is a direct consequence of the "protection" that the dealership provides. Because the dealer posts bid and ask prices that tend to straddle the correct p^*, the transaction price is never too different from this latter price; hence, no much fair share can be lost. The result that the λ's maximizing total excess gain are decreasing in the natural ordering can be heuristically explained by the combination of two effects. Intuitively, PI traders are most effective to exploit TT traders when their proportion is neither too low (there must be enough exploiters around) neither too high (there must be enough people to exploit). But we can put a bit more flesh on this explanation.

Consider the continuous double auction. The overall fair share for the TT group that PI traders can appropriate is roughly proportional to $(1 - \pi)$. On the other hand, taken as a group, the TT traders can lose a piece of their fair share only when one of them trades with a PI agent at a price different from p^*. The probability of a PI agent being matched for trade with a TT agent is roughly proportional to $\pi(1-\pi)$. Therefore, the excess gain appropriated by the PI group in the continuous double auction are approximately proportional to $\pi(1-\pi)^2$ and the maximum should be attained around $\hat{\pi} = 1/3$, corresponding to $\lambda = n\hat{\pi} = 333$ in our exemplar. The actual value is somewhat lower because some matchings between PI and TT agents do not lead to any trade.

Consider now the dealership. The overall fair share that PI traders can appropriate is still roughly proportional to $(1 - \pi)$. Moreover, because they can only trade with an impersonal dealer, the probability of a trade involving a PI agent is roughly proportional to the fraction π. Therefore, the excess gain for the PI group is now approximately proportional to $\pi(1 - \pi)$ and the maximum should be attained around $\hat{\pi} = 1/2$, corresponding to $\lambda = 500$ in our exemplar. As before, the exact value of the maximizer is affected by microstructural considerations that this heuristic argument does not capture. Finally, the corresponding values for the hybrid protocol are a convex combination of those of the parent protocols.

The third comment is that there are no important differences among sequential protocols when π (or λ) is sufficiently large, because there are too few TT traders to be exploited. The overall fair share to be appropriated is roughly proportional to $(1 - \pi)$ and for large π there is simply too little to be taken away by the PI group. Moreover, markets with a high proportion of PI traders tend to exhibit a similar degree of allocative fairness because a PI agent never loses on his fair share. Therefore, we restrict the following comparisons to $\pi \leq 40\%$, corresponding to $\lambda \leq 400$ in our exemplar. For any proportion $\pi \leq 40\%$, the ranking over sequential mechanisms concerning their ability to prevent PI agents from eroding TT traders' fair shares is clear-cut and follows the natural ordering.

The right-hand side of Figure 6.3 reports the relative extra gain $(M_S^T - M_S^*)/M_S^*$ collectively achieved by the PI traders as a function of their number λ for the three sequential protocols. Unsurprisingly, this shows that increasing the number of exploiters makes their "looting" less effective for each protocol. Moreover, the ranking is again clearcut and follows the natural ordering. Finally, this effect is essentially unchanged in all the additional tests reported in the following section.

6.4.1 Tests of robustness

We have run some robustness tests by changing one parameter at a time in the exemplar. The first test looks at differences in the total endowment of stock, leading to a different equilibrium price p^*. The exemplar has a ratio $S/K = 2$ yielding $p^* = 1000 - 120(S/K) = 760$ and generates the left-hand side of Figure 6.3. We keep the same k_i for each trader i, but endow him with a different multiple of his original endowment s_i. This changes the ratio s_i/k_i and of course S/K as well. Figure 6.4 reports data when $S/K = 1$ (on the left) and $S/K = 3$ (on the right), corresponding respectively to a smaller and to a larger total endowment of stock. The equilibrium prices are now 880 and 640, respectively. We adjust the initial dealer's quotes accordingly, making sure that they always exactly straddle the equilibrium price.

Comparing the two figures from Figure 6.4 (as well as the right-hand side of Figure 6.3) shows that a larger stock endowment S increases the relative excess gain $(M_G^T - M_G^*)/M_G^*$ of PI for each protocol and each λ. We do not report the figures for the absolute excess gain to preserve space, but they exhibit a similar increasing effect. In fact, the following argument shows that, over our range of choices for S/K, an increasing relative excess gain implies an increasing absolute excess gain. The quantity M_G^* is roughly proportional to πM^*; in turn, M^* is increasing in (S/K) as far as $\tau\mu \geq (S/K)$ — as seen by differentiating (6.4) with respect to S. As this inequality holds for our choices of S/K,

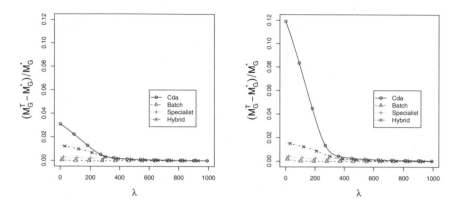

Fig. 6.4. Different equilibrium prices: $S/K = 1$ (left) and $S/K = 3$ (right).

the denominator of the relative excess gain is increasing and the claim follows. Put differently, this shows that a higher stock endowment S brings about a roughly proportional increase in the absolute excess gain.

The increase in the relative excess gain exhibited by Figure 6.4 is a stronger property that is explained by a second perhaps less obvious effect. *Ceteris paribus,* a larger S increases the number of trades that need to be carried out in order to reach the allocative efficiency. Each of these trades is a potential opportunity for PI agents to exploit, making them more likely to extract excess gain from the TT agents. This second effect accounts for the increase in the relative excess gain.

The second test considers the effect of changing the dealer's fixed spread in the nondiscretionary dealership, while keeping his initial quotes centered around the equilibrium price. The exemplar has a fixed spread of 10. Figure 6.5 reports the absolute excess gain when the fixed spread is 6 (bottom), 10 (middle), or 30 (top). The lower the spread, the more influential is the dealer's ability to constrain prices within a narrow band that individually rational trading naturally tends to keep around the equilibrium price p^*. Forcing the transaction price to lie in a band, of course, protects TT agents from more serious mispricings and hence reduces the ability of PI traders to exploit them. Accordingly, we see in Figure 6.5 that the absolute excess gain is increasing in the dealer's fixed spread for any number λ of PI traders.

A third test checks the effect of changing the dealer's fixed spread in the hybrid protocol dealership where an agent has access both to the dealer's quotes and to a book fed with limit orders from other traders.

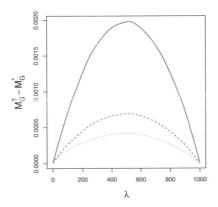

Fig. 6.5. Different fixed spreads in the dealership: 6, 10, 30 (bottom to top).

The exemplar has a fixed spread of 30. Figure 6.6 reports the absolute excess gain when this fixed spread takes five different values from 4 (bottom) to 300 (top). The absolute excess gain is increasing in the dealer's fixed spread for any number λ of PI traders. This effect and its explanation are analogous to the above. There is a second more interesting effect to note. In terms of the ability to control the absolute excess gain, the continuous double auction is the limit case of the hybrid protocol as the fixed spread goes to $+\infty$. When the dealer posts bid and ask that are too far apart, trading takes place only on the book. Accordingly, as we move from a low to a high spread, the excess gain curve morphs from the shape associated with a dealership to the shape associated with a continuous double auction; for instance, the peak increases and shifts leftward.

6.5 Conclusions

We have studied the performance of four market protocols with regard to their ability to equitably distribute the gains from trade among two groups of participants in an exchange economy. We assume Walrasian tatônemment as benchmark and define the fair share that should accrue to a trader as the certainty equivalent he would attain under this procedure.

When necessary, the first group of traders bids or asks their reservation value; this makes sure that trading never decreases their own certainty equivalent but exposes them to a possible loss on their fair

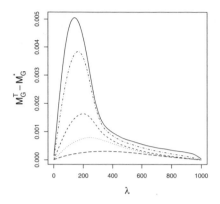

Fig. 6.6. Different dealer's spreads in the hybrid protocol: 4, 10, 30, 100, 300 (bottom to top).

share. The second group of traders knows (or can compute) the equilibrium price p^* and uses this information to make sure that trading cannot reduce either their certainty equivalent or their own fair share.

We test the allocative fairness of protocols by running (computerized) experiments where these two families of traders interact with each other. We find that there is a clear-cut ranking of protocols with respect to allocative fairness, defined as their ability to prevent PI agents from eroding TT traders' fair shares. Going from best to worst, this ranking is: batch auction, nondiscretionary dealership, the hybridization of a dealership and a continuous double auction, and finally the pure continuous double auction. The same ranking holds when we replace the absolute excess gain for PI traders with their relative excess gain.

Acknowledgement. We thank two referees for their comments and acknowledge financial support from MIUR.

References

E. Fehr, G. Kirchsteiger, and A. Riedl. Does fairness prevent market clearing? an experimental investigation. *The Quarterly Journal of Economics,* 108(2):437–459, May 1993.
D. K. Gode and S. Sunder. Allocative efficiency of markets with zero-intelligence traders: Market as a partial substitute for individual ra-

tionality. *Journal of Political Economy*, 101(1):119–137, February 1993.

L. Hurwicz. Economic design, adjustment and mechanism. *Economic Design*, 1:1–14, 1994.

M. LiCalzi and P. Pellizzari. The allocative effectiveness of market protocols under intelligent trading. In C. Bruun, editor, *Advances in Artificial Economics*, pages 17–29. Springer, 2006.

M. LiCalzi and P. Pellizzari. Simple market protocols for efficient risk sharing. *Journal of Economic Dynamics and Control*, 2007. Forthcoming.

W. N. Venables and B. D. Ripley. *Modern Applied Statistics with S.* Springer, fourth edition, 2002.

R. Wilson. The theory of syndicates. *Econometrica*, pages 119–132, 1968.

Part III

Market Dynamics and Efficiency

An Artificial Economics View of the Walrasian and Marshallian Stability

Marta Posada, Cesáreo Hernández, and Adolfo López-Paredes

INSISOC, University of Valladolid, Spain
{posada,cesareo,adolfo}@insisoc.org

7.1 Introduction

The experiments discussed below are an attempt to examine two concepts of instability which stem from two different models of market adjustment used in Economics: Walrasian (W) and Marshallian (M) instability. The M model views volume as adjusting in response to the difference between demand price and supply price at that volume. The W model views price as changing in response to excess demand at that price. Do the M and the W models have a firm foundation on micromotives, or are they just macro abstractions that we could dispense of in Microeconomics?

If there is an awkward question one has to suffer when teaching economics, this is *who does the job of the so called market adjustment?* In contrast with the usual microeconomic models, these processes of adjustment do not represent any optimization of the economic agents' behavior, but just differential equations brought out from nowhere. As Nicholson (1997, chapter 19) states in his well known microeconomics book: *"in the last instance this speculation on the adjustment mechanism hardly makes any sense, because neither the Walrasian nor the Marshalian adjustment reflect the real behavior of the economic agents"*. Being virtual market adjustment models taken from the mechanical analogy of vector fields, they can be compatible with different micro behaviors of the participant agents. Nevertheless it is interesting to further asses the relevance of both concepts of instability, and to which extent they emerge from individual agents' behavior. To this end we will use the empirical evidence obtained from the simulation with an Multi Agent Based Model (MABS).

MABS has become a popular tool to theorize about distributed but interacting phenomena as markets and economic activity are. Economics is a Social Science. Being social inherits complexity and being a science calls for experimentation. Historical records are not enough to test economic theories. Experimental Economics with humans has provided a replicable Lab that provides further empirical data to suggest new solutions to economic problems and to test standing models and theories. But human behavior in the experiments is not directly controllable and the question of what the agents' behavior is remains open. Artificial Economics, mainly MABS, has broadened the scope of Experimental Economics, allowing the experimenter to check alternative individual behavior. In this sense MABS is a "killer application" of Economic Theory.

This paper addresses four questions: Can both stable and unstable equilibria be observed in a Continuous Double Auction? If markets do exhibit instability, which of the two models, M/W, will lead to the right equilibria prediction? How robust are the results against alternative learning agents? In view of these results, what is the interest of both instability concepts for policy modeling and simulation?

7.2 Scope and related work

Some comments are convenient to asses the scope of the paper. There are two strands of researchers in Artificial Economics: people interested in the computational properties and policy issues of a given aggregated market and those interested in growing markets with desirable properties from agents with micromotives. Since in microeconomics we work with aggregated markets at a higher level of abstraction than in MABS, an important issue is often overlooked. The market has three dimensions (Smith, 1989): the institution (it is both the exchange rules and the way the contracts are closed, and the information network), the environment (agents' endowments and values, resources and knowledge) and the agents' behavior. These dimensions are frequently overlooked in Economics, leading to confusing terms such as market adjustment.

In the theory of general equilibrium it was undoubtedly the imposition of high standards of mathematical formalism that led to the almost exclusive concern with the existence and characterization of equilibria rather than the adjustment process that lead to them. In the nineties there was an upsurge in interest to determining the adjustment process and how the economic agents might learn their way into equilibria. But these works have been focused on the question of learning about the parameters of the model as captured by some (Walrasian or not) equilibrium model. They have concentrated on proving the existence of such an equilibrium and perhaps some evolutionary mechanism that will lead to the fixed point equilibrium, under the forceful assumption of rational expectations.

Real markets are information gathering tools that will allow many reasonable and realistic heuristic learning-decision models from agents yet achieving market convergence and equilibrium. Assuming that learning is primary focused towards finding the true parameters, that may describe the macroscopic market behavior as a "virtual" entity, is just totally unnecessary and even unrealistic. Why should the agents have a "virtual correct" macro model in mind and try to capture the parameters of the model? Their search may be local and no super agent such as the Walrasian auctioneer is needed for a market clearing-price as the evidence form Experimental Economics has proved.

The advantage to move from human to artificial agents (from Experimental to Artificial Economics) is that in our experiment we have control over the agents' behavior (Lopez-Paredes et al., 2002).

An extreme case was the Zero-Intelligent agents model of Gode and Sunder (1993) and Sunder (2004). It is a simple artificial model that does a reasonable job of capturing the dynamics of the competitive market and assures convergence and efficiency without any tâtonnement process. Of course such a challenging fact has been questioned recently by Brewer et al. (2002); Cliff and Bruten (1997); Gjerstad and Dickhaut (1998); Posada (2006). The main conclusions are that the institutional design matters and so does the agents' intelligence. That perfect competition is compatible with strategic agent's behaviour.

Our paper is not about solving an M or a W set of general equilibrium system of equations, along the lines of Colander (1995) although we grow a model that, yes, at the same time computes the solution. We do not intend to inquire about the microfoundations of top-down models e.g. differences between Keynesian and Walrasian economics, although again, this will be an interesting application of MABS in a similar vein to this paper.

In this paper we replicate and generalize with artificial agents the results of Plott and George (1992) and Brewer et al. (2002) experiments of M/W instability with humans and a forward falling supply function. They found that in a continuous double auction the M stability model captures the observed phenomena whereas the W model does not. We wonder as well if their results depend on the particular human agents' behavior because nothing is said about this issue.

The choice of the environment to introduce instability is essential to isolate the two sources of instability: either from the agents' behavior or from the environment. In environments where the supply is positively sloped and the demand is negatively sloped (as in Figure 1.a), there is only one equilibrium and it is both W and M stable (MS/WS). The controversy arises when a priori there are several points that should be M (W) stable (unstable). For example, in Figure 1.b, if the supply is negatively sloped and if the demand cuts the supply from above (below), the equilibrium is W unstable (MU) and M stable (WS) and Marshallian unstable (MU).

The forward falling supply is not an exceptionally abnormal supply, although this issue is of a secondary relevance for our arguments. It is the case, for instance, in information technologies products where marginal costs are practically zero and externalities and learning are present.

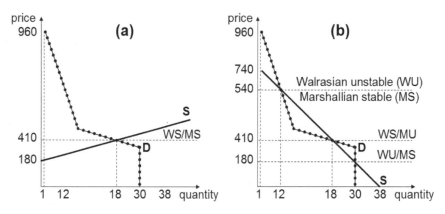

Fig. 7.1. Environments: (a) standard, (b) forward falling supply

7.3 The model

The main features of our model are described using the triple (IxExA):

a) *The institution, I.* Under the continuous double auction (CDA) rules, any trader can send (or accept) an order at any time during the trading period. A new bid/ask has to improve previous pre-existing bid/ask. A trade occurs when a new ask is made that is less than a pre-existing bid, or when a new bid is made that is greater than a pre-existing ask. The trading is equal to that of the pre-existing bid/ask, whose acceptance is triggered automatically by the new entry.

b) *The environment, E.* We use a forward falling supply (Figure 1b). We have used the same valuations which were used in Plott and George (1992)'s experiments with human agents.

In the demand side, there are six buyers (each one with six units). There are two buyers of each type. Each buyer of a given type has identical reserve price given by [960, 600, 440, 350, 330, 0], [880, 640, 410, 390, 310, 0] and [800, 720, 410, 390, 290, 0], respectively. Buyers know their reserve price with certainty.

In the supply side, there are six sellers. Each seller is uncertain about his marginal costs because they depend on their own output and the output of all other sellers. The externality implies that, as market volume increases, the marginal cost decreases even though the individual seller's marginal cost increases with an increase in his own volume. Each seller has eight units to trade. There are two sellers of each type (a, b, c). In Table 1 we show the marginal costs of type-a sellers. Each seller of a given type has identical marginal cost. The marginal cost of the first unit when the volume of others is 0, is 820 (for type-b is 800 and for type-c is 780). As unit increases, the marginal cost value increases by 80. Note that as the volume of others increases, the marginal cost value decreases by 30 per unit. The exceptions are every fifth unit starting at 5 (at 3 for type-b and at 1 for type-c) at which point the increment is 80 as opposed to 30.

Table 7.1. Marginal costs of a type-a sellers

	Volume of others							
	0	1	2	3	4	5	6 ...	18
1st unit	820	790	760	730	700	620	590 ...	130
2nd unit	900	870	840	810	780	700	670 ...	210
3rd unit	980	950	920	890	860	780	750 ...	290
	⋮	⋮	⋮	⋮	⋮	⋮	⋮	⋮ ⋰	⋮
8th unit	1380	1350	1320	1290	1260	1180	1150 ...	690

Table 7.2 lists the equilibria according to both Walrasian and Marshallian theories.

c) *Agent's behavior, A.* The first decision which is taken by each seller is to estimate the volume sold in the market by others. Sellers are uncertain about their marginal costs, because they depend on their output and the output of all the other sellers. Sellers form expectations $\hat{q}_{n+1}$ on the volume using their own past experience. They update their volume expectations according to the actual volume observed in the

Table 7.2. Equilibria according to both Walrasian and Marshallian theories

Price	Quantity	Marshall	Walras
500-540	12	stable	unstable
380-410	18	unstable	stable
140-180	30	stable	unstable

market (q_n). In particular, any seller uses the following simple updating rule:

$$\hat{q}_{n+1} = (1 - \lambda)\hat{q}_n + \lambda q_n .$$

The learning rate λ measures the responsiveness of sellers' volume estimates to new data (a memory weighting factor). If $\lambda = 1$ the agents believe that the quantity sold by others in the next period will be equal to the traded volumes observed in the current period, and they will under-estimate their marginal cost. If $\lambda = 0$ the agents do not use the information generated in the market to improve the estimation of the initial traded volume (myopic behaviour).

Buyers do not need to estimate their reserve prices because they know them with certainty.

In the next step, agents (sellers and buyers) face the following three decisions: How much should they bid or ask? When should they submit an order? When should they accept an outstanding order? To take these decisions each agent only knows his own valuations, which are private, and the information generated in the market.

How much should he offer? We try two alternative bidding strategies: ZI (Gode and Sunder [6]) and GD (Gjerstad and Dickhaut [4]). Each bidding strategy has different answers to this question. Each ZI agent chooses his order randomly between his private valuations and the best order outstanding in the market. Each GD agent chooses the order that maximizes his expected surplus, defined as the product of the gain from trade (price minus private valuation) and the probability $\prod_a$ for an order to be accepted:

$$\max \prod_a (price - MaC) , \tag{7.1}$$

where GD agents estimate the probability $\prod_a$ learning to modify their beliefs using the history of the recent market activity. GD sellers calculate a belief value $q(a)$ for an order a using AAG (accepted asks greater than a), BG (bids greater than a) and RAL (rejected asks less than a). Interpolation is used for values at which no orders are registered.

$$q(a) = \frac{AAG(a) + BG(a)}{AAG(a) + BG(a) + RAL(a)} . \tag{7.2}$$

When should he submit an order? When an agent is active, he may submit an order (a new or a replacement an open order). The agents have a constant activation probability of 25%. Of course, orders must be also in agreement with spread reduction rule of the institution.

When should he accept an outstanding order? A seller accepts the current bid if his ask (submitted or not) is equal to or greater than the current bid. A buyer accepts the current ask if his bid (submitted or not) is equal to or less than the current ask.

7.4 Some results

Note that the agents have two basic learning tasks: learning about the externality as represented by the total amount to be traded, and learning how to bid/ask. How is the performance of humans, ZI and GD agents in these two tasks? Following we discuss the meaning of the results of prices and volume.

Price volatility. Figure 2 shows the price distributions of the transactions in ten trading periods (each one with 100 rounds). Here we can see that for homogeneous ZI populations, the transaction prices are more volatile than for homogeneous GD populations, where the price convergence is very clear. The learning rate plays an important role on the convergence to the Marshallian stable equilibrium. All transactions in GD populations are much closer to the Marshallian stable equilibrium (540-500) when their λ learning rate is 0.9 than when their λ learning rate is 0.1 (myopic behaviour).

Price convergence. Although the transaction prices in homogeneous ZI populations are widely distributed, there is a false convergence appearance. In Figure 3 we show the time series of price transactions. We observe that for ZI homogeneous populations, there is no price convergence to the equilibrium price.

Figure 4 shows the time series of transaction with a GD population. We have represented with a discontinue line the price range (540-500) which is Marshallian stable and Walrasian unstable equilibrium. Here we observe that the transaction prices remain slightly over 540 when $\lambda = 0.1$, with a positive bias, as it happens with the experiment with humans . The transaction prices are unbiased and they cluster around the theoretical equilibrium of (540-500) when $\lambda = 0.9$.

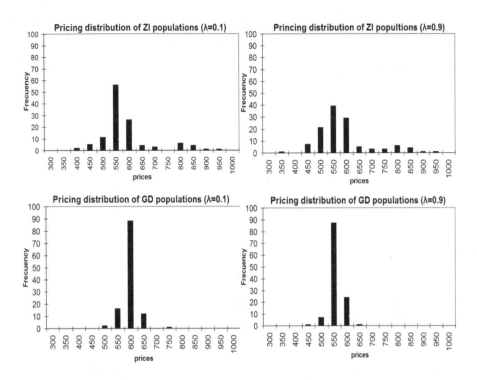

Fig. 7.2. Pricing distribution of both ZI and GD homogeneous populations under extreme learning rates ($\lambda = 0.1$ and $\lambda = 0.9$)

Do humans make mistakes when they estimate the volume sold by others as GD sellers with a low learning rate make? In CDA markets, efficiency is achieved even by ZI agents. This is a consequence of the robustness of the CDA institution against learning. It was not surprising to find in our experiment a market volume of 12 which is Marshallian stable and Walrasian unstable, in every period and for any population.

In GD populations the bias comes from a poor estimation of the externality effect, as measured by the traded volume. The ZI agents make their offers randomly, but they estimate well the traded volume. If we assume that the human agents are more intelligent than the ZI agents, we can conclude that they also achieve the right estimates of the traded volume. We may then conjecture that for humans the source of the bias towards the M equilibrium comes from the offering decisions. This example shows that Experimental Economics and MABS can be used for testing economic aggregated models. But MABS allows us also to calibrate to what extent the results from Experimental Economics

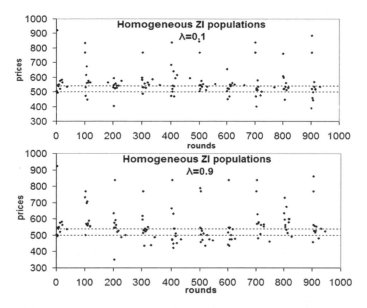

Fig. 7.3. Price dynamics for Homogeneous ZI populations

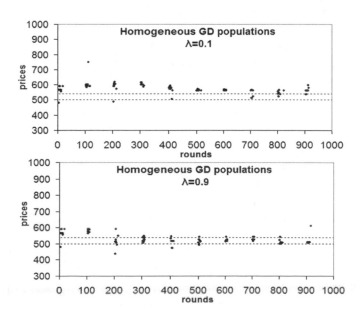

Fig. 7.4. Price dynamics for Homogeneous GD populations

are robust against the unknown behaviour of the participants in the experiment.

7.5 Conclusions

MABS is a "killer" application in Economics. We can validate and calibrate the results from Experimental Economics with humans that have enlightened Economics for the last two decades, since we can control for agents' behavior. If we go down to micro behavior we can grow a market model for some fixed set of AxIxE.

Grown markets, as the real ones, are information gathering tools that will allow many reasonable and realistic heuristic learning-decision models from agents yet achieving market convergence and equilibrium The agents search may be local and no super agent such as the Walrasian auctioneer is needed for a market clearing-price as our experiment shows. This focus opens the way to a new strand of research into microfoundations of aggregated economic models.

Growing Agent-Based Models in Economics, we could dispense of some of the concepts used to describe microeconomic equilibrium since we can trace the full process towards equilibrium and can calibrate it for different arrangements of the AxIxE. Nevertheless aggregate models are, no doubt, useful for policy design. However, to assume that the behavior that is true for the agents is also true for the aggregated system, may be wrong and should always be checked.

Our simulation results show that the theoretical predictions of the Walrasian market adjustment are wrong and that the agents behavior is compatible with the Marshalian model for the chosen environment (E), confirming previous results in Experimental Economics. The results are not robust against alternative agents learning models. M and W equilibrium adjustment is an analogy taken from vector fields that is unnecessary if not confusing. We have the tools (MABS) to model a market fully, allowing individual and social learning, and richer equilibrium concepts.

In view of the results, the following comment by Axtell (2005) is very appropriate: "*In the end we advocate not the jettisoning of this useful abstraction* (Walrasian equilibrium) *but merely its circumspect use whenever focused on questions for which it has limited ability to adjudicate an appropriate answer: distributional issues and actual prices. a direct consequence of the results described above is to at least cast a pale on the utility of such analysis, if not vitiate them altogether.*"

Acknowledgement. This work has received financial support from the Spanish MEC, 2005-05676, and from Junta de Castilla y León, VA029B06. We acknowledge the reviewers comments that helped us to clear the object and the scope of the paper.

References

R. Axtell. The complexity of exchange. *Economic Journal*, 115(504): 193–210, June 2005.

P. Brewer, M. Huang, B. Nelson, and C. R. Plott. On the behavioral foundations of the law of supply and demand: Human convergence and robot randomness. *Experimental Economics*, 5(3):179–208, December 2002.

D. Cliff and J. Bruten. Zero is not enough: On the lower limit of agent intelligence for continuous double auction markets. Technical Report HP-1997-141, Hewlett Packard Laboratories, Bristol, England, 1997.

D. Colander. Marshallian general equilibrium analysis. *Eastern Economic Journal*, 21(3):281–293, Summer 1995.

S. Gjerstad and J. Dickhaut. Price formation in double auctions. *Games and Economic Behavior*, 22:1–29, 1998.

D. K. Gode and S. Sunder. Allocative efficiency of markets with zero-intelligence traders: Market as a partial substitute for individual rationality. *Journal of Political Economy*, 101(1):119–137, February 1993.

A. Lopez-Paredes, C. Hernandez-Iglesias, and J. Gutierrez Pajares. Towards a new experimental socio-economics: Complex behaviour in bargaining. *The Journal of Socio-Economics*, 31(4):423–429, 2002.

W. Nicholson. *Microeconomic Theory*. Dryden Press, 1997.

C. R. Plott and G. George. Marshallian vs. walrasian stability in an experimental market. *Economic Journal*, 102(412):437–460, May 1992.

M. Posada. Strategic software agents in continuous double auction under dynamic environments. In Berlin Heidelberg New York, editor, *Lecture Notes in Computer Science*, volume 4224, pages 1223–1233. Springer-Verlag, 2006.

V. L. Smith. Theory, experiment and economics. *Journal of Economic Perspectives*, 3(1):151–169, Winter 1989.

S. Sunder. Markets as artifacts. In M. Augier and J. March, editors, *Models of a Man: essays in memory of Herbert A. Simon*. MIT Press, 2004.

8

The Performance of Option–Trading Software Agents: Initial Results

Omar Baqueiro, Wiebe Van der Hoek, and Peter McBurney

Department of Computer Science, University of Liverpool, UK {omar, wiebe, peter}@csc.liv.ac.uk

8.1 Introduction

The growth of e-commerce and the development of distributed processing systems have led to interest among computer scientists in methods for resource allocations across multiple participants (Chevaleyre and Dunne, 2005). GRID systems, for example, allow multiple users access to some resource, such as computer processing power or use of an electron microscope (Foster and Kesselman, 1999).

If resources are limited, each agent in a GRID system or other online marketplace faces the possibility of not being able to obtain resources when needed. If resources are allocated according to a market mechanism (either with real-world money or with tokens), agents also face the possibility of not being able to afford to purchase resources, even when they are available. As computational resource allocation systems become increasingly common, participants will require agents able to reserve future resources on their behalf, and hedge against future risks.

Derivatives are financial products whose values depend on the value of some other asset, usually a physical product. Option derivatives provide traders with the right to purchase or the right to sell the underlying assets at agreed future times, under agreed conditions. In this way, traders attempt to hedge against falls in the price of the underlying asset or to gain from price rises, and so manage the risks associated with the uncertainty of asset prices.

Elsewhere, a multi–agent framework has been presented in which BDI–type agents could be vested with decision rules allowing them to trade some product (Espinosa et al., 2005). We use this framework to create agents with similar decision rules for trading of option derivatives, and then undertake a Monte Carlo simulation to compare the marketplace performance of agents trading options with those which do not.

Our contribution comprises the results of the Monte Carlo simulation for which the paper concludes with a discussion of the work. It is important to stress that our focus throughout is not on the exchange mechanism by which agents trade options, or its properties; rather, our concern is with the relative benefits or disbenefits to agents undertaking Options trading.

8.2 Model description

We created a multi agent market framework based on the model of Palmer and Arthur (1994). In our model we consider *goods* instead of *stock*, the goods cannot be divided, we only consider one type of good or asset and the price of the asset is fixed from a external price series. In addition to the standard asset trading mechanism, our model provides means to exchange Option contracts among the agents. We make use of the basic properties of real financial Option contracts to define the Options that agents can trade. Price series of the underlying asset is set from an exogenous discrete time series and Option prices are calculated at each step using the Black and Scholes (1973) model for Option pricing.

8.2.1 The market

The market is composed of a set of agents $A = \{1, 2, 3..., N\}$. A_i is composed of two subsets of agents, agents that can trade options and goods A_o and agents that can only trade goods (assets) A_g.

We consider discrete time points $t = \{0, 1, 2, 3..., T\}$ and refer to a period of time as the tth period (or step t) $[t, t+1]$. The market has also a risk free rate of return r.

At each t each agent i has a number of goods $g_i(t)$ and an amount of cash $c_i(t)$. The total number of goods in the model is fixed, being $\sum_i g_i(t) = G$ for all t. Each agent also has an Option portfolio $\mathcal{O}_i = O_i^w \cup O_i^h$ which is composed by the Options the agent holds (O^h) and the ones it wrote (O^w).

An Option α is defined as:

$$\alpha = \langle X^\alpha, t^\alpha, v^\alpha, \tau^\alpha \rangle \tag{8.1}$$

Where X^α is the exercise price of that Option (the price agreed to pay for each good); t^α is the expiration time; v^α is the volume (the quantity of goods to trade with that Option) and τ^α is the type of Option (call or put). Each Option α has a corresponding premium price $p_\alpha(t)$. This is the price an agent will have to pay its counter–party to hold the Option.

The Options provided by the market are a set of standard *templates* for Option contracts that the agents can trade. Agents are only allowed to exchange Options that comply with the specified templates, this is similar to a real Option regulated market. The number of available Option templates is constant over all time steps.

Pricing mechanism

The asset price $p(t)$ will be provided to the model from an external time series. Option pricing is calculated each step using the Black-Scholes model for option pricing defined in Black and Scholes (1973)[1]. Using this model, the price of an Option is calculated from the price of the good $p(t)$, the variance of the asset price (σ) and a predefined exercise price X^α. The exercise price of an Option is obtained by the following formula:

$$X^\alpha = p(t) \times (1 + k)$$

Where k is a uniformly distributed pseudo-random number within the range $[-SP_k, SP_k]$.

Market timeline

Each period of time starts when the market *publishes* the new price for the asset. After obtaining this price the *Option clearing* phase will run where the market will receive instructions from the agents to exercise any Option that expires at this time. The agents holding any expiring Option must either decide to exercise or lose the Option at this time. Any non exercised Option should be removed from agent's held Options set O_i^h. Any request to exercise an already expired Option will be ignored by the market. In the event of an Option being exercised, the agents will clear the Option, trading the corresponding asset immediately.

---

[1] It is worth noting that other option pricing mechanisms could have been used, in fact some experiments were also ran using the binomial option pricing model by Cox et al. (1979) without any relevant difference in the outcomes.

Afterwards, the market will publish the different Option templates to trade on that period and the *trading phase* will start where the agents will submit their offers to buy and sell assets or hold and write Options. Next, the market will try to match match randomly the asset buy and sell offers and will also try to match the hold and write offers. Finally, the market will clear the matched offers by making the agents exchange the assets or confirming the matched Option contracts. A graphical representation of the time-line is shown in Figure 8.1.

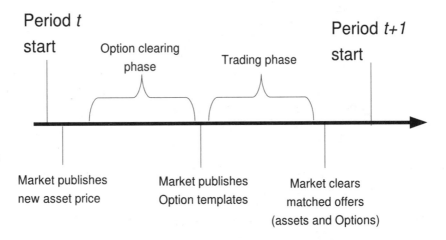

Fig. 8.1. Timeline for one time step of the market

8.2.2 Trading Agents

An agent i is defined by the tuple:

$$\langle g_i, c_i, w_i, \mathcal{O}_i, \mathcal{S}_i, \mathcal{F}_i \rangle \tag{8.2}$$

At time t, the term $g_i(t)$ is the number of goods the agent owns at time t; $c_i(t)$ denotes the quantity of cash the agent has. The term $w(t)$ denotes the *wealth* of the agent which is obtained by the equation:

$$w(t) = p(t) \times g(t) + c(t) \tag{8.3}$$

The agent also owns a set of Option contracts $\mathcal{O}$ which represent a contract to buy or sell one asset at a specific time. The set of Options is composed by two subsets, O^α is the set containing the held Options and O^β contains the Options written. Specifically $\mathcal{O} = O^\alpha \cup O^\beta$.

The term $\mathcal{S}$ is the agent's strategy (See 8.2.4) comprising an action or chain of actions to execute. The set of actions an agent can execute are listed in Table 8.1. Finally, $\mathcal{F}_i$ is the forecast strategy used by the agent.

Action	Description
$buy(g,t)$	Make an offer to buy an asset at time t.
$sell(g,t)$	Make an offer to sell an asset at time t
$hold(\alpha,t)$	Make an offer to hold Option α at time t
$write(\alpha,t)$	Make an offer to write an Option at time t

Table 8.1. Available actions for the agents at time t.

8.2.3 Forecasting and perceived risk

The forecasting process of the agent is comprised by two parts, firstly the agent obtains forecasted price of the asset for future time steps and secondly it uses these forecasts to obtain its perceived risk of executing the possible actions. At each time step agents calculate a forecasted price for future time steps. Agents obtain this price using a forecasting function. Although other types of time series forecasting formulae could be used, our model implements two forecasting mechanisms.

Simple moving average forecasting

The first forecasting mechanism is based on the Simple Moving Average (SMA). Prices at future times are obtained by first calculating the SMA for the interval $[t - n, t]$ as $p_{SMA}(t)$ and then the price at future time steps is obtained by extrapolating the price at current time using the formula:

$$p_i(t + m) = p(t) + m \times (p(t) - p_{SMA}(t)) \qquad (8.4)$$

Where $p_i(t + m)$ is the agent's forecasted price for time $t + m$ and $p(t)$ is the market price at time t.

α–perfect forecasting

Using the second forecasting mechanism called the α–perfect forecast the agent will obtain the future prices from the real time series with some added random variability (noise). The forecasted price will be calculated as:

$$p_i(t + m) = p(t + m) \times (1 + r_\alpha) \qquad (8.5)$$

Where $p_i(t+m)$ is the agent's forecasted price at $t+m$, $p(t+m)$ is the real market asset price at time $t + m$ and r_α is a uniformly distributed pseudo–random number within the range $[1 - \alpha, \alpha - 1]$, being α within the range of $[0, 1]$. Using this mechanism, it is possible for the agent to have complete knowledge of the future prices when α equals 0.

Perceived risk

Inspired by Holton (2004), we model risk as the probability that the agent loses wealth when it carries out a specific action. We assume prices are distributed Normally. Under this assumption each agent can calculate the probability of wealth loss $\rho(a)$ for each possible action a at each step in time t.

This is achieved by using the cumulative standard normal distribution to obtain the cumulative probability of the agent forecasted price being in the wrong direction, assuming that the distribution's mean is $p_i(t + m)$ (the price at the forecasted time step).

8.2.4 Trading strategies

There are two types of agents trading in the market, asset traders and Option traders; asset traders can only trade the underlying asset in the market whereas Option traders can trade assets and Option contracts.

Asset trading strategies

Asset traders trade in the market using one of two strategies: the Random trading strategy in which the agents select an action randomly and Speculator strategy in which agents select an action to buy or sell an asset according to their forecast of the price at the next step.

Option trading strategies

Option traders can trade using the *Minimize Risk* strategy in which agents create an action tree with all the possible combinations of actions for a specific number of time steps and select the path which yields the minimum combined risk. An agent that uses this strategy will choose the sequence of actions from the action tree (a path) where the combination of the actions' risk loss factor ρ is the minimum from all possible combinations. Let a strategy S be defined by the sequence of actions $\langle a_1, a_2, ...a_n \rangle$ and also let $\rho(a_i)$ be the risk loss factor for doing some action, the combined risk loss $\rho_s(S)$ for such strategy is defined as:

$$\rho_s(S) = \prod_i^n \rho(a_i) \tag{8.6}$$

Option trading agents can also use the *Maximize wealth* strategy with which they select the next action after selecting the path which yields the maximum sum of wealth from an action tree. An agent that uses this strategy will choose the sequence of action from the action tree where the combination of each of the action's wealth difference is the maximum from all possible combinations. Let a strategy S be defined by the sequence of actions $\langle a_1, a_2, ...a_n \rangle$ and let $\Delta w(a_i)$ be the perceived wealth difference for doing an action (the wealth before executing the action substracted from the wealth after executing the action), the combined wealth $\Delta w(S)$ is defined as:

$$\Delta w(S) = \sum_i^n \Delta w(a_i) \tag{8.7}$$

8.3 Experiments

Several experiments were run to compare the performance of agents under two different aspects. Firstly to test which of the strategies generated higher profits and secondly to compare the correlation between the agents' wealth and the price of the asset. Our hypothesis was that, the wealth of agents using Options would be lower than that of the ones trading only assets.

8.3.1 Environment setup

A simulation run for our model requires the specification of the parameters of Table 8.2 for the market setup and for the agents. The parameters are explained in Section 8.2 excepting O_s which is used to set the distance between the expiration time (t^α) of the Options generated at each step and $\sigma(0)$ which is the initial value for the standard deviation of the price series. These parameters were fixed for all the experiments.

Initial parameters for the market	
Parameter	Initial value
Simulation duration (T)	500
Number of available Option templates ($|O|$)	3
Steps between available Options (O_s)	1
Strike Price multiplier (SP_k)	15
Risk free rate (r)	0.005
Initial price variance ($\sigma(0)$)	1
Initial parameters for agents	
Parameter	Initial value
Initial cash ($c_i(0)$)	1000
Initial goods ($g_i(0)$)	100

Table 8.2. Initial parameters for the experiments

For all the experiments we also populated the market with 4 sets of 20 agents. All agents within one set were initialized with the same parameters (including strategy and forecast function). Each set used one of the four defined strategies. All the experiment were done using each of the price series to be described.

Price series

To set the price of the underlying asset we used several price series in order to test the performance of the agents under different market conditions. We defined three categories for the price series: stock prices series, which were obtained from the closing prices of different stocks [2]; random prices, which are uniformly distributed pseudo–randomly generated series; and linear prices which are manually generated.

Some statistical information for the price series is summarized in Table 8.3. The Dell, Microsoft, HP, and IBM price series were obtained from the stock prices of the corresponding companies; the RANDOM1 and RANDOM2 price are the pseudo–randomly generated; finally, the Increment price series was generated as a constantly increasing time series and the Decrement was generated as a constantly decreasing time series.

8.3.2 Experiments using SMA forecasting

For the experiments with the Simple Moving Average forecasting, all the agents were assigned this same forecasting function ($\mathcal{F}_i$) with the number of periods $t_{\mathcal{F}_i} = 10$. We ran 50 repetitions of each experiment

---
[2] Freely available online at http://finance.yahoo.com/

	N	Minimum	Maximum	Mean	Std. Deviation
DELL	500	16.15	30.63	25.78	2.44
HP	500	10.75	37.80	21.46	6.34
IBM	500	54.65	125.00	95.66	17.37
MICORSOFT	502	41.75	73.70	58.43	7.40
RANDOM1	500	1.20	200.00	103.18	58.30
RANDOM2	500	4.00	996.80	501.54	293.44
INCREMENT	500	10.00	510.00	260.00	144.77
DECREMENT	500	10.00	509.00	259.50	144.48

Table 8.3. Descriptive statistics of the used price series

and averaged the results. We also calculated the mean of the wealth for each set of agents to obtain the performance for each strategy.

Performance of strategies

We measured the performance of each strategy by obtaining the difference between the wealth of the agent at the last time step and the first time step, this resulted in the profits that each agent obtained for each simulation (see Table 8.4). In order to compare the profits among the

	Opton Traders		Asset Traders		
	MinRisk	MaxWealth	Speculator	Random	Mean
DELL	210.890	-171.660	-74.060	34.830	960.000
IBM	-177.342	45.537	-9.782	141.587	-558.827
HP	-363.480	292.750	38.980	31.750	-1393.000
MICROSOFT	-3.892	-1.262	-39.422	44.578	817.003
RANDOM1	-259.283	265.357	-2384.593	2378.518	-11979.998
RANDOM2	2373.450	-946.150	-21119.950	19692.650	51073.250
INCREMENT	9922.925	-8430.975	8441.825	-9933.775	49899.975
DECREMENT	-3547.801	-2561.132	509.389	5599.545	-47310.719

Table 8.4. Average profit for each strategy with SMA forecasting.

agents we calculated the mean of the average profits (last column in Table 8.4) and subtracted it from the strategy profit. Figure 8.2 shows the relative profits for each strategy among the simulations; from this figure it can be seen that there is no clear advantage in the profits using any strategy.

Performance correlation with price

The second test we performed was an analysis correlation between the price series and the wealth of the agents. This test was conducted to

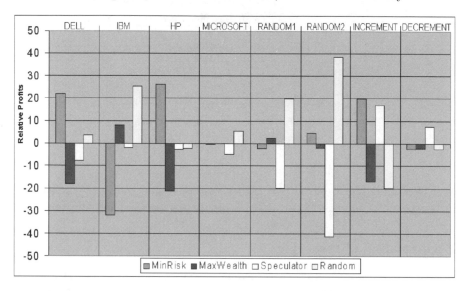

Fig. 8.2. Relative profit for each strategy with SMA forecasting

see whether the fluctuations on the price of the asset had less incidence in the wealth of an agent trading Options, the results[3] on Table 8.5 suggest so, as the correlation between the wealth of the Option trading strategies is slightly less than of the asset trading strategies for three of the four stock market strategies.

	Opton Traders		Asset Traders	
	MinRisk	MaxWealth	Speculator	Z.I.
DELL	0.994	0.974	0.998	0.999
HP	0.999	0.997	1.000	1.000
IBM	1.000	1.000	1.000	1.000
MICROSOFT	0.999	0.999	1.000	1.000
RANDOM1	0.999	1.000	0.970	0.985
RANDOM2	1.000	1.000	0.982	0.990
INCREMENT	1.000	1.000	1.000	1.000
DECREMENT	1.000	1.000	1.000	1.000

Table 8.5. Correlation between agents' wealth and price series with SMA.

---

[3] All correlations were calculated as two tailed Pearson correlation significant to the 0.01 level.

8.3.3 Experiments using α–perfect forecasting

For the experiments with the α–Perfect forecasting function, all the agents were assigned this forecasting function $(\mathcal{F}_i)$ with three different α values of 10, 20 and 40. We ran 50 repetitions of each experiment and averaged the results. We also calculated the mean of the wealth for each set of agents to obtain the performance for each strategy.

Strategies performance

As with the SMA experiments, the performance of each strategy was measured by obtaining the difference between the wealth of the agent at the last time step and the first time step, resulting in the profits that each agent obtained for each simulation. Figures 8.3 shows the resulting relative profit for each strategy with the different α values.

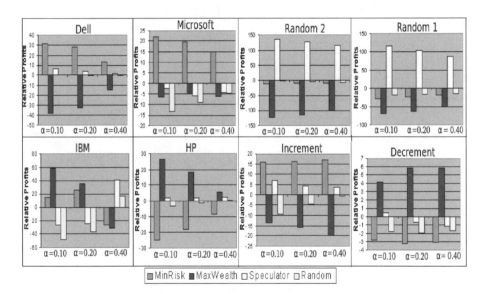

Fig. 8.3. Relative profit for each strategy with α–Perfect forecasting with different α values.

The wide difference in the performance of the Option trading strategies against the asset trading strategies suggests a clear advantage on the use of Options in the case of the α–Perfect forecasting.

Performance correlation with price

Finally, the correlation between the price series and the wealth of the agents was calculated for the α–Perfect experiments. The results of this are listed on Table 8.6, the lower correlation of the Option Trading strategies particularly appear to indicate that the use of Options decreases the influence of the price in the wealth of the agents trading them.

	Correlation for $\alpha = 0.10$					Correlation for $\alpha = 0.20$			
	Opton Traders		Asset Traders			Opton Traders		Asset Traders	
	MinRisk	MaxWealth	Speculator	Random.		MinRisk	MaxWealth	Speculator	Random.
DELL	0.988	0.831	0.998	0.999	DELL	0.984	0.884	0.999	1.000
HP	0.999	0.993	1.000	1.000	HP	0.998	0.991	1.000	1.000
IBM	0.999	0.997	1.000	1.000	IBM	0.999	0.997	1.000	1.000
MICROSOFT	0.997	0.992	1.000	0.999	MICROSOFT	0.997	0.992	1.000	1.000
RANDOM1	0.999	0.718	0.841	1.000	RANDOM1	0.999	0.761	0.861	1.000
RANDOM2	0.999	0.718	0.841	1.000	RANDOM2	0.999	0.765	0.879	1.000
INCREMENT	1.000	1.000	1.000	1.000	INCREMENT	1.000	1.000	1.000	1.000
DECREMENT	1.000	1.000	1.000	1.000	DECREMENT	1.000	1.000	1.000	1.000

	Correlation for $\alpha = 0.40$			
	Opton Traders		Asset Traders	
	MinRisk	MaxWealth	Speculator	Random.
DELL	0.994	0.985	0.998	1.000
HP	0.997	0.992	1.000	1.000
IBM	1.000	0.999	1.000	1.000
MICROSOFT	0.998	0.998	1.000	1.000
RANDOM1	1.000	0.833	0.889	1.000
RANDOM2	0.999	0.833	0.904	1.000
INCREMENT	1.000	0.999	1.000	1.000
DECREMENT	1.000	1.000	1.000	1.000

Table 8.6. Correlation between agents' wealth and price series with α–Perfect forecasting.

8.4 Conclusions

In this paper we demonstrated some of the results from the experiments performed in our proposed Option Market framework. The experiments so far show promising results. It is worth nothing that, although the differences in the results of the tests between Option traders and asset traders are low, we argue that the reason for this could be due to the simplicity of the market. Allowing the agents to trade more than one asset at each step in time and providing them with Options with a higher volume (more than one asset traded on each Option) might increase the differences among the agent's performance. Also, it would be interesting to introduce the concept of *magnitude* of risk into the agents reasoning process.

Acknowledgement. This work has been partially funded by the Mexican Council of Science and Technology (Sponsorship No. 187564) and the Market Based Control project (EPSRC GR/T10664/01). The authors also wish to thank the anonymous reviewers for their very insightful comments and suggestions.

References

F. Black and M.S. Scholes. The pricing of options and corporate liabilities. *Journal of Political Economy*, 81(3):637–54, 1973.

Y. Chevaleyre and P.E. Dunne. Multiagent resource allocation. *Knowledge Engineering Review*, 20(2):143–149, 2005.

J.C. Cox, S.A. Ross, and M. Rubinstein. Option pricing: A simplified approach. *Journal of Financial Economics*, 7(3):229–263, 1979.

B. Espinosa, O.W. van der Hoek, and P. McBurney. Designing agents for derivatives markets. a preliminary framework. In P. Gmytrasiewicz and S. Parsons, editors, *Game Theoretic and Decision Theoretic Agents*, pages 1–14, 2005.

I. Foster and C. Kesselman. *The Grid: Blueprint for a New Computing Infrastructure*. Morgan-Kaufmann, 1999.

G.A. Holton. Defining risk. *Financial Analysts Journal*, 60:19–25, 2004.

R.G. Palmer and W.B. Arthur. Artificial economic life: a simple model of a stockmarket. *Physica D*, 75:264–274, 1994.

9

Studies on the Impact of the Option Market on the Underlying Stock Market

Sabrina Ecca, Mario Locci, and Michele Marchesi

DIEE, University of Cagliari, Italy
{sabrina.ecca, mario.locci, michele}@diee.unica.it

9.1 Introduction

In the past thirty years, options have become an important financial instrument, and now they account for a substantial percentage of total trading activity. From a research perspective, a lot of research have been carried out about the theoretical computation of option prices, starting from the seminal works of Black and Scholes (1973) and Merton (1973). Several researchers also examined the issue of to which extent options interact with their underlying stocks, and in particular their possible effects on stock returns and volatility, and on the overall quality of the underlying security market.

Some studies claim that option trading may have a positive impact on the underlying asset market, reporting a decrease in volatility after the introduction of option trading. Among them, we may quote Nathan Associates (1974), perhaps the first to study the impact of listing options on the Chicago Board of Exchange. They reported that the introduction of options seemed to have helped stabilizing trading in the underlying stocks. Ross (1976) and Hakansson (1982) affirm that the options introduction improve incomplete asset markets by expanding the opportunity set facing investors, and reduce the volatility of the underlying stock. Kumar et al. (1998) claim that option listings have a beneficial impact on the stock market quality in terms of higher liquidity and greater pricing efficiency.

Other researchers affirm, on the other hand, that option trading causes an increase in volatility. because it favors large positions and increases the bid-ask spread. For instance, Wei et al. (1997) report an increase in volatility of options on OTC stocks in the USA.

A third opinion among researchers claims that option trading has no significant impact on price volatility of the underlying stock market. Among these, Bollen (1998) affirms that option introduction does not significantly affect stock return variance, while Kabir (2000) examined option listing in the Netherlands, studying the impact of option trading on the underlying market. He founds a significant decline in stock price, but no significant effect on the volatility.

In the past ten years, a significant new stream of research works introduced modeling and simulation using heterogeneous, boundedly-rational interacting agents as a new tool for studying financial markets (see LeBaron, 2006, for a recent survey). This new approach, while it is still debated and challenged, especially among classical economists relying on the "efficient market hypothesis", is able to give new insight into how markets work. For instance, it is able to explain the so called "stylized facts"[1] shown by virtually every market price series, using endogenous mechanisms. Very many papers appeared proposing different models based on heterogeneous agents, and studying many different aspects of financial market trading. However, to our knowledge, no one has yet tried to study the effect of option trading using this approach.

This paper uses the heterogeneous agents, simulation approach to study the interaction between a stock option market and the underlying stock market. We analyze the effects of realistic option trading strategies on the stylized facts of financial time series, the long wealth distribution of traders and the price volatility. We consider three basic kinds of traders: traders who trade only in the stock market, traders who trade in the stock market, covering their positions using the option market, and a central Bank which issues option contracts in the option market, and trades in the stock market to cover these contracts, upon their expiration. There are four types of trading strategies in the stock market: random, fundamentalist, momentum and contrarian trading. Each trader consistently applies just one strategy, and cannot change it.

A given percentage of traders – spanning over all kinds of strategies – use options to cover their positions. Each time one of these traders places an order in the stock market, she also cover herself buying option contracts from the Bank, or uses a strategy based on the combination of call and put options, like a "Straddle".

---

[1] The main "stylized facts" are: (i) unit root property of asset prices; (ii) power-law distribution of returns at weekly, daily and higher frequencies; (iii) volatility clustering of prices.

9.2 Method and model

In our model there is a market in which N agents trade a single stock, which pays no dividends, in exchange for cash, with no transaction costs. Each trader is modeled as an autonomous agent and is characterized by a wealth, constituted by the sum of her cash and stocks, valued at the current price. Traders' initial endowment – both in cash and stocks – is obtained by dividing agents into groups of 20 traders, and applying Zipf's law to each group, so that the difference in wealth among the richest and poorest traders at the start of the simulation is about twenty-fold.

The agents are divided into sub-populations that adopt different trading strategies. Besides the stock itself, which is traded in the stock market, there is an *European* option contract on the stock. A fixed percentage of traders is also enabled to buy and exercise options. We call them *option traders*.

Another, special type of trader is the *Bank*; only one Bank is present in the market. The Bank issues option contracts and, upon their expiration, guarantees their exercise.

At each simulation step, which roughly corresponds to a day of trading, each trader can place a buy or sell limit order to the stock market. This happens with a probability of 10%, so each trader is active on average every 10 time steps. The pricing mechanism of the stock market is based on the intersection of the demand-supply curve (Raberto et al., 2003).

At each time step, option traders may also buy from the Bank one or more European option contracts, in order to hedge their investment. These traders have a *long position* in the option market. Since we deal only with European options, their owners are allowed to exercise their rights only at the expiration date. The pricing of options is based on Black-Scholes formula.

Upon expiration, options can be classified as being *in the money* (ITM), *at the money* (ATM) and *out of the money* (OTM). A call (put) option is ITM if the strike price is less (greater) than the current market price of the stock, so it is profitable to exercise the option. On the other hand, OTM options are not exercised because they are not profitable, resulting in a net loss of the traders who bought them. A call or put option is ATM if the strike price is exactly equal to the current market price, making irrelevant to exercise or not the option. In practice ATM options are not exercised, and are equivalent to OTM ones.

Traders owning ITM options exercise them, asking the Bank to sell them, or to buy from them, the corresponding stocks at the strike price. If the total number of stocks sold to these traders is not equal to the total number of stocks bought from them, the Bank places on the stock market a market order to cover the imbalance.

The Bank sets all components of the option contract: strike price (which depends on the current price of the stock $p(t)$, expiration date, underlying quantity, premium (Hull, 2002). The computation of the price of the options is made using the formula first introduced by Black and Scholes (1973).

9.2.1 Trading strategies

Stock market traders play the market according to four different kinds of strategies, that roughly mimic traders' behaviors in real markets. These strategies are described in depth in Raberto et al. (2003), and are summarized below. Some strategies require a time window to compute some significant parameters. In this case, each trader has a specific time window whose length is an integer randomly extracted from a uniform distribution, in the interval $2 - 10$.

Random traders: Random traders are characterized by the simplest trading strategy, representing the "bulk" of traders who do not try to beat the market, but trade for exogenous reasons linked to their needs. They are traders with zero intelligence, issuing random orders. If a random trader decides to issue an order, this may be a buy or sell limit order with equal probability. The order amount is computed at random with uniform probability, but cannot exceed the trader's cash and stock availability. The limit price is set at random too, in such a way to increase the probability the order is satisfied.

Fundamentalist traders: Fundamentalist traders believe that stocks have a fundamental price due to factors external to the market, and that, in the long run, the price of the stock will revert to this fundamental price, p_f. Consequently, they sell stocks if the price $p(t)$ is higher than fundamental price and buy stocks in the opposite case. The fundamental price is the same for all fundamentalists and corresponds to the "equilibrium" price, when the total cash owned by all traders, C_{tot} is equal to the value of all the stocks owned by all traders, S_{tot}. The order amount is proportional to the distance between the current price and p_f. The limit price is equal to p_f, or to the current price $p(t)$ plus or minus 20%, whichever is closer to the current price.

Momentum traders: Momentum traders speculate that, if prices are rising, they will keep rising, and if prices are falling, they will keep falling. Their orders are buy orders if the past price trend is positive, and sell orders if the trend is negative. The order amount is computed at random in the same way as random traders, while the limit price is set by extrapolating the price trend.

Contrarian traders: Contrarian traders speculate that, if the stock price is rising, it will stop rising and will decrease, so it is better to sell near the maximum, and vice-versa. So, their orders are sell orders if the past price trend is positive, and buy orders if the trend is negative. The order amounts are computed in the same way as random traders, while limit prices are set by reversing the trend, using as pivot the current price.

9.2.2 The Bank

The Bank is a special trader with infinite wealth, able to issue and sell call and put European options to other traders. The components of an option contract are:

Expiration date: it is fixed on the third Friday of the month. In our model, all months are nominally 20 working days long, thus the expiration dates are days $15, 35, 55, ..., 20k + 15, ...$ We use realistic expiration dates, that depend whether the option is bought before or after the third Friday of the current month (see Hull, 2002). In the former case, the expiration month can be the current month, or the month whose index is equal to the current one, plus 1, 3 or 6. In the latter case, the expiration month can be the month whose index is equal to the current one, plus 1, 2, 3 or 6.

Premium: the premium to be paid for an option is computed using the Black and Scholes formula (Black and Scholes, 1973; Hull, 2002). This formula uses five parameters: the stock price $p(t)$ at the time the option is valued, the strike price X, the time to expiration ΔT, the price volatility, computed in a given time window whose length is in our case 50 time steps, and the short-term interest rate, which in our case is set to zero. The basic idea underlying Black and Scholes formula is that the prices of the stocks follow a random walk, implying that the underlying asset prices are lognormally distributed with a constant mean and standard deviation. In our artificial stock market model, however, the price process is characterized by a strong mean reverting behavior toward a price, p_f, equal to the ratio between the total number of stocks and the total cash owned by traders (Raberto et al., 2001), due to the finiteness of resources of the traders. This leads to overpricing the options, causing steady losses to option traders. For this reason, the option premium computed using Black and Scholes formula is multiplied by a correction factor C that depends on time to expiration ΔT and typically varies between 0.75 (in the case $\Delta T = 120$) and 0.96 (in the case $\Delta T = 10$). These values has been empirically computed through many simulations. Using the correction factor $C(\Delta T)$, we were able to use an option premium that is fair with respect to our finite resources, mean reverting market model.

Strike price: it is the price X at which the option can be exercised. It depends on the current price $p(t)$ of the stock. We consider three different possible strike prices, given by eq. 9.1.

$$X \in \{p(t) - \delta, p(t), p(t) + \delta\} \qquad (9.1)$$

The value of δ depends in turn on $p(t)$. In US Dollar-quoted markets, δ is given by the following formula (Hull, 2002):

$$\delta = \begin{cases} 1.5\$ \text{ if } p(t) \leq 25\$ \\ 3\$ \text{ if } 25\$ < p(t) \leq 200\$ \\ 6\$ \text{ if } p(t) > 200\$ \end{cases} \qquad (9.2)$$

For instance, if $p(t) = 42.7\$$, then $\delta = 3$, and the possible three strike prices are $X = 39.7\$$, $X = 42.7\$$, or $X = 45.7\$$.

When the Bank sells an option contract, it earns the premium, updating its cash. On expiration dates, that is every 20 simulation steps, if option traders have expiring ITM options, they ask the Bank to honor the contracts, selling them the stocks at the strike price in the case of call options, and buying from them the stocks at the strike price in the case of put options. If required, the Bank places a buy or a sell limit order on the market, at the market stock price, plus or minus a proper percentage (set to 2% in our model), to cover its position and be able to satisfy all its obligations. The Bank has unlimited wealth. In practice, it starts with a cash and a number of stocks set to zero, but these values are unbounded, and can assume any value, even negative.

9.2.3 Option traders

Option traders are those traders who are allowed to trade both in the option market and in the underlying stock market. As regards the stock market, they exhibit one of the four possible trading strategies described in section 9.2.1. When they trade in the option market, they can only buy options and possibly exercise them on their expiration dates. Option traders can buy option contracts from the Bank only if their residual cash is higher than the premium of the option contract.

To be more specific, let us call $m_i(t)$ the cash owned by option trader i at simulation step t, and $s_i(t)$ the stocks owned by the same trader at the same step. Let us also suppose that, at step t, option trader i has p_i put option contracts not yet expired. These put options refer to quantity q_j^p, at a strike price of x_j^p, $j = 1, 2, ..., p_i$ respectively. Conversely, let us suppose that at step t, option trader i has c_i call option contracts not yet expired. These call options refer to quantity q_j^c, at a strike price of x_j^c, $j = 1, 2, ..., c_i$ respectively.

The total cash balance expected when all undersigned options are expired, m_B is estimated by eq. 9.3.

$$m_B = \sum_{j=1}^{p_i} q_j^p x_j^p - \sum_{j=1}^{c_i} q_j^c x_j^c \qquad (9.3)$$

The total stock balance expected when all undersigned options are expired, s_B is estimated by eq. 9.4.

$$s_B = \sum_{j=1}^{c_i} q_j^c - \sum_{j=1}^{p_i} q_j^p \qquad (9.4)$$

Note that in computing the balances we don't consider the options to be ITM or OTM with respect to the current price $p(t)$, but for the sake of simplicity we give all the options the chance to be ITM.

On the expiration date, if the option is ITM and if the trader holding it has enough money or stocks, she exercises it. Otherwise, she gets back the difference between the actual price and the strike price from the Bank.

If the option is OTM, the trader places on the stock market a buy limit order (if the option is a call), or a sell limit order (if the option is a put) at the current stock price for the underlying quantity. This quantity is reduced if the trader has no cash or stock enough to cover it completely.

Using options to cover a position

If options are used to cover a position, when option traders decide to place a buy or sell order, they also buy from the Bank a corresponding option to cover their position, provided they have cash enough to buy the option. The expiration date is always three months from the current month, so $\Delta T \approx 90$. If the order is a buy, they buy a put option, with a strike price X equal to the current price $p(t)$ minus δ as in eq. 9.2. If the order is a sell, they buy a call option with $X = p(t) + \delta$. In this way, option traders are guaranteed against losses exceeding δ, but have to pay the option premium, that is in any case subtracted from their cash.

Using straddles

If option traders use straddles, they simultaneous buy a put and call on the same underlying security, with the identical strike price and expiration month. The value of the strike price is the same of the current price of the underlying asset. So, both call and put options are ATM at the moment of purchase. Typically, the buyer of a straddle anticipates a substantial movement in the stock price, but is uncertain what direction it will be. Because the trader is betting on an large stock movement, the odds of losing are high. The buyer of a straddle risks only the amount of the premium. The maximum loss occurs when the price of the stock on the expiration date of the options is exactly equal to the strike price. In our model, in order to ease comparison with the case when option are bought to cover a position, option traders buy a straddle when they place an order on the stock market. The stock quantity of the straddle is the same of the stock market order, provided that the trader has cash enough to pay for the straddle premium.

9.3 Results and conclusion

In this section we describe the results of the computational experiments we performed. Each simulation was run with 5000 time steps and 400 agents. We varied the composition of the population performing various runs, and eventually decided to hold at 10% the percentage of fundamentalist, momentum and contrarian traders. Option traders can be 0%, 20% or 40%, equally divided in the four possible types. Random traders account for the remaining percentage.

The price volatility used in Black and Scholes formula is computed using a time window of 20 trading days. Also in the presence of option trading, our artificial stock market consistently exhibits realistic price series from a statistical point of view, showing the classical stylized facts, with fat tails of returns and volatility clustering.

During the simulation, when option traders decide to buy or sell stocks, they also buy options from the Bank. In doing this, these traders do not directly interfere with the stock market. The only indirect effect on the stock market is that they spend money to undersign options, so that in subsequent buy orders they can buy a smaller amount of stocks.

On expiration dates, on the contrary, the option traders interact with the underlying stock market. This may happen in three ways. The first is when the Bank needs to buy or to sell stocks to cover its cumulative position with respect to the owners of expiring ITM options. These stocks are bought or sold in the stock market, creating an unbalance.

The second way is when option traders have OTM options. In this case, they often buy or sell the stock, placing a buy or sell order of the amount of the option on the stock market.

The third, indirect way is that, by exercising the options, option traders change the composition of their portfolios, and this has an impact on their subsequent trading activity.

We divided the performed simulations in two main categories – option traders covering their positions, and option traders buying straddles. In principle, the effects of these two strategies could be quite different, because covering a position implies buying a single option contract at a time, while buying straddles is a more speculative strategy, and options are bought in pairs.

In both cases, we found that, despite the high percentage of option traders, the price series exhibit the "stylized facts" of real financial markets, and do not substantially differ from the case with no option trader.

9.3.1 Results when options cover a position

In the case option traders use options to cover their positions, as described in section 9.2.3, we performed many simulations, checking the behavior of trader wealth and of price volatility. Fig. 9.1 shows the wealth dynamics for a typical simulation.

Note that contrarian and fundamentalist traders, who use the "right" strategy for a mean-reverting price behavior, tend to increase their wealth, as already reported and discussed in Raberto et al. (2003).

136   Sabrina Ecca, Mario Locci, and Michele Marchesi

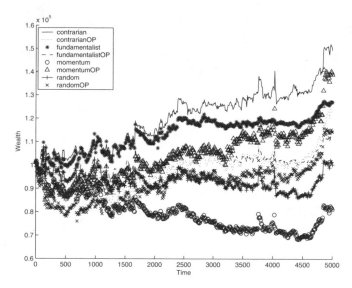

Fig. 9.1. Dynamics of wealth of all kinds of traders for a typical simulation where option traders cover their positions using options. The total percentage of option traders is 40%.

On the other hand, the same kinds of traders using options to cover their positions tend to be much less profitable. This is because they spend money to buy options to cover positions that are unlikely to yield strong losses. The situation of momentum and random traders is completely different. These traders employ losing strategies, and in fact tend to lose wealth. Their option counterparts, however, tend to be much more profitable, because it is convenient to cover themselves with options, when the underlying strategy is bad.

9.3.2 Results when option traders use "straddles"

In another series of simulations, we considered a market where option traders use "straddles", as defined in section 9.2.3. Fig. 9.2 shows the wealth dynamics for a typical simulation. Here the traders tends to gain less than in the other case, and only contrarian traders and fundamentalists – the latter both using and not using options – gain something. All other kinds of traders tend to lose money. All traders, but fundamentalists, who use straddles tend to lose money with respect to traders with the same strategy, not active in the option market. This is not unexpected, however, because in a limited resources, mean-reverting market, a strategy betting on high price variations, like the 'straddle", is unlikely to win.

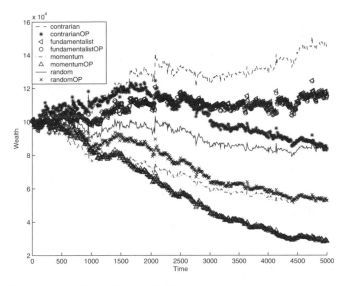

Fig. 9.2. Dynamics of wealth of all kinds of traders for a typical simulation where option traders use "straddles". The total percentage of option traders is 40%.

Table 9.1. Price volatility with and without option trading; each reported value refers to 20 simulation runs. The values are multiplied by 10^3.

Strategy	Quantity	No option trader	20% option traders	40% option traders
Cover	mean	0.45	0.3	0.25
Cover	std. dev.	0.13	0.07	0.06
Straddle	mean	0.45	0.23	0.14
Straddle	st. dev.	0.13	0.07	0.03

In Table 9.1 we show how price volatility changes in the presence of option trading. In general, our simulations show a consistent, strong decrease in price volatility when options are traded. This despite the fact that once in every month the Bank places an order that might be very large, at a limit price able to cause strong price variations. When straddles are used, the number of traded options is doubled, and the volatility decreases even more. The presented figures refer to averaging volatility, computed every 50 time steps, on the whole simulation, and then averaging on 20 different simulation runs. Note that volatility does not show significant trends across a single simulation. These results seem to confirm the empirical findings that option trading stabilizes the market and reduces the volatility (Hakansson, 1982; Nathan Associates, 1974; Ross, 1976).

Clearly, all the presented results are still preliminary, and more tests are needed to assess them. Future research directions we are working on include: (i) modeling dividends and interest rates; (ii) opening the market to external influences so that is is no longer mean-reverting, at least in the short run; (iii) studying other strategies using options; (iv) giving traders the ability to sell options.

Acknowledgement. This work was supported by RAMSES (Research on Agent-based Modeling and Simulation of Economic Systems) research project, sponsored by FIRB research fund of MIUR, grant number: RBAU01KZ7Z, by MIUR PRIN 2004 Project #2004131501, by ComplexMarkets E.U. STREP project #516446, under FP6-2003-NEST-PATH-1, and by EURACE E.U. STREP project #035086, under FP6-2005-IST-2005-2.3.4 -(xi) FET Proactive Initiative: Complex Systems.

References

F. Black and M.S. Scholes. The pricing of options and corporate liabilities. *Journal of Political Economy*, 81(3):637–54, 1973.

N.P.B. Bollen. A note on the impact of options on stock return volatility. *Journal of Banking and Finance*, 22:1181–1191, 1998.

N.H. Hakansson. Changes in the financial market: Welfare and price effects and the basic theorems of value conservation. *The Journal of Finance*, 37(4):977–1004, 1982.

J.C. Hull. *Options, Futures, and Other Derivatives.* Prentice-Hall International, 5 edition, 2002.

R. Kabir. The price and the volatility effects of stock option introductions: A reexamination. In I. Hasan and W.C. Hunter, editors, *Research in Banking and Finance*. Elsevier, 2000.

R. Kumar, A. Sarin, and K. Shastri. The impact of options trading on the market quality of the underlying security: An empirical analysis. *The Journal of Finance*, 53(2), 1998.

B. LeBaron. Agent-based computational finance. In K.L. Judd and L. Tesfatsion, editors, *Handbook of Computational Economics*. North-Holland, 2006.

R. Merton. The theory of rational option pricing. *Bell Journal of Economics and Management Science*, 4:141–183, 1973.

Nathan Associates. Review of initial trading experience at the chicago board options exchange, 1974.

M. Raberto, S. Cincotti, S.M. Focardi, and M. Marchesi. Agent-based simulation of a financial market. *Physica A*, 299:320–328, 2001.

M. Raberto, S. Cincotti, S.M. Focardi, and M. Marchesi. Traders' long-run wealth in an artificial financial market. *Computational Economics*, 22:255–272, 2003.

S. Ross. Options and efficiency. *Quarterly Journal of Economics*, 90: 75–80, 1976.

P. Wei, P.S. Poon, and S. Zee. The effect of option listing on bid-ask spreads, price volatility and trading activity of the underlying otc stocks. *Review of Quantitative Finance and Accounting*, pages 165–180, 1997.

10

On Rational Noise Trading and Market Impact

Florian Hauser

Innsbruck University School of Management, Department of Banking and
Finance
florian.hauser@uibk.ac.at

10.1 Introduction

Since Black (1986) introduced noise as "expectations that need not
follow rational rules", noise traders are welcome in modelling financial
markets as they provide liquidity and solve theoretical problems like
the information-paradox formulated by Grossman and Stiglitz (1980).
Unfortunately, those traders cannot expect to be honored for their contributions, or, as Black (1986) states, "if they expect to make profits
from noise trading, they are incorrect".

This paper presents a simulation model where traders can decide
endogenously whether to rely on costly information or to act as a noise
trader by adopting a random trading strategy. We show that, especially for traders with a low market impact, a random strategy may be
the only rational choice as it promises higher returns than trading on
incomplete information.

The paper is structured as follows: Sect. 10.2 presents the simulation model. To check the value of additional information in this model,
Sect. 10.3 discusses an exogenously defined strategy allocation. Sects.
10.4 and 10.5 analyze equilibrium situations where every trader endogenously chooses his optimal strategy in terms of returns and market
efficiency. Robustness checks are discussed in Sect. 10.6, and Sect. 10.7
concludes.

10.2 Simulation model

We simulate a one-period call market where one security is traded. The
market consists of 1,023 computerized traders who can be classified
according to their market impact. Category $T_{j \in \{1,2,\dots,10\}}$ consists of

2^{10-j} traders, each of them trading 2^{j-1} shares each period. With this categorization, the market impact of all traders in the market roughly follows Zipf's law (see Zipf, 1949). It results in one single trader in group T_{10}, transacting 512 shares per period, while each of the 512 traders in category T_1 trades only one security per period.

All traders are risk-neutral expected wealth maximizers and are free to act as random traders ($I = 0$) by deciding to buy or sell the security in period 0 with equal probability, or to use a fundamental trading strategy by adopting one of ten discrete information levels ($I \in \{1, 2, \ldots, 10\}$). To keep our traders in the market even though some of them will suffer losses, it is assumed that all traders have an exogenous motivation to trade. However, they have to make a decision whether to base trades on a fundamental strategy or to behave as a noise trader.

To model the information system, we state that the intrinsic value V in period 1 is given by the product of 11 individual signals α_i, written as

$$V = \prod_{i=1}^{11} \exp(\alpha_i); \ \alpha \sim N(\mu = 0, \ \sigma = 0.05) . \qquad (10.1)$$

Like in real markets we assume that what the poorly informed traders know should be known to the better informed traders as well. Therefore, a trader adopting information level I will receive the signal $\alpha_{i=I}$ as well as all signals $\alpha_{i<I}$. Assuming a risk-free interest rate of zero, this trader will predict the fair price in period 0 as

$$E(V) = \prod_{i=1}^{I} \exp(\alpha_i) \ + \varepsilon; \ \varepsilon \sim N(\mu = 0, \ \sigma = 0.00001) .^1 \qquad (10.2)$$

As (10.1) describes a random process,[2] the expected relative prediction error $\varsigma = \ln(E(V)) - \ln(V)$ is normally distributed with a mean of 0 and a standard deviation of $0.05 \times \sqrt{(11 - I)}$ (see Table 10.1 for exact values). The cost of information levels is rising progressively with the quality of the information, given by

---

[1] Contrary to α, the error term ε is individually computed for every trader in each run. This creates a certain divergence of opinion among traders adopting the same information level.

[2] Note that the formula used to model the signals can also be used to model a random-walk process (geometric Brownian motion). Many dynamic models apply the same method by assuming that informed traders can predict the value of a security (following a random-walk process) in future periods.

$$C_I = (2^I - 1) \times c; \ c = 0.02 . \tag{10.3}$$

As can be seen in Table 10.1, adopting information level $I = 1$ is quite cheap. For a trader in class T_1, the expenses will lower his absolute returns by 0.02. The cost function increases progressively, so adopting higher information levels will only be reasonable to traders in higher classes. As a trader in T_{10} trades 512 shares, adopting $I = 9$ will lower his absolute returns per share also only by 0.02.

Table 10.1. Relative prediction error ς and absolute costs C of information levels.

I	0	1	2	3	4	5	6	7	8	9	10
ς	0.69	0.16	0.15	0.14	0.13	0.12	0.11	0.10	0.09	0.07	0.05
C	0.00	0.02	0.06	0.14	0.30	0.62	1.26	2.54	5.10	10.22	20.46

After each trader has chosen his information level (we will explain how our traders learn to find their optimal strategies in Sect. 10.4), all informed traders place limit orders to buy the security if the market price $P < E(V)$ and to sell the security if $P > E(V)$. Random traders will decide to buy the security (placing a limit buy order for $P < 2$) or to sell for $P > 0.5$ with a 50% chance for both options. Orders are matched at the price allowing for the highest possible market volume. If this condition is met by a steady interval of prices, the market price is computed as the geometric mean of this interval. If the number of buyers and sellers differs, orders are only partially executed.[3] As every trader class places limit orders for 512 shares, maximum market volume is 2,560 securities per period.

In period 1, all shares are liquidated at the intrinsic value V. According to this, relative gains/losses per share for buyers in class T_j (trading $s = 2^{j-1}$ shares) are calculated as

$$R_{T_j} = \ln(\frac{V \times s - C}{P \times s}) . \tag{10.4}$$

As going short in the security implies that traders receive P in period 0 and pay V in period 1 to buy back the security, returns for sellers are given by

---

[3] As a trader in T_{10} trades 512 securities with the same reservation price, the median of all reservation prices is likely to correspond to this trader's prediction. In this case, the number of buyers and sellers will differ.

$$R_{T_j} = \ln(\frac{P \times s - C}{V \times s}) \,. \tag{10.5}$$

For all results presented in the following sections, settings with 1,000 simulation runs were computed. To derive stable results, all random numbers used in a setting were pre-calculated and recycled when the simulation had to be re-looped.[4]

10.3 Reference setting

To get first insights into the value of information in this model, a reference setting with exogenously defined strategies is analyzed. Suppose that all traders in class T_j choose information level $I = j - 1$, so traders in T_1 adopt a random strategy while all other traders rely on fundamental information. Average returns $\overline{R}$ for trader classes in 1,000 runs with and without costs (black bars and grey bars respectively) are shown in Figure 10.1.

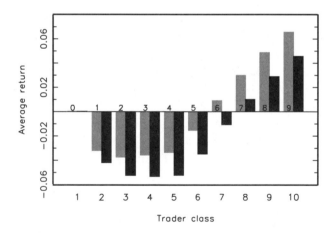

Fig. 10.1. Average returns per trader class with/without costs (black/grey bars). The adopted information level I is plotted above the horizontal axis.

As can be seen, the random traders in T_1 receive an average return of zero although they cannot predict the fundamental value of the security

---

[4] This is especially important for the calculation of equilibria, as an equilibrium that is stable with a certain set of random numbers might get unstable if random numbers are re-calculated.

at all. This is not surprising if we consider that all 512 traders in T_1 will randomly decide whether to go long or short. On average we find 50% of them on each side of the market, so their orders have hardly any impact on market prices. Hence, on average, we will also find 50% of them to have made the right decision.

If we look at returns before costs (grey bars), the market is a zero-sum game. We have seen that random traders will receive average returns of zero, as they make an independent, random decision. Looking at the results for fundamental traders, we find the well-informed trader classes $T_{[7;10]}$ are able to realize positive returns before costs while the less-informed traders in $T_{[2;6]}$ suffer losses. Remarkably, the least informed fundamental traders in T_2 are not the ones receiving the lowest returns. Before (and after) costs, this trader class performs clearly better than T_3 and T_4.

The idea that additional information can worsen the investors' performance is already discussed in several studies (see e.g. Huber et al., 2007; Samuelson, 2004; Schredelseker, 2001). To explain this result with the given model, we have to consider two different effects. First, a higher information level will lower a trader's prediction error. However, as a second effect, additional information will also increase the chance of a trader to make joint mistakes with other trader classes relying on the same signals α_i. Traders in T_3 and T_4 suffer the most from this kind of herding behavior, as their price predictions are on the same time rather unprecise and highly correlated with predictions of other trader classes. For the least informed traders in T_2, the second effect is less pronounced: as they receive only one signal, their price prediction is almost independent of that of the rest of the market.

10.4 Equilibrium

So far we have seen that a random strategy is likely to beat low-information strategies. This leaves us with the question why any trader should stick with a low-information strategy if he is better off as a random trader. Picking up this idea, we are interested in equilibrium situations, meaning strategy allocations where no trader has an incentive to change his strategy if all other traders stick with their strategies as well.

In a first step, we search for equilibria under the condition that all traders in one class choose the same strategy. To find equilibria, every trader class starts with an information level drawn from a discrete uniform distribution ($I_{T_j,\text{start}} \sim U(0, 10)$). For every single trader class, the incentive to change strategy is calculated as $R_{T_j,\text{best}} - R_{T_j,\text{start}}$, with $R_{T_j,\text{best}}$ being the highest possible return for this class when all other classes stick with their original strategy $I_{T_j,\text{start}}$. Then, the trader class with the highest incentive to change adopts the best strategy and the simulation is re-looped. Equilibrium is reached when no trader class has any further incentive to change strategy.

The calculation of equilibrium is re-looped for several hundred times. For the setting presented here, we find only one stable equilibrium with a strategy allocation I_T shown in Table 10.2. One can see that in equilibrium, the 3 traders of T_9 and T_{10} are the only ones who process information. For all other trader classes it is rational to stick with a random strategy.

Table 10.2. Strategy allocation in equilibrium.

Class T_j	T_1	T_2	T_3	T_4	T_5	T_6	T_7	T_8	T_9	T_{10}
I_T	0	0	0	0	0	0	0	0	7	9

This method to find equilibria is then re-applied to several settings, having the same model parameters but different signals α_j and a new set of random numbers. Not in all settings do we find stable equilibria. If equilibria are found, strategy allocations turn out to be quite similar to the setting shown in Table 10.2. Most importantly, in all equilibria only traders in T_9 and T_{10} process information with the higher information level always being associated with T_{10}.

Average returns in equilibrium are shown in Fig. 10.2. As can be seen, only T_{10} is able to realize positive returns after costs while average returns before costs are positive for all 3 traders of T_9 and T_{10}. For all other traders, their random strategies now produce negative returns. Despite that, the equilibrium calculation shows that it is rational for them to stick with a random strategy as all other strategies will make their performance even worse. According to this, noise trading is no longer the result of irrational trading behavior, it may under certain circumstances be the only rational strategy for an investor.

For all trader classes adopting a random strategy, one can see that a higher market impact clearly worsens their performance. This is due to the fact that for a trader in T_8, a random strategy implies that he has to decide whether to go long or short with all 128 shares. Hence, systematic behavior (e.g. all 4 traders in T_8 go long) is much more likely for this category than for T_1, where 512 traders can decide independently whether to go long or short with one share. Because of this, market

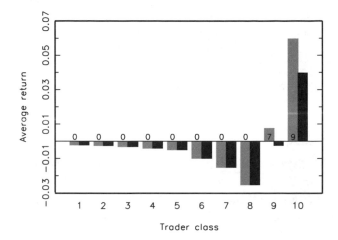

Fig. 10.2. Average returns per trader class with/without costs (black/grey bars) for a strategy allocation as shown in Table 10.2. The adopted information level I is plotted above the horizontal axis.

impact in our model has a twofold effect on the strategy selection of traders: a higher market impact makes a fundamental strategy more profitable as the costs of information per share decline, and it makes a random strategy less profitable as the price impact increases.

Relating to capital markets, this questions if it is rational for private investors to buy index-driven products. As many other investors do the same, those investors choose to play a random strategy with a high market impact. Considering the results in our model, those products may perform worse than the market average, as also shown by Hanke and Schredelseker (2005).

As a second step, we allow for heterogenous choice of strategies in every trader class. Starting with the allocation in Table 10.2, we subsequently check for all trader classes $T_{j \in \{10,9,\ldots,1\}}$ whether every single trader in T_j already adopts his optimal strategy. If not, the trader with the highest incentive to change in this class adopts his optimal strategy and we start again with T_{10}.

After a few loops, a strategy allocation is reached where not a single one of the 1,023 traders has any better option than the strategy he already uses. The exact strategy allocation as well as average returns after costs for $T_{[8;10]}$ are shown in Table 10.3, average returns for all trader classes in this situation are presented in Fig. 10.3.

As a first result, note that the strategy allocation does hardly change compared to the equilibrium with homogenous strategies. While one

Table 10.3. Strategy allocation and average returns in equilibrium with heterogenous strategy choice in every trader class.

Class T_j	$j \leq 7$	T_8				T_9		T_{10}
Trader t	all	1	2	3	4	1	2	1
I_t	0	0	0	0	1	5	7	9
$\overline{R}$ in %		-1.1	-0.8	-0.8	-1.2	-1.8	-1.3	1.9

trader in T_8 leaves his random strategy to adopt $I = 1$, one of the two traders in T_9 now chooses a lower information level of $I = 5$. This leaves us with a situation where only 22.5% of all shares in the market are traded on information. Note that all fundamental traders in the market now use an individual strategy.

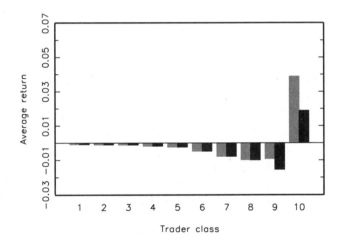

Fig. 10.3. Average returns per trader class with/without costs (black/grey bars) for a strategy allocation as shown in Table 10.3.

For the random traders, returns in the new equilibrium have increased markedly. As a higher share of stocks is traded on information now and the heterogeneity of information increased, the overall market impact of all random traders declined. Although in the new equilibrium still more than 75% of all shares are traded upon a random strategy, the losses of the random traders are quite moderate. Random traders in T_8 (the ones with the highest market impact) on average perform less than 1% worse than the market average, and they realize higher returns than the fundamental traders in T_8 and T_9.

While returns for T_{10} did not change significantly, traders in T_9 are now the ones suffering the highest losses. Note that in the new equilibrium, they are the ones relying on the medium information levels. As shown in the reference setting (see Sect. 10.3), this strategy is fraught with problems: the information processed by T_9 is not good enough to compete with T_{10}. As the signals processed by both traders in T_9 are correlated, they will often make joint mistakes against T_{10}. The reason for them to lose against traders in $T_{[1;8]}$ is rooted in their market impact: contrary to the random traders, their correlated predictions will let them act as price-makers, driving market prices away from fundamental values and hence leading to higher negative returns. Nevertheless, the strategy chosen by traders in T_9 is their best available option: their market impact is too low to adopt very high information levels like $I = 9$, and it is too high to adopt a random- or low-information strategy.

Related to capital markets, the results may explain why Malkiel (2005) finds that actively managed investment funds on average perform worse than their reference indices. The relatively good (and costly) information processed by fund managers in combination with their market impact will work against them and can easily drive their returns below market average.

10.5 Market efficiency

While analyzing several different settings (see Sect. 10.6), we also find equilibria in heterogenous strategies where all traders realize negative returns after costs. In those situations, the simulation shows a market that is truly efficient in the sense of Jensen (1978): with respect to the information system and the cost of information, no trader in this market is able to realize systematic, above-average gains. But, according to Fama (1970), an efficient market should reflect all available information. Concerning the low number of traders that process information in equilibrium (see Section 10.4), one might ask how good this market performs in predicting fundamental values. We therefore use raw returns, calculated as $r = \ln(V) - \ln(P)$, to measure the relative deviation of prices from intrinsic values.

In equilibrium, raw returns from all 1,000 runs have a mean of 0 and a standard deviation of 0.10, corresponding to the prediction error ς made by traders processing information level $I = 7$ (see Table 10.1 for prediction errors). Considering that less than a quarter of all shares in the market are traded on information, prices reflect the intrinsic values quite well.

Next, we check what happens when we leave equilibrium. The left panel of Fig. 10.4 shows the standard deviation of returns, depending on the (homogenous) strategy used by T_1. As can be seen, the price accuracy gets worse if traders in T_1 start to process information. Compared to the random strategy played in equilibrium, price accuracy only increases if traders adopt information levels $I \geq 8$.

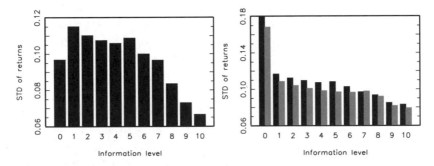

Fig. 10.4. Standard deviation of returns when trader class T_1 (left panel) or a single trader in T_9 (right panel) varies his strategy.

The maximum standard deviation is reached at information level $I = 1$. As one trader in T_8 plays the same strategy, this information is already reflected in market prices. If further traders base trading decisions on the same information, they make joint mistakes and prices become biased. The same explanation holds for the peak at $I = 5$. As one trader in T_9 already processes this information, further traders adopting the same information level will make it more likely for all traders with this strategy to act as price-makers. Although the individual prediction error of T_1 rises when changing his strategy to $I = 3$ or $I = 4$, price fluctuations are lower in those cases. According to that, herding behavior does not only affect the performance of the herd, it is also likely to drive prices further away from fundamental values than trading on noise. This result is inline with the findings in Schredelseker (2001).

The right panel of Fig. 10.4 shows price fluctuations depending on the strategy adopted by the two traders in T_9. Strategy changes of the trader playing $I = 7$ ($I = 5$) in equilibrium are plotted with black (grey) bars. The graph shows that the dependence of price accuracy and information level is transitive for both traders, with one exception in each case: for the first trader, $I = 4$ causes a lower price fluctuation than $I = 5$, as the second trader already adopts $I = 5$. For the second trader, adopting $I = 6$ results in a lower price fluctuation than with $I = 7$, which is the equilibrium strategy of the first trader.

The graph also shows that the maximum number of noise traders is reached not only in terms of possible gains; if one trader in T_9 leaves his equilibrium strategy to become a noise trader, the average price fluctuation increases beyond the prediction error of $I = 1$.

Although this model states that in equilibrium, certain traders do have an incentive to process information, it cannot deliver a solution to the information-paradox as formulated by Grossman and Stiglitz (1980). By using the intrinsic value to calculate returns, we implicitly assume that prices converge to the fundamental value. But the model shows that one might need a large number of noise traders to drive prices away from fundamental values.

10.6 Robustness checks

We check the robustness of our results by varying model parameters in several ways: equilibria for homogenous strategies of trader classes are computed for linear transformations of the original cost function by changing c in (10.3). We find that the number of random traders in equilibrium does not change when the cost of information is increased. Traders in T_9 and T_{10} then adopt lower information levels, which makes it more difficult to find settings with stable equilibria. When decreasing costs beyond a certain level, we find that a higher number of traders process information in equilibrium. With very low costs, also traders in T_8 and T_9 can easily afford to adopt an information level of $I = 10$. In these situations, T_{10} cannot stand out from the crowd anymore, leading to several trader classes using the same (maximum) information level. According to this, the model seems to be well balanced with $c = 0.02$, as the highest information level adopted gets close but does not reach the maximum of $I = 10$. Equilibria for different values for c are shown in Table 10.4.

We also check equilibria for various linear cost functions, following the equation

$$C_I = I \times c. \tag{10.6}$$

As this makes medium- and low information levels more expensive, traders in T_9 then adopt lower information levels in equilibrium. How-

Table 10.4. Strategy allocation in equilibrium for different cost functions.

T	1	2	3	4	5	6	7	8	9	10
$I_{T,c=0.0002}$	0	0	0	0	0	0	2	10	10	10
$I_{T,c=0.002}$	0	0	0	0	0	0	0	5	10	10
$I_{T,c=0.02}$	0	0	0	0	0	0	0	0	7	9
$I_{T,c=0.2}$	0	0	0	0	0	0	0	0	3	5
$I_{T,c=2}$	0	0	0	0	0	0	0	0	1	2

ever, the proportion of fundamental traders and random traders in equilibrium does not change.

The information system is also varied in several ways. As shown in Table 10.1, the prediction error declines progressively with higher information levels. Using information systems where the prediction error is a linear or logarithmic function of the information level does not affect the main results.

The way random traders place their orders does affect equilibria. If one limits the price impact of random traders too strictly (e.g. by setting the rule that in case of more than 50% of all orders in the order book being buy-orders from random traders, market price is set to the best sell-order), random trading gets even more profitable. Due to this, the share of traders processing information in equilibrium declines below 20% and equilibria become less stable.

Several ways how traders' strategies converge to equilibrium are tried, e.g. by varying and randomizing the choice which traders change strategies first. All equilibria found share the same characteristics as presented in Sect. 10.4.

10.7 Conclusions

This paper presents a simulation model where traders with heterogenous market impact can endogenously choose to act as random traders, or to adopt a fundamental strategy by processing costly information. In equilibrium, less than a quarter of all shares are traded on information. As the proportion of fundamental traders and random traders in equilibrium was found to be robust against several variations of the model, we suggest that for traders with a low or medium investment volume, a random strategy is likely to perform better than low-information strategies, and it should on average outperform actively as well as passively managed investment funds.

By analyzing market efficiency in equilibrium, we show that a small share of traders processing information is sufficient to keep market prices close to fundamental values. In equilibrium, prices reflect the fundamental values even better than in situations where additional traders process low- and medium-quality information. Referring to Black (1986), we should rather blame the low- and medium-informed fundamental traders for making prices behave like "a drunk, tending to wander farther and farther from his starting point".

Acknowledgement. I thank Michael Hanke, Jürgen Huber, Sonja Huber, Michael Kirchler, Klaus Schredelseker and two anonymous referees for helpful suggestions.

References

F. Black. Noise. *The Journal of Finance*, 41:529–543, 1986.

E. F. Fama. Efficient capital markets: A review of theory and empirical work. *The Journal of Finance*, 25:761–777, 1970.

S. J. Grossman and J. E. Stiglitz. On the impossibility of informationally efficient markets. *American Economic Review*, 70:393–408, 1980.

M. Hanke and K. Schredelseker. Index funds should be expected to underperform the index. Working Paper, University of Innsbruck, 2005.

J. Huber, M. Kirchler, and M. Sutter. Is more information always better? experimental financial markets with cumulative information. *Journal of Economic Behavior and Organization*, forthcoming, 2007.

M. Jensen. Some anomalous evidence regarding market efficiency. *Journal of Financial Economics*, 6:95–101, 1978.

B. C. Malkiel. Reflections on the efficient market hypothesis: 30 years later. *The Financial Review*, 40:1–9, 2005.

L. Samuelson. Modeling knowledge in economic analysis. *Journal of Economic Literature*, 42:367–403, 2004.

K. Schredelseker. Is the usefulness approach useful? some reflections on the utility of public information. In *Contemporary Issues in Accounting Regulation*. Kluwer Academic Publishers, 2001.

G.K. Zipf. *Human Behavior and the Principle of Least Effort*. Addison-Wesley (Reading MA), 1949.

Part IV

Analysis of Economic and Social Networks

A Note on Symmetry in Job Contact Networks

Andrea Mario Lavezzi[1] and Nicola Meccheri[2]

[1] University of Palermo, Department of Studies on Politics, Law and
Society, Italy.
lavezzi@unipa.it
[2] University of Pisa, Department of Economics, Italy.
meccheri@ec.unipi.it

11.1 Introduction

Since the seminal work of Granovetter (1995), the sociological literature
highlighted the importance of social relationships, like friends, relatives
and acquaintances, as sources of information on jobs in labor markets.
Such importance is also confirmed by a number of empirical studies.[3]
More recently, economists have devoted considerable attention to this
topic,[4] so that the study of individual and aggregate economic outcomes
produced by the presence of social relationships in labor markets is
becoming a fruitful research area in economics.

An important issue in the studies on social networks refers to how
the network structure matters, that is how network characteristics, such
as topology and type of connections play a role in explaining the economic effects of the networks. For instance, the effects of networks
symmetry have been often discussed qualitatively in the sociological
literature (e.g. Granovetter (2005)). On the other hand, the quantitative effects that such network's property may produce on output and
wage inequality have still not received the same attention.

In this paper we tackle this issue and study the effect of symmetry
on workers' aggregate output and inequality.[5] In particular, we adopt a
version with heterogeneous jobs of the model by Calvo-Armengol and

---

[3] See Montgomery (1991) for further discussion and references.

[4] See Ioannides and Loury (2004) for a survey.

[5] In the extended version of this paper (Lavezzi and Meccheri, 2005a) we also begin
to study the role of other networks' properties on output and inequality, such as
social exclusion and network density (see Lavezzi and Meccheri, 2005a, also for
more details on the related literature).

Jackson (2007), in which exogenous social networks facilitate the transmission of information on job vacancies among workers.[6] We find that: a) symmetric networks produce higher output and lower inequality than asymmetric networks and, b) the introduction of social links, having the function of "structural holes" (see Burt, 1992), has a larger positive effect on output and inequality if they are associated with symmetric networks.

The paper is organized as follows: Section 11.2 presents the theoretical model; Section 11.3 contains the results of the simulations; Section 11.4 concludes.

11.2 A Model of labor market with social networks

11.2.1 Production, wages and turnover

Time is discrete and indexed by $t = 0, 1, 2...$ The economy is populated by homogenous, risk-neutral, infinitely-lived agents (workers) indexed by $i \in \{1, 2, ..., N\}$. In each period a worker can be either unemployed or employed in a "good" or "bad" job. Thus, by indicating with s_{it} the employment status of worker i in period t, we have three possible agents' states:

$$s_{it} = \begin{cases} g, & \text{employed in a good job} \\ b, & \text{employed in a bad job} \\ u, & \text{unemployed} \end{cases}$$

On the production side, we consider one-to-one employment relationships and assume a very simple form of a production function, in which productivity depends on the job offered by a firm to a worker. In particular, we denote by y_{it} the output of a firm employing worker i at time t or, in other words, the surplus generated by the match between a worker and a firm (output price is normalized to one).

We simply assume that output in a good job is higher than in a bad job, for instance because it is a hi-tech job. According to these assumptions, the parameter $y^s, s \in (g, b, u)$, indexing the productivity of a match, follows the rule:

$$y^g > y^b > 0 (= y^u).$$

---

[6] Calvo-Armengol and Jackson (2004) provides some simulations on the role of networks' topology for the simpler case of homogeneous workers and jobs.

Wages are a fraction of the match surplus, and are denoted by $w^s = \beta y^s$ with $\beta \in (0,1)$.[7] This produces an ordering of wages obtainable in a given match, which follows the ordering of outputs. Obviously, unemployed workers earn zero wages, and we normalize their reservation utility to zero.

The labor market is subject to the following turnover. Initially, all workers are unemployed. Every period (from $t = 0$ onwards) has two phases: at the beginning of the period each worker receives an offer of a job of type f, with $f \in \{g, b\}$, with arrival probability $a_f \in (0,1)$.[8] Parameter a_f captures all the information on vacancies which is not transmitted through the network, that is information from firms, agencies, newspapers, etc. When an agent receives an offer and she is already employed and not interested in the offer, in the sense that the offered job does not increase her wage, she passes the information to a friend/relative/acquaintance who is either unemployed or employed but receiving a lower wage then the one paid for the offered job. At the end of the period every employed worker loses the job with breakdown probability $d \in (0,1)$.

11.2.2 Social links and job information transmission

social networks may be characterized by a graph G representing agents' links, where $G_{ij} = 1$ if i and j know each other, and $G_{ij} = 0$ indicates if they do not. It is assumed that $G_{ij} = G_{ji}$, meaning that the acquaintance relationship is reciprocal. Given the assumptions on wages and arrival probabilities, the probability of the joint event that agent i learns about a job and this job ends up in agent's j hands, is described by p_{ij}:

$$
p_{ij}(s_{it}^\theta, f) = \begin{cases}
a_b \text{ if } f = b \cup j = i \cup s_i = u \\
a_g \text{ if } f = g \cup j = i \cup (s_i = u \cap s_i = b) \\
a_b \dfrac{G_{ij}}{\sum_{k:s_k=u} G_{ik}} \text{ if } f = b \cup (s_i = b \cap s_i = g) \cup s_j = u \\
a_g \dfrac{G_{ij}}{\sum_{k:s_k \neq g} G_{ik}} \text{ if } f = g \cup s_i = g \cup (s_j = u \cap s_j = b) \\
0 \text{ otherwise}
\end{cases}
$$

In the first two cases, worker i receives an offer with probability a_f, $f \in \{g, b\}$, and takes the offer for herself. This holds if she is either unemployed or employed in a bad job and receives an offer for a good job.

---

[7] For instance β may represent the bargaining power of workers when wages are set by Nash bargaining, as is usual in search models. Clearly, profits are $(1 - \beta)y^s$.

[8] That is, each agent can receive both an offer for a good and a bad job.

In the third case the worker i is employed and receives with probability a_b an offer for a bad job, that she passes only to an unemployed worker $j(\neq i)$. We assume that among all unemployed workers connected with i by a social link, i chooses j randomly. Hence, the probability that worker j receives the information by worker i is equal to $\frac{G_{ij}}{\sum_{k:s_k=u} G_{ik}}$. In the fourth case worker i receives with probability a_g an offer for a good job when she is already employed in a good job, thus she passes the offer, with probability $\frac{G_{ij}}{\sum_{k:s_k \neq g} G_{ik}}$, to a worker connected to her who is either unemployed or employed in a bad job. Clearly, $p_{ij} = 0$ in all remaining cases.

To sum up, a worker who receives an offer makes direct use of it if the new job opportunity increases her wage. Otherwise, she passes the information to someone who is connected to her. The choice of the worker to whom pass the information is "selective", in the sense that the information is never passed to someone who does not need it,[9] but it is random with respect to the subset of the connected workers who improve their condition (wage) exploiting such information (for example, a worker receiving a good job offer is indifferent to pass it to an unemployed contact or a contact employed in a bad job). Finally, we assume that a worker receiving both an offer for a bad and a good job when she does not need them, decides to transmit first the information about the bad job and then, possibly to the same agent, the information about the good job, and we exclude that each job information may be transmitted to more than one (connected) worker.[10]

Figure 11.1 shows the timing of the events for a generic period t (for convenience, the period has been represented as composed by four different consecutive sub-periods, with sub-periods $t.1$, $t.2$ and $t.4$ having negligible length).

---

[9] For the sake of simplicity, we assume that a worker observe the state of her connections at the end of the previous period to make a decision on passing information. In other words, she cannot observe if her connections have already received an offer from someone else. If all of the worker's acquaintances do not need the job information, then it is simply lost.

[10] Calvo-Armengol and Jackson (2007) provide various extensions on the process of transmission of job information.

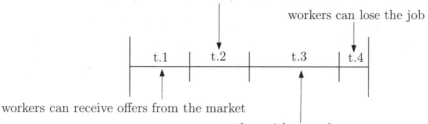

workers can pass/receive offers to/from the network

workers can lose the job

workers can receive offers from the market

workers either produce or are unemployed

Fig. 11.1. Timing

11.3 On networks symmetry

In this section we present the results of our simulations.[11] Our aim is to assess how the structure of social networks affects the dynamics of output and wage inequality in the long run, as well as the correlation of workers' wages. We measure output by averaging over time the average output of the n workers in every period. Inequality is measured by the average Gini index over time.

As a preliminary general remark, it is important to point out that in this framework the network structure basically affects the possibility for the system to be in a state of maximum output (*SMO* henceforth), that is a state in which all agents are employed in the good job. Given our assumptions, *SMO* would be a steady state if the probability of losing the job was zero, as workers would be in the best possible position and would turn down any offer they received, directly or indirectly. In other words, without the exogenous breakdown probability, *SMO* would be an absorbing state for the system. In this respect, the network structure regulates the possibility to attain *SMO* and the speed at which the system recovers to it, after the occurrence of stochastic perturbations given by breakdowns of job relationships. Therefore, as we shall see, high average levels of output and low levels of inequality obtain when the system, driven by the network structure, reaches faster and persistently remains in *SMO* (note that in *SMO* inequality is clearly absent).

---

[11] Simulations are run for 500,000 periods and the parameters are: $u_b = 0.15$, $a_g = 0.10$, $d = 0.015$, $\beta = 0.4$, $y^g = 5$, $y^b = 1$. All simulations are programmed in R (http://www.r-project.org/). Codes are available upon request from the authors.

11.3.1 Symmetric vs. asymmetric networks

We begin by considering a simple case of symmetric vs. asymmetric networks. Technically speaking, symmetry implies that all agents are connected to the same number of other agents. Consider the network

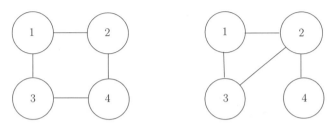

Fig. 11.2. Networks G_A and G_B

structures in Figure 11.2, G_A and G_B.[12] Both networks have the same number of agents, n, and links, N ($N = n = 4$), and the same average number of links for each agent, that is $\mu = 2$.[13] However, they have a different geometry: network G_B is obtained from G_A by simply rewiring one link. This introduces an asymmetry, as in network G_B agent 2 has three links and agent 3 has one link, while agents 1 and 4 maintain the same number of links. In other words, agents 1, 2 and 4 form a cluster of interconnected agents, from which agent 3 is partially excluded. In addition, there exists a difference in the number of links of the agents to whom every agent is connected. In network G_A any agent has two links with agents who have two links. Differently, in network G_B agents 1 and 4 have one link with an agent with two links (respectively agents 4 and 1), and one link with an agent with three links, agent 2. Agent 2 has two links with two agents, 1 and 4, who have two links, and one link with agent 3, who has one link. As we show in Table 11.1, this has consequences for both output and inequality.

We observe that, moving from G_A to G_B, output decreases and inequality increases. The emergence of a local cluster makes the network asymmetric, and affects both output and wage inequality. In particular, the decrease in output and the increase on inequality depend on the

---

[12] This case corresponds to Example 1 in Calvo-Armengol (2004) where, differently from here, workers and jobs are both homogeneous. In general, in our examples we will consider networks where not all possible links are formed as a simple way to consider the fact that link formation is costly. See Calvo-Armengol (2004) for a full treatment of network formation with costly links.

[13] The simple formula to obtain μ, the average number of links per agent, is $2N/n$.

relative isolation of agent 3. Agent 3's average wage is sharply lower in network G_B. In this case the increase in the average wage of agent 2, due to an increase in the number of her connections, is not sufficient to counterbalance the decrease in the average wage of agent 3. Also notice that the variance of agent 2's wage is lower while the variance of agent 3's wage is higher in network G_B.

Table 11.1. Output, inequality and wages, networks G_A and G_B

Network	Output	Ineq.	Av. wages [1, 2, 3, 4]	Var. wages [1, 2, 3, 4]
G_A	4.818	0.034	1.927, 1.927, 1.928, 1.928	0.122, 0.123, 0.121, 0.120
G_B	4.802	0.038	1.924, 1.945, 1.889, 1.924	0.126, 0.091, 0.183, 0.127

Results are also different for agents 1 and 4 although the number of their connections is the same. In particular their average wage is lower and the variance is higher in network G_B. This can be explained by the fact that the number of links of their "connections" is different in network G_B, in particular they are both connected to agent 2 who has three links. This implies that their probability of receiving information on vacancies from agent 2 is lower in network G_B, as they have more "competitors" for information. This result is not so obvious since there could be also a positive effect deriving from a connection with an agent with many links, which should guarantee a more stable position in the state of employment and therefore have a higher propensity to transmit information on vacancies. We term the first effect as *competition effect*, and the second as *connection effect*, and note that the former dominates the latter in network G_B.

These results highlight the complexity of capturing the externalities produced by the structure of the network. In the present framework, the network exerts externalities on agents' utilities as it affects their job opportunities. However, to put these network externalities in closed form is not an easy task, as they derive from a network stochastic process.[14] Our numerical results, however, clearly show that such externalities differ across individuals depending on their location in the network. Moreover, switching from a symmetric to an asymmetric structure, it appears that the negative externalities that derive seem to prevail on positive externalities, since in symmetric networks aggregate results improve.

---

[14] In a different setting, strategic and static, Ballester et al. (2006) studies analytically the variance of network externalities.

worker	1	2	3	4
1	1	0.031	0.026	0.025
2	0.031	1	0.027	0.026
3	0.026	0.027	1	0.020
4	0.025	0.026	0.020	1

worker	1	2	3	4
1	1	0.038	0.014	0.048
2	0.038	1	0.022	0.038
3	0.014	0.022	1	0.010
4	0.048	0.038	0.010	1

Table 11.2. Correlation of workers' wages. Left panel, network G_A; right panel, network G_B.

The creation of a local cluster also affects the distribution of wage correlations across each pair of agents in the network; from Table 11.2 we see that, as predictable, the values of the correlation of wages of the agents in the cluster (i.e. agents 1, 2 and 4) increase.[15] In network G_B agent 3's correlations with any other agent decreases. Note that the correlation between agent 3 and 2's wages is lower, despite the fact that the two agents share a link as in network G_A. In network G_B, however, agent 2 has one extra link and, in practice, this weakens the connection between 2 and 3. Finally, the correlation between 3 and 4 is lower in network G_B because they are not directly connected.[16]

To sum up, the introduction of asymmetry in a network which preserves the same average number of links, causes output to decrease and inequality to increase.[17] Next section takes a step further.

11.3.2 Symmetry and relational heterogeneity

In this section we go deeper on the role of social networks' symmetry in explaining economic outcomes. In fact, as remarked for instance by Ioannides and Loury (2004, p. 1064), there exist results related to social networks structure that may be explained by symmetry, while they have been often attributed to other network properties. Indeed, much of the early sociological research on the effects of job networks' properties

---

[15] All these numerical results are in accordance with the analytics of Calvo-Armengol and Jackson (2007).

[16] Other examples with larger networks, not reported here but available upon request, confirm these results.

[17] These results are in line with those of Calvo-Armengol (2004) on welfare and unemployment. However, this depends on the fact that we introduced heterogeneity in jobs but preserved the homogeneity of workers. In fact, in the setting with heterogeneous jobs and workers of Lavezzi and Meccheri (2005b), we provide an example in which, when productivity differentials are sufficiently high, more symmetry can be associated to lower output. A full treatment of this aspect is beyond the scope of the present work.

mainly focused on *relational heterogeneity*, emphasizing that not all social relations (contacts) have the same role or strength in affecting employment outcomes. Here we aim to disentangle in our framework the effects of network symmetry on output and inequality with respect to some traditional concepts related to relational heterogeneity.

An important argument in the theory of social networks refers to the role of *structural holes*. As is well-known, Burt (1992) defines structural holes as the "gap" of non-redundant links: agents placed at structural holes of a network allow information to flow between otherwise unconnected groups of agents. The structural holes argument implies that networks with more non-redundant links (i.e. more agents placed at structural holes) can provide more information than network *of the same size*, but with more redundant links (see Ioannides and Loury, 2004, p. 1063). Thus, networks in which (structural holes) agents link otherwise unconnected groups should be characterized by more efficient outcomes, since information in such networks circulates more widely.[18]

Consider the different network structures in Figure 11.3, with $n = 8$, $N = 12$ and $\mu = 3$.

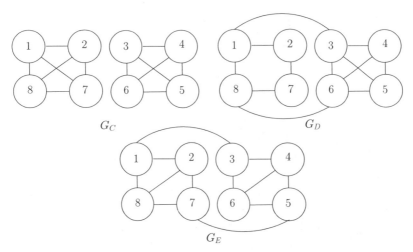

Fig. 11.3. Networks G_C, G_D, G_E: symmetry and structural holes

---

[18] Note that the "structural hole effect" amplifies when information can be transmitted to indirect relationships (more than two-links away) by means of sequential passages, while in our simulations information may be transmitted only one time between direct contacts. However, in a long-run perspective, since the transmission of information can improve the state of one (connected) agent in a given period and this allows her to be more prone to transmit information to others in future periods, the same effect should apply.

In network G_C, there are two separated groups of four agents and, in each group, each agent is linked to each other. Clearly, this is a symmetric network, since all agents are connected to the same number of other agents (three, in this case). It is important to point out that, according to the theory of structural holes, some links in network G_C are, at least partially, redundant, since each pair of agents could be (indirectly) linked anyway via other agents in their group (e.g. agents 1 and 2 are linked via agent 7), and it would be more efficient to have some links to agents in the other group.

In network G_D some agents become structural holes: 1 and 8 for the first subgroup, 3 and 6 for the second. The two groups are linked through a bridge provided by structural holes. The network is not symmetric, since there are agents with a different number of links: i.e. agents 3 and 6 have now four links, while agents 2 and 7 have just two links. Finally, network G_E is a symmetric network with the same number of "structural holes agents" $(1, 3, 5$ and 7 in this case) of G_D.

Running simulations for these networks, we obtain the following aggregate results:

Table 11.3. Networks G_C, G_D, G_E: output and inequality

Network	Output	Inequality
G_C	4.863	0.027
G_D	4.862	0.027
G_E	4.867	0.026

We note that the introduction of structural holes and asymmetry in network G_D slightly reduces output and leaves inequality unchanged, while output is higher and inequality slightly lower in G_E. Also, even if the results are fairly close, this example seems to suggest that, in the aggregate, the positive effect on output which may derive from the introduction of "bridges" between different groups (as can be the case in a passage from G_C to G_E) could be counterbalanced if those bridges are created by rendering asymmetric the structure of the network and, consequently, the position of different agents.

This appears more transparent if we look at Table 11.4, in which we report individual (average) wages of three workers (1, 2 and 3)[19]

---

[19] The situation of the chosen workers changes differently when we move from network G_C to network G_D; in this sense, they have been chosen as representing typical cases. Of course, the same qualitative results also hold for other workers in analogous situations.

in G_C, G_D and G_E. Table 11.4 also shows the wage correlation of two workers with no direct connections (1 and 6) in the different networks.

Table 11.4. Networks G_C and G_D: individual wages [1,2,3] and correlation [1;6]

Network	Av. wage [1]	Av. wage [2]	Av. wage [3]	Corr. wages [1;6]
G_C	1.944	1.944	1.944	0.000
G_D	1.947	1.929	1.959	0.010
G_E	1.947	1.947	1.948	0.012

Wages of agents 1 and 3 increase in network G_D. While the increase of agent 3's wage is largely due to the fact that she has now one extra link, the increase of agent 1's wage is related to a "structural hole" effect: given that the number of her connections is unchanged, now she is linked to the other group and can take advantage, directly or indirectly, from the presence of all workers in the economy. Agent 2 loses one link in G_D and her wage becomes lower than in G_C. In principle agent 2 could have benefited from the presence of a bridge connecting her group to the other, but this appears not sufficient to outweigh the negative effect of losing one link. Moreover, this negative effect appears so powerful that, although some agents become structural holes and have more links, aggregate output (which is proportional to wages) slightly decreases in network G_D.[20]

In network G_E agents maintain the same number of links as in G_C, but some agents (1, 3, 5 and 7) become structural holes. The wage of agents 1 and 3 increases with respect to G_C, indicating that these agents benefit from a better circulation of information. The wage of agent 2, who is not a structural hole, increases as well with respect to G_C even if the number of links is the same, and is much higher than in G_D. The latter effect clearly depends on 2 having more links in G_E than in G_D.

Finally, note from Table 11.4's last column that the presence of bridges between the two groups of workers affects the structure of wages correlations. While wages of workers 1 and 6 are not correlated in network G_C, where they belong to two separated groups, the correlation becomes positive in networks G_D and G_E, even if those workers are not directly connected.

---

[20] This suggests the presence of decreasing returns from increases in the number of social links. This aspect is analyzed in more detail in Lavezzi and Meccheri (2005a).

Overall, the positive effects of bridges creation can be better appreciated in network G_E in which symmetry is preserved. In such a case, output increases and inequality slightly decreases with respect to other networks. This happens because the advantages of a wider circulation of information can be exploited at no costs for agents, in the sense that they maintain the same number of links.

11.4 Conclusions

In this paper we have provided an initial study of the effects of network symmetry on output and inequality. In particular, our results allow for a first set of considerations.

The relevance of symmetric social architectures, which appeared in our examples, points to the relevance of having an "egalitarian" society in which individuals are relatively similar in their degree of social interaction. Moreover, the importance of symmetry also appears in relation to the presence of structural holes, which effects may depend on their being related to symmetry or asymmetry of the network. More precisely, the importance of structural holes is in fact related to the possibility of connecting two or more otherwise disconnected groups of individuals by establishing a symmetric geometry.[21]

References

C. Ballester, A. Calvó-Armengol, and Y Zenou. Who's who in networks. wanted: the key player. *Econometrica*, 74(5):1403–1471, 2006.

R. S. Burt. *Structural Holes*. Harvard University Press, 1992.

A. Calvo-Armengol. Job contact networks. *Journal of Economic Theory*, 115(1):191–206, March 2004.

A. Calvo-Armengol and M. O. Jackson. Networks in labor markets: Wage and employment dynamics and inequality. *Journal of Economic Theory*, 127(1):27–46, January 2007.

A. Calvo-Armengol and M. O. Jackson. The effects of social networks on employment and inequality. *American Economic Review*, 94(3): 426–454, June 2004.

M. S. Granovetter. The impact of social structure on economic outcomes. *Journal of Economic Perspectives*, 19(1):33–50, Winter 2005.

---

[21] In Lavezzi and Meccheri (2005a) we study symmetry with respect to the "strength of weak ties hypotheses" of Granovetter (1973).

M. S. Granovetter. The strength of weak ties. *American Journal of Sociology*, 78(6):1360–1380, 1973.

M. S. Granovetter. *Getting a Job: a Study of Contacts and Careers.* University of Chicago Press, 1995.

Y. M. Ioannides and L. D. Loury. Job information networks, neighborhood effects, and inequality. *Journal of Economic Literature*, 42(4): 1056–1093, December 2004.

A. M. Lavezzi and N. Meccheri. Social networks in labor markets: The effects of symmetry, randomness and exclusion on output and inequality. Computing in Economics and Finance 2005 277, Society for Computational Economics, Nov 2005a.

A. M. Lavezzi and N. Meccheri. Job contact networks, inequality and aggregate output. In N. Salvadori and R. Balducci, editors, *Innovation, Unemployment and Policy in the Theories of Growth and Distribution*, pages 145–167. Edward Elgar, 2005b.

J. D. Montgomery. Social networks and labor-market outcomes: Toward an economic analysis. *American Economic Review*, 81(5):1407–1418, December 1991.

12

Innovation and Knowledge Spillovers in a Networked Industry

Jose I. Santos[1], Ricardo del Olmo[1], and Javier Pajares[2]

[1] University of Burgos, Spain
{jisantos,rdelolmo}@ubu.es
[2] University of Valladolid, Spain
pajares@eis.uva.es

12.1 Introduction

Knowledge and proximity are key concepts in the Geography of Innovation literature (Boschma, 2005). Innovating processes are uncertain because they often take place under unsure conditions and fierce business competitiveness. Geographical proximity can reduce this uncertainty since it potentially facilitates labor movement and knowledge interchange through personal contacts. Supporting this hypothesis, some scholars have highlighted the greater agglomeration of RD activities in technological industries where knowledge plays a significant economic role (Audretsch and Feldman, 1996a).

Our concept of *proximity* is not strictly geographical. There are other dimensions beyond spatial nearness, such as social proximity and cognitive proximity that could have diverse effects on innovation (Boschma, 2005). The social dimension can be modeled using a network of relations that shape agents' opportunities to interact, whereas the cognitive dimension can be captured using the absorptive capacity concept (Cohen and Levinthal, 1990): a firm's capacity to understand, learn and apply the knowledge generated outside itself.

The objective of this paper is to study the impact of network structure and knowledge proximity on the process of innovation and diffusion of knowledge through spillovers. We use agent-based modeling and computer simulation to implement and explore a formal model of an innovative industry, which could not be studied using other analytical approaches (Pajares et al., 2004).

12.2 The Model

In order to have a clearer vision of the proposed problem, we use a simplified abstraction of an innovative industry: a set of N innovating firms indexed in i and endowed with a scalar knowledge $K_i \in R$ which is assumed to affect their innovative effort.

Firms are organized in an undirected graph built following the well-known algorithm proposed by Watts and Strogatz (1998). We start with a one-dimensional ring of N vertices where each vertex links to its k closest neighbors; then, we randomly rewire every individual edge in the graph with probability p. This simple algorithm generates a family of networks that exhibit different values for their average path length and their clustering coefficient, depending on the value of the parameter p: from a fixed, highly clustered and ordered network where the average path length is large ($p = 0$), to the set of pure random networks ($p = 1$), which is characterized by low clustering coefficients and relatively short average path lengths.

Each firm can innovate and increase its knowledge. Following an evolutionary economic approach (Nelson and Winter, 1982) the innovating activity is modeled as a stochastic process. We define firm i's probability of innovating at time t, $P_i^{in}(t)$, as an exponential function:

$$P_i^{in}(t) = p_{max}^{in} - \left(p_{max}^{in} - p_{min}^{in}\right) \exp\left(-\alpha \max\left(0, \overline{K}_{Vi} - \overline{K}\right)\right) \quad (12.1)$$

This equation integrates two common concepts of the Innovation literature: the technological opportunities and the innovative effort. Innovating can be more difficult in some industries than in others (Klevorick et al., 1995); the possibilities to create significant technological novelties define the technological opportunities of an industry. The parameters p_{max}^{in} and p_{min}^{in}, which represent the maximum and minimum probability of innovating, determine the technological opportunity regime in the model.

Not every firm invests the same resources and time in innovative activities, and they are not equally efficient. In our model the intensity of the innovative effort varies from one firm to another according to the firm's relative advantage in knowledge over the industry, which is quantified as the difference between the average knowledge in the firm's neighborhood[1] $\overline{K}_{Vi}$ and the average knowledge in the industry $\overline{K}$. The equation (12.1) shows a positive effect of knowledge spillovers because

---

[1] It is the average knowledge of a firm and its immediate neighbors: vertices directly linked to it in the network.

knowledge interchange between a firm and its neighbors reinforces their innovative efforts, and therefore their probabilities of innovating. The effectiveness of this innovative effort depends on the parameter α that governs the growth rate of the probability function.

The assumption about the innovative effort responds to a simple cumulative causation: having comparatively greater knowledge gives firms an economic advantage that enhances their very process of innovation, and it therefore reinforces the probability of creating even greater knowledge. Thus, there is a positive feedback in the process of innovation: the more you innovate the more likely you are to innovate even more.

The increase in knowledge derived from a successful innovation is calculated using (12.2), where β controls the innovation jump.

$$K_i(t+1) = K_i(t)(1+\beta) \tag{12.2}$$

Before the firm i has an opportunity to innovate, it can learn form its immediate neighbors j in the network, according to (12.3).

$$\Delta K_i(t+1) = AC_{ij}(t) \max\left(0, K_j(t) - K_i(t)\right) \tag{12.3}$$

The expression above describes a knowledge spillover from firm j to firm i as an interactive diffusion process modulated by the absorptive capacity AC_{ij} between the firms. The absorptive capacity AC_{ij} denotes the fraction of the (positive) difference in knowledge between the two firms $(K_j - K_i)$ that firm i acquires. The value of AC_{ij} depends on the corresponding knowledge proximity $(K_i - K_j)$, according to another exponential function (12.4).

$$AC_{ij}(t) = \frac{c_0}{1 + \exp\left(\gamma\left(K_j(t) - K_i(t) - d\right)\right)} \tag{12.4}$$

The absorptive capacity AC_{ij} is close to the default value c_0 for short knowledge distances, gets the value $c_0/2$ for a knowledge distance equal to d and falls down to zero for larger distances. The parameter γ controls the sharpness of the fall, and the parameter d determines the distance where this fall happens. The last parameter is a measure of the firm's sensitivity to knowledge distance, the larger it is the more different knowledge a firm can learn. Fig. 12.1 depicts the functions (12.3) and (12.4) for different values of the parameter γ.

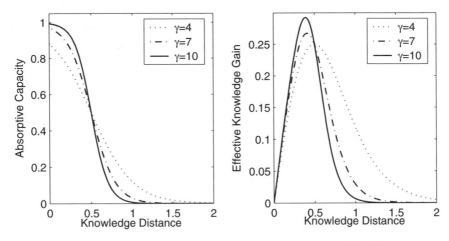

Fig. 12.1. On the left, the absorptive capacity function (12.4) for $c_0 = 1$, $d = 0.5$ and different values of γ; on the right, the corresponding effective knowledge gain function (12.3).

Scheduling can be summarized as follows: each time-step one randomly chosen firm is given the opportunity to learn from its neighborhood and innovate, as described above. The model allows us to simulate complementary scenarios:

- Considering the technological opportunity regime: an industry with a few $(p_{max}^{in} \approx p_{min}^{in} \approx 0)$ or many technological opportunities $(p_{max}^{in} >> p_{min}^{in} \approx 0)$.
- Looking at the knowledge spillovers process: a tacit knowledge regime with low values of the parameter d versus a codified knowledge regime with high values of d.
- Modifying the structure of the network with the parameter p we can compare innovation processes in highly regular networks of diffusion (low values of p) versus innovation processes in random networks of diffusion (values of p close to 1).

12.3 Simulations

Under the hypothesis of homogeneous firms (endowed with similar initial knowledge and capacity to learn through spillovers), we are interested in studying the impact of network structure (using parameter p) on innovation dynamics in an industry, using the rest of the model parameters to define different industry scenarios. In this section we summarize the main simulation results that allow us to advance some conclusions of this work[2].

The industry dynamics are summarized here using the average knowledge (computed as the mean of the firms' knowledge). This industrial rate follows an increasing path without steady states, so we evaluate them close to the horizon of simulations, arbitrary fixed[3].

In the proposed model the innovative advantage of any firm depends mainly on its innovative effort, measured by the difference between the average knowledge in the firm's neighborhood and the average knowledge in the industry. We can intuitively infer that clustered networks ($p << 1$) will get better rates because individual innovations diffuse to close neighbors, reinforcing their knowledge advantage above the rest faster than random networks ($p >> 0$) where diffusion are like scattered showers. But inferences are not so obvious when we analyze the technological opportunities and the knowledge proximity effects on industry dynamics.

12.3.1 Innovation, networks and technological opportunities

We define a first scenario of an industry with few technological opportunities, which corresponds to the following parameterization: $p_{max}^{in} = 0.11$, $p_{min}^{in} = 0.1$ and $AC_{ij} = c_o = 0.1$. Fig. 12.2 shows the evolution of the average and the coefficient of variation of knowledge for a clustered network ($p = 0$) and a random network ($p = 1$). The graph depicts an expected phenomenon: knowledge dispersion drops due to knowledge diffusion, and the average knowledge grows due to firms' innovations. The simulation horizon of 300 time units is enough to evaluate the parameters' effects on the industry performance. We infer an interesting conclusion: when an industry is characterized by a few technological opportunities, modeled as a low probability of innovating similar for all agents, network structure does not play a critical role, although, unlike expected, a random network gets better results than a clustered network because the clustering effect is non significant in these cases.

---

[2] The model has been implemented in Repast (North et al., 2006) and replicated in Netlogo. The simulation model is composed of $N = 500$ firms endowed with a scalar knowledge, which is initialized from a Uniform distribution $U(0, 1)$. We set the value of $k = 6$, $\beta = 0.01$, $c_0 = 0.1$ and $\gamma = 10$.

[3] A simulation run is composed of 300 periods, and 50 replications are recorded for each one. The standard error is less than 1% for all average statistics shown in the graphs of this paper.

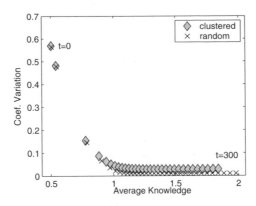

Fig. 12.2. The evolution of the average and the coefficient of variation of knowledge for a clustered network ($p = 0$) and a random network ($p = 1$) when there are a few technological opportunities in the industry ($p^{in}_{max} = 0.11$, $p^{in}_{min} = 0.1$). The industry evolution is very similar for all network structures, although a random networked industry always gets better results than a clustered industry.

The next scenario represents an industry characterized by more technological opportunities: $p^{in}_{max} = 0.3$, $p^{in}_{min} = 0.05$ and $AC_{ij} = c_o = 0.1$. Now the parameter α in (12.1), which modulates the firm's innovative effort, has an important meaning: the firm's ability to apply its innovative effort successfully. Note that we have translated the absorptive capacity concept (Cohen and Levinthal, 1990) into the corresponding absorptive capacity coefficient (12.4) and this skill, represented by α, which can be interpreted as the necessary firm's know-how to turn the knowledge advantage into more possibilities to innovate (12.1).

Fig. 12.3 shows the effect of network structure on the industry average knowledge for different values of the parameter α.

For low values of α we get similar results than the scenario with a few technological opportunities: most firms get the same probability of innovating (close to p^{in}_{min}) whatever their innovative effort, and randomness in network relationships improves the industry performance. For higher values of α clustered networks ($p << 1$) always get better industrial rates than random networks ($p >> 0$). This result is in agreement with empirical studies of industrial clusters (Audretsch and Feldman, 1996b). According to our model, this phenomenon would be related with the existence of technological opportunities in an industry and firms with the ability to exploit them.

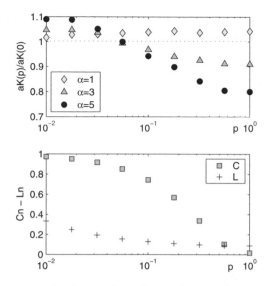

Fig. 12.3. In the graph above, the effect of network structure (p) on the average knowledge for different values of the parameter α when there are significant technological opportunities $(p^{in}_{max} = 0.3, p^{in}_{min} = 0.05)$. In order to highlight the network structure effect, magnitudes are normalized dividing by the corresponding value at $p = 0$. For high values of α clustered networks $(p << 1)$ always get better industrial rates than random networks $(p >> 0)$. Moreover, small world networks $(0 << p < 0.1)$, characterized by high clustering and low average path, get better results than a pure clustered network $(p = 0)$ for values of α high enough. In the graph bellow, the corresponding normalized network features: clustering C and average path length L.

Another interesting inference is that small world networks $(0 << p < 0.1)$, characterized by high clustering and low average path, get better results than a pure clustered network $(p = 0)$. When firms randomly rewired a few local links, they keep the cluster advantage and also benefit from learning from distant sources.

12.3.2 Innovation, networks and knowledge distance

We can imagine a scenario where the knowledge proximity sensitivity (d) is imposed to the industry, and firms can decide the randomness of their relations (p), thus determining the network structure[4]. This approach would be in line with the product life cycle theory, which

---

[4] An interesting evolutionary agent-based model that studies in detail the life cycle approach to innovative industry dynamics is proposed in Pajares et al. (2003).

argues that knowledge is tacit in the first stages of the life cycle and more codified in the mature phases (Klepper, 1996).

Fig. 12.4 shows the effect of network structure, considering the knowledge proximity parameter d as an exogenous variable. Here, either there is no doubt that clustered networks ($p << 1$) get better industrial rates than random networks ($p >> 0$) for every value of d. We see from (12.4) that low values of d, e.g. $d = 1$, limit the diffusion though knowledge spillovers and thus accentuating the positive effect of clustering in the innovation process. The results are very sensitive to the parameter d, for a bit higher value, e.g. $d = 2$, the industry evolution is similar to a scenario where the knowledge proximity between firms does not affect their absorptive capacity ($d = \infty$).

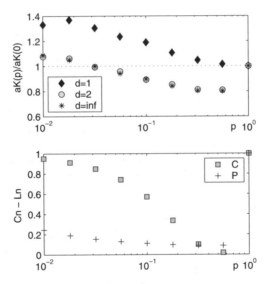

Fig. 12.4. In the graph above, the effect of network structure (p) on the average knowledge for different values of the parameter d when there are significant technological opportunities ($p_{max}^{in} = 0.3$, $p_{min}^{in} = 0.05$). Magnitudes are normalized dividing by the corresponding value at $p = 0$. The positive effect of clustering in the innovation process is accentuated when the knowledge proximity between firms affects significantly their absorptive capacity ($d = 1$). In the graph bellow, the corresponding normalized network features: clustering C and average path length L.

12.4 Conclusions

We have proposed a formal model of an innovative networked industry with knowledge spillovers. Innovation is modeled as a stochastic process where firms' probability of innovating depends on its innovative effort and technological opportunities in the industry. The intensity of the innovative effort varies from one firm to another according to the firm's relative advantage in knowledge over the industry, which is quantified as the difference between the average knowledge in the firm's neighborhood and the average knowledge in the industry.

Knowledge spillovers are modeled as a simple knowledge diffusion process restricted by the firms' absorptive capacity, which depends on the knowledge proximity between firms. Knowledge spillovers have two opposite effects on industry dynamics: a positive one since knowledge interchange between a firm and its neighbors reinforces their innovative efforts, and a negative one since the diffusion process limits knowledge appropriability cutting any initial innovative advantage.

We study the impact of network structure and knowledge proximity on industry dynamics. With these hypotheses if an industry is characterized by a few technological opportunities, the clustering effect is non significant and randomness in network relationships improves industry dynamics. However, when there are significant technological opportunities, clustered networks get better results than random networks. This result is in agreement with empirical studies of industrial clusters; according to our model, this phenomenon would be related with the existence of both technological opportunities in an industry and firms with the ability to exploit them. In most cases small world networks that exhibit high clustering and low average path get better results than a pure clustered network. Finally, when the knowledge proximity between firms affects their absorptive capacity and thus limiting the diffusion through knowledge spillovers, the positive effect of clustering on the innovation process is reinforced.

Acknowledgement. This work has been supported by the Spanish MICYT, research project DPI2004-06590 and SIGAME project DPI2005-05676.

References

D. B. Audretsch and M. P. Feldman. R&d spillovers and the geography of innovation and production. *American Economic Review*, 86(3): 630–640, June 1996a.

D. B. Audretsch and M. P. Feldman. Innovative clusters and the industry life cycle. *Review of Industrial Organization*, 11(2):253–273, 1996b.

R. A. Boschma. Proximity and innovation: A critical assessment. *Regional Studies*, 39(1):61–74, January 2005.

W. M. Cohen and D. A. Levinthal. Absorptive capacity: A new perspective on learning and innovation. *Administrative Science Quarterly, Special Issue: Technology, Organizations and Innovation*, 35(1):128–152, March 1990.

S. Klepper. Entry, exit, growth, and innovation over the product life cycle. *American Economic Review*, 86(3):562–583, June 1996.

A. K. Klevorick, R. C. Levin, R. R. Nelson, and S. G. Winter. On the sources and significance of interindustry differences in technological opportunities. *Research Policy*, 24(2):185–205, March 1995.

R. R. Nelson and S. G. Winter. *An Evolutionary Theory of Economical Change*. Harvard University Press, 1982.

M. J. North, N. T. Collier, and J. R. Vos. Experiences creating three implementations of the repast agent modeling toolkit. *Transactions on Modeling and Computer Simulation*, 16(1):1–25, January 2006.

J. Pajares, , A. Lopez-Paredes, and C. Hernandez-Iglesias. Industry as an organisation of agents: Innovation and r&d management. *Journal of Artificial Societies and Social Simulation*, 10, 2003. Available at http://jasss.soc.surrey.ac.uk/6/2/7.html.

J. Pajares, C. Hernandez-Iglesias, and A. Lopez-Paredes. Modelling learning and r&d in innovative environments: a cognitive multi-agent approach. *Journal of Artificial Societies and Social Simulation*, 7(2), 2004. Available at http://jasss.soc.surrey.ac.uk/7/2/7.html.

D. J. Watts and S. H. Strogatz. Collective dynamics of 'small-world' networks. *Nature*, 393(6684):440–442, June 1998.

13

Heterogeneous Agents with Local Social Influence Networks: Path Dependence and Plurality of Equilibria in the ACE Noiseless Case

Denis Phan

GEMAS UMR, 8598 CNRS & University Paris IV
Sorbonne CREM UMR, 6211 CNRS & University of Rennes 1, France.
dphan@msh-paris.fr

13.1 Introduction

In this paper we explore numerically by means of ACE the impact of local social influence on binary choices. The basic model of binary choices with externality presented here (the "GNP model") is based on Gordon et al. (2005); Nadal et al. (2005); Phan and Pajot (2006) (see Phan and Semeshenko (2007) for an introduction and a review of literature). GNP model has been generalized to a large class of distributions in Gordon et al. (2006). It allows to study the collective behavior of a population of interacting heterogeneous agents. Numerous papers in this field concern homogeneous agents with stochastic choices, in particular, among others: Brock and Durlauf (2001)—hereafter BD model. Our GNP class of models differs by the nature of the disorder. The former belongs to the classes of Random Utility Models (RUM): the utility is stochastic. The individual preferences have an identical deterministic part and the heterogeneity across agents comes from the random term of the RUM. In our *noiseless* GNP *model*, agents are heterogeneous with respect to their idiosyncratic preferences (IWA) which remain fixed and do not contain stochastic term. This model belongs to the class of the *Quenched Random Field Ising Models*, know in statistical physics.

The question of the local topologies of interactions has been recently examined by Ioannides (2006). In the following, we present equilibria results for models with a local regular network (cyclical, one and two dimensional with nearest neighbor). This work is an extension of the GNP

model presented previously to the case with local interactions. Therefore, the reader is assumed to be familiar with these references. Several
important aspects of the analysis and simulation of the model which are
discussed in this paper are not presented here but are mentioned briefly
for the sake of completeness. Section 13.2 introduces the GNP model
and shows how this framework is related to the population games,
by summarizing previous contributions (Phan and Semeshenko, 2007).
Section 13.3 presents and compares both probabilistic calculi for *infinite
size* population and ACE based simulations for *finite size* populations
in the case of a simple *regular local influence network* (lattice). Calculi in Section 13.3.1 and 13.3.2 are based upon a probabilistic method
recently introduced by Shukla (2000) to calculate exactly the hysteresis path both starting from a homogeneous state (nobody adopts) and
from any arbitrary initial state. The simulations were conducted using
the multi-agent platform "Moduleco-Madkit" (Gutknecht and Ferber,
2000; Phan, 2004). A special attention is devoted to Sethna's inner
hysteresis (Sethna et al., 1993). For a given value of the external parameter (i.e. price), there is a multiplicity of equilibria, depending on
the previous state of the system (*path-dependence*). Moreover, if this
parameter returns back to the initial value, the system returns precisely
to the same state from which it left. The inner loop illustrates the *return point memory effect*, in which the system remembers its former
state.

13.2 GNP framework with local setting

13.2.1 Modelling the individual choice in a social context

We consider a set of N agents $i \in \Lambda_N \equiv \{1, 2, \dots, N\}$ with a classical
linear willingness-to-adopt function. Each agent makes a simple binary
choice, either to adopt ($\omega_i = 1$) or not ($\omega_i = 0$) (e.g., to buy or not one
unit of a single good on a market, to adopt or not the social behavior,
etc.). A rational agent chooses ω_i in order to to maximize its surplus:

$$\max_{\omega_i \in \{0,1\}} \left[\omega_i V_i(\tilde{\omega}_{-i}) \right], \tag{13.1a}$$

$$\text{where: } V_i(\tilde{\omega}_{-i}) = (H_i - C) + \frac{J_{ik}}{N_{\vartheta_i}} \sum_{k \in \vartheta_i} \tilde{\omega}_k, \tag{13.1b}$$

C is the cost of adoption, assumed to be the same for all agents, and
H_i represents the idiosyncratic preference component.

The cost of adoption be subjective or objective - it may e.g. represent the price of one unit of a good. Each agent i is influenced by the (expected) choices $\tilde{\omega}_k$ of its neighbors $k \in \vartheta_i$ within a neighborhood $\vartheta_i \in \Lambda_N$ of size N_{ϑ_i}. Denoting J_{ik}/N_{ϑ_i} the corresponding weight, i.e. the marginal social influence on agent i from the decision of agent $k \in \vartheta_i$, the social influence is then a weighted sum of $\tilde{\omega}_k$ choices. When the weights are assumed to be positive, $J_{ik} > 0$, it is possible, according to Brock and Durlauf (2001), to identify this external effect as *strategic complementarities* in the agents' choices.

In the GNP model agents are heterogeneous with respect to their idiosyncratic preferences, which remain fixed and do not contain additively stochastic term. The *Idiosyncratic Willingness to Adopt* (IWA) of each agent is distributed according to the Probability Density Function (pdf) $f_y(y)$ of the auxiliary centered random variable Y, such as H is the average IWA of the population:

$$H_i = H + Y_i, \tag{13.2a}$$

$$\text{where:} \quad \lim_{N \to \infty} \frac{1}{N} \sum_N Y_i = 0 \Rightarrow \lim_{N \to \infty} \frac{1}{N} \sum_N H_i = H. \tag{13.2b}$$

If Y_i remains fixed, the resulting distribution of agents over the network of relations is a *quenched random field*: the agents' choices are purely deterministic. As mentioned before, this contrasts with the random utility approach in the BD model. These two approaches may lead to different behaviors (Galam, 1997; Sethna et al., 1993, 2005). One advantage of the GNP model is that it does not constrain the distribution of the idiosyncratic willingness to adopt to be a priori logistic. Moreover, the qualitative feature of the results may be generalized to a large class of distributions (Gordon et al., 2006). We can assume hereafter without loss of generality that the idiosyncratic preferences are distributed according to a bounded, triangular pdf. This allows the analytical exact determination of the equilibrium properties in the case of complete connectivity (Phan and Semeshenko, 2007). In the following, we restrict to the case of regular nearest neighborhood, cyclical network of dimension one (circle, with $N_{\vartheta_i} = 2$) and two dimension (torus, with $N_{\vartheta_i} = 4$, von Neuman's neighborhood)). Moreover, for the sake of simplicity, we restrict to the case of *positive homogeneous influences*: $\forall i \in \Lambda_N, \forall k \in \vartheta_i : J_{ik} = J > 0$. For a given neighbor k the social influence is J/N_{ϑ_i} if the neighbor is an adopter ($\omega_k = 1$), and zero otherwise. Let η_i^e be i's expected adoption rate within the neighborhood

$$\eta_i^e \equiv \eta_i^e(\tilde{\omega}_{-i}) \equiv \frac{1}{N_{\vartheta_i}} \sum_{k \in \vartheta_i} \tilde{\omega}_k. \qquad (13.3)$$

With these assumptions the surplus of agent i if he adopted is: $H_i - C + J\eta_i^e$. The conditional probability of adoption, for a given η_i^e is:

$$P\left(\omega_i = 1 | \eta_i^e\right) = P\left(H_i > C - J\eta_i^e\right) \qquad (13.4)$$

13.2.2 Interactions in the neighborhood as a population game

The interest of studying such idiosyncratic (exogenous) heterogeneity becomes clear if one reinterprets the GNP model within a game theoretic framework. Each agent i has only *two possible strategies*: to adopt ($\omega_i = 1$) or not adopt ($\omega_i = 0$). In the following, we assume agents have myopic expectations about the behavior of their neighbors: $\tilde{\omega}_{-i}(t) = \omega_{-i}(t-1) \equiv w_{-i}$: then $\eta_i^e(t) = \eta_i(t)$. The best response of an agent playing against its neighbors is formally equivalent to that of an agent playing against a *Neighborhood Representative Player* (NR) (Phan and Pajot, 2006; Phan and Semeshenko, 2007). NR player in turn plays a *mixed strategy* $\omega_{nr} = \eta_i \in [0,1]$. In the present case of *finite neighborhood local interaction*, ω_{nr} takes its value in a discrete subset of $[0,1]$. For example for $N_{\vartheta_i} = 2$, we have $\omega_{nr} = \eta_i \in \{0, 1/2, 1\}$ and for $N_{\vartheta_i} = 4$, we have $\omega_{nr} = \eta_i \in \{0, 1/4, 1/2, 3/4, 1\}$. The "*normal form*" payoff matrix $G1$ gives the total payoff for an agent i playing against this *fictitious* NR player. According to Monderer and Shapley (1996), the best-reply sets and dominance-orderings of the game $G1$ are unaffected if a constant term is added to a column (i.e. $C - H_i$). The coordination game matrix $G2$ in Table 13.1 (right) is said to be "best reply equivalent" to the matrix $G1$ of Table 13.1 (left). However, the values in $G2$ do not indicate the cumulated payoffs, contrary to the values in $G1$, but are a direct measure of the cost—the risk in the sense of Harsanyi and Selten (1998)—of a unilateral deviation from the coordinated solution ($\omega_i = \omega_{nr}$) in the case of the pure strategy framework.

Figure 13.1 (right) presents a (symmetric triangular) distribution and related best reply for a given cost C and a particular value of the IWA. If $C - J > H_i$, then *never adopt* ($\omega_i = 0$) is the strictly dominant strategy for all possible values of η_i (agents of type *(0)* in the light grey zone on the left). If $H_i > C$, *always adopt* ($\omega_i = 1$) is the strictly dominant strategy for all possible values of η_i^e (agents of type *(1)* in the dark grey zone on the right). If $C > H_i > C - J$ then the agent's virtual

a-game $G1$	$\omega_{nr} = 0$	$\omega_{nr} = 1$
$\omega_i = 0$	0	0
$\omega_i = 1$	$H_i - C$	$H_i - C + J$

b-game $G2$	$\omega_{nr} = 0$	$\omega_{nr} = 1$
$\omega_i = 0$	$C - H_i$	0
$\omega_i = 1$	0	$H_i - C + J$

Table 13.1. Payoff matrix for an agent i (left) and best reply equivalent potential game (right). Player i in rows, fictitious NR Player—indexed nr—in columns.

surplus $V_i \equiv H_i - C + J\eta_i$ may be either positive or negative depending on the rate of adoption within the neighborhood η_i. These agents are *conditional adopters* and said to be of type *(2)*. Within these agents, only those with $V_i > 0$ will adopt thanks to the social influence (hashed region). The relevant economic cases are the ones with (at least some) agents of type *(2)*.

Figure 13.1 (left) exhibits a distribution of agents' type in the space $(J, H - C)$ for the symmetric triangular distribution on the interval $[-a, a]$. In the south-west light grey zone there are only agents of type *(0)*, while in the north-dark-zone there are only agents of type *(1)*. In the white zone there is a mixture of at least 2 types of agents, with necessarily some agents of type *(2)*. If $H - C > a - J$, there is no agents of type *(0)*. Conversely in the south zone, where $H - C < -a$, there is no agent of type *(1)*. If both conditions hold then *all agents* are of type *(2)*, corresponding to the hashed triangular zone in the east on Figure 13.2. This implies a sufficiently strength intensity of social effect, with respect to the dispersion of the preferences, that needs to be relatively moderate: $J > 2a$.

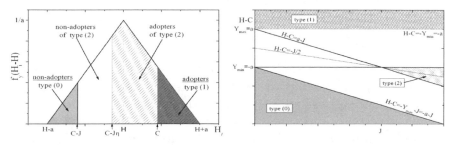

Fig. 13.1. Distribution of agents with respect to their type, on the pdf (right) and in the space $(J, H - C)$ (left) for the symmetric triangular distribution on the interval $[-a, a]$. *Source: Phan and Semeshenko (2007)*.

In the case of global social influence (full connectivity) and bounded distribution of IWA, dominance-ordering analysis allows us to predict the issues of some classic configurations (i.e. symmetric Nash equilibrium), where all agents have the same structure of best reply. But this may be done for only some special cases. In general situations, one needs to use the methods from statistical mechanics. In the case of local neighborhood considered here, any simple result of that kind is available and probabilistic approach or numerical simulations are required. Within an approach of ACE as *complement* of traditional mathematical models, in the next section we compare results using the probabilistic approach for *infinite size* population with results from agent based simulation for *finite size* population.

13.3 Collective Behavior, hysteresis and local frozen domains with local externality: probabilistic approach for *infinite size* population and simulation approach for *finite size* population

As suggested before, the GNP model, as a socio-economic version of Quenched RFIM model, has some significantly different properties with respect to the BD model. First, when changing the external field (i.e. cost variation) an equilibrium depends on the previous equilibrium, but does not depend on the order in which the agents change their behaviour (i.e. adoption or not) through the process called avalanche. In other words, from the simulation point of view, both parallel and sequential updating lead the system to the same equilibrium. Second, the interesting property of Sethna's inner hysteresis phenomenon (Sethna et al., 1993) can be observed. This result from the *return point memory effect*: starting from an equilibrium state, if we change the cost by a given value and reverse the field by the same value, the system remembers its former state and returns exactly to the equilibrium point of departure. The corresponding trajectory is called "inner loop" "minor hysteresis" (Sethna et al., 2005). Finally, in the special case where we change the cost monotonically for a homogeneous state (everybody adopts or no-body adopts) the final equilibrium does not depend on the rate of variation in cost. A dramatic change from $C1$ to $C2$ or a succession of smaller monotonic changes from $C1$ to $C2$ leads to the same state. In this section, we experiment the effect of local social influence in discrete choice adoption process based on the GNP model by means of finite size population, agent-based simulation on the multi-agent platform "Moduleco-Madkit" (Gutknecht and Ferber, 2000; Phan, 2004).

Sections 13.3.1 and 13.3.2 compare analytical results with simulated outcome in the case of the cyclical one-dimensional nearest neighborhood network (circle). Section 3.2. is devoted to the calculus of the inner loop. Section 3.3. presents simulation outcome in the case of the cyclical two-dimensional regular network (von Neuman neighborhood on a torus).

13.3.1 Starting from a homogeneous state without adoption adoption and going to the complete adoption and return: the larger hysteresis loop

Hysteresis within the Quenched RFIM is somewhat different in nature from the hysteresis used by economists that arise from a delayed response of a system (time lags) to a change in the external parameter (here cost). First accounts of such difference are (Amable et al., 1994) for the study of the wage-price spiral and zero-rot dynamics. Previous application of hysteresis in Quenched RFIM in socio-economic models are Galam (1997); Phan et al. (2004). In the case of a finite population, there are a very large number of equilibria and related thresholds between them. In this section, we use methodology and results from physics (Shukla, 2000) established for the ferromagnetic case ($J > 0$) for one dimensional, nearest neighborhood, cyclical and infinite size network. In that case the conditional probability of adoption (equation 13.4) can be expressed in a finite number of occurrences; see Figure 13.2) and relations (13.5)

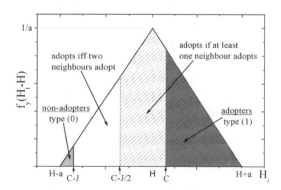

Fig. 13.2. Agents' choices with respect to their IWA and neighborhood state (symmetric triangular distribution).

Probability of adoption for a given state of neighborhood $\eta_i \in \{0, 1/2, 1\}$ with $P_i \equiv P_i(C)$

$$P_0 = P(H_i > C) = P(\text{type } 1, \omega_i = 1 \text{ if } \eta = 0) \qquad (13.5\text{a})$$
$$P_1 = P(H_i > C - J/2) = P(\omega_i = 1 \text{ if } \eta = 1/2) \qquad (13.5\text{b})$$
$$P_2 = P(H_i > C - J) = P(\omega_i = 1 \text{ if } \eta = 1) \qquad (13.5\text{c})$$
$$P_1 - P_0(C) = P(C > H_i > C - J/2)$$
$$= P(\text{to be of type 2 AND } \omega_i = 1 \text{ if } \eta = 1/2). \qquad (13.5\text{d})$$

For a given cost C, the probability of adoption of an agent is:

$$P(\omega_i = 1|C) = P(\eta_i = 1) \, P_2 + P(\eta_i = 1/2) \, P_1 + P(\eta_i = 0) \, P_0 \quad (13.6)$$

where:

$$\eta(C) = P(\omega_i = 1|C) \qquad (13.7\text{a})$$
$$P(\eta_i = 1) = P(\omega_{i\pm1} = 1|C, \omega_i = 0)^2 \qquad (13.7\text{b})$$
$$P(\eta_i = 1/2) = 2 \, P(\omega_{i\pm1} = 1)|C, \omega_i = 0) \, P(\omega_{i\pm1} = 0)|C, \omega_i = 0)$$
$$\qquad (13.7\text{c})$$
$$P(\eta_i = 0) = P(\omega_{i\pm1} = 0|C, \omega_i = 0)^2. \qquad (13.7\text{d})$$

Note that, $P(\omega_{i\pm1} = 1|\omega_i = 0) \equiv P^*(C)$ can be calculated exactly in the infinite case. The probability that my neighbor adopts before me is equal to P_0 (the probability of type *(1)*, then adopts even if no neighbor has adopted before). One must add again the probability for my neighbor to be of type *(2)* but to adopt as soon as the next neighbor has adopted, since this next agent $(\omega_{i\pm2})$ is of type *(1)*. The corresponding joint probability is equal to $[P_1 - P_0]P_0$. At the level 3, one must add again the probability for my neighbor and the next agent to be of type (2) but to adopt as soon as the next neighbor has adopted, given the probability that this next agent $(\omega_{i\pm3}$ is of type *(1)*. This joint probability is equal to $[P_1 - P_0]^2 P_0$, and so on. Summing over all cases:

$$P^*(C) \equiv P(\omega_{i\pm1} = 1|C, \omega_i = 0)$$
$$= \lim_{m\to\infty} P_0 \sum_{k=0}^{m} [P_1 - P_0]^k = \frac{P_0}{1 - [P_1 - P_0]} \qquad (13.8\text{a})$$
$$[1 - P^*(C)] \equiv P(\omega_{i\pm1} = 0|C, \omega_i = 0) = \frac{1 - P_1}{1 - [P_1 - P_0]} \qquad (13.8\text{b})$$

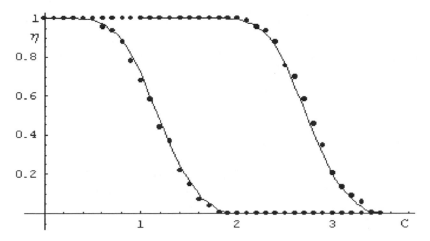

Fig. 13.3. Theoretic (line) and simulated (dot) values for the main hysteresis with: $N = 1156$ agents, $N_\vartheta = 2$ (circle), $J = 4$, $H = 0$.

Using equations (13.6), (13.8a), and (13.8b) the global equilibrium rate of adoption in the population for a given cost C is equal to the probability of adoption of an agent taken at random within a symmetric triangular distribution of IWA:

$$\eta_+(C) = P(\omega_i = 1|C) \tag{13.9}$$

The upper half branch of the main hysteresis, for decreasing C from complete adoption to zero can be obtained by symmetry: $\eta_-(C) \sim -\eta_+(-C)$. Figure 13.3 provides a comparison between these theoretic values of the main hysteresis and the simulated ones, based on experiments with finite population (here 1156 agents).

13.3.2 The inner hysteresis loop: reversing the Cost from an arbitrary point on the exterior loop

In the limit of quasi-static driving (the change in prices remains constant within an avalanche), starting from a point on the upstream trajectory (grey) for $\eta = 40\%$ and $C = 1.25$ a backtracking increase in cost C induces a less than proportional decrease (avalanche) in the number of customers (black curve, upper inner loop) until $C = 2.49$ and $\eta = 30\%$. Then after reversing the cost changes at $C = 2.49$, as the cost decreases back to the initial value (grey curve, lower inner loop) the system returns precisely to the same state from which it left the outer loop ($C = 1.25$, $\eta = 40\%$). The inner loop can also go from a branch of the main hysteresis loop to the other. For example, starting at $C = 1$ and $\eta = 68\%$, a backtracking increase in cost C induces a cross-trajectory between the upstream and the downstream branch of the main hysteresis loop. This cross-trajectory finishes at $C = 2.93$ and $\eta = 30\%$, when the equilibrium points are those of the main hysteresis. As established analytically, that confirms that there is a multiplicity of equilibria, depending on the previous state of the system (*path dependence*). Figure 13.4 (right panel) exhibits separated homogeneous domains (or cluster) in the network, due to the dominance of positive or negative effects of social influence as well as a particular distribution of heterogeneous IWA, enforced by both locality and finite size effect.

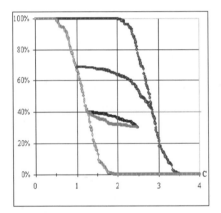 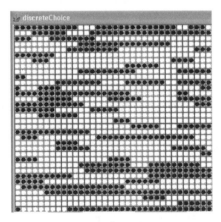

Fig. 13.4. Right panel, Sethna's inner hysteresis $J = 4$, $N = 2$ (circle). Left panel, homogeneous domains (1D-clusters) within the network for $\eta = 40\%$ and $C = 1.27$.

As previously mentioned, it is possible to provide some hints to calculate the probability of adoption starting from an arbitrary point on the exterior loop. The method used here follows the lines of Shukla (2000). For the reversing formula and complete calculations in the case of the symmetric triangular pdf, see the long version of this work (to be presented at CEF 2007). This calculus is more difficult than in the previous case, because the choice of adoption depends now in a non trivial way on the rate of adoption in the neighborhood, which depends itself directly or indirectly on the state of the other agents over the network. The probability of adoption between the two branches of the external hysteresis is conditional to the cost C for which the backtrack starts. These analytical results fit correctly the numerical simulations in the case of finite population experiments (see the long version for CEF 2007)). For a given cost C', with backtracking at C, the probability of adoption of an agent is:

$$P(\omega_i = 1|C,C') = P(\omega_i = 1,C) - Q_2(C',C)+ \\ - Q_1(C',C) - Q_0(C',C), \tag{13.10}$$

where:

$$\eta(C',C) = P(\omega_i = 1|C,C') \tag{13.11a}$$

$$Q_2(C',C) = P^*(C)^2 \left(P_2(C) - P_2(C')\right) \tag{13.11b}$$

$$Q_1(C',C) = 2\,P^*(C) \left[Q_a(C',C) + Q_b(C',C)\right] \left(P_1(C) - P_1(C')\right)$$

$$Q_0(C',C) = \left[Q_a(C',C) + Q_b(C',C)\right]^2 \left(P_0(C) - P_0(C')\right) \tag{13.11c}$$

$$Q_a(C',C) = \frac{P^*(C)\left(1 - P_2(C)\right) + \left[1 - P^*(C)\right]\left(1 - P_1(C)\right)}{1 - \left(P_1(C) - P_1(C')\right)} \tag{13.11d}$$

$$Q_b(C',C) = \frac{P^*(C)\left(P_2(C) - P_2(C')\right)}{1 - \left(P_1(C) - P_1(C')\right)} \tag{13.11e}$$

13.3.3 The two-dimensional von Neuman neighborhood network (Torus)

There is no analytical result at this time for the two-dimensional, cyclical network with von Neuman neighborhood (Torus). But the example on Figure 13.5 suggests that both Sethna's inner loop and homogeneous domains remain quite similar.

13.4 Conclusion

Using methods from statistical physics, we illustrated the stationary properties for particular cases of symmetric triangular distribution of IWA in the presence of local interactions. Simulation results allow us to observe numerous complex configurations on the adoption side, such as hysteresis and Sethnas inner-loop hysteresis. This complex social phenomenon depends significantly on the structure and parameters of the relevant network. Finally, the last section opens the question of finite size effects, also addressed by Glaeser and Scheinkman (2002); Krauth (2006) among others. The preliminary results in the case of a simple, regular network suggest new fields of investigation, as opposed to a standard focus on conditions of uniqueness of equilibrium, under a

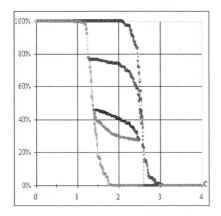 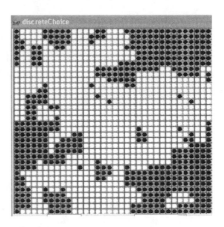

Fig. 13.5. Right panel, Sethna's inner hysteresis $J = 4$, $N = 2$ (torus). Left panel, homogeneous domains (2D-clusters) within the network for $\eta = 40\%$ and $C = 1.41$.

moderate social influence assumption (Glaeser and Scheinkman, 2002). It would be interesting to compare more systematically the analytical predictions against the simulation results and to study the statistical properties of such a phenomenon for different values of J and different network's structure.

Acknowledgement. The author acknowledges M. B. Gordon, J.P. Nadal, and V. Semeshenko for their significant intellectual contribution to the development of methods used in this paper (see bibliography), to C. Deissenberg for valuable remarks on a previous version of this work and to Alexandra Frénod for significant corrections on the original draft, D.P. is CNRS member.

References

B. Amable, J. Henry, F. Lordon, and R. Topol. Strong hysteresis versus zero-root dynamics. *Economics Letters*, 44(1–2):43–47, 1994.

W. A. Brock and S. N. Durlauf. Discrete choice with social interactions. *Review of Economic Studies*, 68(2):235–260, April 2001.

S. Galam. Rational group decision making: A random field ising model at t = 0. *Physica A: Statistical and Theoretical Physics*, 238(1–4): 66–80, April 1997.

E. L. Glaeser and J. A. Scheinkman. Non-market interactions. In Turnovsky. Eds. Dewatripont, Hansen., editor, *Advances in Economics and Econometrics: Theory and Applications*. Cambridge University Press, 2002.

M. B. Gordon, J. P. Nadal, D. Phan, and J. Vannimenus. Seller's dilemma due to social interactions between customers. *Physica A: Statistical Mechanics and its Applications*, 356:628–640, October 2005.

M. B. Gordon, J. P. Nadal, D. Phan, and V. Semeshenko. Discrete choices under social influence: Generic properties. In *Proceeding of WEHIA 2006*, 2006.

O. Gutknecht and J. Ferber. Madkit: a generic multi-agent platform. In *AGENTS '00: Proceedings of the Fourth International Conference on Autonomous Agents*, pages 78–79, New York, NY, USA, 2000. ACM Press.

J.C. Harsanyi and R. Selten. *A General Theory of Equilibrium Selection in Games*. MIT Press, 1998.

Y. M. Ioannides. Topologies of social interactions. *Economic Theory*, 28(3):559–584, 2006.

B. Krauth. Social interactions in small groups. *Canadian Journal of Economics*, 39(2):414–433, May 2006.

D. Monderer and L.S. Shapley. Potential games. *Games and Economic Behavior*, 14(1):124–143, May 1996.

J. P. Nadal, D. Phan, M. B. Gordon, and J. Vannimenus. Multiple equilibria in a monopoly market with heterogeneous agents and externalities. *Quantitative Finance*, 5(6):557–568, December 2005.

D. Phan. *From Agent-Based Computational Economics Toward Cognitive Economics*, chapter 22, pages 371–398. Springer, Berlin, 2004.

D. Phan and S. Pajot. Complex behaviours in binary choice models with global or local social influence. In C. Bruun, editor, *Advances in Artificial Economics*, pages 203–220. Springer, 2006.

D. Phan and V. Semeshenko. Equilibria in models of binary choice with heterogeneous agents and social influence. *European Journal of Economic and Social Systems*, 2007. revised version accepted.

D. Phan, M.B. Gordon, and J.P. Nadal. *Social Interactions in Economic Theory: an Insight from Statistical Mechanics*, chapter 20, pages 335–358. Springer, Berlin, 2004.

J. P. Sethna, K Dahmen, S. Kartha, J. A. Krumhansl, B. W Roberts, and J. D. Shore. Hysteresis and hierarchies: Dynamics of disorder-driven first-order phase transformations. *Physical Review Letters*, 70: 3347–3350, 1993.

J. P. Sethna, K. A. Dahmen, and O. Perkovic. *Random-Field Ising Models of Hysteresis*, volume 2, chapter 2. Elsevier, Amsterdam, 2005.

P. Shukla. Exact solution of return hysteresis loops in one dimensional random field ising model at zero temperature. *Physical Review E*, 62 (4):4725–4729, 2000.

14

Economy-Driven Shaping of Social Networks and Emerging Class Behaviors

Philippe Caillou, Frederic Dubut, and Michele Sebag

LRI, Université Paris Sud, France
{caillou,dubut,sebag}@lri.fr

14.1 Introduction

Agent-based Computational Economics (ACE) is a powerful framework for studying emergent complex systems resulting from the interactions of agents either mildly rational, or with incomplete information (Axelrod, 2004; Tesfatsion, 2002, 2006) or driven by the social network (Bala and Goyal, 2003; Carayol and Roux, 2004; Slikker and van den Nouweland, 2000).

This paper focuses on the interrelationship between social networks and economic activities. Compared to the state of the art, the main originality is that the social network dynamically evolves based on the rational decisions of agents: a loan granting activity is enabled by the network and the agents continuously re-shape the network to optimize their utility. Three classes of agents (rational agents, free riders and "investors") are considered. The global welfare is investigated in relation with the agent diversity, examining the differential advantages/disadvantages of the agent classes depending on their distribution in the agent population. Lastly, the stability of e.g. the average interest rate is contrasted with the instability of the network structure.

After describing the state of the art and the problem tackled in this paper (section 14.2), we present a loan granting game played by a society of rational agents with a long-term utility function, conditioned by and shaping their social network (section 14.3). Section 14.4 reports on the simulation results; the main contributions of the approach are discussed together with perspectives for further studies in section 14.5.

14.2 State of the Art and Goal of the Study

Introduced by Epstein and Axtell (1996), Agent-based Computational Economics established two major results (the interested reader is referred to Tesfatsion (2002, 2006) for a comprehensive presentation). Firstly, the lack of a centralized walrasian auctioneer does not prevent a society of 0th-intelligence agents from converging towards an economical equilibrium when agents interact and exchange in a decentralized manner; secondly, this result does not hold any longer if the agents can die or evolve.

Meanwhile, after the pioneering Milgram (1967)'s experiment and many further studies (e.g. Watts and Strogatz, 1998), the structure of social networks is acknowledged a major factor of economics efficiency. A framework for analyzing social network economics was defined by Jackson and Wolinsky (1996), and exploited through either analytical approaches, or various simulation-based extensions (Bala and Goyal, 2003; Carayol and Roux, 2004; Slikker and van den Nouweland, 2000).

While both domains of ACE and social networks are clearly related, to our best knowledge little attention has been devoted to the interdependent evolution of social and economical activities, considering the social network as both a result and an enabling support of the economical activity. In such a unified perspective, the stress is put on the complex system emerging through the interaction of social and economical activities. Along this line, this paper investigates the complex system made of a population of agents engaged in a loan granting activity, where the activity is simultaneously conditioned by, and shaping, the social network. Basically, every agent is endowed with an individual utility function parameterized after its fixed preference toward immediate rewards; it accordingly decides between borrowing or lending money from/to its neighbors at every time step. While the network thus governs the instant rational optimization problem faced by the agents, agents can decide to create/delete links and thereby modify the network. This setting contrasts with former studies (Bala and Goyal, 2003; Carayol and Roux, 2004; Jackson and Wolinsky, 1996; Slikker and van den Nouweland, 2000) modeling the social network as the end of the socio-economic game, that is, where the network only supports the exchange of information and agents are assessed based on their position in the network.

Furthermore, agents will not reveal their preference − as opposed to e.g. Epstein and Axtell (1996) where the exchange price is based on the preferences of both agents. The fact that agents do not reveal their preference is relevant to the study of socio-economic games in two respects; firstly it is more realistic from a non-cooperative game per-spective; secondly, the incompleteness of information might adversely affect the convergence of the game.

Finally, the study examines the impact of the agent models and strategies on the global welfare in a long term perspective. This con-trasts with e.g. Jackson and Wolinsky (1996) focussing on the immedi-ate network efficiency, and discarding the long term impact of current decisions.

14.3 Overview

This section presents the agent model, the interaction setting and the observed variables of the system. Due to space limitations, the reader is referred to Caillou et al. (2007) for details.

14.3.1 Agent model

The agent utility function models the intertemporal choice of the con-sumer after the standard economic theory (Fisher, 1930). Formally, agent A_i maximizes the sum over all time steps of its weighted instant utilities. The utility weight at time t, set to p_i^t ($0 < p_i < 1$), reflects the agent preference toward the present (parameter p_i). The instant utility reflects the current consumption level $C_{i,t}$, with a diminishing marginal utility modeled through parameter b_i ($0 < b_i < 1$), standing for the fact that the agent satisfaction is sublinear with its consumption level (Menger, 1871). Letting M_i denote the lifelength of agent A_i, it comes:

$$U_i = \sum_{t=0}^{M_i} (p_i^t C_{i,t}^{b_i})$$ (14.1)

The instant neighborhood of agent A_i, noted $V_{i,t}$ involves all agents A_j such that link (i, j) belongs to the social network at time t. Additional agent parameters comprise:

- **Salary R_i:** A_i receives a fixed salary R_i at the beginning of each time step, and uses it to grant or pay back loans, to buy links, or for consumption.
- **Sociability factor s_i** ($0 < s_i < 1$): A_i creates a new link (i, j) (where j is uniformly chosen) with a probability s_i at each time step; in case A_i is isolated, a new link is automatically created.

- **Strategy** S_i: The social network comes at a cost, i.e. every link (i, j) must be paid by agents A_i or A_j or both. Three social strategies (classes of agents) are defined:
  Optimizers accept to pay for a link iff it was profitable during the last five time steps (if the utility increase due to this link offsets the link cost). This strategy, referred to as rational strategy, deletes all links which are not sufficiently useful.
  Free Riders never pay for a link. While the free rider minimizes its social cost (the link cost), it does not optimize its neighborhood which might adversely affect its utility (see below).
  Investors always accept to pay for a link. On the one hand this strategy gives the agent every means to optimize its economic activities, and possibly maintain beneficial relations with isolated agents; on the other hand, it suffers the cost of possibly many useless links.

Under mild assumptions (Caillou et al., 2007), agent A_i can compute its threshold interest rate r_i (lower bound for grant activities and upper bound for loan activities). Note that this rate needs be updated after every elementary transaction as it depends on the agent current and expected capital.

14.3.2 Interaction protocol

Every agent lives a sequence of epochs, where each epoch involves four phases: i) salary and loans payback, ii) negotiation, iii) consumption, iv) social activity (link creation/deletion).

During the first phase, agent A_i receives its salary R_i, reimburses the money borrowed (plus interests) and is reimbursed for the money lent (plus interests). The negotiation phase involves a variable number of transactions. At each step, A_i determines the best possible borrowing and lending rate; it maintains its estimation $r_{i,j}$ of the interest rate for a transaction (borrow or grant) with every agent A_j in its neighborhood, and proposes the best possible transaction for one currency unit. Depending on whether the transaction is accepted, $r_{i,j}$ is updated (Alg. 1). Agent A_j accepts a borrow transaction if the proposed rate is lower than i) its limit rate r_j and ii) its last borrow rates during this negotiation phase (similar conditions hold for lend transactions).

The transactions proceed until no more transactions are realized.

```
BestRate r*=0;
foreach A_j ∈ V_i such that r_ij > r_i do
    Propose Loan(rate=r_ij);
    if accepted then
        if r_ij > r* then r* = r_ij;
        Increase(r_ij)
    else
        Decrease(r_ij)
    end
end
if r* > 0 then Lend one currency unit at rate r*
```

Algorithm 1: Lending transactions (borrowing transactions proceed likewise)

During the consumption phase, the agent computes its optimal fraction of consumption (see Caillou et al., 2007, and scores the corresponding utility)) .

During the social phase, each agent decides whether it maintains its links depending on its strategy and whether the link has been profitable in the last five epochs. Link (i, j) is either maintained by agents A_i and/or A_j, or deleted. Independently, A_i creates a new link (i, j) with probability s_i (its sociability factor), where j is uniformly randomly selected. If A_i has no neighbor, a link (i, j) is automatically created.

After M_i epochs, agent A_i dies. It is then replaced by a new agent (reinitializing all agent parameters) *with same neighborhood.*

14.3.3 Fitness and Global Welfare

The socio-economical system will be assessed from the global welfare of the agents. As the agent utilities cannot be directly compared (parameters p_i and b_i depend on the agent), they are normalized w.r.t. the canonical consumer-only alternative strategy. Each A_i, would it have adopted the consumer-only strategy, would get utility The consumer-only agent, spending its whole salary in each time step, gets utility:

$$U_i^* = \sum_{t=0}^{M_i}(p_i^t R_i^{b_i}) = R_i^{b_i}\frac{1 - p_i^{M_i+1}}{1 - p_i}$$

Accordingly, the normalized fitness of A_i is defined as:

$$F_i = \left(\frac{U_i}{U_i^*}\right)^{\frac{1}{b_i}} - 1$$

Note that if A_i had spent a fixed fraction α, $0 \leq \alpha \leq 1$ of its salary in each time step (without engaging in any borrowing or lending transactions), it would score a normalized fitness $\alpha - 1$. In brief, agent A_i benefits from the social network iff its fitness F_i is positive.

The efficiency of the socio-economical system is thus measured from the average normalized fitness of the individuals, and its standard deviation. Further, each class (optimizers, free-riders and investors) will also be assessed from the average normalized fitness of the individuals belonging to this class.

14.4 Results

After the description of the experimental setting, this section reports on the impact of the network and agent dynamics on the global efficiency of the system.

14.4.1 Experimental settings

The socio-economical game is implemented and simulated within the Moduleco framework (Phan, 2004). The initial structure of the social network is a ring, where each agent is connected to its two neighbors. Agents are initialized by independently drawing their parameters using Gaussian or uniform laws as follows.

- Time preference $p_i \sim \mathcal{N}(0.8, 0.075)$
- Utility factor $b_i \sim \mathcal{N}(0.5, 0.1)$,
- Sociability factor $s_i \sim \mathcal{N}(0.05, 0.05)$,
- Salary $R_i \sim \mathcal{N}(20, 5)$,
- Life expectancy $M_i \sim U(20, 100)$,

The link cost is set to .2 in the remainder of the paper. Complementary experiments with varying values of the link cost are reported in Caillou et al. (2007). Experiments were conducted with a population size ranging from 25 to 100, with similar results. All reported results are averaged over 25 independent experiments conducted with 25 agents over 1000 epochs. The global (respectively, class) fitness is computed by averaging the normalized fitness of agents (resp. belonging to the class) that died before the 1000th. epoch.

14.4.2 Complete and costless information

The classical economic theory relies on the assumption of a complete and costless information, e.g. gathered and disseminated by the "walrasian auctioneer", enforcing the convergence of the interest rate toward the equilibrium rate. As formally shown in Caillou et al. (2007), the equilibrium rate can be analytically derived from the agent utility functions.

The first experiment, as a sanity check, thus considers the fully connected social network and compares the empirical interest rate toward the equilibrium rate. As expected, the average interest rate rapidly converges toward the equilibrium value τ ($\tau = .24$ in the experimental setting, Fig. 14.1). The standard deviation ($< .0025$ after 5 epochs in the fully connected case) is explained from the experimental noise, discrete loan amount and limited number of agents.

Interestingly, randomly removing edges in the social network only delays the convergence toward the equilibrium rate, although the standard deviation of the interest rate significantly increases for social networks with low density. Fig. 14.1 displays the standard deviation vs the percentage of edges in the social network after 20 epochs.

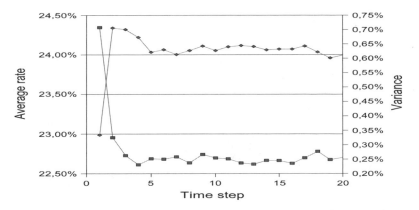

Fig. 14.1. Interest rate and standard deviation within a complete network

14.4.3 Rational and immortal agents

The second experiment focuses on rational agents (optimizer strategy) with infinite lifelength. Despite the fact that the social network can evolve with the rational agent decisions, the empirical interest rate still

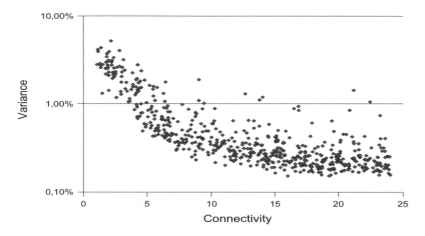

Fig. 14.2. Impact of the network connectivity on the standard deviation of interest rate after 20 epochs

converges toward the equilibrium rate. Still, the convergence is slower than in the previous case, and the standard deviation remains high after 1000 epochs (Fig. 14.3).

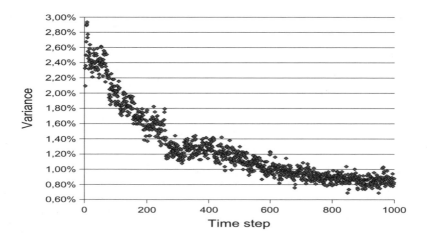

Fig. 14.3. Rational and Immortal Agents: Standard Deviation of the Interest Rate

Most surprisingly, while the interest rate reaches the equilibrium, it does so with a continuously changing social network; no edge in the network appears to last more than a few epochs, as agents endlessly optimize their neighborhood. Indeed, in either competitive or monopolistic situations, there always exists some profitable link creation or deletion. The canonical case of a 3-agent network, depicted in Fig. 14.4, involves three possible configurations (being reminded that a link is created automatically when an agent is isolated), all of which are unstable. In the n-agent case, instability is increased by cascading effects, the creation/deletion of a link leading to further link deletions or creations.

Fig. 14.4. 3-agent network configurations; arrows indicate the lender-borrower pair

1 In the triangle (clique) case, there are two possible situations:
  – If A can lend the desired amount to C with a rate higher than the B limit rate r_b, A is not interested in maintaining link AB, which will thus be deleted.
  – If the C limit rate r_c decreases (because of the loans contracted by C) and becomes lower than r_b, A will grant loans to B and C (with a rate lower than r_b). Therefore B will be unable to lend money to C, since C will refuse to borrow money with rate higher than r_b. Thus the BC link becomes useless and will be deleted.
2 In the line case, B borrows from A at rate $\tau_{AB} < r_B$. C borrows from B at rate $\tau_{BC} > r_B$. When A or C will create the link AC, it will be stable because A will accept to grant loans to C at a rate $\tau_{BC} - \epsilon$ which will be higher (and thus more profitable) than τ_{AB}. We are back to case 1.
3 In the star case (case 3a), agent A is the only one lending money. In this monopolistic situation, A will progressively increase the loan granting rate, until the BC link becomes profitable and thus stable when it will be created. We are back to case 1. Same analysis holds for case 3b (C will decrease its borrow rate).

14.4.4 Mixed populations and global welfare

Let us consider the mixed population cases. Each possible distribution of the strategies (or classes) in the population is represented as a point in the 2D plane, where the x (resp. y) coordinate stands for the proportion of Free Riders (resp. Investors) in the population (Fig. 14.5). Point (x, y) is associated with the global population welfare or fitness. Considering the three pure strategies (optimizers only, (0,0); investors only (0,1); free-riders only (1,0)), the Optimizer strategy is by far the best one; this fact is explained as the free-rider-only population generates a sparse random network, while the investor-only population generates a clique (and pays the price for it).

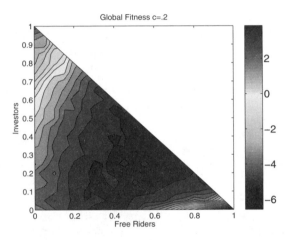

Fig. 14.5. Average Fitness vs Strategy Distribution in the Population. Point (x, y) correspond to the distribution of $x\%$ free-riders, $y\%$ investors and $1 - x - y \%$ optimizers. Each fitness level differs by .5 from the neighbor fitness levels.

Most interestingly, in the case of mortal agents, mixed populations outperform optimizer-only populations; e.g. the uniform distribution (1/3 optimizers, 1/3 free-riders and 1/3 investors) gets an average fitness significantly higher than the optimizer-only population (complementary experiments show that this result also holds when the link cost is significantly higher or lower, see Caillou et al. (2007)). This fact is explained as the useless links paid for by investors, are actually very useful to quickly reorganize the network when an agent dies.

14.4.5 Class behaviors

While agent diversity is beneficial on average, it remains to examine whether "class behaviors" appear in the population. Two issues will be specifically investigated. Firstly, do the average class fitness depend on its representativity, ie, its percentage of the population (intra-class effects); secondly, do the class representativity affect the average fitness of the other classes (inter-class effects).

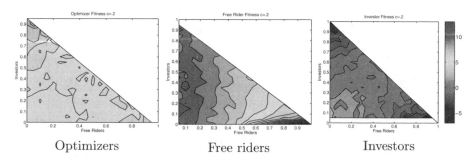

Optimizers   Free riders   Investors

Fig. 14.6. Strategy average fitness; each level represents an increase/decrease of 1 for the strategy average fitness

The free-rider class does present a class behavior (Fig. 14.6): their fitness is excellent when they are a minority, and it decreases rapidly as the free-rider representativity increases. The investor class also displays a class behavior: their fitness is good when the representativity of optimizers is sufficiently high, as the optimizers share the costs of the links. In summary, the average fitness of investors and free-riders depends on the class distribution; quite the opposite, the optimizer fitness does not.

We finally examine the impact on the global and class welfare, of the arrival of a new agent depending on its class (Fig. 14.7).

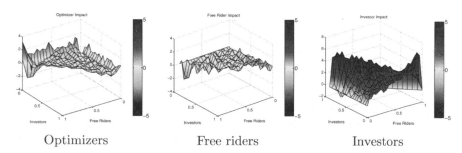

Optimizers   Free riders   Investors

Fig. 14.7. Adding a new agent: impacts on the fitness of the other classes

The arrival of an investor is globally beneficial to other classes. and even more so when there a few optimizers. Indeed, investors fund the infrastructure used by the other agents; their impact is greater when the network is poor (when there are few optimizers).

The arrival of a free rider has a negative impact on the rest of the economy, except when there are many investors. In this case, the free rider decreases the graph connectivity level (and cost) and allows a faster reorganization of the network.

Optimizers, which are not influenced by economic class structure, do not influence it either. Their impact is mostly neutral, though it might be positive in the extreme cases where there are no investors or no free riders.

14.5 Conclusion and perspectives

The socio-economic game presented in this paper, based on autonomous and diversified agents, leads to two lessons. The first one concerns the fact that the convergence of economic macro-variables such as the interest rate is compatible with the instability of the social network supporting the economic activities. Secondly, the benefits of the population diversity have been empirically demonstrated and interpreted in terms of the emerging class behaviors. While investors and free-riders display class behaviors (their fitness depends on the population structure, they have an impact on the welfare of the other classes), the optimizer class seems to be almost unaffected by the population structure, and exerts little influence in return.

Further research perspectives are concerned with the dynamics of the class structure, examining how the best fit agents can influence the distribution, preferences and strategies of the new-born agents.

Acknowledgement. We warmly thank D. Phan for making available his Moduleco Framework. This work was supported in part by the IST Programme of the European Community, under the PASCAL Network of Excellence, IST-2002-506778.

References

R. Axelrod. Advancing the art of simulation in the social sciences. *Advances in Complex Systems*, 7(1):77–92, 2004.
Venkatesh Bala and Sanjeev Goyal. A noncooperative model of network formation. *Japanese Journal for Management Information Systems*, 12(3), 2003.

P. Caillou, F. Dubut, and M. Sebag. Loans in social networks: when sub-optimality increases global welfare. Technical report, LRI, 2007.

N. Carayol and P. Roux. Behavioral foundations and equilibrium notions for social network formation processes. *Advances in Complex Systems*, 7(1):77–92, 2004.

J. Epstein and R. Axtell. *Growing Artificial Societies. Social Science From the Bottom Up*. The MIT Press, 1996.

I. Fisher. *The Theory of Interest*. Macmillan, 1930.

M. O. Jackson and A. Wolinsky. A strategic model of social and economic networks. *Journal of Economic Theory*, 71(1):44–74, October 1996.

C. Menger. *Principles of Economics*. Dingwall and BF Hoselitz, 1871.

S. Milgram. The small-world problem. *Psychology today*, 2:60–67, 1967.

D. Phan. From agent-based computational economics towards cognitive economics. In P. Bourgine and J.P. Nadal, editors, *Cognitive Economics*, Handbook of Computational Economics, pages 371–398. Springer Verlag, 2004.

M. Slikker and A. van den Nouweland. Network formation models with costs for establishing links. *Review of Economic Design*, 5(3): 333–362, 2000.

L. Tesfatsion. Agent-based computational economics: Growing economies from the bottom up. *Artificial Life*, 8(1):55–82, 2002.

L.S. Tesfatsion. A constructive approach to economic theory. In L. Kenneth, J. Tesfatsion, and L. Tesfatsion, editors, *Handbook of Computational Economics*, volume 2 of *Handbooks in Economic Series*. North-Holland, 2006.

D.J. Watts and S.H. Strogatz. Collective dynamics of 'small-world' networks. *Nature*, 393:440–442, 1998.

15

Group Effect, Productivity and Segregation Optimality

Raúl Conejeros[1] and Miguel Vargas[2]

[1] Department of Biochemical Engineering
   Catholic University of Valparaíso, Chile
   rconejer@ucv.cl
[2] Diego Portales University School of Business, Chile
   miguel.vargas@udp.cl

15.1 Introduction

In literature on residential segregation (**RS** hereafter) there are two important results about the social optimality of this phenomenon. Firstly, the maximum level of **RS** can constitute a social optimum if one part of the population generates negative externalities on the remaining one. The population suffering the negative externalities can be called a prejudiced population. Under these circumstances traditional bid-rent models with externalities and general equilibrium models have showed the optimality of **RS**[3]. On the other hand, when the individuals' preferences are to live in balanced neighborhoods, high levels of **RS** diminish the aggregated utility, consequently, full integration is the social optimum. The well known Schelling's model has stressed this issue, showing how a population, in an artificial world, can evolve to a segregated society although individuals want to live in a perfectly balanced neighborhood, reaching a bad, but the only stable, equilibrium. If the prejudiced population coexist with a population preferring balanced neighborhood, the literature has proposed the payment of compensating transfers by the prejudiced population to the non-prejudiced ones to accept the exclusion (Anas, 2002).

These results rely upon the fact of these models considering just the individuals' utility depending on the neighborhood's characteristics and segregated individuals suffering **RS**'s negatives consequences

---

[3] See for instance Anas (2002); Ando (1981); Bailey (1959); Kanemoto (1980); Papageorgiou (1978); Rose-Ackerman (1975); Schnare (1976); Yinger (1976).

just on their own[4]. Notwithstanding, here it is argued that the negative consequences of **RS** would affect the utility of the non-segregated population too. This is a quite reasonable statement if the kind of **RS** consequences are studied. As a matter of fact, literature has pointed out that **RS** can have impact upon the the level of joblessness, out-of-wedlock births, level of criminality, low educational achievement, income inequality and poverty traps, amongst others. **RS** can produce these effects mainly by two mechanisms, namely, lowering the consumption of public good, for instance poor neighborhoods have, in general, bad quality schools[5]; and peer-effects. As an example of the latter, there is fair evidence telling us that the school performance does not depend just on the individual capabilities, but also upon the desire of the rest of the classmates for having a good school performance[6].

If one part of society is being affected by these sort of difficulties, it is almost sure that all the population is going to be affected too. For example, if **RS** generates spots of criminality, this criminality will reach, also, the non-segregated population. As another example can be considered the fact that if **RS** has a negative impact on educational achievement, ghettos of low-skilled laborers can emerge, a process that can be reinforced by itself. Consequently, the society will loss productivity, and therefore, all individuals' level of consumption will be lower, diminishing the welfare of every single individual, being segregated or not. If that is the case, the prejudiced population is going to face a trade-off between the desire of living just amongst peers and the lower level of consumption that **RS** produces.

Benabou (1993) is the first attempt to formalize the link among location decision, education investment and productivity. According to this article, segregation diminishes some communities' chances to reach good labor skills and therefore the labor force quality will be lower, affecting poor and rich households welfare. Education is assumed to be a local public good affected by community composition. Consequently, segregation arises because rich households want to live in communities with a high level of investment in education, bidding out poor families. Segregation efficiency depends on the form of the function cost of poor households education.

---

[4] See for instance Charles et al. (2004); Clapp and Ross (2004); Dawkins et al. (2005); LaVeist (2003); Massey (2001); Wilson and Hammer (2001); Yinger (2001).

[5] For instance, Berglas (1976) introduces skills to the Tiebout's model.

[6] Arnot and Rowse (1987) compute the school optimal composition for different forms of peer group effects. De Bartolome (1990) studies the inefficiency in the communities composition due to peer groups effects on education.

Nevertheless, with the important insights that Benabou (1993) has provided, there are some aspect of urban structure that standard classical models cannot treat properly. Meen and Meen (2003) have provided a detailed discussion on these characteristic, explaining why a model considering them, must be used to model urban systems. Specifically, the characteristic stressed by Meen and Meen (2003) are self-organization, heterogeneity between agents, multiple equilibria, unstable equilibria, with the system being out-of-equilibrium for long periods of time (therefore dynamics are more interesting than long-run equilibria). Cellular automata, or agent-based models, have been largely used in literature to deal with system of this sort. These models are attractive for this purpose because they consider explicitly agents heterogeneity and their interactions, which can be more complex than in traditional game theory models. Because of these interactions complexity and self-organization can emerge from agent-based models, where individual action generates ordered pattern of behavior. Besides, multiple equilibria and out-of-equilibrium situations can be studied as an equilibrium formation process: a dynamic process with random events. Hence, for instance, it is possible to study the probability of a particular equilibriums emergence.

Because of the elements explained in the above paragraph, a cellular automaton has been developed here to investigate upon optimality properties of segregation, formalizing the link between location decision and productivity, focusing on peer-groups effects. This is the first time that a model featuring these characteristics is implemented to study the segregation phenomenon.

In section 15.2 the theoretical model is developed, explaining its main characteristics. In section 15.3 through the use of simulations the equilibria and social optima properties are studied and the effects of some public policies. In section 15.4 conclusions and final remarks are given.

15.2 The model

The model developed here is an extension of Schelling (1971) and its first mathematical formalization due to Zhang (2004). Therefore the first step, it is to define an artificial society made up of an advantaged prejudiced population and a non-prejudiced disadvantaged population. Each agent belongs just to a one particular population group. The proportion of these two populations are given by π_j with $j \in \{0, 1\}$, indexing the population's types. If $j = 1$ the agent is a disadvantaged one and with $j = 0$ a non-disadvantaged one. Each one of this society members, or agents, is allocated in the vertex of a NxN lattice graph with a periodic boundary condition or, what it is the same under this feature, embedded on a torus.

Utility. Each agent j's utility U is made up of two parts: a deterministic one u_i and a stochastic term ϵ. This stochastic term reflects the assumption of bounded rationality, because agents can make mistakes, but also guarantee agents' heterogeneity. The deterministic part depends on how many like-type neighbors he has in the local neighborhood and in his level of consumption. The stochastic part is assumed being independent across agents and locations. As Zhang (2004) points out, the latter it is because agents value different characteristics, and different locations have different idiosyncratic traits. The utility function u is assumed additively separable in two components: a location term ℓ and a consumption term c. The location term differs depending on the agent's type.

$$
\ell_j = \begin{cases} A_j \left(\dfrac{x}{n_j} \right) & \text{if } x \leq n_j \\ (2A_j - B_j) + (B_j - A_j)\dfrac{x}{n_j} & \text{otherwise} \end{cases}
\tag{15.1}
$$

where $A > B > 0$ are parameters guaranteeing a linear kinked shape, increasing on the left side of n_j and decreasing on the right, being n_j the peak as it is showed in Figure 15.1. Therefore, n_j is the number of like-type neighbors in the local neighborhood that maximize ℓ_j. The total number of the local neighborhoods inhabitants can be represented by $Z_j n_j$, where $Z_j \in \mathbb{N}$. x is the actual number of like-type neighbors in the local neighborhood.

The consumption term for both agent's type is just the normalized level of consumption. Therefore, the deterministic term of the utility function is given by:

$$
u_j = \beta \ell_j + \alpha c
\tag{15.2}
$$

being β and α positives parameters indicating the importance of location and consumption for agents. The utility function for any agent i of type j is:

$$
U_{ij} = u_j + \epsilon
\tag{15.3}
$$

Finally, the aggregated utility is:

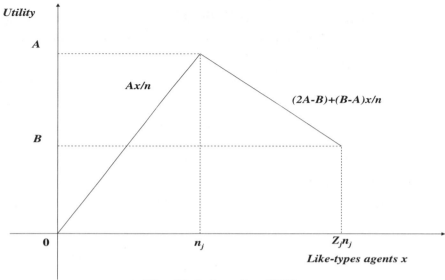

Fig. 15.1. Location Utility

$$\mathbf{U} = \sum_{1}^{NxN} U_i \qquad (15.4)$$

Production. Each agent is endowed in every period of time with one unit of "productivity". In every period of time the agent can have just one unit of "productivity". An important assumption it is made here is that the agent's productivity can be affected by the local neighborhood's characteristics (group effects). In particular, it is assumed that if in a local neighborhood the majority of inhabitants (more that the 50%) belong to the disadvantaged population, then the productivity of that type of agent decreases. Hence, the productivity for a non-disadvantaged agent is always 1, and for a disadvantaged one is:

$$p_1 = \begin{cases} \dfrac{x - Z_1 n_1}{\tau - Z_1 n_1} & \text{if } x > \tau \\ 1 & \text{otherwise} \end{cases} \qquad (15.5)$$

where τ is the threshold value of like-types neighbors that triggers the productivity diminishing process as is depicted in Figure 15.2. The aggregated production is:

$$\mathbf{P} = \sum_{1}^{NxN} p_i \qquad (15.6)$$

the level of consumption of every agent is $\dfrac{P}{N}$. This means that all the agents, prejudiced and non-prejudiced, are going to be affected negatively by segregation.

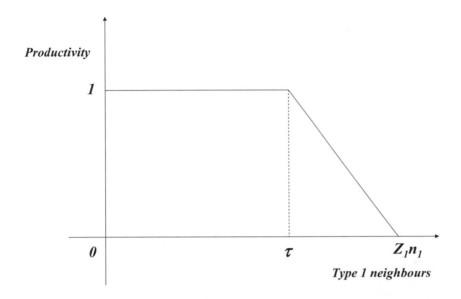

Fig. 15.2. Disadvantaged Agents Productivity Function

Log-linear behavioral rule. A Log-linear behavior is observed when agents change their location based upon their own personal interests. In each period two agents coming from different neighborhoods are selected and in order to perform a change, every agent will bid in an sort of auction for a better location, consequently the focus is on the sum of two chosen agents' utility. If the sum of switching is bigger than the sum of not switching, then agents will swap their locations. If the switch situation is called S and the opposite NS, and, for following exposition, the chosen agents are agent 1 and agent 2, and they do not swap locations, then:

$$U_1(\cdot|NS)+\epsilon_1+U_2(\cdot|NS)+\epsilon_2 = U_1(\cdot|NS)+U_2(\cdot|NS)+\epsilon_1+\epsilon_2 = V^{NS}+\eta$$

but if they do, then:

$$U_1(\cdot|S) + \epsilon_1 + U_2(\cdot|S) + \epsilon_2 = U_1(\cdot|S) + U_2(\cdot|S) + \epsilon_1 + \epsilon_2 = V^S + \varepsilon$$

Agents will change location if and only if $V^{NS}+\eta < V^S+\varepsilon$. It is assumed that η and ε are independent, and that they follow an identical extreme value distribution. Then, based on McFadden (1973), and following Zhang (2004), a log-linear switch rule can be settled as follow:

$$Pr(S) = Pr(V^{NS} + \eta < V^S + \varepsilon) = Pr(\eta < V^S - V^{NS} + \varepsilon) =$$

$$= \int_{-\infty}^{+\infty} F(V^S - V^{NS} + \varepsilon)f(\varepsilon)d\varepsilon = \int_{-\infty}^{+\infty} e^{-e^{-V^S+V^{NS}-\varepsilon}}$$

$$e^{-\varepsilon-e^{-\varepsilon}}d\varepsilon = \int_{-\infty}^{+\infty} \exp\left[-\varepsilon - e^{-\varepsilon}\left(\frac{e^{V^{NS}} + e^{V^S}}{e^{V^{NS}}}\right)\right]d\varepsilon =$$

$$= \int_{-\infty}^{+\infty} \exp\left[-\varepsilon - e^{-\varepsilon}e^{\Phi}\right]d\varepsilon =$$

$$= e^{(-\Phi)}\int_{-\infty}^{+\infty} \exp\left[-(-\varepsilon - \Phi) - e^{-\varepsilon-\Phi}\right]d(\varepsilon - \Phi) =$$

$$= \exp(-\Phi)\int_{-\infty}^{+\infty} f(\varepsilon - \Phi)d(\varepsilon - \Phi) =$$

$$= \exp(-\Phi)\cdot 1 = \left(\frac{e^{V^{NS}} + e^{V^S}}{e^{V^{NS}}}\right).$$

Being $\Phi = ln\left(\frac{e^{V^{NS}}+e^{V^S}}{e^{V^{NS}}}\right)$, hence,

$$Pr(S) = \left(\frac{e^{V^{NS}} + e^{V^S}}{e^{V^{NS}}}\right)$$

This behavioral rule depends just upon the deterministic utilities, therefore, it is possible to work avoiding the stochastic utilities, which are unobservable.

A segregation measure. In order to measure the level of segregation the index of dissimilarity is used. This index, due to Duncan and Duncan (1955), can be interpreted as the percentage of a group's population that would have to change residence for each local neighborhood to have the same percentage of that group as the metropolitan area overall. The index ranges from 0.0 (complete integration) to 1.0 (complete segregation), and is given by the following formula:

$$D = \sum_{i=1}^{m} \left[\frac{g_i |k_i - K|}{2GK(1 - K)} \right] \qquad (15.7)$$

where m is the total number of local neighborhoods, g_i is the i local neighborhood's total population, G is the total population, k_i is the group of interest percentage in the local neighborhood i, and K is the group of interest total percentage in the city.

15.3 Simulations and well-being analysis

For simulations purposes an artificial society made up by 100 agents is considered. Hence, $N=10$. Both type of agents are equally distributed across the population, therefore $\pi_0=\pi_1=0.5$. The local neighborhoods used are Moore neighborhoods, that, for every agent, include the eight adjacent agents as neighbors. The reasons underlying the latter is because, as Zhang (2004) shows, using this kind of neighborhood the model converges faster, besides, the final outcome is independent of the neighborhood type. It is assumed too, that non-disadvantaged agents are prejudiced against the disadvantaged ones, therefore the former prefer just like-type neighbors, meanwhile disadvantaged ones prefer balanced neighbourhoods[7]. Consequently, $n_1 = 4$ and $4 < n_0 \leq 8$. As one of the main aims of the present research is the search for the conditions that define a social optimum linked to a positive level of segregation, but not absolute segregation, α and β values must be relatively balanced between each other, otherwise either integration or complete segregation will be the social optimum. Intuition tells us in a straightforward fashion, that agents must have balanced preferences between location and consumption. For instance, considering the case where agents have higher preferences on neighborhoods characteristics than on consumption, i.e. $\alpha \to 0$, with a prejudiced population, the social optimum will imply complete social exclusion. On the other hand, if neighborhoods characteristics are not important, i.e $\beta \to 0$, then complete integration will be the social optimum. In order to facilitate calculations and normalize utility functions is picked $A_0 = 1$, $B_0 = \dfrac{n_0}{n_0 + x}$, $A_1 = 1$ and $B_1 = 0.6$.

The variable of interest is the optimal level of segregation OS and the stable equilibrium level of segregation ES. In the first one is the

---

[7] The other two kind of neighborhoods used in the agent-based literature are Von Neumann and $r(2)$, where the former considers the four surrounding agents as neighbors and the latter covers 12 agents inside a circle with radius 2.

level of segregation associated to the maximum level of aggregated utility, and in the second one is the level of segregation that the system reaches by itself. The basic structure of the algorithm used to obtain the ES has been already explained in the previous section 15.2. The way to obtain the OS deserves some further explanation. As the natural evolution of the problem does not settle at the optimal social utility, a stochastic search method has been used, namely the Threshold Acceptance (TA) algorithm, in order to find the best utility neighboring distribution. This algorithm is related to the general class of Simulated Annealing (SA) type algorithms, enabling the stochastic search for effective solutions to highly combinatorial optimization problems but with a much easier implementation. The algorithm is shown in Figure 15.3.

```
1. Get an initial system configuration S and an initial threshold
   Δnew = Δold
2. While outer loop stop criterion not satisfied do:
   a) While inner loop stop criterion not satisfied do:
      • Select a trial solution S'
      • If  C(S') ≤ C(S) + Δnew,   let  S = S'
   End of inner loop
   b) If S has changed reduce threshold:
      • Δold = Δnew ,
      • Δnew = α · Δold .
   End of outer loop
3. Report best solution found
```
Fig. 15.3. The threshold acceptance algorithm

As this is an stochastic algorithm, every time that a maximum it has been searched for in the inner loop, it has been run 100 times, and the maximum value amongst these 100 "maxima" has been picked up.

Agents' relevant elements, in order to choose a location, are the value of the location utility ℓ and the value of consumption utility c. The parameters values that have been chosen are: $\dfrac{\alpha}{\beta} = \dfrac{3}{4}$, $n_0 \in \{5, 6, 7, 8\}$ and $\tau \in \{4, 5, 6, 7, 8\}$. The results of these simulations are shown in Table 15.1.

The most striking fact arising from simulations is that the system always converges to the lowest level of segregation after a random perturbation (see Figure 15.4). This means that full integration comes to

Table 15.1. Optimal and equilibrium segregation

$n_0=8$	$\tau=4$	$\tau=5$	$\tau=6$	$\tau=7$	$\tau=8$	$n_0=7$	$\tau=4$	$\tau=5$	$\tau=6$	$\tau=7$	$\tau=8$
OS	0.00	0.12	0.36	0.48	0.96	OS	0.00	0.08	0.32	0.36	0.84
ES	0.04	0.04	0.04	0.04	0.04	ES	0.04	0.04	0.04	0.04	0.04
ES-OS	0.04	-0.08	-0.32	-0.44	-0.92	ES-OS	0.04	-0.04	-0.28	-0.32	-0.80
$n_0=6$	$\tau=4$	$\tau=5$	$\tau=6$	$\tau=7$	$\tau=8$	$n_0=5$	$\tau=4$	$\tau=5$	$\tau=6$	$\tau=7$	$\tau=8$
OS	0.00	0.08	0.12	0.36	0.84	OS	0.00	0.04	0.04	0.20	0.80
ES	0.04	0.04	0.04	0.04	0.04	ES	0.04	0.04	0.04	0.04	0.04
ES-OS	0.04	-0.04	-0.08	-0.28	-0.80	ES-OS	0.04	0.00	0.00	-0.16	-0.76

be a stable equilibrium. This finding is quite different from previous literature results, where the main fact that has been pointed out is exactly the opposite: the system always converging to the highest levels of segregation. The element that makes the difference is the agents taking into account of the segregation's negative effect on their own level of consumption.

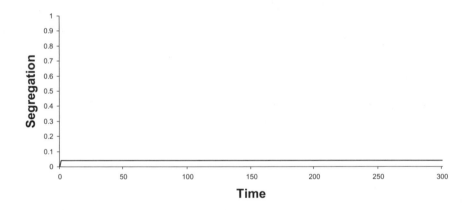

Fig. 15.4. Evolution of segregation

As the equilibrium segregation is the lowest possible, the difference between optimal and equilibrium segregation is almost all the time negative. This difference gets lower when the level of advantaged agents' prejudice diminishes, because optimal segregation also diminishes (see Figure 15.5).

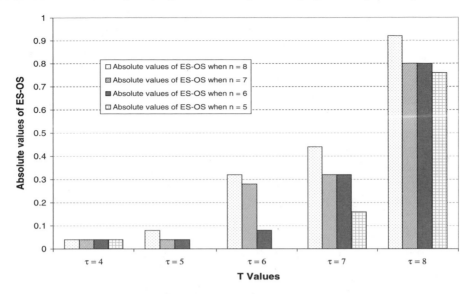

Fig. 15.5. Equilibrium v/s optimal segregation

An interesting thing is that if the relative consumption importance gets lower, the system could converge to higher levels of segregation greater than 0, by means of adjusting the consumption relative importance parameter α. An interesting question is if, following this process, the system can reach a stable equilibrium where equilibrium and optimal segregation are equal. After some trials, it was possible to find a combination of parameters' values where this situation is fulfilled. The specific parameters' values used to find this particular equilibrium were the following: $\frac{\alpha}{\beta} = \frac{1}{5}$, $\tau = 4$ and $n_0 = 8$. Under this setting the system converges to an equilibrium level of segregation of 0.64, the same value of the optimal segregation (see Figure 15.6). Therefore, optimal segregation is not necessarily an out-of-equilibrium situation or a corner solution.

15.4 Concluding remarks

The first interesting finding of the present research is that positive levels of segregation, lower than complete segregation, can be a social optimum. This is quite different to the previous literature, where just either full integration or full segregation can be a social optimum.

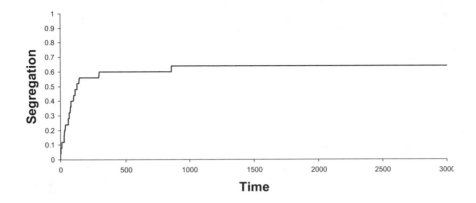

Fig. 15.6. Evolution to the optimum level of segregation

The optimal segregation value depends on the extend of prejudices and negative impact of group effects on productivity. For instance, with highly prejudiced agents and irrelevant groups effects, the social optimum will be full segregation. In the opposite case, the social optimum will be full integration. However, with more balanced parameters values the optimal segregation will be lying between 0 and 1 but not reaching the extremes.

The most striking result is full integration being a stable equilibrium. The reason that has made the difference is the agents taking into account of the segregation's negative effect on their own level of consumption at the moment of taking their location decisions. Also, it has been possible to find a combination of parameters' values where the system converges to an optimum level of segregation greater than 0 but less than 1 too. Therefore, a society can reach by itself an optimal level of segregation different from the less realistic cases of full integration and full segregation.

All these findings can have interesting policy implications. First of all, segregation must not be seen as a bad situation a priori. What is going to be the optimal level of segregation is something depending upon of how prejudiced are prejudiced agents, the extend of groups effects impact and the relative importance amongst local neighborhood characteristics and consumption on agents' utility. Consequently, it can be argued that there is not such a thing like a unique optimal level of segregation or an absolute segregation target. If the aim is to improve welfare, policymakers must have a clear picture of individual preferences, group effects and other elements, that have not been treated in this research but it is worthy to mention them, as provision of local and non local public goods, before to implement any policy with the objective of reducing segregation. Besides, it is clear that two cities, or regions, have not the same characteristics, hence, every different city have different level of optimal segregation, and, therefore needs different policies.

References

A. Anas. Prejudice, exclusion, and compensating transfers: the economic of ethnic segregation. *Journal of Urban Economics*, 52:409–432, 2002.

A. Ando. *Development of a unified theory of urban land use*. PhD thesis, University of Pennsylvania, 1981.

R. Arnot and R. Rowse. Peer group effects and educational attainment. *Journal of Public Economics*, 32:287–305, 1987.

M. Bailey. Note on the economics of residential zoning and urban renewal. *Land Economics*, 35:288–292, 1959.

R. Benabou. The workings of a city: Location, education, and production. *Quartely Journal of Economics*, 108(3):619–652, 1993.

E. Berglas. Distribution of tastes and skills and the provision of local public goods. *Journal of Public Economics*, 6:409–423, 1976.

C. Charles, G. Dinwiddie, and D. Massey. The continuing consequences of segregation: Family stress and college academic performance. *Social Science Quarterly*, 85(5):1353–1373, 2004.

J. Clapp and S. Ross. Schools and housing markets: An examination of school segregation and performance in connecticut. *Economic Journal*, 114(499):425–440, 2004.

J. Dawkins, Q. Shen, and T. Sanchez. Race, space, and unemployment duration. *Journal of Urban Economics*, 58:91–113, 2005.

C. De Bartolome. Equilibrium and inefficiency in a community model with peer group effects. *Journal of Political Economy*, 48:110–133, 1990.

O. Duncan and B. Duncan. A methodological analysis of segregation indices. *American Sociological Review*, 20:210–217, 1955.

Y. Kanemoto. *Theories of Urban Externalities*. North Holland, 1980.

T. LaVeist. Racial segregation and longevity among african americans: An individual-level analysis. *Health Services Research*, 38:1719–1733, 2003.

D. Massey. Segregation and violent crime in urban america. In *Problem of the century: Racial stratification in the United States*. Russell Sage Foundation, 2001.

D. McFadden. Conditional logit analysis of qualitative choice behavior. In *Frontiers of Econometrics*. Academic Press, New York, 1973.

D. Meen and G. Meen. Social behaviour as a basis for modelling the urban housing market: A review. *Urban Studies*, 40:917–35, 2003.

J. Papageorgiou. Spatial externalities. i: theory. *Annals of the Association of American Geographers*, 68:465–476, 1978.

S. Rose-Ackerman. Racism and urban structure. *Journal of Urban Economics*, 7:233–250, 1975.

T. Schelling. Dynamics models of segregation. *Journal of Mathematical Sociology*, 1:143–186, 1971.

A. Schnare. Racial and ethnic price differentials in an urban housing market. *Urban Studies*, 13:107–120, 1976.

F. Wilson and R. Hammer. Ethnic residential segregation and its consequences. In *Urban inequality: Evidence from four cities*. Russell Sage Foundation, 2001.

J. Yinger. Racial prejudice and racial residential segregation in an urban model. *Journal of Urban Economics*, 3:383–396, 1976.

J. Yinger. Housing discrimination and residential segregation as causes of poverty. In *Understanding poverty*. Harvard University Press, 2001.

J. Zhang. Residential segregation in an all-integrationist world. *Journal of Mathematical Behavior and Organization*, 54(4):533–550, 2004.

The Grass is Always Greener on the Other Side of the Fence: The Effect of Misperceived Signalling in a Network Formation Process

Simone Giansante[1], Alan Kirman[2], Sheri Markose[1], and Paolo Pin[3]

[1] CCFEA, University of Essex, UK
   {sgians,scher}@essex.ac.uk
[2] GREQAM, Université d'Aix Marseille, France
   kirman@ehess.univ-mrs.fr
[3] Economics Department, University of Venice, and ICTP, Trieste, Italy
   pin@unive.it

16.1 Introduction

Social and economic networks are becoming increasingly popular in the last ten years, because of both the application of game theory to the network formation processes[4], and the study of stochastic processes that fit the statistical properties of real world social networks.[5] In the very recent years there have also been attempts to combine the contribution of these two streams of research, trying to find strategic models whose equilibria resemble the empirical data.[6] A well known source of debate in the game theoretical approach is the incompatibility between stability and efficiency: in most of the models Nash equilibria are actually not the network architectures that maximize the overall sum of utilities, as surveyed in Jackson (2003). On the other hand the econophysics approach is not interested in the utility of single nodes but has other measures of efficiency, which are essentially the probabilities of the network to maintain certain properties after random deletion of links or nodes.

---

[4] The seminal paper is by Jackson and Wolinsky (1996), see Jackson (2006) for a survey of this literature.

[5] The starting point of this second stream of research can be considered Albert and Barabási (1999), see Newman (2003) for a survey. Let us refer to this second scientific contribution as the econophysics approach.

[6] As an example see Jackson and Rogers (2007).

We will consider a similar trade–off between stability and efficiency, in a game theoretical network formation model. The nature of our model is however such that both the efficient networks, and the most likely outcomes in real world applications, are different from how classical social networks look like. The social networks that are usually brought as examples are those of human informal relations (as friendships). They are strongly connected networks with short minimal paths between any two of their nodes. There are however different environments and related theoretical models where the outcomes are likely to be segregated clusters. Reasonable applications where likely outcomes are actually segregated clusters could be those where the nodes tend to mutually control each others. Think for example as an R&D setup where firms cooperate on secret projects, trying to keep low the risk of industrial espionage. Consider moreover informal contracts of mutual insurance (such as those in rural villages analyzed by Bramoullé and Kranton (2007) where reciprocal control is necessary to avoid moral hazard issues. A third example could be the market of perishable goods described in Weisbuch et al. (2000). Also Jackson and Wolinsky (1996), in their original coauthor–model, imagine a set of researchers that have a utility from working with other colleagues that is increasing in the number of coauthors, but decreasing in the coauthors of their coauthors. Moreover there are some costs for maintaining links. For low enough costs both the efficient outcome and the equilibria of the co–author model are networks segregated in fully connected clusters.

The present paper considers a particular case of the model proposed by Kirman et al. (2007), where agents try to maximize the total number of reciprocal links in their neighborhood. The nodes have a maximum number of links they can send to others. Directed networks are considered so that the notion of Nash equilibrium can be straightforward applied. This model has a Nash equilibrium network architecture which is also the efficient one, that is the case where agents cluster in isolated but complete (i.e. fully connected) subnetworks. However there are also other, less efficient, equilibria, so that the problem is a classical one of coordination among players. We use computer driven simulations, where agents are faced with the possibility to change some of their connections if better profits are present. It comes out that the coordination toward the efficient equilibrium is not always the case, especially if the players have many links to possibly cast, or if they are heterogeneous in their maximum possible number of links. We have found out that, amplifying the signal from a change in strategies, so that it may happen that agents change because they think to improve their situation but this does not happen, the probability for the final outcome to be efficient, and in general the expected cumulative utility, increase.

Next Section formalize the model and the algorithm used in the simulations, while Section 16.3 shows the results. The main result may seem not surprising to those who know some theoretical physics or computer science: every heuristic optimization algorithm work with experimentation to avoid local minima. We will conclude and analyze this comparison in Section 16.4, arguing that it is not completely exact.

16.2 The model

The game we are considering is a one shot network formation game between N agents. The network resulting from any strategy–profile is a directed irreflexive unweighed one, in the spirit of Bala and Goyal (2000). Each agent i can casts up to l_i links (this number l_i will be the only specification of the agents' type) to other agents.[7] This is the only action we have considered, so that the strategy set for agent i represents all the subset of the remaining $N - 1$ agents, with cardinality up to l_i. Let us identify the action of every agent with one such subset, and call it R_i. The strategy profile of the game will determine an undirected network of N nodes (the agents) and up to $\sum_i^N l_i$ links (the maximum possible number of links). The structure of the network determines the payoff for each agent. This payoff is a measure of how well interconnected is the neighborhood of degree one of each agent. Agent i counts all the links between all the nodes in $R_i \cup \{i\}$ (the nodes in her out-degree neighborhood and herself), in both directions, call this number π_i, i's payoff is then exactly π_i.[8]

Let us start our analysis from the homogeneous case where all the l_i are equal to a certain value l. To simplify the analysis let us also assume that N is a multiple of $l + 1$. Given these hypothesis (that we will maintain in our first group of simulations), it becomes easy to analyze the welfare of the system. The most efficient network structure is the one in which the nodes are clustered in segregated fully connected sub–networks of $l + 1$ nodes each. It is easy to check that this is the only possible architecture that guarantees the maximum profit to every node: every cluster is for everyone of its members exactly the $R_i \cup \{i\}$

---

[7] The limit in the number of links can have many economic explanations, all of them reducible to a story of limited resources and costly link formations.

[8] This game is the "level 2 neighborhood" case of the general model considered in Kirman et al. (2007).

neighborhood, in which a maximum of $(l+1) \cdot l$ links is present. Since the efficient network is feasible and inside it no agent can improve her payoff, it is straightforward to check that the efficient network is also a Nash equilibrium. Unfortunately this is not the only Nash equilibrium, even when l is low (so that coordination does not seem hard), as shown in Figure 16.1, where l is set to 2, while $N = 6$.

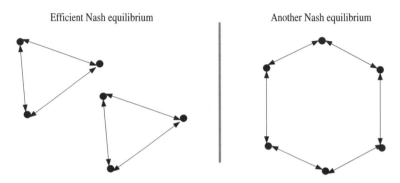

Fig. 16.1. Comparison between the efficient Nash equilibrium (left) and a possible non–efficient one. Here $N = 6$ and $l_i = 2 \ \forall i \in \{1, \ldots 6\}$.

The right hand side equilibrium in Figure 16.1 gives an equal utility to all the agents that is only $\frac{2}{3}$ of that received in the optimal left hand side case (4 links in the neighborhood instead of 6) because every node's neighbors are not connected between each other, and changing neighbors would only make things worse. The suggestion we get from this comparison is that, without the possibility of coordination between the agents, suboptimal outcomes cannot be avoided.

As intuition would suggest, the coordination problems will increase as soon as we introduce heterogeneity in the players of our game. Suppose for example that our N agents are divided in two sub–population of which one has a given value l' for the maximum number of allowed links, while the other has another value l''. In order to simplify thinks let us assume that the N' agents whose value is l' are such that N' is a multiple of $l'+1$, and the same for N'' and l'' (clearly $N' + N'' = N$). With similar consideration as the ones for the simpler case, it comes out that the only efficient network is the one in which agents cluster in fully connected sub–networks of cardinality $l'+1$ (the N' agents of the first type) and $l''+1$ (the remaining N'' agents). Since this config-uration maximizes the payoff of every player and no agent can improve her own profit, the efficient network is also a Nash equilibrium.

As in the previous case, however, the efficient equilibrium is not the only one. Consider $N = 30$ and $l_i = 2 \ \forall i \in \{1, \ldots 15\}$, while $l_j = 4 \ \forall j \in \{16, \ldots 30\}$. The efficient Nash equilibrium would be: 8 segregated clusters (3 quintuplets and 5 triplets). This is however not the only one. Examples of non–efficient Nash equilibria can be easily set up for this example as has been done in the homogeneous case

16.2.1 The adaptive mechanism

We describe here a very simple algorithm that would allow us to span the possible network configurations and search for the equilibria of the game described above. Imagine a discrete time process where at every time step we have a network configuration. The initial configuration is just a random network with the constraint that every node i casts exactly l_i links to other nodes (from the way payoff are computed we can exclude a priori that a rational agent would cast less links than allowed). At every time step every node: (i) considers all her links and compute which is the worst one in terms of marginal payoff (in case it is more than one uniform probabilities are applied); (ii) considers a random node to whom she is not already linked and compute the marginal payoff from changing her worst connection for this new one; (iii) if this change is profitable to her she changes her link for the better target.

It is not given that, if this algorithm is blocked in a stall network for all the possible deviations, then this network is a Nash equilibrium, since a deviation in strategies could happen also changing more than one single link.[9] We know however what the efficient Nash equilibrium is. Thus the aggregate wealth of every configuration can always easily be computed, and also the ratio between the aggregate payoff (obtained when the algorithm stops) and the optimal achievable one.

Formally, at every time step, every node i computes the marginal payoff from deleting every one (but only that single one) of her links, call this value $\Delta_\lambda \pi_i$ for every link $\lambda \in \{1, \ldots l_i\}$. She picks a link that minimizes this payoff: $\underline{\lambda} \in \arg\min\{\Delta_\lambda \pi_i\}$. Node i is then assigned randomly (with uniform probabilities) a node $j \notin R_i$ (j is not in i's neighborhood) and she is informed on what would be her marginal payoff from severing link $\underline{\lambda}$ and connecting to j with a link $\lambda_{\to j}$. She computes the difference

$$D_{\underline{\lambda} \to j} = \Delta_{\lambda_{\to j}} \pi_i - \Delta_{\underline{\lambda}} \pi_i \ ,$$

---

[9] The reverse is however true, the algorithm would surely stop in a Nash equilibrium.

if it is positive she makes the change.

The object of our empirical analysis is then: what would happen if the perception of the marginal payoff from the new connection is positively biased? In the formulas it would be as if we had a parameter $\alpha \geq 1$ (the value of bias) that linearly distort the external information. The perceived difference would become

$$D^{\alpha}_{\underline{\lambda} \to j} = \left(\alpha \cdot \Delta_{\lambda \to j} \pi_i \right) - \Delta_{\underline{\lambda}} \pi_i \ .$$

If this new formula is positive the agent will change her connection, but it is not guaranteed that also the real difference $D_{\underline{\lambda} \to j} \leq D^{\alpha}_{\underline{\lambda} \to j}$ is non–negative.

16.3 Results

We apply the adaptive mechanism described in previous Section to computer–based simulations, for different values of $\alpha \geq 1$. α is the positive bias in the perception of the payoff from new links, its value is exogenously fixed in every simulation and is the same for all the agents in the system.

The measurement that we will make for those simulations are two. First of all we will check if the algorithm eventually stops to an absorbing network configuration.[10] As discussed above a stall network is however not guaranteed to be a Nash equilibrium. This holds even for $\alpha > 1$.[11] It is plausible to expect from the simulations that, as the value of α increases from 1, the probability that the algorithm will not stop in some fixed configuration becomes higher and higher. There will moreover be a value of α for which the system will never stop because, no matter the shape of the network and the resulting payoffs, there will always be an agent willing to change one of her links. Since we are running several simulations for every starting population and value of α, we keep track of the percentage of those simulations that happen to stop in some network configuration. We call this first measure the *Stability* of a simulation.

As clarified in Section 16.2 we know what is the optimal achievable payoff for every agent i, as soon as we know her link–capacity l_i. This

---

[10] Technically we check if the system does not change for a long enough number of time–steps.

[11] For $\alpha > 1$ neither the reverse implication can be made: if the system is in a Nash equilibrium, it can still change configuration because some agents may get wrong signals and adopt a non–profitable change of a link.

maximal payoff is the one she gets in a fully connected cluster of similar agents and is the number of links in such a cluster, namely $l_i \cdot (l_i - 1)$. We choose the starting population so that there is surely an efficient Nash equilibrium where all the agents reach their optimal payoff. The second measure we take will identify how far the agents' final payoff are from the ideal efficient case. We measure the final utility of each agent and consider the ratio with the optimal one, then we express as a percentage the average value of this ratio across all the population.[12] This second measure will be called the *Wealth* of a simulation. We have then two indices, Stability and Wealth (both expressed in percentage), for every starting population and bias α.

The first group of simulation has been made with a population of 60 homogeneous agents, each with a link capacity $l_i = 2$. This is a 10 times larger group than the one considered in the example of Figure 16.1, but the efficient Nash equilibrium is still one in segregated triplets. Figure 16.2 shows the result when α is ranging from 1 to 2.5. For values of $\alpha > 1.5$ the stability of the system is not sure anymore. Full wealth optimality is never reached on average (the Wealth measure is always below 90%), but a simple second order polynomial interpolation of the results suggest that an expected maximum Wealth is reached between $\alpha = 1.5$ and $\alpha = 2$. The result is surprising for two reasons. First of all the higher expected wealth is not reached for $\alpha = 1$, but for a higher value. Secondarily this optimum seems to stand where the algorithm is not surely stable anymore. The effect of bias undermines stability after a certain α^U but, up to a certain point $\alpha^* > \alpha^U$, it improves the expected payoff of the agents. As we will see the qualitative outcome of this first group of simulations will hold also in the following ones.

Figure 16.3 shows the result of simulations when the population of 60 players is still homogeneous, but now the link capacity of the agents is $l_i = 4$. The efficient Nash equilibrium is a network divided in 12 segregated quintuplets. As expected now the agents' coordination problem gets more tricky: the value α^U over which instability may arise becomes smaller, while the value α^* where there is an optimum expected wealth seems to increase. As a consequence we get the same kind of results (i.e. $1 < \alpha^U < \alpha^*$) as in the previous simpler model.

We have ran simulations also for the case of non–homogeneous populations, mixing between the two previous cases. We have considered the three quartile distributions with 60 agents: 15 agents with a link capacity of $l_i = 2$ and 45 with a link capacity of $l_j = 4$; the $30 - 30$

---

[12] When the algorithm is not stable and there is not a final configuration, we measure the average wealth of the agents on a sufficiently large final time window.

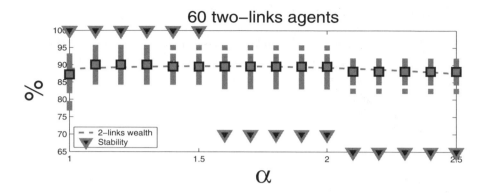

Fig. 16.2. Simulations on a homogeneous population of 60 agents, with $l_i = 2$. α ranges from 1 to 2.5, with a grid of 0.1. For every value of α in this grid 20 simulations are ran. Small squares show Wealth in every simulation; big squares are for the average Wealth, which is interpolated with a second order polynomial; triangles indicate stability.

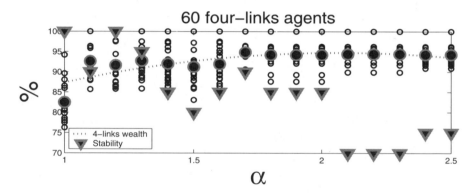

Fig. 16.3. Simulations on a homogeneous population of 60 agents, with $l_i = 4$. α ranges from 1 to 2.5, with a grid of 0.1. For every value of α in this grid 20 simulations are ran. Small circles show Wealth in every simulation; big circles are for the average Wealth, which is interpolated with a second order polynomial; triangles indicate stability.

case and the $45 - 15$ case. All of them have efficient Nash equilibria where all the two–linked agents ($l_i = 2$) cluster in triplets, while the four–linked ones ($l_j = 4$) segregate in quintuplets. Figure 16.4 (page 231) shows the results. As when increasing link capacity with homogeneous populations, an even higher complexity reduces the likelihood of

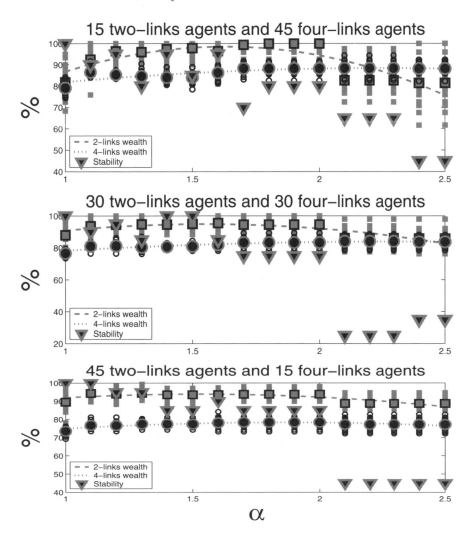

Fig. 16.4. Simulations on a heterogeneous population of 60 agents: 15, 30 and 45 respectively with $l_i = 2$, the remaining ones with $l_j = 4$. α ranges from 1 to 2.5, with a grid of 0.1. For every value of α in this grid 20 simulations are ran. Small squares show Wealth of the 2-links agents in every simulation; big squares are for their average Wealth, which is interpolated with a second order polynomial; circles are used for the 4-links agents; triangles indicate stability.

coordination, that is less stability and less expected wealth. In all of the three cases Stability suffer a substantial reduction above $\alpha = 2$,[13] but

---

[13] We observe what physicians call a phase transition.

already at $\alpha = 1.1$ stability is not guaranteed (i.e. Stability$< 100\%$), so that we can locate α^U slightly above 1. The points α_2^* and α_4^*, where the maxima of expected wealth are located, are now shifted to the right, even if the agents with only two links seem to suffer less from the cohabitation, at least when stability is kept safely above 0.

From simulations we have the *unexpected* result that a value of $\alpha > 1$, i.e. an encouragement for trying new connections, leads instead to a more probable and faster type–biased segregation, that is the efficient equilibrium. The idea is that if agents receive exaggerated incentives linking, i.e. the false perception of better conditions than the actual ones, in the long run they do not facilitate connected networks but instead drive themselves with higher probability to segregation.

16.4 Conclusion

We have a game theoretical network–formation model with multiplicity of equilibria, of which only a very few are the efficient ones. We are facing a typical coordination problem. We briefly discussed in the Introduction which economic applications may have segregated equilibria as the optimal ones.

The result could have two possible implications, a regulatory one and a behavioral one. Think for example to openness and mobility in the job market. Incentives to mobility, even if positively biased in a misleading way, so that people find worse conditions than expected, may lead in the long run to more efficient allocations of the resources. The fact that human beings seem to overestimate the conditions of their similar in different neighborhoods, and the profit they could get elsewhere, could be an inborn attitude to implement experimentation.

The model and the results proposed here have clear analogies, at one side, with other segregation models, at the other side, with the heuristic optimization techniques that allow non–optimal steps in order to exclude local minima (sub–optimal but stable network configuration in our case). Our setup of heterogenous agents that cluster in closed homogeneous subgroups seems very close to the Schelling (1971) Segregation Model (SSM), even if differences should be pointed out. Here the topology of the problem is unbounded, every agent can cast links (up to her maximum threshold) to every other agent and there is no fixed grid. The geometrical constraint is much stronger in that model. In SSM, moreover, a single agent's deviation is a jump to a completely different neighborhood, while our agents can change only one neighbor at time. In this way also the effect on the other agents is reduced here in comparison to SSM. Another difference between our hetero-geneous setup and SSM is that for us the distinction across the two sub–populations is not in preferences, but in the spread of their neighborhood. We do not reach segregation because of different utilities but because of different resources.

We think that the achieved result (that is: biased perception increases average wealth) are a counter–intuitive novelty, at least in an economic setting of individual profit maximization. They may however not seem so if we consider how our adaptive algorithm has clear analogies with the optimizing simulated annealing algorithm at non–zero temperature (See Kirkpatrick et al., 1983). Since the latter works well in finding optima also our process should increase the average wealth. There are however two considerations that should be made. The first one is that the simulated annealing works well at a stable temperature only if the global optimum is distant (i.e. different) enough from the local ones. This is not something that we have for granted in our model, where the value of bias α is kept fixed along any single simulation. The second, more important, point is that in heuristic optimization, when evaluating a new move, marginal global utility is considered and not the marginal utility of a single agent. The heuristic optimization would work exactly in a cooperative game, but not in our non–cooperative network formation process. In short: when an agent of ours decides to change a link she does not care about what would happen to her neighborhood, neither the old nor the new one. So, there are at least two reasons for which our results are in principle not predictable by the optimizing stochastic processes considered by theoretical physics and theoretical computer science.

References

R. Albert and A. L. Barabási. Emerging of scaling in random networks. *Science*, 286:509–512, 1999.

V. Bala and S. Goyal. A noncooperative model of network formation. *Econometrica*, 68(5):1181–1230, September 2000.

Y. Bramoullé and R. Kranton. Risk-sharing across communities. Technical report, Mimeo, January 2007.

M. O. Jackson and B. W. Rogers. Meeting strangers and friends of friends: How random are social networks? *American Economic Review*, 2007. Forthcoming.

M. O. Jackson and A. Wolinsky. A strategic model of social and economic networks. *Journal of Economic Theory*, 71(1):44–74, October 1996.

M.O. Jackson. The stability and efficiency of economic and social networks. In M. R. Sertel and S. Koray, editors, *Advances in Economic Design*, pages 319–362. Springer, 2003.

M.O. Jackson. The economics of social networks. In Blundell R., Newey W., and Persson T., editors, *Advances in Economics and Econometrics, Theory and Applications*, volume 1, chapter 1. Cambridge University Press, 2006.

S. Kirkpatrick, C. D. Gelatt, and M. P. Vecchi. Optimization by simulated annealing. *Science, Number 4598, 13 May 1983*, 220(4598): 671–680, May 1983.

A. Kirman, S. Markose, S. Giasante, and P. Pin. Marginal contribution, reciprocity and equity in segregated groups: Bounded rationality and self-organization in social networks. *Journal of Economic Dynamics and Control*, 2007. Forthcoming.

M. E. J. Newman. The structure and function of complex networks. *SIAM Review*, 45:167–256, 2003.

C. Weisbuch, A. Kirman, and D. Herreiner. Market organization and trading relationships. *Economic Journal*, 110:411–436, 2000.

Part V

Methodological Issues and Applications

Market Selection of Competent Venture Capitalists

David Mas

ERMES-CNRS, Université Panthéon-Assas Paris II, France
David.Mas@u-paris2.fr

17.1 Introduction

Venture capital is actually considered a very efficient mean for financing innovation. Kortum and Lerner (2000) estimate that a dollar invested in venture capital is three times more effective in stimulating patenting than a dollar invested in traditional R&D. Understanding venture capital is therefore a central matter for designing innovation policies. Venture capital has a very peculiar functioning. Venture capitalists finance young firms whose only activity is to develop radical innovations (start-ups). These new firms have no access to the banking system because they are too risky and have no collateral. But their future is also too uncertain to allow them to enter the financial market. Venture capitalists are assuming this uncertainty because they are looking for high-risk/high-reward investments. Venture capitalist are not wealthy individuals risking their own money (business angels), but fund managers. This means they provide institutional investors (pension funds, insurance companies, investment bank) with the possibility to invest in an asset, the venture capital fund, whose risk is manageable with traditional financial methods, like portfolio diversification. Venture capital is in fact turning the uncertainty of investing in radical innovations into a simple, though high, risk.

I propose a model that explicitly describe this essential feature of the venture capital market. This model is intended to understand what are the conditions for the existence and for an efficient functioning of a venture capital market. Following Carlsson and Eliasson (2003), I consider that venture capitalists are competent actors whose function is to select and finance the most promising start-ups. This means that venture capitalists reduce uncertainty in choosing the right start-ups to invest in. To formalize this idea, I propose a model of venture capital as a market of heterogeneous interacting agents. On the one hand there are start-up projects of different qualities that need financing, and on the other hand there are venture capitalists of different levels of competence trying to detect and finance the best start-up. The evaluation of start-up quality by venture capitalist is imperfect, and its accuracy depends on venture capitalist's competence. Despite the simplicity of the model, the interaction of heterogeneous agents in a stochastic environment makes it tractable only with a simple distribution of agents' qualities and some restrictive hypotheses. The use of simulation allows to overcome this limitation.

In a previous paper Mas and Vignes (2006) show under which conditions the competence of venture capitalists allow for an efficient screening of start-ups. In this paper I investigate the market selection of venture capitalists and show how an efficient venture capital industry can emerge from an initial random population of heterogeneous venture capitalists. I also identify and study the role of a particular institution of venture capital, the limited partnership, in venture capitalists selection. I show i) that the accuracy of the selection as well a the risk taken by institutional investors increases with the size of the limited partnership, i.e. with the number of investments a venture capitalist can make before having to raise an other fund, ii) that the size of the limited partnership has almost no influence on the final distribution of competence, iii) that the optimal choice for the size of the limited partnership can be determined by the computation of selection costs taking type I and type II errors into account.

17.2 Related literature

Kaplan and Stromberg (2001) distinguish three main roles for venture capitalists, which are screening, contracting and monitoring. The contracting role has been extensively studied both from a theoretical point of view and from an empirical point of view (Kaplan and Stromberg, 2000). The optimal contract approach has successfully proposed rationales for some stylized facts of venture capital, like the control right allocation in venture capital contracts (Hellmann, 1998) and the staging of venture capital investment (Gompers, 1995). The monitoring role of venture capitalists is often considered as the specific added value provided by venture capitalists. The early empirical studies (Gorman and Sahlman, 1989; Sapienza, 1992) emphasize the time spent by venture capitalists interacting with the firms of their portfolio. The later ones

(Hellmann and Puri, 2000, 2002; Lerner, 1995) show evidences of the active involvement of venture capitalists in the management of start-ups and the positive impact of this involvement on the start-up success. But the screening role of venture capitalists has received much less attention. I consider though, like Carlsson and Eliasson (2003), that the screening of start-ups is the main role of venture capitalists. The model presented in this paper places this role at the core of the venture capital market.

My work can be related to two other models. Chan (1983) proposes a model of the venture capital market in which information about the quality of investment is costly. These information costs justify the existence of venture capitalists. In this paper I propose an alternative for the role of venture capitalists : instead of costly information, I consider that information about start-up quality is only (imperfectly) available to competent venture capitalists. Amit et al. (1999) propose a model of venture capital that takes all agency risk (moral hazard and asymmetry of information) into account. They also propose a screening competence, called 'due diligence', that would allow to predict the quality of a given start-up project (and thus to minimize the asymmetry of information) : but they have not developed the model based on this hypothesis. In this paper I adopt a very similar hypothesis for the screening competence of venture capitalists, I build a model based on that idea and I simulate its functioning.

17.3 The model

The model contains two types of heterogeneous agents, the start-ups and the venture capitalists. I first present each agent and then the dynamics of the model. I only provide the essential equations, see Mas and Vignes (2006) for a more detailed presentation.

17.3.1 The start-ups

Start-up projects are heterogeneous in quality. The quality of a start-up project i determines her probability of success p_i.

$$p_i = q_i \, \bar{p} \qquad (17.1)$$

I assume that the mean quality of the start-up projects q is one, so that $\bar{p}$ is the mean probability of success of the start-ups projects. Investing in a start-up is risky, it only generates profit in case of success.

For an initial investment I in a start-up i the expected profit is given by the following equation.

$$E(\pi_i) = (p_i\, g - 1)\, I \qquad (17.2)$$

Equations (17.1) and (17.2) simply state that the higher the quality, the higher the probability of success and the higher the expected profit.

17.3.2 Venture capitalists

Competence is defined as the ability of a venture capitalist to evaluate the quality of a start-up project. For a venture capitalist of competence c_j, the evaluation of the start-up project quality q_i is :

$$\tilde{q}_{ij} = c_j\, q_i + (1 - c_j)\, u_{ij} \qquad (17.3)$$

Here u_{ij} is a random noise with the same distribution as q_i. The accuracy of the evaluation varies from perfect information, when $c_j = 1$, to pure noise, when $c_j = 0$. The venture capitalists screen the start-up projects in sequence. Each venture capitalist evaluates the available start-up projects and picks the best one according to his own evaluation.

17.3.3 Dynamics

Start-ups only live for one period. They are created as projects and screened by venture capitalists. If they are selected, they may succeed and generate profits. Venture capitalists stay on the market as long as they have enough capital to invest. The failed venture capitalists are replaced by new ones. The number of start-up projects S and of venture capitalists V is constant in time.

Each venture capitalist raises a fund LP (Limited Partnership) that he invests totally, always financing one start-up per period. The eventual profits are accumulated by the limited partners. Once the fund is totally invested the limited partners may decide to give the venture capitalist a new fund to manage or not, according to his performance.

At each period n, we repeat the following steps:

1. new start-up projects are created.
2. venture capitalists screen the start-ups
3. the financed start-ups generate profits or losses.
4. venture capitalists accumulate the profits or losses realized by their start-up.
5. venture capitalists whose fund has been totally invested raise a new fund or are replaced by new ones.

17.4 Formal analysis

The aim of this section is to find the best estimator of the performance
of venture capitalists and to study its influence on the selection process.

17.4.1 Best selection criterion

The competence of a venture capitalist determines in a non linear way
the expected quality of the start-ups he finances, and hence their expected probability of success. This probability is also affected by the
market conditions and structure (Mas and Vignes (2006)). Thus I can
define for each venture capitalist j the expected probability of success
p_j of his start-ups s_j as a function of his competence c and of the market conditions M. With given market conditions M, p_j only depends
on c_j, and $\frac{\partial p_j}{\partial c_j} > 0$.

$$p_j = E(q_{s_j}) \; \bar{p} = f(c_j, M) \tag{17.4}$$

The outcome of an investment for the venture capitalist j is a
Bernoulli trial of probability p_j. Thus the number of successful investments out of n follows a binomial law $B(n, p_j)$. From these considerations it follows that the average profits of all the investments made by
a venture capitalists converge towards a value that depends linearly on
p_j.

$$\hat{\pi}_j = \frac{1}{n} \sum_t \pi_{j,t} \xrightarrow[n \to \infty]{} (p_j \, g - 1) \, I \tag{17.5}$$

$$E(\hat{\pi}_j) = \frac{1}{n}(E(B(n, p_j))g - n) \, I = (p_j \, g - 1) \, I \tag{17.6}$$

$$var(\hat{\pi}_j) = \frac{1}{n^2} \, var(B(n, p_j)) \, g^2 \, I^2 = \frac{1}{n} \, p_j \, (1 - p_j) \, g^2 \, I^2 \tag{17.7}$$

The expected profits of a venture capitalist depend through p_j on
his competence c_j. After any number of investments made by a venture capitalist, the average of his realized profits is the best estimator
of his performance. Therefore the best selection criterion for venture
capitalists is $\hat{\pi}_j > 0$.

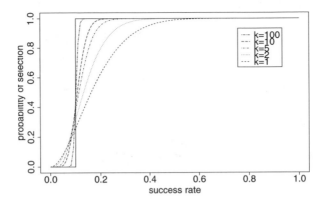

Fig. 17.1. Probability of selection of a venture capitalist at the end of his first limited partnership as a function of his expected success rate p_j for various number of investments per fund $LP = k\,g$ with $g = 10$.

17.4.2 Influence of the size of the limited partnership

For the institutional investor who gives the venture capitalists a fund to manage, the finite time horizon of the limited partnership provides both a powerful incentive to the venture capitalist to do his best and an opportunity to monitor his performance. The institutional investor can chose the size of the fund LP which correspond to a given number of investments after which he can choose to give an other fund to the venture capitalist or to give his chance to a new one. What is the impact of this choice on the selection of venture capitalists?

Let assume for simplicity that the size of the limited partnership is a multiple of the return in case of success $LP = k\,g$. From the previous analysis I can compute the probability of meeting the selection criterion at the end of the first fund.

$$P(S|p_j, LP) = P\left(B(k\,g, p_j)\,g - k\,g\right)I > 0) \qquad (17.8)$$
$$= P(B(k\,g, p_j) > k) \qquad (17.9)$$
$$= 1 - F_{B(k\,g, p_j)}(k) \qquad (17.10)$$

For a given size of the limited partnership $LP = k\,g$ the probability of selection can be expressed as the value at k of the complementary cumulative distribution function (ccdf) of a binomial law of parameters $k\,g$ and p_j. Figure 17.1 shows the evolution of the selection function for various size of funds. As k increases it converges towards an Heaviside's function $h(p_y - \frac{1}{g})$. The bigger the size of the limited partnership, the more accurate is the selection. But a bigger size of the fund corresponds also to a bigger risk for the institutional investor. Thus the choice of the size of the limited partnership is a balance between the accuracy of the selection and the risk taken by the institutional investor.

17.4.3 Global selection function

The outcome of the complete selection process is not tractable. In order to study it, I will simulate the model. After the end of the run it is possible to retrieve the global selection function using Bayes' rules. Let S be the event that the venture capitalist has been selected. Then the global selection function is :

$$P(S|c) = \frac{P(c|S)\ P(S)}{P(c)} \qquad (17.11)$$

Where $P(c|S)$ is the final distribution of competence, $P(S)$ the ratio of the number of selected venture capitalists over the number of the venture capitalists that once entered the market and $P(c)$ is the initial distribution of competence.

17.5 Simulations results

I simulate the model with four different settings, with either a gaussian or an exponential distribution for the quality of start-ups and with a uniform or triangular distribution for the competence of venture capitalists. I then vary the size of the limited partnership. Following the formal analysis, I choose $LP = k\ g$, with $g = 10$. In each case I ran one hundred simulations of five thousand periods, with a population of one hundred venture capitalists that screen five hundred start-ups projects at each period.

The parameters of the model have been chosen such that the minimum level of competence required to achieve positive profits is $c_G = 0.5$ for the gaussian distribution of quality, and $c_E = 0.6$ for the exponential distribution. The essential difference between the two distributions of quality is the spread of the function $p_j = f(c_j, M)$. With the exponential distribution the difference between more competent investors and lesser ones is bigger. It should leads to a more discriminative selection. The difference between the distributions of venture capitalists' competence, uniform and triangular, is the proportion of very competent venture capitalists. With the triangular distribution sufficiently competent venture capitalists are rarer, making the selection more challenging.

244   David Mas

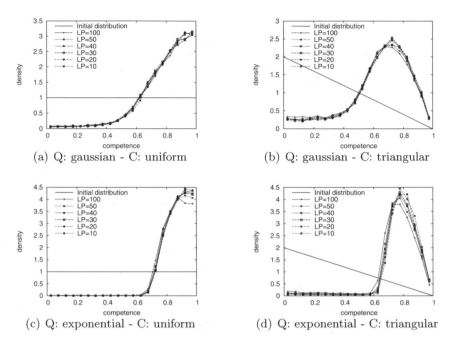

Fig. 17.2. Distributions of competence after 5000 periods

17.5.1 Final distribution of competence

Figure 17.2 shows the resulting distribution of competence after five thousand time periods. These distributions are averaged across the hundred simulation run with each setting. The plain line represents the initial distribution of competence.

The first result is that the selection is efficient. For each setting, even with few very competent venture capitalists in the initial distribution, the final population in the market is essentially composed of sufficiently competent venture capitalists.

The second result is that the final distributions of competence are almost the same for all sizes of the limited partnership. This is surprising because the formal analysis shows that bigger sizes should lead to a more accurate selection. This means that even if each selection step is different, the result of the global selection process does not depends of the size of the limited partnership.

17.5.2 Market selection function

Figure 17.3 shows the global selection function for each process, computed using Equation (17.11). The plain line represents the perfect

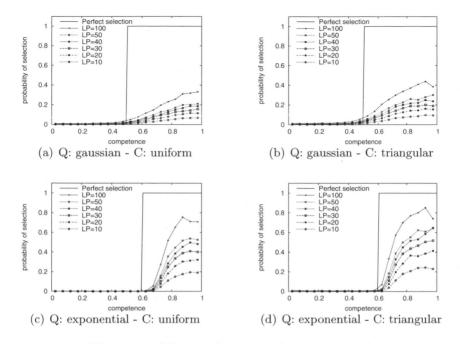

Fig. 17.3. Selection functions after 5000 periods

selection function. The selection functions are approaching the perfect selection function, getting closer to it as the size of the limited partnership increases.

The selection functions are clearly better with the exponential distribution of quality, which corresponds to a more discriminative spread of the performance of venture capitalists. The market has its own selection capability, determined by the market conditions which are essentially the distribution of agents' characteristics. The choice of the size of the limited partnership magnifies this selection capability.

This analysis confirms that even if the size of the limited partnership does not change the final distribution of competence, it affects the accuracy of the selection.

17.5.3 Optimal size of the limited partnership

The optimal size for the limited partnership LP corresponds to the optimal balance between selection accuracy and risk. In order to determine it, I compute the total selection costs paid to obtain the (identical) final distribution of competence with the following formula :

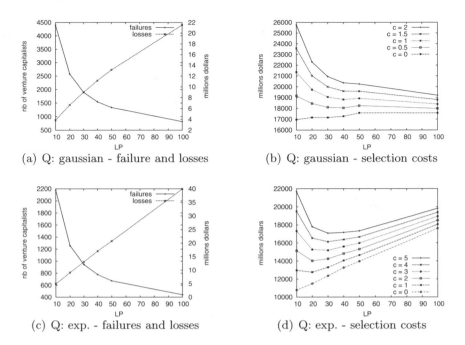

(a) Q: gaussian - failure and losses

(b) Q: gaussian - selection costs

(c) Q: exp. - failures and losses

(d) Q: exp. - selection costs

Fig. 17.4. Selections costs as a function of the size of the limited partnership $LP = k\,g$, $g = 10$

$$C_{selection} = E(losses) * failures + c_{search} * failures \qquad (17.12)$$

The first term is the total losses incurred by the institutional investors before finding a sufficiently competent venture capitalists. It corresponds to the costs associated with type I errors (financing a bad venture capitalist). The second term is the total search costs incurred when the institutional investors have to look for a new venture capitalists to replace a failed one. It corresponds to the costs associated with type II errors (missing a good venture capitalists).

Figure 17.4 shows on the left the evolution of the number of failures and of the expected losses in case of failure with the size of the limited partnership. In both cases, gaussian and exponential distribution of start-up qualities[1], expected losses increases linearly with LP, while the number of failures fails as a negative power of LP. As already stated, increasing LP increases both the risk and the accuracy of the selection.

---

[1] For concision the results are only showed for the uniform distribution of competence. They do not change with the triangular distribution of competence.

The graphs on the right of Figure 17.4 allow to determine the optimal size for the limited partnership for different values of the unitary search cost c. In both cases the institutional investor will prefer the smallest size in the absence of search costs. If they don't pay for type II errors, it is rational for them to minimize the number of type I errors only. As the search costs increase, the optimal size for LP also increases. In the gaussian case, the selections costs with no search costs are very close. Thus the optimal size increases very rapidly with c. In the exponential case, on the contrary the initial difference is much bigger, and only slowly compensated by increasing search costs. With the same value of unitary search cost $c = 1$, the institutional investors will prefer the size $LP = 20$ in the exponential case when they already prefer the size $LP = 100$ in the gaussian case.

17.6 Conclusion

The analysis of this agent based model provides a characterization of the selection process of competent venture capitalists with a noisy selection criterion. It shows that the market selection based on venture capitalists' past performance is efficient. It also shows that the accuracy of the selection increases with the size of the limited partnership, i.e. with the number of observations used for the evaluation. The final distribution of venture capitalists' competence, however, is independent of the size of the limited partnership.

The choice of the size of the limited partnership for the institutional investor is a balance between the accuracy of the selection and the risk he incurs. The optimal size can be determined by the computation of selection costs. It depends on the relative costs of type I and type II errors.

Acknowledgement. This research was supported by CO3 NEST 012410 EC grant.

References

Raphael Amit, James Brander, and Christoph Zott. Venture-capital financing of entrepreneurship: Theory, empirical evidence and a research agenda, 1999.

Bo Carlsson and Gunnar Eliasson. Industrial dynamics and endogenous growth. *Industry and Innovation*, 10(4), 2003.

Yuk-Shee Chan. On the positive role of financial intermediation in allocation of venture capital in a market with inperfect information. *The Journal of Finance*, 37(5), 1983.

Paul A. Gompers. Optimal investment, monitoring and the staging of venture-capital. *The Journal of Finance*, 50(5), 1995.

Michael Gorman and William Sahlman. What do venture capitalists do ? *Journal of Business Venturing*, 1989.

Thomas Hellmann. The allocation of control rights in venture capital contracts. *The Rand Journal of Economics*, 29(1), 1998.

Thomas Hellmann and Manju Puri. The interaction between product market and financing strategy : The role of venture capital. *The Review of Financial Studies*, 13(4), 2000.

Thomas Hellmann and Manju Puri. Venture capital and the professionalization of start-up firms: Empirical evidence. *The Journal of Finance*, 57(1), 2002.

Steven Kaplan and Per Stromberg. Venture capitalists as principals: Contracting, screening, and monitoring. *The American Economic Review*, 91(2), 2001.

Steven Niel Kaplan and Per Johan Stromberg. Financial contracting theory meets the real world: An empirical analysis of venture capital contracts. Working paper, University of Chicago, Graduate School of Business, 2000.

S. Kortum and J. Lerner. Assessing the contribution of venture capital to innovation. *The Rand Journal of Economics*, 31(4), 2000.

Joshua Lerner. Venture capitalists and the oversight of private firms. *The Journal of Finance*, 50(1), 1995.

David Mas and Annick Vignes. Why do we need venture capitalists ? the role of competent intermediaries in the creation process. Working paper, ERMES-CNRS, 2006.

Harry Sapienza. When do venture capitalists add value ? *Journal of Business Venturing*, 7, 1992.

A Binary Particle Swarm Optimization Algorithm for a Double Auction Market

Calogero Vetro and Domenico Tegolo

Department of Mathematics and Applications, University of Palermo, Italy
{vetro,tegolo}@math.unipa.it

18.1 Introduction

In this paper, we shall show the design of a multi-unit double auction (MDA) market. It should be enough robust, flexible and sufficiently efficient in facilitating exchanges. In a MDA market, sellers and buyers submit respectively asks and bids. A trade is made if a buyers bid exceeds a sellers ask. A sellers ask may match several buyers bids and a buyers bid may satisfy several sellers asks. The trading rule of a market defines the organization, information exchange process, trading procedure and clearance rules of the market. The mechanism is announced before the opening of the market so that every agent knows how the market will operate in advance. These autonomous agents pursue their own interests maximizing their own utilities. Therefore, we can view our market as a multi-agent system where the market mechanism defines the structure and rules of the environment in which agents will play the market game. An efficient market maximizes the total profit obtained by all participating agents (Fudenberg and Tirole, 1991). However, voluminous game theory literature focuses on auction markets. Satterthwaite and Williams (1989) were among the early researchers studying double auction markets. They designed a single-unit double auction (SDA) market where they eliminated the strategic behavior on the sellers side. McAfee (1992) allowed strategic behavior on both sides of a SDA market and required a market maker to balance the budget. Gjerstad and Dickhaut (1998) allowed agents to use simple rules to form beliefs about their opponents offers and showed that the market price converged to competitive equilibrium quickly. Das et al. (2001) carried over a series of experiments where humans and software agents competed with each other. Sandholm and Suri (2001) showed that if a double auction market allows agents to submit discriminatory bids, the problem of clearing the market faced by the market maker is NP-Complete.

In this paper, a binary particle swarm optimization algorithm has been proposed to solve a quadratic assignment problem to achieve an optimal solution to a double auction market.

In section 2 it will be proposed the mathematical model, section 3 will introduce the *PSO* methodology as proposed by Kennedy and Eberhart, a special binary version of PSO will be shown in section 4, and finally sections 5 and 6 will respectively give results and conclusions.

18.2 Mathematical model

One ideal way of organizing an efficient MDA market is to let the buyers/sellers submit bids/asks about how many items they want to purchase/sell and at what reservation prices. Based on this information, the market maker solves an optimization problem to determine how many units each agent should purchase/sell and at what price to maximize the total profit of the market. In a MDA market with m buyers and n sellers, each buyer i wants to purchase Z_i unit items and each seller j has Y_j unit items to sell. We assume both Z_i and Y_j are known to every agent. The reservation prices, which are private, for buyer i and seller j are b_i and s_j. We assume the reservation price for each agent is static. Let q_{ij} denote the quantity buyer i buys from seller j. If all information is public, the maximum total market value can be obtained by solving the following linear programming problem:

$$\max \sum_{i=1}^{m} \sum_{j=1}^{n} q_{ij}(b_i - s_j), \tag{18.1}$$

where

$$\sum_{i=1}^{m} q_{ij} \leq Y_j \ \ \forall \, j \tag{18.2}$$

and

$$\sum_{j=1}^{n} q_{ij} \leq Z_i \ \ \forall \, i \tag{18.3}$$

with

$$q_{ij} \geq 0 \ \ \text{for every } i, j. \tag{18.4}$$

Constraints (2) and (3) state that a seller sells no more than what he possesses and a buyer will not buy more than he needs. It is interesting to note that the trading price does not show up in the problem. In fact, if buyer i buys quantity q_{ij} from seller j at price p_{ij}, then the market value this transaction implements is the sum of buyer i utility plus seller j utility, which is $q_{ij}(b_i - s_j)$ independent of the trading price p_{ij}. However, it is clear that the trading price will affect each agents utility.

18.3 Particle swarm optimization

Particle Swarm Optimization (PSO) is a parallel population-based computation technique developed by Kennedy and Eberhart (1995). Their biological inspiration is based on the organisms behavior such as flocking of birds and schooling of fishes. In these groups the moviment of the whole swarm is based on his own knowledge and on a leader, the one with the best performance. From this, one can learn that PSO shares many common points with genetic algorithm, in fact, they start with a randomly generated population, evaluate the population with a fitness function, update the population, search for the optimum with random techniques and do not guarantee optimality. PSO's major difference from genetic algorithm is that PSO uses the physical movements of the individuals in the swarm as a flexible mechanism to combine global search and local search avoiding local optima, whereas genetic algorithm uses genetic operators like mutation and crossover. Each individual of the swarm has a position in the solution hyperspace and a velocity, that is changed, at each step, to update individual position. Each particle knows its position and the value of the fitness function for that position. Besides each particle keeps track of its coordinates in the problem space, which are associated with the best fitness value it has achieved so far. Every particle knows also the best position among all of the particles and its fitness value. The update of the particle position is the result of a compromise among three alternatives: following its current pattern of exploration; going back towards its best previous position; going towards the overall best position. The updating processes are accomplished according to the following equations:

$$x_{ij}(k+1) = x_{ij}(k) + v_{ij}(k) \tag{18.5}$$

$$v_{ij}(k) = F \cdot [w \cdot v_{ij}(k-1) + v_{ijlocbest}(k-1) + v_{ijglobest}(k-1)] \tag{18.6}$$

$$v_{ijlocbest}(k) = c_1 \cdot r \cdot (x_{ijlocbest}(k) - x_{ij}(k)) \tag{18.7}$$

$$v_{ijglobest}(k) = c_2 \cdot r \cdot (x_{ijglobest}(k) - x_{ij}(k)). \qquad (18.8)$$

At each step, equation (6) calculates a new velocity for each particle in the swarm based on its velocity at previous step, the best position it has been achieved (locbest) and the best position (globest) the population has been achieved. Then, using the resultant velocity value the position of each particle is updated by equation (5). About the coefficients in equation (6), F is a constrictor factor to insure convergence, the use of an inertia weight w provides to improve performance in a number of applications, while the (0,1)-random constants r and the coefficients c_1 and c_2 represent the weighting of the stochastic acceleration terms that pull each particle towards xlocbest and xglobest locations. The PSO algorithm is stopped when the best particle position of the entire swarm cannot be improved further after a sufficiently large number of iterations. PSO algorithms were proposed, in many research fields, to solve continuous optimization problems. Now, it is very interesting the possibility to solve discrete optimization problems. We do this adopting the quantum discrete algorithm (Yang et al., 2004). The basic idea is that, in quantum theory, the minimum unit carrying information is a bit, that can be in any superposition of state 0 and 1. let R the swarm size and S the particle's length, we define the following quantum particle vector $V = [V_1, V_2, ..., V_R]$ with $V_i = [v_{i1}, v_{i2}, ..., v_{iS}]$ with $0 \leq v_{ij} \leq 1$ to represent the probability of the bit j of the particle i to be 0. Denoting with $X = [X_1, X_2, ..., X_R]$ with $X_i = [x_{i1}, x_{i2}, ..., x_{iS}]$ where $x_{ij} = \{0, 1\}$ a position vector associated with V, to update the position we made use of the following rule 1:

"for each v generate a random number ρ in $[0,1]$ and a sigmoid(v) using equation (12), then if $\rho < sigmoid(v)$ then $x = 1$ else $x = 0$".

The equations for updating processes are modified as follows:

$$v_{ij}(k+1) = w \cdot v_{ij}(k) + c_1 \cdot v_{ijlocbest(k)} + c_2 \cdot v_{ijglobest(k)} \qquad (18.9)$$

$$v_{ijglobest}(k) = \alpha \cdot x_{ijglobest}(k) + \beta \cdot (1 - x_{ijglobest}(k)) \qquad (18.10)$$

$$v_{ijlocbest}(k) = \alpha \cdot x_{ijlocbest}(k) + \beta \cdot (1 - x_{ijlocbest}(k)) \qquad (18.11)$$

$$sigmoid(v_{ij}) = (1 + exp(-v_{ij}))^{-1} \qquad (18.12)$$

where $\alpha + \beta = 1, 0 < \alpha, \beta < 1, 0 < w, c_1, c_2 \leq 2$.

18.4 Binary particle swarm optimization for double auction market

To maximize the collective utility using a Binary PSO algorithm (BPSO), we solved the following quadratic programming problem:

$$\max \sum_{i=1}^{m} \sum_{j=1}^{n} q_{ij} x_{ij} (b_i - s_j) \tag{18.13}$$

Where

$$\sum_{i=1}^{m} q_{ij} x_{ij} \leq Y_j \ \forall \, j \tag{18.14}$$

$$\sum_{j=1}^{n} q_{ij} x_{ij} \leq Z_i \ \forall \, i \tag{18.15}$$

with

$$x_{ij} = \{0, 1\}, \ and \ \ q_{ij} \geq 0 \text{ for every } i, j. \tag{18.16}$$

In the objective function we have two sets of variables x_{ij} and q_{ij}. We introduced a binary variable x_{ij} that is equal to 1 if there is a transaction between buyer i and seller j independently by the number of units, q_{ij}, each agent should purchase/sell. Then we can solve our problem as an assignment problem. It is possible summarize the algorithm as follows:

1. Random initialization of the particles (candidate solutions);
2. Evaluation of their fitness using equation (13);
3. Updating of particles velocity and position using equations (9)-(12) and rule 1 until a maximal number of iterations.

18.5 Results

Validation of an analytical method through a series of experiments demonstrates that the method is suitable for its intended purpose. The algorithm was implemented on a Pentium Centrino Duo in Matlab 6.5. To realize a robust algorithm, it was very important to obtain proper values for the control parameters according to problem characteristics. To do this, the algorithm was run from random initial solutions under many different parameter settings. After many experiments, the parameters were set as in table 1.

Table 18.1. control parameters for BPSO algorithm

parameter	value
α	0.7
β	0.3
w	1
c_1	2
c_2	2
F	0.729

Problems of different size were solved to test the efficiency of the proposed algorithm and to evaluate its performance. Each instance was run 20 times from different initial solutions. Our result (average of 20 running) is displayed in Fig.1 and proves as, after about 20 iterations, the process reaches stability. Then we proposed the information entropy for measuring the similarity convergence among the particle vectors. We calculated the conditional probability that value 1 happens at the bit j given the total number of bits that take value 1 in the entire swarm as follows:

$$prob_j = \frac{\sum_{i=1}^{R} x_{ij}}{\sum_{i=1}^{R} \sum_{h=1}^{S} x_{ih}}. \tag{18.17}$$

Then the particle vector entropy can be defined as:

$$E = - \sum_{j=1}^{S} (prob_j \cdot log_2(prob_j)). \tag{18.18}$$

If the particle vectors are highly similar to one another, the values of those non-zero $prob_j$ would be high, resulting in less entropy value. Fig.2 depicts the particle vector entropy versus the number of iterations. This is to testify that the swarm evolves to the same optimization goal and the best solution is not obtained by chance due to a lucky particle. Obviously, this is because each particle can adjust its direction and velocity depending on the results of its neighbors. The results are quite promising and show that the algorithm is applicable to nonlinear problems.

18.6 Conclusions

In this paper we introduce PSO mechanism into double auction market with discriminatory bids and asks. The algorithm doesn't need complex

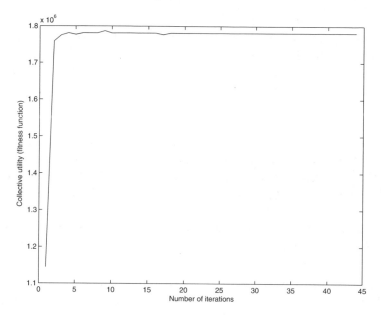

Fig. 18.1. Convergence graph for a 25 x 35 buyers-sellers problem

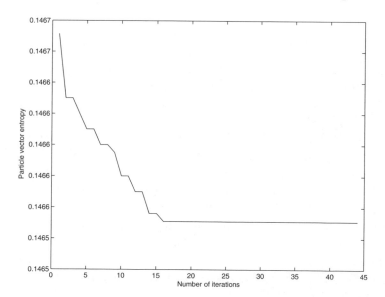

Fig. 18.2. The particle vector entropy versus the number of iterations

encoding and decoding processes and also for this is efficient in running time. Many problems are left for future research. In particular, it's necessary further theoretical analysis for getting a better BPSO convergency and to investigate how uncertainty in transactions can influence the solution's stability. The presented example are merely illustrative. However, the modeling results seem to be very promising for analysis and planning especially in markets that use fixing procedures. Future work can be extended to self-adaptive algorithms for dynamic environments. Moreover, PSO method can be defined as a evolutionary technique and it encourages studies about social interaction among peoples. Some features applications of PSO could focus the own attention on a study concerning special methodologies for prey-predator problems or for finding the best path to reach a target in robotic field (DiGesù et al., 2006).

Acknowledgement. This paper has been partially supported by *60%* project and *PI2S2* project by *COMETA Consortium*. Moreover special thanks have to be given to reviewers for the useful comments.

References

R. Das, J. Hanson, J. Kephart, and G. Tesauro. Agent-human interactions in the continuous double auction. In *Proceedings of the 7th International Joint Conference on Artificial Intelligence*, pages 1169–1176, 2001.

V. DiGesù, B. Lenzitti, G. Lo Bosco, and Tegolo D. Comparison of different cooperation strategies in the prey-predator problem. In *Proceedings of IEEE International Workshop on Computer Architecture for Machine Perception and Sensing*, pages 105–111, 2006.

D. Fudenberg and J. Tirole. *Game Theory*. The MIT Press, 1991.

S. Gjerstad and J. Dickhaut. Price formation in double auctions. *Games and Economic Behavior*, 22(1):1–29, 1998.

J. Kennedy and R. Eberhart. Particle swarm optimization. In *Proceeding of the 1995 IEEE International Conference on Neural Network*, pages 1942–1948, 1995.

R. McAfee. A dominant strategy double auction. *Journal of Economic Theory*, 56(2):434–450, 1992.

T. Sandholm and S. Suri. Market clearability. In *Proceedings of the 7th International Joint Conference on Artificial Intelligence*, pages 1145–1151, 2001.

M. Satterthwaite and S. Williams. The rate of convergence to efficiency in the buyer bid double auction as the market becomes large. *The Review of Economic Studies*, 56(4):477–498, 1989.

S.W. Yang, M. Wang, and L.C. Jiao. A quantum particle swarm optimization. In *Proceeding of the 2004 IEEE Congress on Evolutionary Computation*, pages 320–324, 2004.

Better-Reply Strategies with Bounded Recall

Andriy Zapechelnyuk

Center for Rationality, the Hebrew University, Israel
andriy@vms.huji.ac.il

19.1 Introduction

In every (discrete) period of time a decision maker (for short, an *agent*) makes a decision and, simultaneously, Nature selects a state of the world. The agent receives a payoff which depends on both his action and the state. Nature's behavior is ex-ante unknown to the agent, it may be as simple as an i.i.d. environment or as sophisticated as a strategic play of a rational player. The agent's objective is to select a sequence of decisions which guarantees to him the long-run average payoff as large as the best-reply payoff against Nature's empirical distribution of play, *no matter what Nature does*. A behavior rule of the agent which fulfills this objective is called *universally consistent*[1]: the rule is "consistent" if it is optimized against the empirical play of Nature; the word " universally" refers to its applicability to *any* behavior of Nature.

A range of problems can be described within this framework. One example, known as the *on-line decision problem*, deals with predicting a sequence of states of Nature, where at every period t the agent makes a prediction based on information known before t. The classical problem of predicting the sequence of 0's and 1's with " few" mistakes has been a subject of study in statistics, computer science and game theory for more than 40 years. In a more general problem, an agent's goal is to predict a sequence of states of Nature at least as well as the best expert from a given pool of experts[2](see Cesa-Bianchi et al., 1997; Freund and Schapire, 1996; Littlestone and Warmuth, 1994; Vovk, 1998). Another

---

[1] The term "universal consistency" is due to Fudenberg and Levine (1995).

[2] By an " expert" we understand a given deterministic on-line prediction algorithm. Thus, " to do as well as the best expert" means to make predictions, on average, as close to the true sequence of states as the best of the given prediction algoritms.

example is *no-regret learning* in game-theory. A regret [3] of an agent for action a is his average gain had he played constant action a instead of his actual past play; the agent's goal is to play a sequence of actions so that he has "no regrets" (e.g., Cesa-Bianchi and Lugosi, 2003; Foster and Vohra, 1999; Fudenberg and Levine, 1995; Hannan, 1957; Hart and Mas-Colell, 2000, 2001).

Action a is called a *better reply* to Nature's empirical play if the agent could have improved upon his average past play had he played action a instead of what he actually played in the past. In this paper, we assume that in every period the agent plays a *better reply* to Nature's past play. The better-reply play is a natural adaptive behavior of an unsophisticated, myopic, non-Bayesian decision maker. The class of better-reply strategies encompasses a big variety of behavior rules, such as fictitious play and smooth fictitious play.[4] Hart and Mas-Colell (2000)'s "no-regret" strategy of playing an action with probability proportional to the regret for that action; the logistic (or exponential-weighted) algorithms used in both game theory and computer science (see Cesa-Bianchi et al., 1997; Freund and Schapire, 1996; Littlestone and Warmuth, 1994; Vovk, 1998); the polynomial (l_p-norm) "no-regret" strategies and potential-based strategies of Hart and Mas-Colell (2001) (see also Cesa-Bianchi and Lugosi, 2003).

The agent is said to have m-recall if he is capable of remembering the play of m last periods, and the empirical frequency of Nature's play to which the agent " better-replies" is the simple average across the time interval not exceeding the last m periods. A special case of agent with perfect recall ($m = \infty$) is well studied in the literature, and universally consistent better-reply strategies of an agent with perfect recall are well known (see Cesa-Bianchi and Lugosi, 2003; Foster and Vohra, 1999; Hannan, 1957; Hart and Mas-Colell, 2000, 2001).

The question that we pose in this paper is whether there are better-reply strategies for an agent with *bounded recall* ($m < \infty$) which are (nearly) universally consistent if the agent has sufficiently large length of recall. We show that an agent with long enough recall can approach the best reply to any i.i.d. environment. However, by a simple example we demonstrate that an agent cannot optimize his average play against general (non-i.i.d.) environment, no matter how long (yet, bounded)

---

[3] This paper deals with the simplest notion of regret known as *external* (or *unconditional*) regret (see, e.g., Foster and Vohra, 1999).

[4] In the original (Fudenberg and Levine, 1995)'s definition, the smooth fictitious play is *not* a better-reply strategy; however, certain versions of it, such as the l_p-norm strategy with large p and the exponential-adjustment strategy with small η, are better-reply strategies.

recall he has and no matter what better-reply strategy he employs. Formally, we say that a family of better-reply strategies with bounded recall is *asymptotically universally consistent* if for every $\varepsilon > 0$ and every sufficiently large $m = m(\varepsilon)$ an agent with recall length m has an ε-universally consistent strategy in this family. We prove the following statement.

> *There is no family of bounded-recall better-reply strategies which is asymptotically universally consistent.*

The statement is proven by a counterexample. We construct a game where if Nature plays a certain form of the fictitious play, then, regardless of what better-reply strategy the agent uses, for every agent's recall length m the limit play forms a cycle. The average payoff of the agent along the cycle is bounded away from the best-reply payoff by a uniform bound for all m. Intuitively, the reason for a cyclical behavior is that in every period t the agent's learns a new observation, a pair (a_t, ω_t), and forgets another observation, (a_{t-m}, ω_{t-m}). An addition of the new observation shifts, in expectation, the agent's average payoff (across the last m periods) in a " better" direction, however, the loss of (a_{t-m}, ω_{t-m}) shifts it in an arbitrary direction. Since the magnitude of the two effects is the same, $1/m$, it may lead to a cyclical behavior of the play. Note that with unbounded recall, $m = \infty$, the second effect does not exist, i.e., the agent does not forget anything, and, consequently, a cyclical behavior is not possible.

A closely related work of Lehrer and Solan (2003) assumes bounded recall of agents and studies a certain form of a better-reply behavior. Lehrer and Solan describe an ε-universally consistent strategy, where the agent periodically " wipes out" his memory. Comparison of this work with our results brought into our paper an interesting insight that "better memory multiplies regrets": an agent can achieve a better average payoff by not using, or deliberately forgetting some information about the past (see Section 19.6 for further discussion).

19.2 Preliminaries

In every discrete period of time $t = 1, 2, \ldots$ a decision maker (or an *agent*) chooses an action, a_t, from a finite set A of actions, and Nature chooses a state, ω_t, from a finite set Ω of states. Let $u : A \times \Omega \to \mathbb{R}$ be the agent's payoff function; $u(a_t, \omega_t)$ is the agent's payoff at period t. Denote by $h_t := ((a_1, \omega_1), \ldots, (a_t, \omega_t))$ the history of play up to t. Let

$H_t = (A \times \Omega)^t$ be the set of histories of length t and let $H = \bigcup_{t=1}^{\infty} H_t$ be the set of all histories.

Let $p : H \to \Delta(A)$ and $q : H \to \Delta(\Omega)$ be behavior rules of the agent and Nature, respectively. For every period t, we will denote by $p_{t+1} := p(h_t)$ the next-period mixed action of the agent and by $q_{t+1} := q(h_t)$ the next-period distribution of states of Nature. A pair (p, q) and an initial history h_{t_0} induce a probability measure over H_t for all $t > t_0$.

We assume that the agent does not know q, that is, he plays against an unknown environment. We consider better-reply behavior rules, according to which the agent plays actions which are " better" than his actual past play against the observed empirical behavior of Nature. Formally, for every $a \in A$ and every period t define $R_t^m(a) \in \mathbb{R}_+$ as the average gain of the agent had he played a over the last m periods instead of his actual past play. Namely, let[5]

$$R_t^m(a) = \left[\frac{1}{m} \sum_{k=t-m+1}^{t} (u(a, \omega_k) - u(a_k, \omega_k))\right]^+ \quad \text{for all } t \geq m$$

and

$$R_t^m(a) = \left[\frac{1}{t} \sum_{k=1}^{t} (u(a, \omega_k) - u(a_k, \omega_k))\right]^+ \quad \text{for all } t < m.$$

We will refer to $R_t^m(a)$ as the agent's *regret for action a*.

The parameter $m \in \{1, 2, \ldots\} \cup \{\infty\}$ is the agent's length of recall. An agent with a specified m is said to have *m-recall*. We shall distinguish the cases of *perfect recall* $(m = \infty)$ and *bounded recall* $(m < \infty)$.

Consider an agent with m-recall. Action a is called a better reply to Nature's empirical play if the agent could have improved upon his average past play had he played action a instead of what he actually played in the last m periods.

Definition 1. *Action $a \in A$ is a* better-reply action *if $R_t^m(a) > 0$.*

A behavior rule is called a better-reply rule if the agent plays only better-reply actions, as long as there are such.

Definition 2. *Behavior rule p is a* better-reply rule *if for every period t, whenever $\max_{a \in A} R_t^m(a) > 0$,*

$$R_t^m(a) = 0 \quad \Rightarrow \quad p_{t+1}(a) = 0, \quad a \in A.$$

---

[5] We write $[x]^+$ for the positive part of a scalar x, i.e., $[x]^+ = \max\{0, x\}$.

The focus of our study is how well better-reply rules perform against an unknown, possibly, hostile environment. To assess performance of a behavior rule, we use Fudenberg and Levine (1995)'s criterion of ε-universal consistency defined below.

An agent's behavior rule p is said to be *consistent with q* if the agent's long-run average payoff is at least as large as the best-reply payoff to the average empirical play of Nature which plays q.

Definition 3. *Let $\varepsilon > 0$. A behavior rule p of the agent with m-recall is ε-consistent with q if for every initial history h_{t_0} there exists T such that for every[6] $t \geq T$*

$$\Pr_{(p,q,h_{t_0})} \left[\max_{a \in A} R_t^\infty(a) < \varepsilon \right] > 1 - \varepsilon.$$

A behavior rule p is consistent with q *if it is ε-consistent with q for every $\varepsilon > 0$.*

Let $\mathcal{Q}$ be the class of all behavior rules. An agent's behavior rule p is said to be *universally consistent* if it is consistent with *any* behavior of Nature.

Definition 4. *A behavior rule p of the agent with m-recall is (ε-) universally consistent if it is (ε-) consistent with q for every $q \in \mathcal{Q}$.*

19.3 Perfect recall and prior results

Suppose that the agent has perfect recall ($m = \infty$). This case has been extensively studied in the literature, starting from Hannan (1957), who proved the following theorem.[7]

Theorem 19.3.1 (Hannan, 1957) *There exists a better-reply rule which is universally consistent.*

Hart and Mas-Colell (2000) showed that the following rule is universally consistent:

$$p_{t+1}(a) := \begin{cases} \dfrac{R_t^\infty(a)}{\sum_{a' \in A} R_t^\infty(a')}, & \text{if } \sum_{a' \in A} R_t^\infty(a') > 0, \\ \text{arbitrary}, & \text{otherwise.} \end{cases} \tag{19.1}$$

---

[6] $\Pr_{(p,q,h)}[E]$ denotes the probability of event E induced by strategies p and q, and initial history h.

[7] The statements of theorems of Hannan (1957); Hart and Mas-Colell (2000) presented in this section are sufficient for this paper, though the authors obtained stronger results.

According to this rule, the agent assigns probability on action a proportional to his regret for a; if there are no regrets, his play is arbitrary. This result is based on Blackwell (1956)'s Approachability Theorem. We shall refer to p in (19.1) as the *Blackwell strategy*.

The above result has been extended by Hart and Mas-Colell (2001) as follows. A behavior rule p is called a *(stationary) regret-based rule* if for every period t the agent's next-period behavior depends only on the current regret vector. That is, for every history h_t, the next-period mixed action of the agent is a function of $R_t^\infty = (R_t^\infty(a))_{a \in A}$ only: $p_{t+1} = \sigma(R_t^\infty)$. Hart and Mas-Colell proved that among better-reply rules, all " well-behaved" stationary regret-based rules are universally consistent.

Theorem 19.3.2 (Hart and Mas-Colell, 2001) *Suppose that a better-reply rule p satisfies the following:*

(i) p is a stationary regret-based rule given for every t by $p_{t+1} = \sigma(R_t^\infty)$; and

(ii) There exists a continuously differential potential $P : \mathbb{R}_+^{|A|} \to \mathbb{R}_+$ such that $\sigma(x)$ is positively proportional to $\nabla P(x)$ for every $x \in \mathbb{R}_+^{|A|}$, $x \neq 0$.

Then p is universally consistent.

The class of universally consistent behavior rules (or " no regret" strategies) which satisfy conditions of Theorem 19.3.2 includes the logistic (or exponential adjustment) strategy given for every t and every $a \in A$ by

$$p_{t+1}(a) = \frac{\exp(\eta R_t^m(a))}{\sum_{b \in A} \exp(\eta R_t^m(b))},$$

$\eta > 0$, used by Cesa-Bianchi et al. (1997); Freund and Schapire (1996); Littlestone and Warmuth (1994); Vovk (1998) and others; the smooth fictitious play[8]; the polynomial (l_p-norm) strategies and other strategies based on a separable potential (Cesa-Bianchi and Lugosi, 2003; Hart and Mas-Colell, 2001).

19.4 Bounded recall and i.i.d. environment

The previous section shows that the universal consistency can be achieved for agents with perfect recall. Considering the perfect recall

---

[8] See footnote 4.

as the limit of m-recall as $m \to \infty$, one may wonder whether the universal consistency can be approached by bounded-recall agents with sufficiently large m.

We start with a result that establishes existence of better-reply rules which are consistent with any i.i.d. environment. Nature's behavior rule q is called an i.i.d. rule if $q_t = q_{t'}$ for all t, t', independently of the history. Let $\mathcal{Q}_{i.i.d.} \subset \mathcal{Q}$ be the set of all i.i.d. behavior rules. An agent's behavior rule p is said to be *i.i.d. consistent* if it is consistent with any i.i.d. behavior of Nature.

Definition 5. *A behavior rule p of the agent with m-recall is (ε-) i.i.d. consistent if it is (ε-) consistent with q for every $q \in \mathcal{Q}_{i.i.d.}$.*

Denote by $\mathcal{P}^m$ the class of all better-reply rules for an agent with m-recall, $m \in \mathbb{N}$. Consider an indexed family of better-reply rules $\mathbf{p} = (p^1, p^2, \ldots)$, where $p^m \in \mathcal{P}^m$, $m \in \mathbb{N}$.

Definition 6. *A family $\mathbf{p}$ is asymptotically i.i.d consistent if for every $\varepsilon > 0$ there exists m such that for every $m' \geq m$ rule $p^{m'}$ is ε-i.i.d. consistent.*

Theorem 19.4.1 *There exists a family $\mathbf{p}$ of better-reply rules which is asymptotically i.i.d. consistent.*

Proof Let $q^* \in \Delta(\Omega)$ and suppose that $q_t = q^*$ for all t. Denote by $\bar{q}_t^m$ the empirical distribution of Nature's play over the last m periods,

$$\bar{q}_t^m(\omega) = \frac{1}{m} |k \in \{t - m + 1, \ldots, t\} : \omega_k = \omega|, \quad \omega \in \Omega.$$

Suppose that the agent plays the fictitious play with m-recall. Namely, the agent's next-period play, p_{t+1}^m, assigns probability 1 on an action in $\arg\max_{a \in A} u(a, \bar{q}_t^m)$, ties are resolved arbitrarily. Thus, the agent plays in every period a best reply to the average realization of m i.i.d. random variables with mean q^*. Since $\max_{a \in A} u(a, x)$ is continuous in x for $x \in \Delta(\Omega)$, the Law of Large Numbers implies that in every period the agent obtains an expected payoff which is ε_m-close to the best reply payoff to q^* with probability at least $1 - \varepsilon_m$, with $\varepsilon_m \to 0$ as $m \to \infty$.
$\square$

19.5 A negative result

In this section we demonstrate that an agent with bounded recall cannot guarantee his play to be ε-optimized against the empirical play of

Nature, no matter how large recall length he has and no matter what better-reply rule he uses.

Definition 7. *Family* $\mathbf{p} = (p^1, p^2, \ldots)$ *of better-reply rules is asymptotically universally consistent if for every* $\varepsilon > 0$ *there exists* m *such that for every* $m' \geq m$ *rule* $p^{m'}$ *is* ε-*universally consistent.*

Theorem 19.5.1 *There is no family of better-reply rules which is asymptotically universally consistent.*

The theorem is proven by a counterexample.

$$
\begin{array}{c|ccc}
 & \text{L} & \text{M} & \text{R} \\
\hline
\text{U} & 1{,}0 & 0{,}1 & 0{,}\tfrac{3}{4} \\
\text{D} & 0{,}1 & 1{,}0 & 0{,}\tfrac{3}{4}
\end{array}
$$

Fig. 19.1.

Consider a repeated game Γ with the stage game given by Fig. 19.1, where the row player is the agent and the column player is Nature. For every m denote by p^m and q^m be the behavior rules of the agent and Nature, respectively. We shall show that for every $m_0 \in N$ there exists $m \geq m_0$ such that the following holds.

Suppose that the agent with recall length m *and Nature play game* Γ. *Then for every agent's better-reply rule* p^m *there exist behavior rule* q^m *of Nature, initial history* h_{t_0} *and period* T *such that for all* $t \geq T$

$$
\Pr{}_{(p^m, q^m, h_{t_0})} \left[\max_{a \in \{U, D\}} R_t^\infty(a) \geq \frac{1}{32} \right] \geq \frac{1}{32}.
$$

Let $M = \{4j + 2 \mid j = 2, 3, \ldots\}$. For every $m \in M$, let p^m be an arbitrary better-reply rule, and let q^m be the fictitious play with m-recall. Namely, denote by u_N the payoff function of Nature as given by Fig. 19.1, and denote by $\bar{p}_t$ the empirical distribution of the agent's play over the last m periods,

$$
\bar{p}_t(a) = \frac{1}{m} |k \in \{t - m + 1, \ldots, t\} : a_k = a|, \quad a \in A.
$$

Then q_{t+1}^m assigns probability 1 to a state in $\arg\max_{\omega \in \{L, M, R\}} u_N(\bar{p}_t, \omega)$ (ties are resolved arbitrarily). Let P^m be the Markov chain with state space $H^m := (A \times \Omega)^m$ induced by p^m and q^m and an initial state h_{t_0}. A history of the last m periods, $h_t^m \in H^m$ will be called, for short, *history at* t. Denote by $H_C^m \subset H^m$ the set of states generated along the

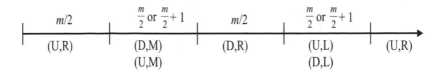

Fig. 19.2. Closed cycle of Markov chain P^m.

following cycle (Fig. 19.2). The cycle has four phases. In two phases labeled (U,R) and (D,R), the play is deterministic, and the duration of each phase is exactly $m/2$ periods. In the two other phases, the play may randomize between two profiles (one written above the other), and the duration of each phase is $m/2$ or $m/2 + 1$ periods. First, we show that this cycle is closed in P^m, i.e., $h_t^m \in H_C^m$ implies $h_{t'}^m \in H_C^m$ for every $t' > t$.

Lemma 19.5.2 *For every $m \in M$, the set H_C^m is closed in P^m.*

The proof is in the Appendix.

Next, we show that the average regrets generated by this cycle are bounded away from zero by a uniform bound for all m.

Lemma 19.5.3 *For every $m \in M$, if $h_{t_0} \in H_C^m$, then there exists period T such that for all $t \geq T$*

$$\Pr_{(p^m, q^m, h_{t_0})} \left[\max_{a \in \{U, D\}} R_t^\infty(a) \geq \frac{1}{32} \right] \geq \frac{1}{32}.$$

The proof is in the Appendix. Lemmata 19.5.2 and 19.5.3 entail the statement of Theorem 19.5.1.

Remark 1 In the proof of Theorem 19.5.1, Nature plays the fictitious play with m-recall, which is a better-reply strategy for every m. Consequently, an agent with bounded recall cannot guarantee a nearly optimized behavior even if Nature's behavior is constrained to be in the class of better-reply strategies.

Remark 2 The result can be strengthened as follows. Suppose that whenever an agent has no regrets, then he plays a fully mixed action, i.e.,

$$\max_{a' \in A} R_t^m(a') = 0 \implies p_{t+1}^m(a) > 0 \quad \text{for all } a \in A. \tag{19.2}$$

The next lemma shows that if in game Γ the agent plays a better-reply strategy p^m which satisfies (19.2) and Nature plays the fictitious play with m-recall, then the Markov chain P^m converges to the cycle H_C^m *regardless of an initial history*. Thus the above negative result is not an isolated phenomenon, it is not peculiar to a small set of initial histories.

Lemma 19.5.4 *For every $m \in M$, if p^m satisfies (19.2), then for every initial history h_{t_0} the process P^m converges to H_C^m with probability 1.*

The proof is in the Appendix.

To see that the statement of Lemma 19.5.4 does not hold if p^m fails to satisfy (19.2), consider again game Γ with the agent playing a better-reply strategy p^m and Nature playing the fictitious play with m-recall, q^m. In addition, suppose that whenever $\max_{a' \in A} R_t^m(a') = 0$, $p_{t+1}^m(U) = 1$ if t is odd and 0 if t is even. Let t be even and let h_t consist of alternating (UR) and (DR). Clearly, $R_t^m(U) = R_t^m(D) = 0$, and Nature's best reply is R, thus, $q_{t+1}(R) = 1$. The following play is deterministic, alternating between (UR) and (DR) forever.

19.6 Concluding remarks

We conclude the paper with a few remarks.

1. Why does the better-reply play of an agent with bounded recall fail to exhibit a (nearly) optimized behavior (against Nature's empirical play)?

For every $a \in A$ denote by $v_t(a)$ the one-period regret for action a,

$$v_t(a) = u(a, \omega_t) - u(a_t, \omega_t),$$

and let $v_t = (v_t(a))_{a \in A}$. Since $R_{t-1}^m = \frac{1}{m} \sum_{k=t-m}^{t-1} v_k$, we can consider how the regret vector changes from period $t-1$ to period t:

$$R_t^m = R_{t-1}^m + \frac{1}{m} v_t - \frac{1}{m} v_{t-m}.$$

Since the play at period t is a better reply to the empirical play over time interval $t-m, \ldots, t-1$, the term $\frac{1}{m} v_t(a)$ shifts the regret vector, in expectation, towards zero, however, the term $-\frac{1}{m} v_{t-m}$ shifts the regret vector in an arbitrary direction. A carefully constructed example, as in Section 19.5, causes the regret vector to display a cyclical behavior.

2. The following model was introduced by Lehrer and Solan (2003). Suppose that the agent has bounded recall m. Divide the time into blocks of size m: the first block contains periods $1, \ldots, m$, the second

block contains periods $m + 1, \ldots, 2m$, etc. Let $n(t)$ be the first period of the current block,[9] $n(t) = m\lceil t/m \rceil + 1$. The agent's regret for action $a \in A$ is defined by

$$\hat{R}_t^m(a) = \frac{1}{t - n(t) + 1} \sum_{\tau=n(t)}^{t} \left(u(a, \omega_\tau) - u(a_\tau, \omega_\tau) \right). \qquad (19.3)$$

That is, $\hat{R}_t^m(a)$ is the agent's average increase in payoff had he played a constantly instead of his actual past play *within* in the current block. Let p^* be the Blackwell strategy (19.1) with better replies computed relative to (19.3). Clearly, this strategy can be implemented by the agent with m-recall. However, the agent behaves as if he remembers only the history of the current block, and at the beginning of a new block he " wipes out" the content of his memory. Notice that the induced probability distribution over histories within every block is identical between blocks and equal to the probability distribution over histories within first m periods in the model with a perfect-recall agent. The Blackwell (1956)'s Approachability Theorem (which is behind the result of Hart and Mas-Colell (2000) on the universal consistency of p^*) gives the rate of convergence of $1/\sqrt{t}$, hence, within each block the agent can approach $1/\sqrt{m}$-best reply to the empirical distribution of Nature's play.

This result is a surprising contrast to the counterexample in Section 19.5. It shows that *an agent can achieve better average payoff by not using, or deliberately forgetting some information about the past.* Indeed, according to the example presented in Section 19.5, if the agent uses full information that he remembers, the play may eventually enter the cycle with far-from-optimal behavior, no matter with what initial history he starts.

3. Hart and Mas-Colell (2001) used a slightly different notion of better reply. Consider an agent with perfect recall and define for every period t and every $a \in A$

$$D_t^m(a) = \frac{1}{t} \sum_{k=1}^{t} \left(u(a, \omega_k) - u(a_k, \omega_k) \right).$$

Note that $R_t^m(a) = [D_t^m(a)]^+$. Action a is a *strict* better reply (to the empirical distribution of Nature's play) if $D_t^m(a) > 0$ and it is a *weak* better reply if $D_t^m(a) \geq 0$. According to Hart and Mas-Colell, behavior rule p is a better-reply rule if whenever there exist actions which are weak better replies, only such actions are played; formally, whenever $\max_{a \in A} D_t^m(a) \geq 0$,

---

[9] $\lceil x \rceil$ denotes a number x rounded up to the nearest integer.

$$D_t^m(a) < 0 \quad \Rightarrow \quad p_{t+1}(a) = 0, \quad a \in A.$$

The definition of a better-reply rule used in this paper is the same as Hart and Mas-Colell's, except that the word " weak" is replaced by " strict"; formally, whenever $\max_{a \in A} D_t^m(a) > 0$,

$$D_t^m(a) \le 0 \quad \Rightarrow \quad p_{t+1}(a) = 0, \quad a \in A.$$

These notions are very close, and one does not imply the other. To the best of our knowledge, all specific better-reply rules mentioned in the literature satisfy both notions of better reply. It can be verified that our results remain intact with either notion.

Appendix

A-1 Proof of Lemma 19.5.2.

Let $k = \frac{m-2}{4}$. Denote by z_t the empirical distribution of play, that is, for every $(a, \omega) \in A \times \Omega$, $z_t(a, \omega)$ is the frequency of (a, ω) in the history at t,

$$z_t(a, \omega) := \frac{1}{m} |\{\tau \in \{t - m + 1, \ldots, t\} : (a_\tau, \omega_\tau) = (a, \omega)\}|.$$

Let ζ_t be is the frequency of play of U in the last m periods, $\zeta_t = z_t(\text{U,L}) + z_t(\text{U,M}) + z_t(\text{U,R})$.

Fact 1. For every period t,

$$\omega_{t+1} = \begin{cases} \text{L, if } \zeta_t < \frac{1}{4}, \\ \text{M, if } \zeta_t > \frac{3}{4}, \\ \text{R, if } \frac{1}{4} < \zeta_t < \frac{3}{4}. \end{cases}$$

Proof. Note that

$$u_N(\bar{p}_t, \text{L}) = z_t(\text{D,L}) + z_t(\text{D,M}) + z_t(\text{D,R}) = 1 - \zeta_t,$$
$$u_N(\bar{p}_t, \text{M}) = z_t(\text{U,L}) + z_t(\text{U,M}) + z_t(\text{U,R}) = \zeta_t,$$
$$u_N(\bar{p}_t, \text{R}) = \frac{3}{4}.$$

Since Nature plays fictitious play, at $t + 1$ it selects

$$\omega_{t+1} \in \arg\max_{\omega \in \{\text{L,M,R}\}} u_N(\bar{p}_t, \omega).$$

Note that ties never occur, since $m \in M$ and ζ_t is a multiple of $\frac{1}{m}$, thus $\zeta_t \ne \frac{1}{4}$ or $\frac{3}{4}$. $\square$ **Fact 2.** Suppose that $h_t^m \in H_C^m$ such that t is

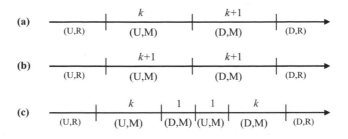

Fig. 19.3. Three forms of the (U,M)/(D,M) phase.

the last period of the (D,R) phase, and suppose that the (U,M)/(D,M) phase preceding the (D,R) phase has form (a), (b) or (c), as shown in Fig. 19.3. Then the play for the next $m/2$, $m/2 + 1$, or $m/2 + 2$ periods constitute the full cycle as shown in Fig. 19.2, where phases (D,L)/(U,L) and (U,M)/(D,M) have forms[10] (a), (b) or (c).

Proof. Suppose that h_t^m contains $m/2$ (D,R)'s, preceded by the (U,M)/(D,M) phase in form (a), (b), or (c). We shall show that the play in the next $m/2$ or $m/2 + 1$ periods constitute phase (D,L)/(U,L) in form (a), (b) or (c), followed by $m/2$ (U,R)'s. Once this is established, by considering the last period of phase (U,R) and repeating the arguments, we obtain Fact 2.

Case 1. Phase (U,M)/(D,M) preceding phase (D,R) has form (a) or (b). Note that whether the (U,M)/(D,M) phase has form (a) or (b), h_t^m is the same, since it contains only $2k + 1 \equiv m/2$ last periods of the (U,M)/(D,M) phase. Let t be the last period of the (D,R) phase. We have $\zeta_t = \frac{k}{m} < \frac{1}{4}$, thus by Fact 1, $\omega_{t+1} =$ L. Also,

$$R_t(U) = z_t(D,L) - z_t(D,M) = -z_t(D,M) = -\frac{k+1}{m},$$

$$R_t(D) = z_t(U,M) - z_t(U,L) = z_t(U,M) = \frac{k}{m},$$

hence $a_{t+1} =$ D. Further, in every period $t+j$, $j = 1, \ldots, k$, $(a_{t+j}, \omega_{t+j}) =$ (D,L) is played and $(a_{t+j-m}, \omega_{t+j-m}) =$ (U,M) disappears from the history. At period $t + k$ we have

---

[10] The forms of the (D,L)/(U,L) phase are symmetric to those of (U,M)/(D,M), obtained by replacement of (U,M) by (D,L) and (D,M) by (U,L).

$$R_{t+k}(U) = z_{t+k}(D,L) - z_{t+k}(D,M) = \frac{k}{m} - \frac{k+1}{m} = -\frac{1}{m},$$
$$R_{t+k}(D) = z_{t+k}(U,M) - z_{t+k}(U,L) = 0 - 0 = 0.$$

There are no regrets, and therefore both (U,L) and (D,L) may occur at $t+k+1$. Suppose that (D,L) occurs. Since $(a_{t+k-m}, \omega_{t+k-m}) = $ (D,M), it will disappear from the history at $t+k+1$, so, we have

$$R_{t+k+1}(U) = \frac{k+1}{m} - \frac{k}{m} = \frac{1}{m},$$
$$R_{t+k+1}(D) = 0 - 0 = 0,$$

and (U,L) occurs in periods $k+2, \ldots, 2k+2$, until we reach $\zeta_{t+2k+2} = \frac{k+1}{m} > 1/4$. Thus, the phase (D,L)/(U,L) has $k+1$ (D,L)'s, then $k+1$ (U,L)'s, i.e., it takes form (b). If instead at $t+k+1$ action profile (U,L) occurs, then

$$R_{t+k+1}(U) = \frac{k}{m} - \frac{k}{m} = 0,$$
$$R_{t+k+1}(D) = 0 - \frac{1}{m} = -\frac{1}{m},$$

and, again, there are no regrets and both (U,L) and (D,L) may occur at $t+1$. If (U,L) occurs, then

$$R_{t+k+2}(U) = \frac{k}{m} - \frac{k-1}{m} = \frac{1}{m},$$
$$R_{t+k+1}(D) = 0 - \frac{2}{m} = -\frac{2}{m},$$

and (U,L) occurs in periods $k+3, \ldots, 2k+1$, until we reach $\zeta_{t+2k+1} = \frac{k+1}{m} > 1/4$. Thus, the phase (D,L)/(U,L) has k (D,L)'s, then $k+1$ (U,L)'s, i.e., it takes form (a). Finally, if at $t+k+2$ (D,L) occurs, then

$$R_{t+k+1}(U) = \frac{k+1}{m} - \frac{k-1}{m} = \frac{2}{m},$$
$$R_{t+k+1}(D) = 0 - \frac{1}{m} = -\frac{1}{m},$$

and (U,L) occurs in periods $k+3, \ldots, 2k+2$, until we reach $\zeta_{t+2k+2} = \frac{k+1}{m} > 1/4$. Thus, the phase (D,L)/(U,L) has k (D,L)'s, then single (U,L), then single (D,L), and then k (U,L)'s, i.e., it takes form (c).

Case 2. Phase (U,M)/(D,M) preceding phase (D,R) has form (c). Then, similarly to Case 1, we have $\zeta_t = \frac{k}{m} < \frac{1}{4}$, and (D,L) is deterministically played $k+1$ times, until

$$R_{t+k+1}(U) = z_{t+k+1}(D,L) - z_{t+k+1}(D,M) = \frac{k+1}{m} - \frac{k}{m} = \frac{1}{m},$$
$$R_{t+k+1}(D) = z_{t+k+1}(U,M) - z_{t+k+1}(U,L) = 0 - 0 = 0.$$

After that, (U,L) is played in periods $k+2,\ldots,2k+2$, until we reach $\zeta_{t+2k+2} = \frac{k+1}{m} > 1/4$. Thus, the phase (D,L)/(U,L) has $k+1$ (D,L)'s and then $k+1$ (U,L)'s, i.e., it takes form (b).

Let $t_1 = t + 2k + 1$ if the phase (D,L)/(U,L) had form (a) and $t_1 = t + 2k + 2$ if (b) or (c). Notice that at the end of the phase (D,L)/(U,L) we have $z_{t_1}(U,M) = z_{t_1}(D,M) = 0$, hence

$$R_{t_1}(U) = z_{t_1}(D,L) - z_{t_1}(D,M) > 0,$$
$$R_{t_1}(D) = z_{t_1}(U,M) - z_{t_1}(U,L) < 0,$$

Thus, (U,R) is played for the next $m/2 = 2k+1$ periods, until we reach $\zeta_{t_1+m/2} = \frac{3k+2}{m} > 3/4$, and phase (U,M)/(D,M) begins. $\square$

A-2 Proof of Lemma 19.5.3.

By Lemma 19.5.2, $h_{t_0} \in H_C^m$ implies $h_t^m \in H_C^m$ for all $t > t_0$. Let $h_t^m \in H_C^m$ such that t is the period at the end of the (D,R) phase. Since the history at t contains only (U,M)/(D,M) and (D,R) phases, we have $z_t(D,L) = z_t(U,L) = 0$. Also, since at the end of the (D,R) phase the number of U in the history is $\frac{m+2}{4}$, it implies that $z_t(U,M) = \frac{1}{4} + \frac{1}{2m}$. Therefore,

$$R_t(D) = z_t(U,M) - z_t(U,L) = z_t(U,M) = \frac{1}{4} + \frac{1}{2m} \equiv C$$

For every period τ, $|R_\tau(D) - R_{\tau+1}(D)| \leq \frac{2}{m}$, therefore, in periods $t-j$ and $t+j$ the regret for D must be at least $R_t(D) - 2j/m$. Since the duration of every cycle is at most $2m+2$, the average regret for D during the cycle is at least

$$\frac{1}{2m+2}\left(C + 2\left[\left(C - \frac{2}{m}\right) + \left(C - \frac{4}{m}\right) + \ldots + \right.\right.$$
$$\left.\left. + \left(C - \frac{2(m/4 - 2)}{m}\right)\right]\right) \geq \frac{1}{2m}\left(\frac{m}{2}C - \frac{2}{m}\frac{m^2 - 4}{32}\right) \geq \frac{1}{32}.$$

Let γ^m be the limit frequency of periods where at least one of the regrets exceeds ε,

$$\gamma^m = \lim_{t\to\infty} \frac{1}{t}\left|\tau \in \{1,\ldots,t\} : \max_{a\in\{U,D\}} R_\tau^m(a) \geq \varepsilon\right|.$$

Clearly, $\gamma^m > \varepsilon$ implies that for all large enough t

$$\Pr_{(p^m, q^m, h_{t_0})} \left[\max_{a \in \{\mathrm{U,D}\}} R_t^\infty(a) \geq \varepsilon \right] \geq \varepsilon.$$

Combining (19.4) with the fact that γ^m is at least as large as the average regret for D during the cycle, we obtain $\gamma^m \geq 1/32$. $\square$

A-3 Proof of Lemma 19.5.4.

We shall prove that, regardless of the initial history, some event $H_E^m \subset H^m$ occurs infinitely often, and whenever it occurs, the process reaches the cycle, H_C^m, within at most $2m$ periods with strictly positive probability. It follows that the process reaches the cycle with probability 1 from any initial history.

Fact 3. Regardless of an initial state, L and M occur infinitely often.

Proof. Suppose that M never occurs from some time on. Then at any t

$$R_t(\mathrm{U}) = z_t(\mathrm{D,L}) - z_t(\mathrm{D,M}) = z_t(\mathrm{D,L}) \geq 0,$$
$$R_t(\mathrm{D}) = z_t(\mathrm{U,M}) - z_t(\mathrm{U,L}) = -z_t(\mathrm{U,L}) \leq 0.$$

Case 1. $z_t(\mathrm{D,L}) > 0$. Suppose that L occurred last time at $t - j$, $0 \leq j \leq m - 1$. After that U must be played with probability 1 in every period $j' = t - j + 1, \ldots$, until frequency of U increases above $\frac{3}{4}$ and, by Fact 1, Nature begins playing M. Contradiction.

Case 2. $z_t(\mathrm{D,L}) = 0$, That is, the agent has no regrets, his play is defined arbitrarily. By assumption (19.2), $p_{t+1}^m(\mathrm{U}) > 0$, and thus there is a positive probability that U occurs sufficiently many times that the frequency of U increases above $\frac{3}{4}$ and M is played. Contradiction.

The proof that L occurs infinitely often is analogous. $\square$

Fact 4. If $\omega_t = \mathrm{L}$ and $\omega_{t+j} = \mathrm{M}$, then $j > \frac{m}{2}$. Symmetrically, if $\omega_t = \mathrm{M}$ and $\omega_{t+j} = \mathrm{L}$, then $j > \frac{m}{2}$.

Proof. Suppose that $\omega_t = \mathrm{L}$, then by Fact 1, $\zeta_{t-1} < \frac{1}{4}$. Clearly, it requires $j > \frac{m}{2}$ periods to reach ζ_{t+j-1} greater than $\frac{3}{4}$, which is required to have $\omega_{t+j} = \mathrm{M}$. The second part of the fact is proved analogously. $\square$

Fact 5. Regardless of an initial state, the event $\{\omega_t = \mathrm{L}$ and there are no more L in $h_t^m\}$ occurs infinitely often.

Proof. By Fact 3, both L and M occur infinitely often. By Fact 4, the minimal interval of occurrence of L and M is $\frac{m}{2}$, hence if L occurs first time after M, previous occurrence of L is at least $m + 1$ periods ago. $\square$

Fact 6. Suppose that $\omega_t = \mathrm{L}$ and there are no more L in the history. Then after $j < m$ periods we obtain $\frac{1}{4} < \zeta_{t+j} < \frac{1}{4} + \frac{1}{m}$, and with strictly positive probability $R_{t+j}(\mathrm{U}) > 0$ and $R_{t+j}(\mathrm{D}) \leq 0$.

Proof. We have

$$R_t(\text{U}) = z_t(\text{D,L}) - z_t(\text{D,M}),$$
$$R_t(\text{D}) = z_t(\text{U,M}) - z_t(\text{U,L}).$$

By Fact 1, $\omega_t =$ L implies $\zeta_{t-1} < \frac{1}{4}$, that is, U occurs at most k times in the history at $t-1$, thus $z_t(\text{U,M}) \leq z_{t-1}(\text{U,M}) \leq \frac{k}{m}$.

Case 1. $R_t(\text{D}) > 0$ and $R_t(\text{U}) > 0$ Then both (D,L) and (U,L) may be played. Since history at $t-1$ does not contain L, regardless of what disappears from the history, we have $R_t(\text{U})$ nondecreasing and $R_t(\text{D})$ nonincreasing. Thus, with positive probability, both (D,L) and (U,L) are played for j periods, until we obtain $\frac{1}{4} < \zeta_{t+j} < \frac{1}{4} + \frac{1}{m}$, $R_{t+j}(\text{U}) > 0$ and $R_{t+j}(\text{D}) \leq 0$. Note that $j < \frac{3}{4}m + 1$, since by Fact 4 the interval between the last occurrence of M and the first occurrence of L is at least $m/2$, thus after period $t + m/2$ there are no M in the history, $R_{t+m/2}(\text{U}) > 0$, $R_{t+m/2}(\text{D}) < 0$, and (U,L) is played at most $k + 1 = \frac{m+2}{4}$ times until the frequency of U becomes above $1/4$.

Case 2. $R_t(\text{D}) > 0$, $R_t(\text{U}) \leq 0$. Then (D,L) is played for the next $j' = (z_t(\text{D,L}) - z_t(\text{D,M})) \cdot m + 1$ periods. At period $t + j'$ we have $R_{t+j'}(\text{D}) > 0$ and $R_{t+j'}(\text{U}) > 0$, and proceed similarly to Case 1.

Case 3. $R_t(\text{D}) \leq 0$, $R_t(\text{U}) \leq 0$. That is, the agent has no regrets, his play is defined arbitrarily. By assumption, $p_{t+1}(\text{D}) > 0$, hence there is a positive probability that (D,L) occurs for $j' = z_t(\text{D,M}) \cdot m$ periods which will yield $R_{t+j'}(\text{U}) > 0$, Case 2.

Case 4. $R_t(\text{D}) \leq 0$, $R_t(\text{U}) > 0$. Then (U,L) is played for $j = 1$ or 2 periods (depending whether $(a_t, \omega_t) = $ (D,L) or (U,L)), and we have $\frac{1}{4} < \zeta_{t+j} < \frac{1}{4} + \frac{1}{m}$, $R_{t+j}(\text{U}) = R_t(\text{U}) > 0$ and $R_{t+j}(\text{D}) < R_t(\text{D}) \leq 0$. $\square$

Using Fact 6, we can now analyze the dynamics of the process. Suppose that $\frac{1}{4} < \zeta_t < \frac{1}{4} + \frac{1}{m}$, $R_t(\text{U}) > 0$, $R_t(\text{D}) \leq 0$. Then

I. (U,R) is played in the next $j_{UR} \geq \frac{m}{2}$ periods, and we obtain $\frac{3}{4} < \zeta_{t+j_{UR}} < \frac{3}{4} + \frac{1}{m}$. Since by now M has disappeared from the history, the regrets are

$$R_{t+j_{UR}}(\text{U}) \geq z_t(\text{D,L}) > 0,$$
$$R_{t+j_{UR}}(\text{D}) \leq -z_t(\text{U,L}) \leq 0.$$

II. (U,M) is played for the next $j_{UM} = k+1$ periods. Since $j_{UR} + j_{UM} \geq \frac{m}{2} + k + 1 = 3k + 1$, it implies that $z_{t+j_{UR}+j_{UM}}(\text{U,L}) \leq k$, and

$$R_{t+j_{UR}+j_{UM}}(\text{D}) = z_{t+j_{UR}+j_{UM}}(\text{U,M}) - z_{t+j_{UR}+j_{UM}}(\text{U,L})$$
$$\geq \frac{k+1}{m} - \frac{k}{m} = \frac{1}{m} > 0.$$

III. With positive probability, (D,M) is played for the next $j_{DM} = k+1$ periods, and, since by now L is not in the history, we have

$$\zeta_{t+j_{UR}+j_{UM}+j_{DM}} = 1 - \frac{j_{DM}}{m} = \frac{3k+1}{m} < \frac{3}{4},$$

$$R_{t+j_{UR}+j_{UM}+j_{DM}}(\text{U}) = -z_{t+j_{UR}+j_{UM}+j_{DM}}(\text{D,M}) < 0,$$

$$R_{t+j_{UR}+j_{UM}+j_{DM}}(\text{D}) = z_{t+j_{UR}+j_{UM}+j_{DM}}(\text{U,M}) > 0.$$

Notice that at period $t+j_{UR}+j_{UM}+j_{DM}$ the last m periods correspond to phases (U,R) and (U,M)/(D,M) of the cycle (the latter is in form (b)). □

Acknowledgement. I thank Dean Foster, Sergiu Hart, Eilon Solan, Tymofiy Mylovanov, Peyton Young, and participants of the seminars at the Hebrew University and Tel Aviv University for helpful comments and suggestions. I gratefully acknowledge the financial support from Lady Davis and Golda Meir Fellowship Funds, the Hebrew University.

References

D. Blackwell. An analog of the minmax theorem for vector payoffs. *Pacific Journal of Mathematics*, 6:1–8, 1956.

N. Cesa-Bianchi and G. Lugosi. Potential-based algorithms in on-line prediction and game theory. *Machine Learning*, 51:239–261, 2003.

N. Cesa-Bianchi, Y. Freund, D. Helmbold, D. Haussler, R. Shapire, and M. Warmuth. How to use expert advice. *Journal of the ACM*, 44: 427–485, 1997.

Dean Foster and Rakesh Vohra. Regret in the online decision problem. *Games and Economic Behavior*, 29:7–35, 1999.

Yoav Freund and Robert Schapire. Game theory, on-line prediction and boosting. In *Proceedings of the Ninth Annual Conference on Computational Learning Theory*, pages 325–332, 1996.

Drew Fudenberg and David Levine. Universal consistency and cautious fictitious play. *Journal of Economic Dynamics and Control*, 19:1065–1089, 1995.

J Hannan. Approximation to Bayes risk in repeated play. In M. Dresher, A. W. Tucker, and P. Wolfe, editors, *Contributions to the Theory of Games, Vol. III*, Annals of Mathematics Studies 39, pages 97–139. Princeton University Press, 1957.

Sergiu Hart and Andreu Mas-Colell. A simple adaptive procedure leading to correlated equilibrium. *Econometrica*, 68:1127–1150, 2000.

Sergiu Hart and Andreu Mas-Colell. A general class of adaptive procedures. *Journal of Economic Theory*, 98:26–54, 2001.

Ehud Lehrer and Eilon Solan. No regret with bounded computational capacity. The Center for Mathematical Studies in Economics and Management Science, Northwestern University. Discussion Paper 1373, 2003.

N. Littlestone and M. Warmuth. The weighted majority algorithm. *Information and Computation*, 108:212–261, 1994.

V. Vovk. A game of prediction with expert advice. *Journal of Computer and System Sciences*, 56:153–173, 1998.

Lecture Notes in Economics and Mathematical Systems

For information about Vols. 1–512
please contact your bookseller or Springer-Verlag

Vol. 513: K. Marti, Stochastic Optimization Techniques. VIII, 364 pages. 2002.

Vol. 514: S. Wang, Y. Xia, Portfolio and Asset Pricing. XII, 200 pages. 2002.

Vol. 515: G. Heisig, Planning Stability in Material Requirements Planning System. XII, 264 pages. 2002.

Vol. 516: B. Schmid, Pricing Credit Linked Financial Instruments. X, 246 pages. 2002.

Vol. 517: H. I. Meinhardt, Cooperative Decision Making in Common Pool Situations. VIII, 205 pages. 2002.

Vol. 518: S. Napel, Bilateral Bargaining. VIII, 188 pages. 2002.

Vol. 519: A. Klose, G. Speranza, L. N. Van Wassenhove (Eds.), Quantitative Approaches to Distribution Logistics and Supply Chain Management. XIII, 421 pages. 2002.

Vol. 520: B. Glaser, Efficiency versus Sustainability in Dynamic Decision Making. IX, 252 pages. 2002.

Vol. 521: R. Cowan, N. Jonard (Eds.), Heterogenous Agents, Interactions and Economic Performance. XIV, 339 pages. 2003.

Vol. 522: C. Neff, Corporate Finance, Innovation, and Strategic Competition. IX, 218 pages. 2003.

Vol. 523: W.-B. Zhang, A Theory of Interregional Dynamics. XI, 231 pages. 2003.

Vol. 524: M. Frölich, Programme Evaluation and Treatment Choise. VIII, 191 pages. 2003.

Vol. 525: S. Spinler, Capacity Reservation for Capital-Intensive Technologies. XVI, 139 pages. 2003.

Vol. 526: C. F. Daganzo, A Theory of Supply Chains. VIII, 123 pages. 2003.

Vol. 527: C. E. Metz, Information Dissemination in Currency Crises. XI, 231 pages. 2003.

Vol. 528: R. Stolletz, Performance Analysis and Optimization of Inbound Call Centers. X, 219 pages. 2003.

Vol. 529: W. Krabs, S. W. Pickl, Analysis, Controllability and Optimization of Time-Discrete Systems and Dynamical Games. XII, 187 pages. 2003.

Vol. 530: R. Wapler, Unemployment, Market Structure and Growth. XXVII, 207 pages. 2003.

Vol. 531: M. Gallegati, A. Kirman, M. Marsili (Eds.), The Complex Dynamics of Economic Interaction. XV, 402 pages, 2004.

Vol. 532: K. Marti, Y. Ermoliev, G. Pflug (Eds.), Dynamic Stochastic Optimization. VIII, 336 pages. 2004.

Vol. 533: G. Dudek, Collaborative Planning in Supply Chains. X, 234 pages. 2004.

Vol. 534: M. Runkel, Environmental and Resource Policy for Consumer Durables. X, 197 pages. 2004.

Vol. 535: X. Gandibleux, M. Sevaux, K. Sörensen, V. T'kindt (Eds.), Metaheuristics for Multiobjective Optimisation. IX, 249 pages. 2004.

Vol. 536: R. Brüggemann, Model Reduction Methods for Vector Autoregressive Processes. X, 218 pages. 2004.

Vol. 537: A. Esser, Pricing in (In)Complete Markets. XI, 122 pages, 2004.

Vol. 538: S. Kokot, The Econometrics of Sequential Trade Models. XI, 193 pages. 2004.

Vol. 539: N. Hautsch, Modelling Irregularly Spaced Financial Data. XII, 291 pages. 2004.

Vol. 540: H. Kraft, Optimal Portfolios with Stochastic Interest Rates and Defaultable Assets. X, 173 pages. 2004.

Vol. 541: G.-y. Chen, X. Huang, X. Yang, Vector Optimization. X, 306 pages. 2005.

Vol. 542: J. Lingens, Union Wage Bargaining and Economic Growth. XIII, 199 pages. 2004.

Vol. 543: C. Benkert, Default Risk in Bond and Credit Derivatives Markets. IX, 135 pages. 2004.

Vol. 544: B. Fleischmann, A. Klose, Distribution Logistics. X, 284 pages. 2004.

Vol. 545: R. Hafner, Stochastic Implied Volatility. XI, 229 pages. 2004.

Vol. 546: D. Quadt, Lot-Sizing and Scheduling for Flexible Flow Lines. XVIII, 227 pages. 2004.

Vol. 547: M. Wildi, Signal Extraction. XI, 279 pages. 2005.

Vol. 548: D. Kuhn, Generalized Bounds for Convex Multistage Stochastic Programs. XI, 190 pages. 2005.

Vol. 549: G. N. Krieg, Kanban-Controlled Manufacturing Systems. IX, 236 pages. 2005.

Vol. 550: T. Lux, S. Reitz, E. Samanidou, Nonlinear Dynamics and Heterogeneous Interacting Agents. XIII, 327 pages. 2005.

Vol. 551: J. Leskow, M. Puchet Anyul, L. F. Punzo, New Tools of Economic Dynamics. XIX, 392 pages. 2005.

Vol. 552: C. Suerie, Time Continuity in Discrete Time Models. XVIII, 229 pages. 2005.

Vol. 553: B. Mönch, Strategic Trading in Illiquid Markets. XIII, 116 pages. 2005.

Vol. 554: R. Foellmi, Consumption Structure and Macro-economics. IX, 152 pages. 2005.

Vol. 555: J. Wenzelburger, Learning in Economic Systems with Expectations Feedback (planned) 2005.

Vol. 556: R. Branzei, D. Dimitrov, S. Tijs, Models in Cooperative Game Theory. VIII, 135 pages. 2005.

Vol. 557: S. Barbaro, Equity and Efficiency Considerations of Public Higer Education. XII, 128 pages. 2005.

Vol. 558: M. Faliva, M. G. Zoia, Topics in Dynamic Model Analysis. X, 144 pages. 2005.

Vol. 559: M. Schulmerich, Real Options Valuation. XVI, 357 pages. 2005.

Vol. 560: A. von Schemde, Index and Stability in Bimatrix Games. X, 151 pages. 2005.

Vol. 561: H. Bobzin, Principles of Network Economics. XX, 390 pages. 2006.

Vol. 562: T. Langenberg, Standardization and Expectations. IX, 132 pages. 2006.

Vol. 563: A. Seeger (Ed.), Recent Advances in Optimization. XI, 455 pages. 2006.

Vol. 564: P. Mathieu, B. Beaufils, O. Brandouy (Eds.), Artificial Economics. XIII, 237 pages. 2005.

Vol. 565: W. Lemke, Term Structure Modeling and Estimation in a State Space Framework. IX, 224 pages. 2006.

Vol. 566: M. Genser, A Structural Framework for the Pricing of Corporate Securities. XIX, 176 pages. 2006.

Vol. 567: A. Namatame, T. Kaizouji, Y. Aruga (Eds.), The Complex Networks of Economic Interactions. XI, 343 pages. 2006.

Vol. 568: M. Caliendo, Microeconometric Evaluation of Labour Market Policies. XVII, 258 pages. 2006.

Vol. 569: L. Neubecker, Strategic Competition in Oligopolies with Fluctuating Demand. IX, 233 pages. 2006.

Vol. 570: J. Woo, The Political Economy of Fiscal Policy. X, 169 pages. 2006.

Vol. 571: T. Herwig, Market-Conform Valuation of Options. VIII, 104 pages. 2006.

Vol. 572: M. F. Jäkel, Pensionomics. XII, 316 pages. 2006

Vol. 573: J. Emami Namini, International Trade and Multinational Activity. X, 159 pages, 2006.

Vol. 574: R. Kleber, Dynamic Inventory Management in Reverse Logistics. XII, 181 pages, 2006.

Vol. 575: R. Hellermann, Capacity Options for Revenue Management. XV, 199 pages, 2006.

Vol. 576: J. Zajac, Economics Dynamics, Information and Equilibnum. X, 284 pages, 2006.

Vol. 577: K. Rudolph, Bargaining Power Effects in Financial Contracting. XVIII, 330 pages, 2006.

Vol. 578: J. Kühn, Optimal Risk-Return Trade-Offs of Commercial Banks. IX, 149 pages, 2006.

Vol. 579: D. Sondermann, Introduction to Stochastic Calculus for Finance. X, 136 pages, 2006.

Vol. 580: S. Seifert, Posted Price Offers in Internet Auction Markets. IX, 186 pages, 2006.

Vol. 581: K. Marti; Y. Ermoliev; M. Makowsk; G. Pflug (Eds.), Coping with Uncertainty. XIII, 330 pages, 2006.

Vol. 582: J. Andritzky, Sovereign Default Risks Valuation: Implications of Debt Crises and Bond Restructurings. VIII, 251 pages, 2006.

Vol. 583: I.V. Konnov, D.T. Luc, A.M. Rubinov[†] (Eds.), Generalized Convexity and Related Topics. IX, 469 pages, 2006.

Vol. 584: C. Bruun, Adances in Artificial Economics: The Economy as a Complex Dynamic System. XVI, 296 pages, 2006.

Vol. 585: R. Pope, J. Leitner, U. Leopold-Wildburger, The Knowledge Ahead Approach to Risk. XVI, 218 pages, 2007 (planned).

Vol. 586: B.Lebreton, Strategic Closed-Loop Supply Chain Management. X, 150 pages, 2007 (planned).

Vol. 587: P. N. Baecker, Real Options and Intellectual Property: Capital Budgeting Under Imperfect Patent Protection. X, 276 pages , 2007.

Vol. 588: D. Grundel, R. Murphey, P. Panos , O. Prokopyev (Eds.), Cooperative Systems: Control and Optimization. IX, 401 pages , 2007.

Vol. 589: M. Schwind, Dynamic Pricing and Automated Resource Allocation for Information Services: Reinforcement Learning and Combinatorial Auctions. XII, 293 pages , 2007.

Vol. 590: S. H. Oda, Developments on Experimental Economics: New Approaches to Solving Real-World Problems. XVI, 262 pages, 2007.

Vol. 591: M. Lehmann-Waffenschmidt, Economic Evolution and Equilibrium: Bridging the Gap. VIII, 272 pages, 2007.

Vol. 592: A. C.-L. Chian, Complex Systems Approach to Economic Dynamics. X, 95 pages, 2007.

Vol. 593: J. Rubart, The Employment Effects of Technological Change: Heterogenous Labor, Wage Inequality and Unemployment. XII, 209 pages, 2007

Vol. 594: R. Hübner, Strategic Supply Chain Management in Process Industries: An Application to Specialty Chemicals Production Network Design. XII, 243 pages, 2007

Vol. 595: H. Gimpel, Preferences in Negotiations: The Attachment Effect. XIV, 268 pages, 2007

Vol. 596: M. Müller-Bungart, Revenue Management with Flexible Products: Models and Methods for the Broadcasting Industry. XXI, 297 pages, 2007

Vol. 597: C. Barz, Risk-Averse Capacity Control in Revenue Management. XIV, 163 pages, 2007

Vol. 598: A. Ule, Partner Choice and Cooperation in Networks: Theory and Experimental Evidence. Approx. 200 pages, 2007

Vol. 599: A. Consiglio, Artificial Markets Modeling: Methods and Applications. XV, 277 pages, 2007

Vol. 600: M. Hickman, P. Mirchandani, S. Voss (Eds.): Computer-Aided Scheduling of Public Transport. Approx. 424 pages, 2007

Vol. 601: D. Radulescu: CGE Models and Capital Income Tax Reforms: The Case of a Dual Income Tax for Germany. XVI, 168 pages, 2007

Vol. 602: N. Ehrentreich: Agent-Based Modeling: The Santa Fe Institute Artificial Stock Market Model Revisited. XVI, 225 pages, 2007

Teacher
Education
AND
Human
Rights

AUDREY OSLER
AND HUGH STARKEY

David Fulton Publishers
London
Published with the support of the Council of Europe

David Fulton Publishers Ltd
2 Barbon Close, London WC1N 3JX

First published in Great Britain by
David Fulton Publishers 1996

Note: The right of Audrey Osler and Hugh Starkey to be identified as the
authors of this work has been asserted by them in accordance with the
Copyright, Designs and Patents Act 1988.

British Library Cataloguing in Publication Data

A catalogue record for this book is available from the British Library

ISBN 1–85346–406–6

Typeset by The Harrington Consultancy, London
Printed in Great Britain by BPC Books & Journals Ltd., Exeter

Contents

Acknowledgements   iv

Preface   v

Part 1. Human rights, international agreements and shared values
1. Human rights as universal standards   1
2. Taking children's rights seriously: implementing the UN Convention on the Rights of the Child   16
3. The Council of Europe and human rights education   34

Part 2. Human rights education and political realities
4. Challenging racism, xenophobia and intolerance   48
5. Education for citizenship and democracy   69
6. Teachers' and student teachers' understandings of human rights, citizenship and identities   87

Part 3. Human rights and the curriculum
7. Curriculum development in teacher education   103
8. Human rights and the professional development of teachers   118
9. Human rights and the school curriculum   142
10. Looking to the future   158

Appendices
1. The United Nations Universal Declaration of Human Rights   173
2. Summary of UN Convention on the Rights of the Child   175
3. Recommendation R(85)7   181

Bibliography   184

Index   195

Acknowledgements

We wish to thank Judy Dandy for her assistance in preparing the manuscript.

The authors and publishers wish to thank the editors of *Educational Review* for their agreement to our use of material in Chapter 2 adapted from 'The UN Convention on the Rights of the Child: some implications for teacher education', by Audrey Osler, Vol. 46, No. 2 (1994). Thanks also to the editors of the *Journal of Moral Education* for their agreement to our use in Chapter 8 of material adapted from 'Fundamental Issues in Teacher Education for Human Rights: a European perspective', by Audrey Osler and Hugh Starkey, Vol. 23, No. 3 (1994).

The Austrian Ministry of Education's guidelines on pp.149–50 are also available in German from: Federal Ministry of Education and Cultural Affairs, Strozzigrasse 2/5, A–1080 Wien, Austria.

Figures and boxes

Figures
1.1 Cassin's model of the Universal Declaration   4
2.1 The Ladder of Participation   33
5.1 Human rights curriculum triangle   85

Boxes
2.1 UN Convention on the Rights of the Child   22
4.1 Equality for rural working women   63
5.1 Four components of citizenship   71
5.2 Components of citizenship education   75
5.3 A school equal opportunities statement   82
5.4 Democracy in schools   84
7.1 Joint module   112
8.1 CIFEDHOP programme   121
8.2 UK summer school 1994   132

Preface

This book addresses three important concerns. First, in the section entitled 'Human rights, international agreements and shared values', we argue that the concept of human rights, as used by the United Nations and the Council of Europe, underlies a basic set of universal ethical standards. We show how these principles can be applied both in teacher education and in schools. We draw on the experiences of teachers and student teachers to illustrate the significance of human rights as a framework of values and note that this can be particularly helpful in secular and multicultural societies. We note the changing status of children and the important advances introduced by the 1989 United Nations Convention on the Rights of the Child. We suggest that knowledge of this and other international human rights instruments should be an entitlement for teachers and for children, who are now also recognised as citizens.

In the second section, entitled 'Human rights education and political realities', we stress the importance of a knowledge of human rights for protecting and enhancing democracy. Societies based on the notion of the 'community of citizens' are likely to have a chance of providing peaceful conditions for living and creative opportunities to find fulfilment for all. Such inclusive societies are rare in reality, as attempts to create them are thwarted by global economic forces, which in recent decades have resulted in large-scale unemployment and accompanying social tensions. These tensions are a threat to the possibility of the good society and they often find expression in anti-democratic forces such as public and private manifestations of racism and xenophobia. Democratic societies depend on their citizens understanding and supporting democratic values, which in turn are based on human rights. For this reason human rights education is an important means of helping to protect individuals by creating a climate of opinion which rejects violence and unjust discrimination. Arguably, a sense of public security is more an outcome of a climate of civility than of policing and law enforcement.

Democracy, for its survival, must continually expand its scope and become more inclusive. A democratic society is based on pluralism and an acceptance of varied forms of cultural and religious expression. An inclusive society is one with which all members identify. We contend that education is the process of acquiring multiple identities. Human rights transcend national, ethnic, cultural and religious differences. Societies based on human rights are able to include and integrate individuals and groups. But all individuals and groups, to feel included, must recognise and acknowledge those common values that unite them. Human rights education is a necessity for a pluralistic society.

The third section of the book, 'Human rights and the curriculum', gives examples of projects and courses in schools and in teacher education. The application of human rights in schools and in teacher education concerns the curriculum, that is the content of what is formally offered to learners but also, and importantly, the ways in which institutions are organised. We examine ways in which schools can be developed as models of democratic pluralist societies. Courses for teachers can also be based on principles of human rights and democracy. We give examples of work in Britain, in the rest of Europe and of courses whose participants are drawn from countries across the world.

Audrey Osler and Hugh Starkey
September, 1996

Part 1. Human rights, international agreements and shared values

1   *Human rights as universal standards*

Introduction

In January 1996 the Chief Executive of the Schools Curriculum and Assessment Authority for England organised a conference to launch a debate on basic moral values at which he proposed the setting up of a forum to 'produce a statement of values, a code of morals – the sort of thing we think schools should be doing on behalf of society'. This proposal appears to acknowledge a lack of consensus about values education in England. The 1988 Education Act which initiated a national curriculum stresses the centrality of Christianity as a national characteristic. Yet European societies, including England, are manifestly both secular and multifaith. Christianity is but one ethical tradition amongst many. In this context it is perhaps not surprising that many question the primacy of a particular faith in schools and that this should lead to uncertainty about what constitutes public and agreed values. Which aspects of private beliefs should legitimately be respected in schools and which should be confined to the home or place of worship? National governments may make decisions and policies, including those on education, for ideological reasons. We recommend that a multifaith and multiethnic society needs a perspective on values that transcends party, national and ethnic traditions. We look to international institutions for guidance.

As teachers, we are constantly making judgements about pupils and their actions or inaction. In this process we are confronted with situations requiring us to make professional and sometimes moral choices. Children will assert their identity and their individuality in ways which may challenge our plans or the school's procedures. We have to decide whether to ignore certain behaviour or whether to intervene. Many of our decisions involve value judgements. How can we establish an appropriate response to insults to other pupils, imprecations against the school, boisterous or violent play or behaviour, absences, lateness, refusal to work or to work with others, or unusual dress? How can we respond to disruptive non-conformity?

A commonly accepted basis for moral and ethical decision-making required in our professional life provides psychological security, enabling us to operate confidently. We may seek assurance that decisions we make can be justified in the eyes of our colleagues and the community. It is, however, inappropriate in a multifaith or secular society to justify public decisions by reference to a particular religious tradition. We cannot rely on a consensus around a particular interpretation of traditional morality. The inhabitants of European states come from and are influenced by many nations and traditions. It is necessary to look to a supra-national level to find a commonly acceptable basis for agreed social values. At such a level, be it regional (Europe) or global (the United Nations and its agencies), we can find a multiplicity of carefully constructed agreed statements of value and principle. These statements have a unifying theme. They are all based on respect for human rights and fundamental freedoms. Since the concepts associated with human rights are founded on a concern for individual human dignity, in other words treating others as you would wish to be treated, the same principles can be applied to any human context or community. The school is one such community.

The origins of international commitments to human rights

The concept of human rights as currently formulated is a comparatively recent invention, dating from the 1940s. A concern for human rights was already part of the Enlightenment Project (Gray, 1995), with its origins in the eighteenth century. Several formulations associated with the declarations made at American independence (1776) and the French Revolution (1789) have passed directly into the codification of the United Nations Charter (1945) and the Universal Declaration of Human Rights (1948).

Whilst human rights have a distinguished ancestry, their twentieth-century formulation is new in that its scope is no longer national (America or France) but universal. The President of the United Nations General Assembly of December 1948 which proclaimed the Universal Declaration of Human Rights, Dr H. E. Evatt of Australia, observed that this was 'the first occasion on which the organised world community had recognised the existence of human rights and fundamental freedoms transcending the laws of sovereign states' (Laqueur and Rubin, 1979).

Human rights are the key part of an international project to promote and maintain world peace. Representatives of fifty-one countries meeting in San Francisco on 26 June 1945, just before the end of the Second World War, signed the United Nations Charter. The Charter begins with a manifesto:

> We the Peoples of the United Nations determined
> to save succeeding generations from the scourge of war, which twice in our lifetime has brought untold sorrow to mankind, and
> to reaffirm faith in fundamental human rights, in the dignity and worth of the human person, in the equal rights of men and women and of nations large and small, and
> to establish conditions under which justice and respect for the obligations arising from treaties and other sources of international law can be maintained, and
> to promote social progress and better standards of life in larger freedom ...

Although the signatory states proclaim their faith in fundamental human rights, these rights were not defined in the Charter itself. It took another three years for a team, including notably René Cassin from France and Eleanor Roosevelt from the USA, to draft the Universal Declaration of Human Rights (UDHR) which was adopted by the General Assembly of the United Nations at its meeting in Paris on 10 December 1948. The Declaration, the founder text of modern human rights, defines in its thirty articles those rights and fundamental freedoms that are the inherent birthright of all human beings.

The first paragraph of the preamble is an encapsulation of the sentiments expressed in the UN Charter above, namely that:

> Recognition of the inherent dignity and of the equal and inalienable rights of all members of the human family is the foundation of freedom, justice and peace in the world.

Human rights principles are those based on a recognition of the equal entitlement of all human beings to respect for their essential dignity and, further, an equal entitlement to all those rights recognised by the international community as human rights.

There are many ways of conceptualising and ordering the articles of the Universal Declaration, but that proposed by René Cassin himself (see Figure 1.1) has the merit of a mnemonic. Cassin sees the Declaration as resembling a classical Greek portico (Féron, 1987: 86–7), such as that used in the logo of UNESCO. The foundations are the preamble and the first article:

> All human beings are born free and equal in dignity and rights. They are endowed with reason and conscience and should act towards one another in a spirit of brotherhood.

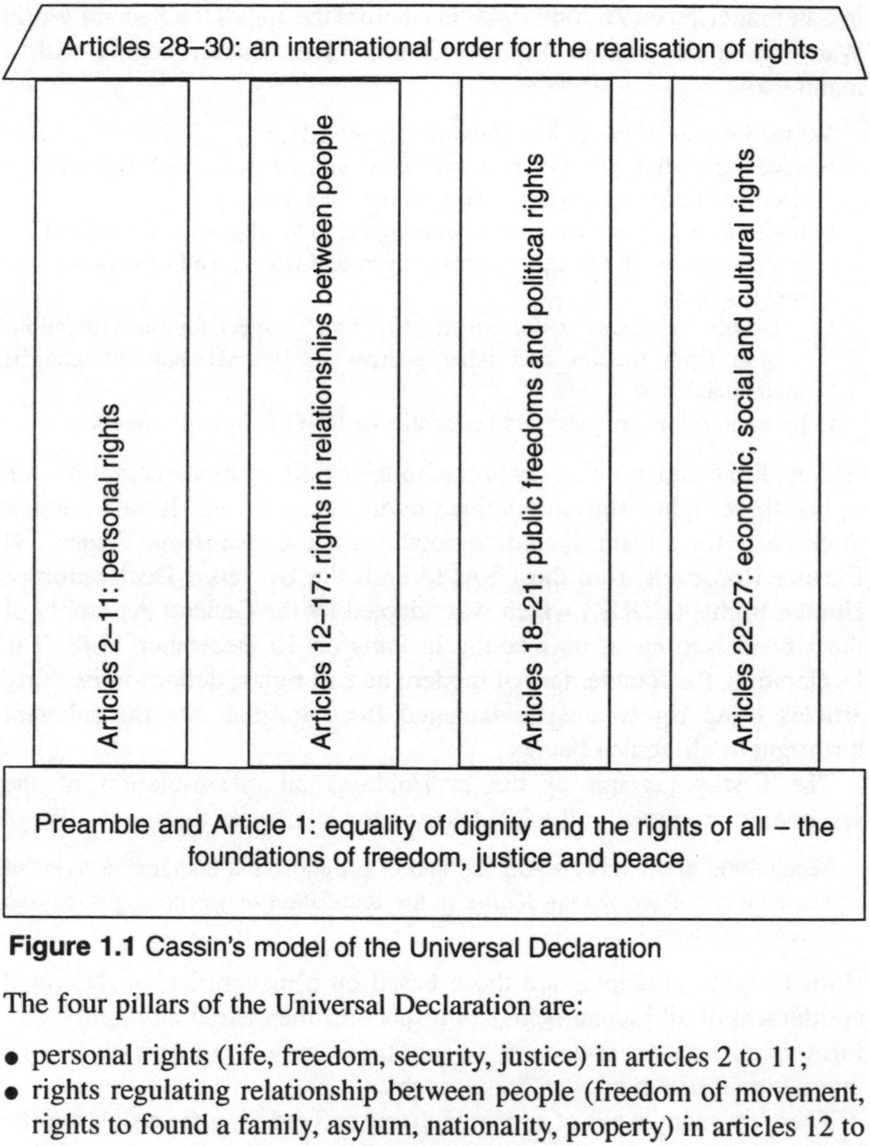

4

Articles 28–30: an international order for the realisation of rights

Articles 2–11: personal rights

Articles 12–17: rights in relationships between people

Articles 18–21: public freedoms and political rights

Articles 22–27: economic, social and cultural rights

Preamble and Article 1: equality of dignity and the rights of all – the foundations of freedom, justice and peace

Figure 1.1 Cassin's model of the Universal Declaration

The four pillars of the Universal Declaration are:

- personal rights (life, freedom, security, justice) in articles 2 to 11;
- rights regulating relationship between people (freedom of movement, rights to found a family, asylum, nationality, property) in articles 12 to 17;
- public freedoms and political rights (thought, religion, conscience, opinion, assembly, participation, democracy) in articles 18 to 21;
- economic, social and cultural rights (social security, work, equal wages, trade unions, rest and leisure, adequate standard of living, education, cultural life) in articles 22 to 27.

To cap the edifice (articles 28–30) there is the pediment of an international order essential for the realisation of rights and the understanding that rights imply duties to the community and freedoms do not extend to those actions which jeopardise the rights of others. The full text of the Universal Declaration is included as Appendix 1.

European commitment to human rights

The principles of the Universal Declaration are also enshrined in the European Convention for the Protection of Human Rights and Fundamental Freedoms, which, since it came into force in 1953, has protected all those living in the democratic countries of Europe. The member states of the Council of Europe, ten of them at its founding in May 1949, now around forty, commit themselves to respect human rights and fundamental freedoms. This commitment is more than just a form of words. It carries obligations. Individuals who feel that their rights have not been respected can appeal to the Court of Human Rights in Strasbourg. Many governments of European states have been obliged to change their laws or their procedures and in some cases offer compensation as a result of decisions of the Court.

The shared principles of European citizenship are enumerated in many official documents signed by heads of state and government or their ministers. The principles have not changed over recent years. In the preamble to the European Convention for the Protection of Human Rights and Fundamental Freedoms member states of the Council of Europe agree to secure the agreed rights and freedoms:

> Considering the Universal Declaration of Human Rights proclaimed by the General Assembly of the United Nations on 10 December 1948;

> Considering that this Declaration aims at securing the universal and effective recognition and observance of the Rights therein declared;

> Considering that the aim of the Council of Europe is the achievement of greater unity between its Members and that one of the methods by which that aim is to be pursued is the maintenance and further realisation of Human Rights and Fundamental Freedoms;

> Reaffirming their profound belief in those Fundamental Freedoms which are the foundation of justice and peace in the world and are best maintained on the one hand by an effective political democracy and on the other by a common understanding and observance of the Human Rights upon which they depend...

Unity, it is believed, can be achieved if states respect human rights and fundamental freedoms. This voluntary but formal commitment is expressed by becoming a full member of the Council of Europe.

The crucial role of educators in promoting this world of justice and peace is also underlined. If the various communities within Europe are to have a 'common understanding' of human rights, this implies that it should be an essential and fundamental component of education. Unfortunately, it would appear that relatively few people, even well-informed people such as teachers, are familiar with the basic texts on which our future is supposed to be founded. The Council of Europe has, with the co-operation of its member states, promoted a very significant programme of education for human rights, which is discussed in Chapter 3.

The other major European organisation, the European Union, formerly the European (Economic) Community, is based on the same principles as the Council of Europe. The Copenhagen Summit of December 1973 produced a document on European identity. The members are:

> determined to defend the principles of representative democracy, of the rule of law, of social justice – which is the ultimate goal of economic progress – and of respect for human rights. All of these are fundamental elements of the European identity. (Duparc, 1993: 30)

The Treaty of European Union (Maastricht Treaty) of 1992, which attempted to define the future direction and shape of the European Union, similarly begins with a preamble which spells out the basic aims of European unity. The heads of state confirm 'their commitment to the principles of freedom, democracy, respect for human rights and fundamental freedoms and the rule of law'.

The universality of commitments to human rights

Europe is part of the world community, whose main institution is the United Nations. The fundamental principles of Europe are not just European, but universal. Human rights are, in this sense, internationally validated moral standards, universally accepted in principle in international discourse and in international law (Palley, 1991: 13), even if they are not always enacted or observed by governments and their agents. The universal status of human rights is also accepted by all major religious groups, even though there are many examples of behaviour apparently justified by religion which clearly contravene the spirit and often the letter of human rights obligations. In fact as Ray (1994: 18) points out, the lists of rights and obligations that were referred to by the United Nations Human Rights Commission in drawing up the Universal Declaration came from religions, secular philosophical movements

(Confucianism, Communism, secular humanism), and legal traditions. At the time of independence, India, a multiethnic and multifaith nation, adopted in 1949 a constitution which, as Ghosh and Attieh (1987: 40) point out, 'was based on the belief that democracy cannot be established unless certain rights are assured to all citizens'. Its preamble reflects the spirit of article 1 of the Universal Declaration that 'All human beings are born free and equal in dignity and rights.' This challenges the conservatism of the traditional Hindu society based on caste, in order to create a new Indian nation in which Hindu religious values still find expression, but where there is room for other faiths and social change is possible. Duties and rights are embedded in Hindu thought, and interpretations of religious understanding can evolve when confronted with economic, political and social changes.

It is the case that some governments and political movements have argued against human rights. Any far-right movement based on a racist or xenophobic ideology clearly does not accept the fundamental equality of dignity and rights of all human beings. The commitment to human rights and democracy by nations is, however, a commitment to prevent such movements and parties coming to power.

Other arguments put forward by governments apparently critical of human rights are often, as Halliday (1995) points out, in fact endorsements of the universality of human rights. The criticism is not of human rights, but of dual standards. States may use human rights rhetoric but tacitly condone abuses when it suits their foreign policy to do so. The speech made at the UN in 1993 by Iran's foreign minister, Ali Akbar Velayati, and quoted by Halliday, illustrates both the attack on the hypocrisy of human rights being used for political advantage and the declared commitment of a government of the Islamic world to universal human rights:

> Based on the supreme teachings of Islam, the Islamic Republic of Iran considers respect for human rights and the lofty character of mankind in all material and spiritual dimensions as a fundamental duty for all governments. According to this belief, the Islamic Republic of Iran, without paying attention to any propaganda hue and cry, will continue its efforts to strengthen the principles which guarantee support for the rights of all citizens ... As the majority of the countries of the world stressed in the course of the [Vienna 1993] international conference on human rights, the only way to lend real support to human rights and promote such principles throughout the world is to end the practices of having double standards and exploiting human rights issues for political objectives. (Halliday, 1995: 145–6.)

It is clear from this speech that the rhetoric of human rights is an essential element of international discourse. The acknowledgement of the importance of human rights standards, even if governments do not fully implement them, makes international negotiations and agreements possible. The reference to the Vienna World Conference on Human Rights in the Iranian statement is significant. On 25 June 1993 the delegates of 171 states, representing 99 per cent of the world's population, adopted unanimously the Vienna Declaration, which in its first article reaffirms the universality of human rights:

> The World Conference on Human Rights reaffirms the solemn commitment of all States to fulfil their obligations to promote universal respect for, and observance and protection of, all human rights and fundamental freedoms for all in accordance with the Charter of the United Nations, other instruments relating to human rights, and international law. The universal nature of these rights and freedoms is beyond question.

One criticism of the notion of the universality of human rights is the argument based on cultural relativism and the contention that different societies are entitled to continue 'traditional' practices even if these offend human rights norms. Exploitation of child labour and mutilation as a judicial punishment have been justified on these grounds. The quotation above demonstrates that the international community of states meeting in formal assembly rejects such claims. The argument is well put by Halliday:

> Even if it can be proved that some particular practice or value or legal prescription is indeed 'traditional' in the sense of having been upheld for a long period of time in a particular community, this need not necessarily entail that it is beyond reform, criticism or outright rejection. ... Equally such invocations of tradition are open to a critique on the basis of history, in that they deny what all studies of 'tradition' contemporarily received show, namely that traditions are themselves modern creations – selections, instrumental reproductions, often inventions concealing contemporary purposes behind the invocation of a time-honoured, and incontestable, continuity. (1995: 239)

Indeed, as Cassese points out, Islamic countries have taken great pains to stress their commitment to equality between men and women in the two Islamic Declarations of Human Rights of 1981 and 1986.

> It is almost as if, despite the awareness of the gap between what is and what ought to be, there was a desire to restate faith in an important international value, as being applicable at 'regional' level. (1990: 66)

China has been criticised for its record on human rights, but, as with Iran, any expression of sensitivity on this issue is likely to reflect a feeling that the criticism is serving a political purpose. The states which indulge in such criticism may themselves be offenders against human rights. Zhou Nan-Zhao (1994), presumably reflecting an official perspective, points out that China is committed in principle to human rights and that the situation is evolving rapidly.

Zhou points out that the Chinese 'tradition' emphasised the collective at the expense of individual rights. As Galtung (1994:10) observes, when the state guarantees total rights in principle it demands total duties in return. 'The total provider is entitled to total commitment.' Since the 1940s the People's Republic of China has held together its multiethnic population by a strong state apparatus based on an official ideology, namely Communism. Individual rights have been suppressed in the name of duties to the state and to the ruling party. However, fifty years on, according to Zhou, the evolution of world society is forcing a re-appraisal, similar to that of India at independence:

> Along with a reassessment of cultural traditions and Western values, a more balanced understanding has been reached by the young generation and the citizenry of the dialectic interrelations of collective and individual rights ... Rights are a historical concept that evolves along with societal changes. (1994: 86)

That acceptance by China both of universality and historical evolution is symbolic of a world consensus which in 1993 was expressed by the UN Secretary-General, Boutros Boutros-Ghali, as follows:

> Let us deal first with the imperative of universality. To be sure, human rights are a product of history. As such they evolve in accordance with history, should evolve simultaneously with history and should give the various peoples and nations a reflection of themselves they recognise as their own. Yet, the fact that human rights keep pace with history should not change what constitutes their very essence, namely their universality! (UNHCR, 1994: 7)

Globalisation and the need for a global ethic

Globalisation is the term used to describe the increasing interdependence of national economies, the integration of financial markets, the increasing power, influence and scale of transnational corporations and media and communications that cover the whole world. A further dimension is provided by the environmental movement. This has raised consciousness of threats to the global commons and the necessity for international co-operation. Globalisation brings with it requirements for regulation, explored in the report of the Commission on Global Governance (1995).

However, simultaneously and possibly as a reaction to globalisation, there is within many societies and states an assertion of specificity. Religious, ethnic and cultural groups vigorously promote their particular claims to differentiate themselves from others and reject the process of homogenisation of world culture. Ismail Serageldin of the World Bank expresses these tensions:

> A third powerful force that clearly was significantly strengthened by the end of the cold war is the universal drive for the respect of human rights and its closely associated set of concerns with the nature of the democratic process. The superpower rivalry in the third world is no longer an excuse for either side to support tyrants that have little support among their people as was routinely done over the last 40 years. This has allowed, for the first time, the local forces in practically every society to assert themselves, seeking greater voice and greater power. The downside of this phenomenon is the emergence of hateful petty nationalisms that transform the rightful call for identity and participation into a call for hating your neighbour and ultimately even 'ethnic cleansing'. (1994: 4)

The Commission on Global Governance reported at the time of the fiftieth anniversary of the United Nations. It concluded:

> We also believe the world's arrangements for the conduct of its affairs must be underpinned by certain common values. Ultimately, no organization will work and no law upheld unless they rest on a foundation made strong by shared values. These values must be informed by a sense of common responsibility for both present and future generations. (1995: xiv)

The values are spelt out in the Commission's report:

> We believe that all humanity could uphold the core values of respect for life, liberty, justice and equity, mutual respect, caring and integrity. (1995: 49)

The Commission proposes a global ethic expressed as a set of rights and responsibilities. The rights currently enshrined in international law are not threatened, but the Commission urges the need for 'due respect for the reciprocal rights of others' which means responsibilities. The list is as follows:

The rights of all people to:
- a secure life
- equitable treatment
- an opportunity to earn a fair living and provide for their own welfare
- the definition and preservation of their differences through peaceful means
- participation in governance at all levels
- free and fair petition for redress of gross injustices

- equal access to information
- equal access to global commons.

At the same time all people share a responsibility to:
- contribute to the common good
- consider the impact of their actions on the security and welfare of others
- promote equity, including gender equity
- protect the interests of future generations by pursuing sustainable development and safeguarding the global commons
- preserve humanity's cultural and intellectual heritage
- be active participants in governance
- work to eliminate corruption.

A further UN report, *Our Creative Diversity*, commissioned by UNESCO and chaired by the former UN Secretary General Pérez de Cuéllar, adds its weight to calls for global ethical standards and their elaboration. It stresses the importance of the cultural element in development. It concludes on the necessity of adopting universal standards:

> The principles of democracy, transparency, accountability and human rights should be universal. (World Commission on Culture and Development, 1996: 285)

It notes that this view may be challenged, but adopts the position that:

> Without an assertion of absolute standards, no recommendation of this commission would be possible, indeed no reasoned discourse could be conducted. (ibid.)

Post-modernism and the denial of universality

The ideal of a global democratic and peaceful society based on underlying universal shared values is not accepted by all, even within the democratic tradition. The main criticism is that the Enlightenment Project, or modernism, whilst claiming universality, is in fact a Western individualistic project imposed on societies for whom collective perspectives are more comfortable. It is the case that the Enlightenment Project is based on rationality, initially so as to free societies from the obfuscating grip of politically entrenched religion. Kant proposed three separate critiques or world views, namely science, religion or morality and the arts, each with their own internal logics and discourse. By separating science from religion the Enlightenment Project aimed to employ the accumulated knowledge of objective science, universal moral values and autonomous artistic expression for the enrichment of everyday life through a just and rational organisation of society.

Critics of modernism claim that the project of modernism has proved destructive to minorities and to the environment and is not therefore capable of benefiting all peoples and communities. This essentially conservative perspective is often referred to as post-modernism. Some criticisms of modernity are well founded. It is the case that some modernising projects have been at the expense of cultural traditions and diversity. For example, universal education in France and Italy almost wiped out regional languages. The modernisation of industry and the economy destroyed communities and natural habitats. Indeed, until the Club of Rome report *Limits to Growth* in 1972, the natural environment was perceived by governments, industry and peoples as a resource to be 'exploited'.

As Luc Ferry, the philosopher who is currently chair of the French national curriculum commission, argues, the line of thought sometimes called post-modern derives from one strand of the 1968 events (Ferry and Renaut, 1988). He points out that post-modernism is an essentially individualist philosophy. It sees the world as fragmented and defined by local and individual cultural expressions. In particular, and ironically, post-modernism rejects the modern individualist movement *par excellence*, namely consumerism, and asserts the spontaneous, the anarchic, the irrational, the emotional and the archaic. It is perhaps well defined as being based on an ironic backward glance, seeing past and present simultaneously by taking neither too seriously.

This worldview puts the peripheral and minorities at the centre. It stresses and celebrates diversity and traditional ways. The struggle for identity and recognition in the face of attempts to modernise economies and social structures is highlighted. Whereas a human rights perspective respects and promotes individual freedoms and collective cultural expression within a wider framework of norms and basic values, post-modernism precisely rejects normative statements.

UNESCO is closely identified with a human rights perspective and argues for 'a world in which diversity and unity are balanced for human growth and well-being'.

> Unity is very different from uniformity; it is not based on the eradication of differences, but on their integration into a harmonious whole ... Humankind has now reached the limits of diversification and a weakness in the countervailing forces of integration can only lead to the erosion of diversity through the arbitrary imposition of some kind of uniformity. As unco-ordinated diversity spells chaos, so undifferentiated uniformity spells not

merely stultifying boredom but also critical instability: mono-culture in society, like mono-culture in agriculture, may seem efficient in the short term but it is unsustainable. (Laszlo, 1993: 201)

The political struggles of minorities to find acceptance of their worldview and cultural expression lead them to challenge structures which appear to impose uniformity rather than unity. In so doing they may deny the possibility of a transcendent view that enables minority groups to find expression within a wider and tolerant social framework. From this perspective, if fragmentation and diversity are the condition of the age, then all judgements are provisional and relative.

Such a perspective is extremely unhelpful in schools. Schools, being in the public domain, need basic minimum standards, the ground rules within which diversity and creativity can flourish without oppressing others. The human rights values of respect for human dignity and equality of rights at least provide a minimum framework for decision-making. To reject such norms in the name of a worldview based on cultural relativism is to surrender the capacity to make rational decisions.

If cultural relativity is accepted without reference to some universal standards or norms, it is possible for any parent or pupil to claim legitimacy for any action if they maintain it is an essential or traditional part of their culture or belief system. They may claim, for instance, that their tradition sanctions the use of violence to settle disputes or that their beliefs lead them to reject contact between one group and another. Cultures may indeed include elements of inequality, but this does not mean that such practices should be sustained in a public education system. Arguments for cultural relativity are often based on a notion of culture which is static, whereas in fact all cultures are in a process of evolution and mutual interaction at all times.

Whatever the failings of the Enlightenment Project in the past, particularly with regard to the environment and to minorities, its advocates have accepted constructive criticism and redirected its energies. The United Nations and the Council of Europe, the leading repositories and exponents of the Enlightenment Project, are also bodies committed to environmental protection, to safeguarding the rights of members of minority communities, to gender equality, to the preservation of cultural heritage. Indeed, for Jürgen Habermas, the affirmation of democracy and enlightenment is essential to enable nations to come to terms with and accept their past without being paralysed by guilt.

Habermas draws on the work of Laurence Kohlberg to draw an analogy between individual moral behaviour and the moral stance of a nation-state. Kohlberg distinguishes between pre-conventional, conventional and post-conventional moral behaviour. The first is based on a concept of right and wrong according to individual cases. The second looks to the group, family, ethnic group or nation to give support to or authority for a moral decision. Thus a terrorist act might be justified by reference to the needs and culture of an oppressed ethnic or political minority. Post-conventional moral behaviour looks beyond the group to a transcendent moral code. It takes its legitimacy not from a group norm but from universal principles. Habermas suggests that what he calls constitutional patriotism based on a post-conventional national identity is the cornerstone of a political system based on free thought and expression. In this way nations can establish new identities based on an acceptance of the past without having to condone the 'chain of irreparable violations' or 'the barbaric dark side of all previous cultural accomplishments'. Such a perspective enables, for example, Germany to come to terms with the Nazi period and Britain with its imperialist past. For Habermas, the affirmation of democracy and enlightenment is 'the greatest intellectual achievement of our post-war period' (Holub, 1991: 183).

The adoption of a set of basic minimum universal values does not deny or undermine cultural and political expression by minorities. On the contrary, it is essential for the preservation of a peaceful order that will enable these forms of expression and assertions of identity and difference. Amitai Etzioni, the architect of Communitarianism, expresses this forcefully:

> Without a firm sense of one supra-community, there is considerable danger that the constituent communities will turn on one another. Indeed, the more one favours strengthening communities, a core of the Communitarian agenda, the more one must concern oneself with ensuring that they see themselves as parts of a more encompassing whole, rather than as fully independent and antagonistic. (1995: 155)

The United Nations and the Council of Europe are such supra-communities. They embody both the assertion of universal values and a concern for culture and the protection of minorities and of heritage. Their status is that accorded them by their members. Their authority is essentially moral.

Summary

As teachers we are likely to find our everyday professional lives easier to manage if we have firm principles on which to base our judgements and decisions. Whatever our personal religious or philosophical beliefs or our background, it should be possible for us to find common ground, on questions of values, with the vast majority of our students and their families if we refer to transcendent values such as those enunciated by representatives of international organisations and the world community. These transcendent values are expressed in declarations and conventions on human rights.

When we are confronted with questions apparently arising from a clash of values, a reference to the values of the world community may enable us to deal rationally and more objectively with events and pressures. Where the pressure comes from a refusal to accept principles of equality, freedom and respect for human dignity and the rule of law, we know that we will need to call upon institutional support.

It is reassuring to be able to express explicitly our fundamental values, in the knowledge that they are non-ideological and so, in principle, non-threatening. A knowledge of human rights principles and basic standards should be part of every teacher's basic tool kit.

2   *Taking children's rights seriously: implementing the UN Convention on the Rights of the Child*

Introduction

The UN Convention on the Rights of the Child is one of the most comprehensive and innovative pieces of human rights legislation ever introduced. It provides exceptional opportunities for the advancement of children's rights in the 1990s and beyond, setting standards on children's issues and providing a valuable set of guidelines for future action. The Convention has particular implications for teachers and for the organisation and management of schools, since it sets out principles and standards relating to children's participation rights, as well as to rights of protection and provision. This chapter examines changing conceptions of children's rights and identifies some key issues for teachers. It considers the implications of the UN Convention on school and classroom organisation and explores how the Convention might be used as an instrument for policy development in teacher education.

Historical overview

The first international attempt to codify children's rights was made in 1924 when the Assembly of the League of Nations endorsed the Declaration of the Rights of the Child proclaimed by the non-governmental organisation (NGO) Save the Children International Union. This document, which was revised and expanded in 1948, formed the basis of the 1959 UN Declaration of the Rights of the Child, a statement of general principles for children's welfare and protection.

Although children's rights have been the subject of public debate for over a century, the discourse on children's rights has changed dramatically over the last twenty-five years or so. In the early 1970s a

British edition of an original Danish publication, *The Little Red Schoolbook* (Hansen and Jensen, 1971), attracted a great deal of publicity and controversy. It provided young people with basic information about education; the emphasis was on rights and participation, with a section on democracy at school and the setting up of school councils. It also contained basic and explicit information about sex and drugs which was not widely available to young people at that time. Opposition to its publication and distribution came from many who were concerned, first and foremost, with its anti-authoritarian stance, and what was seen as a confrontational style. The introductory section is headed: 'All grown ups are paper tigers'. Public interest in the children's liberationist movement was very considerable at this time as is evidenced by the publication of a popular edition of a collection of writings entitled *Children's Rights: towards the liberation of the child* (Hall, 1971). The debates of this period had a significant impact:

> The liberationist movement challenged those who claimed the status of children could be advanced exclusively by conferring on children increased protection. The emphasis shifted from protection to autonomy, from nurturance to self-determination, from welfare to justice. (Freeman, 1992: 3)

A guide published twenty-five years later, the *Young Citizen's Passport* (Thorpe, 1996), which focuses on legal rights and also provides information about sex and drugs, has won official approval in the form of business sponsorship and as winner of the Senior Information Book Award. The author admits however to having been less explicit about sex: 'Some of the children you are addressing are below 16 and are using the book in school, so you have to be sensitive to the moral issue' (Croall, 1996). Nevertheless, the period between the two publications has seen a considerable shift in attitudes towards children, young people and their rights. The movement of the late 1960s and 1970s stressed freeing children from the constraints of a too-rigid social and educational system. It was essentially individualistic, with academic anarchists such as Paul Goodman and Colin Ward finding a ready audience for their ideas. In the 1990s the question being addressed is the reciprocal relationship between young people and society. Rather than assuming conflict between youth and society, the debate is now about young people as citizens, with rights and responsibilities.

In Europe before the sixteenth century, as Verhellen (1989) reminds us, children over the age of six were not generally regarded as a separate class from adults. Hart (1991) traces the development of children's status as the property of their parents over the next 300 years. During this period children had an important economic role, contributing to family work and supporting their parents in their old age. As a result of industrialisation and the increase of children's work outside the family, a series of measures was introduced during the nineteenth century to protect the children of the poor. Children's labour was perceived as a social fact rather than a social problem; protecting children was a means of protecting society from the destabilising effects of anti-social behaviour resulting from mistreatment. Hart concludes that only during the twentieth century does a shift in status of children from that of property to that of persons begin to take place.

During the 1960s and 1970s attitudes towards children and childhood were undergoing rapid change in a number of Western countries. Archard (1993) provides a critical review of the debates of this period, which saw a move away from the traditional view of children as the property of their parents. While some advocates of children's rights argued that they should be given the same rights as adults, others raised questions about the limits to the possibility of autonomy of children in relation to adults, both parents and teachers. These decades also saw a number of experiments with radical alternative models of schooling which emphasised non-authoritarian, co-operative forms of education (Illich, 1971; Lister, 1974; Watts, 1977). However, the text of the 1959 UN Declaration was rarely quoted and so there was little consensus during these decades as to what 'the rights of the child' might imply. As Rodham (1973) famously expressed it, children's rights were 'a slogan in search of a definition'.

1989 UN Convention on the Rights of the Child

1979 marked the International Year of the Child in which children's rights received much-needed publicity and attention. During 1979 a Working Group was set up by the UN Commission on Human Rights to draft a Convention on the Rights of the Child, in response to a formal proposal by Poland. From 1979 until 1987 this drafting group met annually for one week, followed by two fortnight-long meetings in 1988 in order to complete the text for the adoption of the Convention in 1989. The group was made up of representatives of member states, NGOs, and intergovernmental agencies such as the International Labour Organisation and UNICEF. Cantwell (1992) explains how the NGOs organised effectively from 1983 in an ad hoc group to make a very significant contribution to the final legislation. He contrasts their efforts with those of the intergovernmental organisations whose impact he characterises as 'scandalously weak'; UNICEF, for example, only appears to have recognised the potential of the proposed legislation for its work at a relatively late stage. Although the industrialised countries were over-represented throughout the drafting process, this bias towards the North was offset by the particularly active participation of a number of developing countries, notably Algeria, Argentina, Senegal and Venezuela.

The 1989 Convention on the Rights of the Child marks an important development in international law on children's rights since, unlike the Declaration which preceded it, a Convention is legally binding on all states which choose to ratify it. A special treaty body, the UN Committee on the Rights of the Child, exists to support the process of its implementation. State parties are required to report to the Committee on the measures they have taken to implement the Convention two years after its entry into force and subsequently every five years (article 44). The Committee can request further information from those states who fail to provide sufficient information and, under article 45, can take into consideration reports from NGOs and other competent bodies. These measures are important, for the Committee can make suggestions and recommendations based on the reports it receives under articles 44 and 45; no government wishes to receive an unfavourable report on its record of children's human rights.

Doek (1992) notes how quickly an unprecedented number of states worldwide either have ratified the Convention or are signatories, presumably considering ratification. Moreover, despite concerns that social and economic conditions might make many countries, particularly those of the South, reluctant to ratify the Convention, state parties are fairly evenly distributed between the North and the South. It is likely to become the first universally ratified human rights convention in history and one goal is that all members of the UN should have ratified it by the year 2000.

The very existence of the Convention has enhanced the position of children's rights internationally, and increased public awareness of these rights. In September 1990, in the same month that the Convention was adopted, the first World Summit for children was held in New York, bringing together leaders from over seventy countries. An African Charter on the Rights and Welfare of the Child was agreed that same year. The European Convention on the Exercise of Children's Rights, which focuses on procedural rights and seeks to support the UN Convention and contribute to its implementation in member states of the Council of Europe, was opened for signature in January 1996 (Jeleff, 1996). The ending of the Cold War has permitted increased co-operation between states on issues of children's rights. New emergent democracies face a number of pressures, both internal and external, to address human rights issues, and this has helped support a climate in which the protection of children's rights remains a relatively high international priority.

The adoption of the 1989 Convention as an international human rights treaty marks an important step forward for children: first, it provides an internationally agreed set of minimum standards for children, and secondly, children are now widely recognised as a group to which human rights law applies. The Convention is both an agenda for action and a means by which public understanding and education on children's rights can be developed.

One of the special features of the Convention on the Rights of the Child is that it integrates economic and social rights with civil and political rights, effectively recognising the interdependence and indivisibility of these rights. Children's rights, as covered in the Convention, have been categorised as the three 'P's: those of protection, provision (services, material benefits) and participation. The Convention recognises that children, particularly those in exceptionally difficult conditions, need special protection, and that children may have group needs for which specific provision must be made; moreover, children have the right to express their views, and to receive appropriate information and education to enable them to participate in decisions about their own lives and futures.

The principle of indivisibility of rights established in the Convention is perhaps of particular importance to those states where widespread poverty prevents the majority of children from effectively claiming their rights. Under article 28, for example, states which have ratified the Convention are required to engage in international co-operation to implement the child's right to education and to facilitate access to scientific and technical knowledge and modern teaching methods. It states that 'particular account shall be taken of the needs of developing countries'. Article 45, also concerned with international co-operation to secure the implementation of the Convention, permits the Committee on the Rights of the Child to transmit reports from state parties which contain a request or need for technical advice or assistance to the United Nations Children's Fund and other competent bodies, and to include the Committee's observations and suggestions on such requests. Under the Convention, state parties who are unable to fulfil their obligations for social or economic reasons might request the support and co-operation of other state parties in order to secure children's rights.

National education legislation and the rights of the child

While the UN Convention on the Rights of the Child provides us with an important set of principles and standards for children's rights we need to be wary about equating the existence of the Convention with the realisation of these rights. The effectiveness of the Convention depends, first and foremost, on the raising of public awareness concerning its provisions. Whilst legally binding on all state parties, the Convention cannot be enforced in the same way as domestic legislation. For this reason it is important that governments are persuaded of the importance of ensuring that, where national legislation currently fails to secure the minimum standards set in the Convention, appropriate legislation is enacted.

Box 2.1 lists the main provisions of the Convention identified as being of particular relevance to teachers. (A summary of the full Convention is included as Appendix 2.) Since teachers and schools take on a variety of roles in the care and education of children, any selection from the Convention is necessarily somewhat arbitrary; all teachers need to be familiar with the whole of the Convention, and indeed article 42 requires the state to make the rights contained in the Convention widely known to both adults and children. Teachers and teacher educators have a critical role to play in this process, since the formal education system is likely to be the main means by which most children will become familiar with their rights. The successful implementation of article 42 is thus largely dependent on the education and training of teachers in the rights of the child and the provisions of the Convention.

Fundamental to the whole Convention is the requirement (article 3) that in all actions concerning children 'the best interests of the child shall be a primary consideration'. This is important as an agreed international standard in child-rearing which goes beyond the basic requirements of a number of national systems of legislation. Freeman (1988) suggests two measures which he argues would support children's rights in this way: first, the appointment of an ombudsperson for children, similar to the *Barneombudet* in Norway. The function of this official would be to make a continuing assessment of the impact of changing society on the way children grow up and to promote children's interests. The Norwegian ombudsperson, who has an advisory panel and a professional staff from a variety of backgrounds, examines the drafts of policies and legislation to consider their effects on children. S/he identifies relevant issues and responds to those brought by others, including children. Secondly, Freeman advocates a 'child impact statement' which would require all those who draft legislation, policies and practices in areas such as

22

taxation, social security, housing, social services, environment, and education to assess the impact of their proposals on the lives and futures of children. Such statements would be scrutinised by the ombudsperson.

Preamble
Article 2: non-discrimination
Article 3: best interests of the child
Article 5: parental guidance and the child's evolving capabilities
Article 12: the child's opinion
Article 13: freedom of expression
Article 14: freedom of thought, conscience and religion
Article 15: freedom of association
Article 16: protection of privacy
Article 17: access to private information
Article 19: protection from abuse and neglect
Article 22: refugee children
Article 23: disabled children
Article 25: periodic review of placement
Article 28: education
Article 29: aims of education
Article 30: children of minorities and indigenous populations
Article 31: leisure, recreation and cultural activities
Article 32: child labour
Article 37: torture, punishment and protection of liberty
Article 42: implementation and entry into force.

Box 2.1 UN Convention on the Rights of the Child: articles of particular relevance to teachers

In the United Kingdom, as Newell (1991) stresses, not all courts of law affecting children adopt a 'best interests' principle. He points out that while the Children Act (1989) has gone a long way to ensuring that social welfare institutions in England and Wales act in the best interests of the child, the same principle is not generally guaranteed in education and 'there is no duty to observe the best interests of the child in education legislation' (1991: 9). The Children Act has encouraged a number of publications (for example, Gallagher and Cross, 1990; Lindsay, 1990; Hodgson and Whalley, 1992; Rodway, 1993) which consider its implications for schools and local education authorities, but this analysis has generally been limited to children with special educational needs and to those educated in residential settings. While attention has been given to the need to inform and involve such children in decisions which affect their lives and futures, the right of other children to have their opinions taken into consideration in procedures which affect them (article 12) has often been denied.

Article 12, which recognises the child's right to express views and feelings on all matters affecting the child, and to have those opinions taken into consideration, is, as Newell (1991; 1993) demonstrates, the principle most consistently broken in UK education legislation. While parents, as education 'consumers', have had certain rights of access to decision-making and appeal extended, for example in the choice of their child's school, recent legislation has ignored children's voices in decisions affecting their education. Article 12 is breached in the UK by the denial of any right of the child to be heard, for example:

> in the procedures for choosing a school and school-choice appeals; for children with special needs, in assessment and placement decisions, reviews, reassessments and appeals under the Education Act 1981 (and the equivalent legislation for Scotland and Northern Ireland); in the various formal administrative procedures under the National Curriculum and arrangements for excluding certain children from it; in the arrangements for appeal against school exclusions. (Newell, 1991: 41)

As part of the process of monitoring and evaluating how far the rights contained in the Convention are respected in the UK, the Children's Rights Development Unit, an NGO, collaborated with organisations and individuals concerned with children's issues to produce a comprehensive report to the UN Committee, the *UK Agenda for Children* (Lansdown and Newell, 1994). The UN Committee, as well as receiving reports from governments, welcomes other reports on children's rights, such as those from NGOs, when reviewing the achievements of a particular state party. The process which led to the report from the Children's Rights Development Unit was noted by the chair of the UN Committee on the Rights of the Child as representing a significant contribution to the methodology of monitoring children's rights within an individual country which may be of much interest internationally. The report is organised into key sections which comment on law, policy and practice as they relate to children. These include care of children; health and health care services; child labour; education; and youth justice. Within the section on education the summary of recommendations covers issues relating to legislation, local authority administration, school management and administration, curriculum, and pastoral care. The following list draws on these recommendations to indicate how headteachers, governors, teachers and teacher educators might ensure that their policy and practice meets the minimum standards set by the Convention on the Rights of the Child.

Taking children's rights seriously: a checklist for educators

Access and participation

- Are admissions criteria published in an accessible form? Are they available in relevant community languages? Do they comply with the Race Relations Act 1976 and the CRE Code of Practice on the Elimination of Racial Discrimination in Education?
- Is there ethnic monitoring and analysis of applications for admission? Do any practices need changing to avoid discrimination against any groups of children?
- What steps is the school taking to ensure the provision of integrated teaching of English as a second language?
- How does the school/LEA ensure that due consideration is given to the views of individual children on matters affecting them? What procedures are there for children to make complaints when they are dissatisfied with the process or outcome of any decision made about them?
- Are there any procedures in place which allow the child to be heard in decision-making and appeals concerned with school choice, exclusions from school, and special needs assessment and statementing?
- What steps are being taken to reduce the numbers of children excluded from school? Is exclusion only used when a pupil's behaviour is likely to be seriously detrimental to their own or other pupils' education or welfare, or to the welfare of the staff?
- What provision exists (e.g. a school council) to permit children to express their views on matters of concern relating to the running of the schools? Are children's views given due weight in accordance with their age and maturity?

Protection from violence, respect for dignity

- Have pupils and all other members of the school community been involved in the development of a whole-school behavioural policy? How does the policy prevent and respond to bullying? What training on anti-bullying strategies is given to governors and all responsible for supervising playgrounds?
- Are staff provided with guidance on the appropriate use of physical restraint?

Refugee children

- What steps have been taken to ensure that refugee children can benefit fully from the education available? What provision is made for their induction, language tuition, and teacher training?

Equality for children with disabilities

- What provision is made for those children with special needs who are not statemented?
- What information is made available from the LEA and health authority on services available, and the legal rights of children and their parents? Is this information available in community languages?
- What steps is the school taking to ensure the fullest possible integration of children with special needs?
- Have unmet needs been identified and built into the school development plan?

Promoting the child's personality, talents and respect for human rights

- What steps are being taken to ensure the curriculum fully incorporates perspectives on human rights and democracy?
- What school-based support is given to teachers to enable them to carry out their duties without racially discriminating and in a way that meets the demands of schools in a multiracial and multilingual society? Are there clear guidelines on disciplinary procedures to be followed in the event of discrimination?

Teacher education and training

- How is the principle of respect for children and for their personal and physical integrity incorporated into programmes?
- What is being done to prepare teachers to increase democratic practices in the schools and classrooms?
- Are there initial and in-service programmes available to teachers to enhance their capacity to meet the needs of children with special needs within an integrated setting? Is training offered to governors and non-teaching assistants on services for children with special needs?
- How might university departments of law and education work together to increase teachers' understanding of the law, particularly with regard to special educational needs?
- How do initial teacher education courses equip teachers to do their work without racially discriminating and in a way which supports schools in a multicultural and multilingual society?

The UN Committee on the Rights of the Child, in its first report on the implementation of the Convention in the UK, published in 1995, found that the British government is failing children in nearly every aspect of their lives and was particularly critical of policy and practice in education. Among its recommendations relating to education were that corporal punishment in private schools be made illegal and that children be consulted over the running of their school, and be taught about their rights (*The Guardian*, 28 January 1995). Interestingly, the British educational press failed to report on the findings of the UN Committee.

The Convention on the Rights of the Child sets internationally agreed minimum standards and principles for children's education and welfare. As one of the duties of teacher educators in the UK is to prepare new teachers to understand their responsibilities under recent legislation, it would seem that they should also ensure that their students are aware of the implications of the Convention, including its relationship to national legislation; this should include an understanding of issues and procedures which might involve breaches of the Convention. Moreover, compliance with article 12 requires both initial and in-service teacher education to be founded on principles of respect for children and greater democracy within schools.

The human rights school

One way in which we can usefully familiarise ourselves with the Convention on the Rights of the Child and begin to explore its meanings for our practice is to consider how it might influence the design and the workings of a human rights school. We can then compare this ideal with the schools with which we are familiar and consider the implications for school organisation and ethos, pedagogy, and curriculum. Article 2 of the UN Convention, that of non-discrimination, raises issues of significance to each of these three dimensions of the school. It entrusts the state with the role of ensuring that all rights are available to all children without discrimination of any kind, mentioning specifically race, colour, sex, language, religion, political opinion, ethnic or social origin and disability.

In the UK, programmes to promote 'race' and gender equality in schools have continued to be called in question by the political right. Indeed, Conservative government ministers have even suggested that teachers should not concern themselves with the politics of 'race' or gender. For disabled children, the opportunity for education in an ordinary school alongside children without disabilities is still not always seen as a right; the report *Within Reach*, commissioned by the Spastics Society (now SCOPE) and the National Union of Teachers, found that only one in ten secondary schools and one in four primary schools are fully accessible to children with physical disabilities (Pyke, 1993).

Yet all state parties to the Convention have made a commitment to ensure that girls and boys are treated on equal terms; that the rights of children with disabilities are protected (article 23); that children of minority communities have the right to their own culture, language and religion (article 30); and that the provisions of the Convention are widely known to children as well as to adults so that both are aware of their entitlements under international law (article 42). These articles legitimate the efforts of teachers concerned to promote the equal rights of girls and boys, children from minority communities, and those with disabilities or learning difficulties.

Human rights issues are invariably political and there is a danger that teachers who engage with them may be subject to accusations of political bias or indoctrination. The Council of Europe Recommendation R(85)7 on Teaching and Learning about Human Rights in Schools acknowledges this:

> Human rights inevitably involve the domain of politics. Teaching about human rights should, therefore, always have international agreements and covenants as a point of reference, and teachers should take care to avoid imposing their personal convictions on their pupils and involving them in ideological struggles. (Council of Europe, 1985)

This Council of Europe text (included as Appendix 3) provides valuable guidelines for teachers engaged in human rights education and also legitimates the efforts of teachers in member states of the Council of Europe in teaching about human rights in schools (see Chapter 3).

Articles 28 (education) and 29 (aims of education) of the UN Convention both raise a number of issues with regard to both teaching methodology and student–teacher relationships, as do articles 12 (the child's opinion), 13 (freedom of expression), 14 (freedom of thought, conscience and religion), 16 (protection of privacy) and 17 (access to appropriate information). Running through most of these articles is the principle of participation, which to a large degree is dependent on the child acquiring a range of skills, including social skills and skills of communication and judgement; the aims of an education compatible with the principles of the Convention must be to empower the child by providing opportunities to practise and develop these skills of participation. This clearly has implications for the teaching methodologies adopted and may involve the individual teacher in a complete reassessment of her or his role. Listening to pupils' opinions and needs may well have implications for the school as a whole. The Council of Europe Recommendation expresses this same idea in another way:

> Democracy is best learned in a democratic setting where participation is encouraged, where views can be expressed openly and discussed, where there is freedom of expression for pupils and teachers, and where there is fairness and justice. (Council of Europe, 1985)

One principle raised by the Convention which may be challenging to a number of teachers is the rights and responsibilities of parents in providing guidance to the child (article 5). Some teachers hold a deficit model of certain groups of parents, blaming them for real or apparent learning difficulties or behavioural problems (Hughes, 1989; Docking, 1990). A number may be ill-prepared to work with parents of children from ethnic minority groups, although Davey (1986) in a study of parental involvement in schools found little evidence to support teachers' assertions that these parents were not concerned about their children's education. Research into Muslim women's attitudes to their daughters' schooling (Osler and Hussain, 1995) confirms that parents are keenly interested in what is happening in school and that a number recognise the need for further dialogue with teachers. An examination of the rights and responsibilities of parents as defined in both domestic and international legislation would seem to be a useful first step in informing teachers, enabling them to establish a more positive view of parents, and genuinely to work in the best interests of the child.

As teachers and student teachers engaged in the process of exploring the principles of the Convention on the Rights of the Child, it is helpful for us to examine the relationship between the legal and moral aspects of human rights (see Chapter 8). Unless we do we may act on principles which may be in accordance with the rights of the child but be unaware of the legal authority which supports those principles. For example, a Cardiff teacher concerned about the practice of female circumcision among certain of her students raised the issue with them in the context of a course on social and health education; she also discussed the issue with their mothers. Opponents of the practice have sometimes been accused of racism and cultural insensitivity, but the teacher saw genital mutilation as a form of child abuse which needs to be tackled. As she expressed it: 'If it happened to white children, people would say "what can we do?"' (Sone, 1993).

Article 24 on health and health services includes the clause: 'State Parties shall take all effective and appropriate measures with a view to abolishing traditional practices prejudicial to the health of children'. Traditional practices harmful to children were one of a number of issues which tested the impact of cross-cultural factors in setting international human rights norms. Only four other issues challenged the drafting committee in a similar fashion: freedom of religion, inter-country adoption, rights of the unborn, and the duties of children toward their parents. Although a number of states proposed a direct reference to female circumcision, objections were raised since this would have had the effect of targeting Africa, when other traditional practices harmful to the health of children, such as son-preference, have been shown to be much more pervasive. Nevertheless, as Johnson notes, 'there can be no doubt in the Travaux Préparatoires that the article was intended to include female circumcision' (1992: 110).

The Cardiff case illustrates the importance, particularly in multicultural and pluralist societies, of schools adopting a code of ethics to which all members of the community can subscribe. The teacher who sought to provide her students with information which might protect them from a harmful practice was not only acting on the basis of her own moral convictions; her actions were also clearly in accordance with the spirit of internationally agreed legislation.

The ways in which a school resolves conflicts and disputes and deals with matters of student behaviour is likely to be a good indicator of whether or not it is operating as a human rights community. Cunningham (1991) argues that the traditional discipline model of investigation–punishment often operates without reference to principles of justice, equality and peace. He points out that an essential condition of justice, that of separation of powers, does not apply in schools where teachers are often investigators, interrogators, adjudicators, counsellors and sentencers. He advocates an alternative model, that of investigation–resolution–restitution–sanction–communication (see below), designed to cover a variety of school disputes, disagreements and offences. He argues that if teachers adopt such a model they will be contributing to their pupils' understanding of due process and respect for human rights.

Cunningham's human rights model for school justice and disputes

Investigation

Everyone shall be presumed innocent until proven guilty.
Be careful to distinguish between facts and supposition.

1 In interpersonal disputes it is useful to make notes to establish points of difference.
2 Pupils can be asked to name someone they trust to be a fair witness, not a close friend.

3 In pupil–teacher disputes the teacher should be heard first in deference to professional responsibilities.

4 A pupil must be able to put their side of the case.

5 To avoid arguments or a recurrence of the original problem, a senior staff member acts as chair, allowing each party to make an uninterrupted statement.

6 If necessary, allow tempers to cool down.

7 Remember, a physically injured party is not necessarily guiltless.

8 Take care to avoid anger or hostility to a suspected person and remember to avoid moral pressure to get a confession. It is well known that people under stress can make false confessions.

Resolution

Resolution means the dispute is accepted by all parties as finished.

1 A compromise, or apology, may lead to parties being asked if they are satisfied.

2 Set the seal on the agreement by a symbolic gesture such as a hand-shake or written statement about future intentions.

3 In a dispute between students, an adult who has spare time sorting matters out would become an injured party if the agreement were broken.

4 Part of the resolution may be a written contract, clearly stated and entered into freely.

5 Contracts work well if the essential goal is positive and if there is some payoff to the contractor, e.g. a pupil who has been disruptive may 'earn' points for successful lessons. A defined number of points may earn a privilege.

6 It is best to involve parents. Schools only have a limited number of worthwhile rewards. If parents do not understand or approve, the contract will be flawed.

Restitution

Restitution means paying back or making reparations for injury. It is easier to make direct reparation for theft or damage than for bullying.

1 The school may need to act as an intermediary on the injured party's behalf.

2 An offence against a school human rights code challenges the self-

respect and morale of the community. It is fair to expect an offender to pay something back through an activity useful to the school.

3 Restitution allows the perpetrator to gain self-respect, lack of which is often the root cause of misdemeanours.

Sanctions

Cruel, inhuman or degrading punishment as prohibited in article 37 includes all physical punishments and others which might cause humiliation, ridicule or shame.

1 The ultimate sanction is exclusion from the school community, whether temporary or permanent. It should only be used where all steps to avoid it have been taken and where the school is satisfied that unless excluded, the pupil's behaviour is likely to be seriously detrimental to the education or welfare of the pupil or others, or the welfare of staff.

2 Exclusion is a last resort as it effectively denies the pupil's right to education.

3 Sanctions which are over-used become ineffective.

4 The double-jeopardy rule says no-one should be punished twice for the same offence. It is often possible to negotiate with parents a joint course of action.

5 There can be no system of fixed penalties since any offence is in the context of a person's overall development, including his or her successes and contributions. To treat each individual as a blank page is the antithesis of equal treatment.

Communication

1 Any injured party must not be forgotten in the effort to put the offender on the right track. Those who have suffered need some reassurances the school is working for them. They should be kept in touch and, where appropriate, play a part in resolution and restitution.

2 The ideas and advice of parents should be listened to, as they are key partners in any major matter concerning their child. It is therefore dangerous to promise immunity from parental involvement in return for information.

3 Only maintain files that can be open to parents.

4 Remember the rights of young people to privacy and consider their access to files.

Children's participation rights

Hart (1992) argues that the participation rights of children and young people must be set within the context of unequal power relations and the struggle for equal rights. We have seen that English education law falls short in securing children their participation rights; Freeman (1993) reminds us that in England children in care also have more say than those living at home. Hart suggests that if children are to realise fully their right to participate and express their views in matters affecting them, as defined in articles 12 and 13 of the Convention, then they must be given opportunities to participate alongside adults in community projects. Without such participation he argues that they will not gain the experience they require to exercise their rights and responsibilities as citizens. He argues that much of what generally passes for children's participation is, in fact, manipulation or tokenism. His 'Ladder of Participation' (Figure 2.1) identifies how we might move towards children's full participation in community projects. He points out that while it is relatively easy to think of examples from children's play where they conceive and carry out complex projects, it is much more difficult to find examples of child-initiated community projects. His model provides a challenge to teachers to consider how children might become genuine participants in school plans and decision-making.

In his discussion of the democratisation of secondary schools Hannam (1995) considers the potential of schools' councils to be not merely a channel of representation but a genuine means of pupil participation. Further discussion and examples of student participation and decision-making in schools can be found in Chapters 5 and 9.

Summary

Any discussion of teacher education and the rights of the child which takes the 1989 Convention as its framework invariably involves a broad consideration of rights, including the rights of parents and teachers, the rights of people with disabilities and the rights of minority and indigenous communities. The Convention stresses the universality and indivisibility of human rights, and places an important emphasis on the need for international co-operation to secure the rights of the child. Formal education is the main means by which international human rights legislation can become known and understood within communities. The 1989 Convention on the Rights of the Child has set out internationally agreed principles and minimum standards for children's welfare and education, against which current domestic legislation can be assessed and future progress monitored. As teachers and teacher educators we have a vital role to play in ensuring that our programmes incorporate the principles set out in the Convention and ensuring that children are in a strong position to claim their rights.

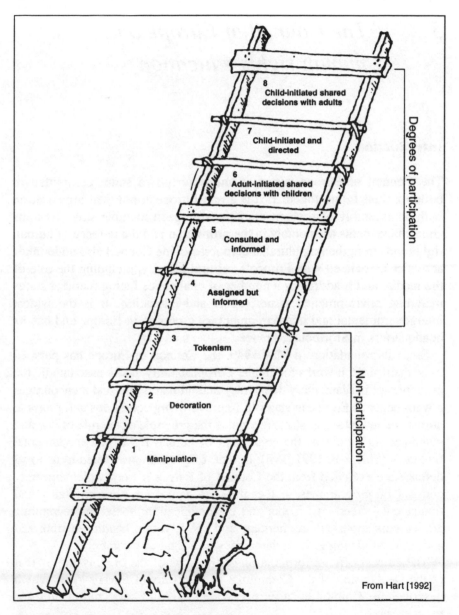

Figure 2.1 The Ladder of Participation

3   *The Council of Europe and human rights education*

Introduction

The Council of Europe currently unites forty-two states committed to building their future together. It is a pan-European political organisation with an assembly of parliamentarians from each member state. Its aims and achievements are notably in the promotion and the defence of human rights and strengthening pluralist democracy. The Council also undertakes activities associated with Europe's cultural identity, including the role of the media, and it addresses a number of challenges facing member states including environmental issues, sport and education. It is the widest intergovernmental and interparliamentary grouping in Europe and has its headquarters in Strasbourg, France.

Since its foundation in May 1949, the Council of Europe has pursued three main aims. It works for greater European unity, it strives to uphold the principles of parliamentary democracy and human rights, and it encourages governments of European states to improve living conditions and promote human values. Member states recognise the principle of the rule of law and guarantee their citizens the enjoyment of human rights and fundamental freedoms (Shennan, 1991: xvii). In fact, only questions related to national defence are excluded from the Council of Europe's work which currently consists of programmes in the areas of democracy, human rights and fundamental freedoms; media and communication; social and economic affairs; education, culture, heritage and sport; youth; health; environment and regional planning; local democracy and legal co-operation.

The current official formulation of the aims of the organisation is that of the Declaration of the Committee of Ministers of 5 May 1989, which describes the Council as 'a Europe-wide system of cooperation' in three main areas:

- safeguarding and reinforcing pluralist democracy and human rights by reference to the European Convention on Human Rights and the European Social Charter;
- fostering awareness of, and enhancing, European cultural identity;
- seeking common or convergent responses to challenges confronting modern European society.

The Council of Europe has considerable influence with governments, but only in the field of the protection of human rights does it have the powerful legal backing that can enforce compliance. In all other respects it must rely on indirect approaches.

The Council's educational work comes under the Council for Cultural Co-operation (CDCC), itself an instrument for the implementation of the European Cultural Convention of 1954. The CDCC is open to European countries that are not members of the Council of Europe. For some states membership of the CDCC is a useful preliminary step towards full membership. At the time of writing there were forty-four states within the Cultural Convention, which co-ordinates activities within the fields of education, culture, heritage and sport. The programmes are overseen by four specialised committees covering education, culture, cultural heritage and university problems. There is also a close working relationship between the CDCC and the regular meetings and conferences of ministers responsible for education, culture and heritage.

Human rights protection in Europe

Human rights in Europe are protected under the European Convention on Human Rights and Fundamental Freedoms, signed in 1950 and entering into force on 3 September 1953. The drafting of the Convention was one of the first tasks of the Council of Europe, which is the organisation responsible for its maintenance and realisation. The Convention is an international treaty and, as such, a form of contract under which states accept certain legal obligations. States recognise that individuals have specific rights which the state has a duty to protect. The feature that makes the European Convention a landmark in international law is that individuals can petition the European *Commission* of Human Rights (which has a mediating role) and seek redress either through an amicable settlement or through the European *Court* of Human Rights.

The Convention, it should be noted, applies, under article 1, to everyone within the jurisdiction of the state, not just to citizens.

Furthermore the Convention guarantees, through its article 14, that enjoyment of the rights is equally available. It specifically outlaws discrimination on the grounds of 'race, colour, language, religion'. The Convention covers the following areas:

- the right to life, liberty and security of person, including the enjoyment of family life and possessions and privacy in the home and in correspondence
- the right to a fair trial
- the right to education
- freedom of thought, conscience and religion
- freedom of expression (including for the press)
- freedom of peaceful assembly and association (the right to form trade unions)
- prohibition of:
  o torture and inhuman or degrading treatment, including slavery and forced labour
  o retroactive criminal legislation
  o the death penalty
  o expulsion or refusal of entry to nationals
  o collective expulsion of aliens.

The European Court of Human Rights and education

The Court is a busy working institution whose judgements may well help to clarify the limits of the powers of a state and may even cause member governments to amend their legislation. Notable examples of this for education are the 1976 Kjeldsen, Busk Madsen and Pedersen v. Denmark case concerning sex education and the 1982 Campbell and Cosans v. United Kingdom case which caused the British government to abolish corporal punishment in state schools.

The right to education as such, under the European Convention, is found in article 2 of Protocol Number 1, which entered into force on 18 May 1954, less than a year after the Convention itself (Brownlie, 1971: 338). The article stipulates:

> No person shall be denied the right to education. In the exercise of any functions which it assumes in relation to education and to teaching, the State shall respect the right of parents to ensure such education and teaching is in conformity with their own religious and philosophical convictions.

It should be noted that the article is formulated negatively. Education is the right to be protected, and the state has a duty to ensure that public provision is inclusive in that it is accessible to all and not delivered in such a way as to offend the consciences of those who entrust their children to the education system.

In the Danish case, parents protested against the inclusion of sex education in the curriculum, claiming that it was offensive to their philosophical or religious convictions. The Court did not uphold their protest, noting that the article of the Convention invoked:

> aims ... at safeguarding the possibility of pluralism in education, which possibility is essential for the preservation of the 'democratic society' as conceived by the Convention ... in view of the power of the modern state it is above all through State teaching that this aim must be realised.

In other words, the Court considered that, given that education is one of the state's instruments for supporting a pluralist democracy, education must itself be pluralist, that is to say, as far as possible, even-handed and objective. Any judgement of the Court implies that the same underlying principle should apply across Europe. In some countries, such as France, this neutrality is ensured by banning religious and party political manifestations from schools. Whatever the structure of national education systems and whatever freedoms may be accorded to schools, member states are deemed to be ultimately responsible for ensuring that their schools are free of indoctrination.

> The State, in fulfilling the functions assumed by it in regard to education and teaching, must take care that information and knowledge included in the curriculum is conveyed in an objective, critical and pluralistic manner. The State is forbidden to pursue an aim of indoctrination that might be considered as not respecting parents' religious and philosophical convictions. That is the limit that must not be exceeded. (Gomien, 1991: 101)

It should be noted that the Convention supports national legislation that allows parents to withdraw their children from particular lessons such as religious education. However, sometimes, as with sex education in Denmark, the potentially controversial issue is conceived as a cross-curricular theme. It will, inevitably, be part of the biology syllabus, but references to sex and to sexuality are also appropriate in personal and health education, physical education, studies of literature and elsewhere in the curriculum. Sex education will also occur in different school years. Withdrawal from particular lessons is not a practical solution in this case, since it would be unreasonable to expect a child to be shielded completely from any reference to sex and sexual behaviour. The judgement therefore reinforces the obligation for states to ensure that sensitive topics like sex education are handled professionally and without undue emphasis on a particular ethical perspective.

The Campbell and Cosans v. UK case, on the other hand, found in favour of the parents. These Scottish parents objected to the use of corporal punishment in the schools attended by their children, as violating their philosophical convictions. Cosans also complained that the exclusion of her child from school, on disciplinary grounds, violated the child's right to education. On the issue of corporal punishment, the Court demonstrated an understanding of the concept of the 'hidden curriculum', stating:

> The use of corporal punishment may, in a sense, be said to belong to the internal administration of a school, but at the same time it is, when used, an integral part of the process whereby a school seeks to achieve the object for which it was established, including the development and moulding of the character and mental powers of its pupils. (Gomien, 1991: 102)

In other words, a school using corporal punishment is giving out a very strong message to its pupils, and one that may well violate the philosophical convictions of parents who may hold, for example, that such punishment constitutes inhuman or degrading treatment. The judgement hangs both on the right to education and on the appropriateness of invoking 'philosophical convictions'. The Court defined these as:

> such convictions as are worthy of respect in a 'democratic society' ... and are not incompatible with human dignity, in addition, they must not conflict with the fundamental right of the child to education.

A philosophical conviction based, for example, on a view of racial superiority or rule by force without consent cannot be invoked. Such convictions are not compatible with the fundamental principles of democracy and human rights. A philosophical view that children should be allowed to grow up 'naturally' without any formal education is also unacceptable, since education itself is a right. On the other hand, a view that refuses to accept that schools may inflict on children physical punishments outlawed in the judicial system, can be said to be one in accordance with principles of equity and respect for human dignity. Or, in the words of the Court:

> The applicants' views relate to a weighty and substantial aspect of human life and behaviour, namely the integrity of the person, the propriety or otherwise of the infliction of corporal punishment and the exclusion of the distress which the risk of such punishment entails.

Legislation, as René Cassin memorably pointed out, does not in itself protect human rights. The court can act only after an abuse has been committed. The Convention is a back-up mechanism, but it is education and opinion-forming that create the climate in which groups can live together in society without the racial violence, the pogroms and the ethnic cleansing which historically have been a feature of European society.

The rationale for a human rights education programme

The Council of Europe is committed to an education programme that underpins democracy and human rights in Europe. The programme was described by its major architect, Maitland Stobart, at a special information seminar held in Moscow in September 1992:

> Our Organisation is also aware of the considerable problems facing the New Europe. At the one level, there are cooperation, integration and solidarity. At another there are disintegration, fragmentation, intolerance, rejection, violence and even warfare. Furthermore, economic change and re-structuring are often accompanied by unemployment and marginalisation, and there are fears that the New Europe could become a two-track society.
>
> In this fluid and challenging situation, the Council of Europe's education programme seeks to find answers to three overarching questions.
>
> The first question is: how can education help to promote human rights and fundamental freedoms and strengthen pluralistic democracy? In response to this question we are carrying out work on human rights education and civic education in schools and on human rights teaching in universities.
>
> The second question is: how can education help bring the peoples of Europe closer together and create a sense of 'being at home' in the wider community that is Europe? In response to this question we are carrying out work on modern languages, history, geography, school links and exchanges and academic mobility and equivalence.
>
> The third question is: how can education help the governments and citizens of Europe to meet the big challenges facing our societies? In response to this question we are carrying out work on education and the multi-cultural society and on adult education and social change. (Stobart, 1992)

Stobart has characterised the vision of education of the Council of Europe as a 'concern for the individual and by a refusal of situations of exclusion, marginalisation, isolation and discrimination'. He argues that:

> although the Council of Europe believes that education can help to bring the peoples of Europe closer together, it is equally convinced that programmes to promote an awareness of Europe should not, in turn, promote Eurocentric attitudes or feelings of cultural superiority. Education systems should, therefore, encourage all young Europeans to see themselves 'not only as

citizens of their own regions and countries, but also as citizens of Europe and the wider world'.

The final phrase in quotation marks is taken from the Recommendation No. R(83)4 of the Committee of Ministers of Education of the Council of Europe, *Concerning the Promotion of an Awareness of Europe in Secondary Schools* (Shennan, 1991: 229).

The Council of Europe thus stresses the role of education in, on the one hand, promoting an active commitment to human rights and the principles of pluralistic democracy and, on the other, combating such challenges to democratic values as intolerance, xenophobia, anti-semitism and racism.

To this end the Council of Europe, through its Directorate of Education, Culture and Sport, has undertaken programmes to develop and disseminate good practice in human rights education. The programmes are always supported by recommendations of the Committee of Ministers and resolutions of the Standing Conference of the European Ministers of Education and even, in October 1993, by a resolution of Heads of State and Government meeting at a summit in Vienna. Amongst the means at its disposal the organisation has acted by sponsoring colloquys of educational research workers, symposia of policy makers with national or regional responsibility for education, meetings of experts, teachers' seminars and consultations of and co-operation with international non-governmental organisations, in particular the School as an Instrument of Peace (Geneva) and the René Cassin Institute (Strasbourg). As well as itself publishing reports and studies, the Council also collaborates with commercial publishers for both academic and pedagogical publications.

In the 1990s the Directorate of Education, Culture and Sport started working particularly closely with the Directorate of Human Rights and the Human Rights Information Centre on a programme to promote education for democracy and human rights in the emerging democracies of Central and Eastern Europe.

Resolutions and Recommendations

A Recommendation that has exercised considerable influence is Recommendation R(85)7 of the Committee of Ministers of the Council of Europe on 'teaching and learning about human rights in schools', which is reproduced as Appendix 3. The Recommendation originated in the conclusions of an international symposium, hosted by the Austrian government in Vienna in May 1983, which brought together representatives appointed by governments, education experts, teachers' unions and NGOs. The conclusions of the symposium were circulated to member states for comment and re-drafted in the light of their suggestions for formal adoption at a meeting of ministers on 14 May 1985.

In their preamble the ministers reaffirm democratic values in the face of intolerance; acts of violence and terrorism; the re-emergence of the public expression of racist and xenophobic attitudes; and the disillusionment of many young people in Europe, who are affected by the economic recession and aware of the continuing poverty and inequality in the world.

The Recommendation emphasises that 'throughout their school career, all young people should learn about human rights'. It identifies certain skills they should acquire such as the identification of bias, prejudice, stereotypes and discrimination, recognising and accepting differences and establishing positive and non-oppressive personal relationships, and resolving conflict in a non-violent way.

Students, the Recommendation suggests, should learn about 'the main categories of human rights, duties, obligations and responsibilities'. They should know about 'the various forms of injustice, inequality and discrimination, including sexism and racism'. In fact 'the study of human rights in schools should lead to an understanding of, and sympathy for, the concepts of justice, equality, freedom, peace, dignity, rights and democracy. Such understanding should be both cognitive and based on experience and feelings.'

Although, in common with the Universal Declaration of Human Rights, the Recommendation is just a sheet of paper, it can justifiably claim to be an influential one. It has been translated into most of the major languages of Europe, including recently Russian, Polish and Romanian. The French minister of education ensured that it was circulated to all schools with an accompanying letter of warm endorsement. Other governments, notably Sweden and Portugal, gave the document similarly wide distribution. In the UK it has been quoted notably by two important commissions (Speaker's Commission on Citizenship, 1990; Runnymede Trust, 1993).

The Council's concern at the growth of open and explicit racist activity led to the convening of a summit meeting in Vienna in October 1993. The conclusions of the summit are discussed in Chapter 4. The Recommendation of 1985 was strengthened by a Resolution of the Standing Conference of European Ministers of Education meeting in Madrid in March 1994. The Ministers

Affirm the important role which education for its part can play in helping young people and adults equip themselves with:
− the motivation, knowledge and skills to operate and improve democratic

42

institutions and to uphold the rule of law;
- a set of values which includes tolerance, solidarity and respect for diversity
- the ability to make independent and balanced judgements and not to be swayed or manipulated by extremist views or biased information;

Emphasise the need for a coherent and sustained approach by schools to education for democratic citizenship. Such an education should start at an early age and make full use of the many possibilities offered by the formal curriculum and extra-curricular activities including contacts with organisations working for human rights ...

Recognise that the effectiveness of programmes of education for democratic citizenship depends on the commitment and skills of the teachers. They need appropriate training and support and there should be an effective partnership between educators, politicians and members of the community – all firmly committed to the values proclaimed in the Universal Declaration of Human Rights and the European Convention. (Council of Europe, 1994)

Symposia, colloquys of educational research workers and teachers' seminars

The Vienna Symposium of 1983 provided an opportunity for representatives of governments and NGOs to discuss the position papers and principles provided by several academic experts. The conclusions have provided the basis of the Council of Europe's subsequent activities in human rights education. Regular meetings of directors of national educational research institutes are also organised by the Council. The 1989 meeting in Portugal covered 'socialisation of school-children and their education for democratic values and human rights' (Starkey, 1991a). The 1992 meeting considered 'education for democratic citizenship' (Fogelman, 1994).

One particularly important line of action is meetings of teachers. These seminars are offered by a member state for its own teachers and the CDCC provides bursaries enabling ten to twelve teachers from other member states to attend. Specialist experts are usually invited to give key-note addresses, but much of the time is devoted to teachers exchanging their first-hand experience on the topic under consideration. A rapporteur is commissioned to sum up the proceedings, which are sometimes published. Every year teachers' seminars on human rights education are held. Topics range from pre-school to upper secondary school and from history to science. The regularity of such seminars indicates the importance that member states and their education authorities give to human rights education. A list of published reports is included in the references.

Work with non-governmental organisations

International courses and summer schools have been organised, with the direct support of the Council of Europe, by organisations such as the René Cassin Institute in Strasbourg, the Education in Human Rights Network in the UK and CIFEDHOP, the training arm of School as an Instrument of Peace, in Geneva. These international courses are by their nature inter-cultural and thus arguably the best possible form of course. A residential course enables participants to learn from each other and often gain the confidence to stage their own training courses in their home region to disseminate the insights, the information and the pedagogical approaches even more widely. For instance, such courses have been staged in Slovakia, Lithuania, Romania, Bulgaria and Slovenia.

The International Institute of Human Rights in Strasbourg, the René Cassin Institute, named after its founder and Nobel Prize winner, runs a large summer programme on human rights for lawyers and those working directly in the field of human rights. During the 1980s, with the active support of Professor Massarenti of the University of Geneva, a week-long session specifically on human rights education in schools was held, alongside the main summer school. The programme has been described by Best (1991). By 1987 the session was operating in two language groups, English and French, but organisational constraints forced the abandonment of this initiative until 1994, when it was revived with the support of Canadian educators.

The international NGO School as an Instrument of Peace was founded in 1967 by the Geneva publisher Jacques Mühlethaler. Conscious of the importance of training teachers for their contribution to peace through human rights, the organisation set up a training arm known as CIFEDHOP which since 1982 has organised a summer training session of one week's duration for teachers and educators. The first of these was, in fact, organised jointly with the René Cassin Institute. The programme and its philosophy is discussed in Chapter 8. The Council of Europe has been closely identified with the session. It has enabled bursaries to be offered under its teacher bursary scheme and under its programme of support for Central and Eastern Europe. It also published a report on the 1995 session (Henaire, 1995). The Directorate of Education, Culture and Sport and the Human Rights Infor-mation Centre have been directly represented at the session since 1989.

The Human Rights Album

It is not easy for an intergovernmental organisation such as the Council of

44

Europe to promote specific pedagogical materials. Guidelines, reports and policy statements are expected and welcome contributions from an international organisation, but teaching materials are rarely suitable for use in countries other than those from which they originate. Nonetheless, the Council found itself in the early 1990s under pressure to produce material that could be used in many contexts.

An approach from a French publisher in 1991 convinced the Council that an appropriate publication for use with children in schools was achievable. The publisher offered the services of an original graphic artist of Polish origin, Wozniak, whose cartoons enliven the French satirical paper the *Canard Enchaîné*, to illustrate articles of the European Convention on Human Rights. The result was a small full-colour exercise-book-size publication, *The Human Rights Album*. Originally published in 1992 in English, French and Polish editions, it has subsequently become available in several other European languages, the translations and further publishing costs being borne by individual member states.

The *Album* has a number of potential uses. Although it is attractive to children and young people, the reading level of the text and the explanations of the work of the Council of Europe and the European Convention on Human Rights puts it beyond the capacity of most pre-teenagers, at least if working by themselves. However, the *Album* was always designed to be used by young people with some adult help and there are also many ways in which younger children can benefit from it. Teachers will find, in its thirty-two pages, a clear description of the Council of Europe, its history, aims, structures, programmes and current concerns. There is information about the European Convention on Human Rights and its machinery, illustrated by quotations from the articles and guidance as to their implications and scope. The *Album* comes complete with a tear-off postcard so that the reader, teacher or pupil, can request further information on human rights issues or the work of the Council.

The *Album* is a very useful complement to other materials designed for classroom use. Its main virtues are its attractiveness and its enigmatic illustrations. When offered to children or teachers the *Album* is always opened and examined. The pictures attract the attention, but unlike many realistic or conventional illustrations of human rights, these pictures yield their meaning gradually. The reader has to give thought to how the illustration and the articles of the Convention are matched. Initially the graphic style may need some deciphering. The search for the meaning of the picture is likely to stimulate questioning and discussion. As in the interpretation of any art, a number of meanings or readings are possible, itself a lesson in pluralism. Teachers on initial or in-service training courses respond well, in our experience, to the opportunities provided by the *Album* for information and discussion. Children, too, enjoy talking about the pictures and they are often encouraged or inspired to make their own illustrations. Wozniak's illustrations have also been used for a desk calendar, and a series of posters and cards promoting human rights.

Stand Up NOW for Human Rights!

Following the production of the *Album*, the Human Rights Information Centre in conjunction with the Directorate of Education, Culture and Sport commissioned a forty-minute video programme, *Stand Up NOW for Human Rights!* to introduce the Council and the European Convention and to illustrate ways in which young people are involved in activities protecting and promoting human rights. The video is designed to appeal to young people across Europe and to encourage them to engage actively in the life of civil society. Much of the impetus for the production of this resource came from demands of governments and human rights educators in Central and Eastern Europe.

The commission was awarded to an independent British producer, Mark Chapman of Dramatic Productions. He was advised by Cheryl Law, who assisted on the location shoot in Belgium, the Czech Republic, France, Germany, Slovakia, Slovenia and the UK and who wrote the accompanying teachers' material. The result is a video with considerable impact that can be used with teachers and with young people. It has a powerful and original music sound-track as well as voiceover, including poetry and quotations, and many examples of young people speaking for themselves.

The programme comes in three major sections. The first ten minutes explain the concept of human rights, using the definitions provided by young activists, articles of the European Convention and some historical background. The middle section, lasting twenty minutes, shows examples of young people working in organisations or schools to help those in need. They work with the elderly, the disabled, the homeless, refugees, prisoners of conscience and young people in personal crisis. They are also shown practising and developing freedom of expression through local radio and freedom of religion through previously forbidden ceremonies. The final section concentrates specifically on young people's action in opposing racism and promoting inclusion and solidarity.

Just as the message of the video is about young people being active citizens in the promotion of democracy and human rights, so the way it is used should be such as to elicit an active learning experience. Although the programme can be watched in one session, it is desirable to spend time fully exploiting each of the sections, following some of the many ideas in the accompanying booklet. The video then becomes, like the *Album*, a stimulus to enquiry, expression and action rather than a statement from a distant international organisation.

Priorities in the 1990s

Since the ending of the Cold War and the accession of states in Central and Eastern Europe to full membership of the Council of Europe and their participation in the activities of the CDCC, the Council has paid particular attention to education for democracy and human rights in those countries where these were for many years largely denied. In November 1993 the Council convened in Strasbourg a Co-ordination Meeting of Co-operation Programmes for Central and Eastern European Countries in the Field of Human Rights Education, including Education for Democratic Values at School Level and Teacher Training. The meeting enabled participating member states to define their needs for support and to make contact with NGOs who could help with education and training.

A further project to promote democracy through education, launched in 1993, stresses the need to ensure that minorities are protected and their right to cultural life accepted. Entitled Democracy, Human Rights and Minorities: Educational and Cultural Aspects, the project's aims are:

> to develop civics, intercultural education and cultural democracy, reinforced through practical field activities; to examine the educational and cultural aspects of the management of minorities in a democratic society; and to pursue the work of reflection and analysis in order to produce, on completion of the project, guidelines for the attention of governments on educational and cultural rights.

One strand of the project, entitled Strategies for Interculturally-oriented Civics Teaching at Primary and Secondary Level, is described by Birzea (1995). Working closely with the Romanian authorities, it supported the establishment of an International Institute for Intercultural Education in Timisoara, inaugurated in December 1994. The project encouraged teachers from across Europe to undertake action research and share their findings (Georgescu, 1994). A working group within this project edited an anthology of texts, provided by member states and illustrating the development, over the centuries, of the humanistic thinking which paved the way for the European Convention on Human Rights (Carpentier, forthcoming).

The Council has also supported informal education for young people through the European Youth Centre. The All Different All Equal Campaign in 1995 mobilised thousands of young people across Europe in anti-racist activities. Some of the materials produced for this campaign are described in Chapter 4.

A new project starting in 1997, entitled Education for Democratic Citizenship, brings together several strands of the Council's work. The project aims to promote education for citizenship both through the formal school sector and as an entitlement of adults in life-long learning. A new protocol to the European Convention on Human Rights develops educational and cultural rights as formal entitlements accepted by those member states which adopt it.

Summary

A multilateral agency such as the Council of Europe operates on a number of levels. It constantly prompts and reminds governments and ministers of their commitment to human rights and to combating anti-democratic activity such as racism or xenophobia. It is also able to give moral support and international networking facilities to teachers and to organisations working in society to promote human rights. This educational process plays an important role in enabling young people throughout Europe to acquire democratic attitudes and behaviours. The success of the programme is ultimately judged by the quality of democracy and the extent of respect for human rights in Europe.

Part 2. Human rights education and political realities

4   *Challenging racism, xenophobia and intolerance*

Introduction

Public manifestations of intolerance appear to intensify in periods of difficulty or economic crisis. Racial and religious extremism is still very much in evidence in many parts of the world. In some places certain groups have resorted to extreme displays of violence and brutality in order to achieve their ends. In parts of Europe we have seen the growth and strengthening of neo-fascist movements and persistent racial attacks on members of ethnic minority communities. At its most extreme, the 1990s have witnessed so-called 'ethnic cleansing' and large-scale massacres in former Yugoslavia, and genocide systematically planned and executed in Rwanda. This chapter focuses on the potential of human rights to create new perspectives in education and particularly to promote mutual respect in a context of cultural diversity. It will begin by considering some of the broad challenges of educating for human rights and democracy which are common to many multicultural societies. It will then identify some of the barriers which prevent the full participation of ethnic minorities in education. Finally it will examine some recent initiatives to promote education for tolerance, racial equality and justice from a number of different countries.

Educating for democracy and tolerance in a multicultural community

Chapter 1 sought to demonstrate how human rights offer an ethical code acceptable to people of different religious and secular traditions. We have argued that in a multicultural society it is important that educators adopt a framework of values which are genuinely universal, and that human rights provide such a framework. As teachers we may operate within a broad value system which is compatible with human rights, but are rarely explicit about our values or their source. There is some evidence to suggest that parents, and particularly parents from minority traditions and communities, are concerned about the values which schools may be overtly or covertly promoting and would welcome closer dialogue on the shared values of home and school (Osler and Hussain, 1995). Indeed they should expect such a dialogue, in keeping with article 5 (the state's duty to respect the rights and responsibilities of parents and family to provide appropriate guidance) and article 14 (the child's right to freedom of thought, conscience and religion, subject to appropriate parental guidance) of the UN Convention on the Rights of the Child.

Some parents, particularly those from minority communities, may feel that their children are vulnerable to indoctrination at state schools or that their home traditions and religion may be undermined. This may be explained partly in terms of differences in perceptions between parents and teachers as to what is actually being taught and clearly has implications for the ways in which teachers communicate with parents. The UK Commission for Racial Equality has highlighted a gulf between the perceptions of black families in rural areas and those of headteachers. Even in those schools in predominantly white areas which have taken steps to introduce multicultural perspectives into the curriculum and to promote diversity, teachers may be unaware of the racist name-calling and taunts which black pupils are likely to experience and may fail to make links between racist name-calling and bullying and more extreme examples of racism in the community (Wallace, 1996). A headteacher may find it difficult to make connections between racist incidents in the local community which attract considerable media attention – such as fire-bombings, serious assault or murder – and the life of the school. It is likely however that parents and children from black and ethnic minority families will readily make the links between such incidents and their own everyday experiences of racism. Article 30 of the UN Convention on the Rights of the Child affirms the right of children from minority communities to enjoy and practise their own culture, religion and language. Children can claim this right when schools ensure that they support children from ethnic minority communities and have in place policies and procedures which deal with racial harassment. Similarly children from majority communities need not only an understanding of cultural diversity and tolerance but also the skills effectively to challenge racism and intolerance when they meet it.

There may be a tendency, in countries where there is an established tradition of democracy, to be complacent about education for human rights and democracy. Research from Canada suggests that, even in societies which are considered to have developed a rights-conscious and rights-respecting culture, the maintenance of this culture is dependent on an active programme of human rights education. Covell and Howe (1995) set out to establish the attitudes of fifteen- to eighteen-year-old Canadians to children's rights, on the assumption that the successful implementation of the UN Convention on the Rights of the Child may well depend on this generation's attitudes to the rights specified within the Convention. Conscious that a number of schools have education programmes which seek to protect young people from physical and sexual abuse, but that fewer actively teach for socio-economic rights or legal rights, such as the right to social security or the right to a fair trial, they were interested to establish whether young people would vary in their levels of support for different categories of rights.

They found that both sexes showed highest support for freedom from physical abuse, and then freedom from sexual exploitation. There was less support for socio-economic rights, while legal rights attracted the least support. In other words, students showed greatest support for rights in those domains where they had received some formal education, and least support for those which had not been addressed in their schooling. Overall, females showed a higher support for rights than males in all domains other than the legal. The researchers looked for a correlation between an individual's support for rights and their assessment of future educational and occupational opportunities. They conclude that the implementation of the Convention is most likely to be successful under conditions of full employment, accessible education, optimism about future opportunities, and the socialisation of males as well as females within a care-for-others orientation. Oscarsson (1996), in a study of social attitudes and future expectations of young Swedes, arrives at similar conclusions: a commitment to rights and democracy amongst the young cannot be assumed; each generation needs to be educated into human rights and democracy.

The subject of 'race' and education has produced an enormous literature over the past two decades. In England, schools and local education authorities (LEAs) introduced a number of initiatives in the 1980s designed to promote intercultural tolerance and challenge racism. Nevertheless, schools in the 1990s, obliged to respond to legislation relating to curriculum, school development, the role of LEAs, resources and training, and in the face of hostile attacks from the political right, have found it difficult to sustain their commitment to the development of a curriculum and ethos which promotes diversity and tolerance, and challenges racism and xenophobia. Yet the need for such an education remains pressing. We argue that human rights can provide a valuable framework for new initiatives in this field. As teachers working to challenge oppressive practices in education and to promote tolerance we recognise that racism in education needs to be challenged both directly and indirectly. Other social injustices such as sexual inequality, homophobia, and poverty often operate together in a complex way. It is important that teachers, student teachers and pupils in school all have opportunities to examine racism as a discrete issue. At the same time we need to recognise the ways in which challenges to social justice are often inter-related.

In order to develop tolerance and mutual respect it is critical that we first confront our own prejudices. Whereas in one setting it may be appropriate to begin by focusing on racial equality, in another it may seem more relevant to challenge homophobia. We believe that everyone, regardless of their culture or background, is likely to respond to each of these issues at an emotional level. Recognising and challenging racial prejudice may involve identifying other issues which appear either less emotionally charged or more immediately relevant to the local community. We suggest that a human rights framework permits teachers and their students to make links between various forms of injustice and allows each individual the opportunity to recognise the importance of solidarity in securing their own rights and protecting those of others.

An intergovernmental response to racism, anti-semitism and xenophobia

The heads of state and government of the member states of the Council of Europe, at their first summit in Vienna in October 1993, recommitted themselves to

> pluralist and parliamentary democracy, the indivisibility and universality of human rights, the rule of law and a common cultural heritage enriched by its diversity. (Council of Europe, 1993)

The summit acknowledged the real threat which expressions of intolerance pose to democracy in Europe where 'diversity of traditions and cultures has for centuries been one of Europe's riches' and expressed its alarm at the resurgence of racism, xenophobia and anti-semitism, aggressive forms of nationalism, violence against migrants and people of immigrant origin, and the degrading discriminatory treatment faced by these groups. It also expressed its concern at the deterioration of the economic situation which threatens societal cohesion and which may generate forms of exclusion likely to foster social tensions and xenophobia.

Accordingly the summit agreed to

condemn in the strongest possible terms racism in all its forms, xenophobia, anti-semitism and intolerance and all forms of religious discrimination;

encourage member States to continue efforts already undertaken to eliminate these phenomena, and commit ourselves to strengthening national laws and international instruments and taking appropriate measures at national and European level;

undertake to combat all ideologies, policies and practices constituting an incitement to racial hatred, violence and discrimination, as well as any action or language likely to strengthen fears and tensions between groups from different racial, ethnic national, religious or social backgrounds;

launch an urgent appeal to European peoples, groups and citizens, and young people in particular, that they resolutely engage in combating all forms of intolerance and that they actively participate in the construction of a European society based on common values, characterised by democracy, tolerance and solidarity. (Council of Europe, 1993)

The summit agreed a plan of action which included a broad European Youth Campaign co-ordinated by the Council of Europe in co-operation with European youth organisations against racism, anti-semitism and intolerance, which acknowledges the equal human dignity of all.

The 1995 Commission on Global Governance (CGG) similarly recognised the serious threat which poverty and gross economic inequalities can pose both in societies which are striving to introduce a new democratic culture and in those which have long-standing democratic traditions:

Societies in which there are deep and expanding social or economic disparities face enormous obstacles, whether in creating or maintaining democracy. Citizens who must struggle daily to meet basic needs and who see no possibility of improving their circumstances are unlikely to have either the interest, or the ability, to work on behalf of democratisation. To be sustainable, democracy must include the continuing prospect of contributing to the prosperity and well-being of citizens. (CGG, 1995: 61)

The 1995 Rowntree inquiry into income and wealth shows that since 1979 there is no industrialised country in the world, other than New Zealand, where economic disparities have grown faster or greater than Britain. The number of people living in relative poverty, as internationally defined, has increased from 10 per cent to 25 per cent over this period and this includes a third of all children. Absolute poverty has also increased. A third of all black and ethnic minority people are to be found among the poorest 20 per cent of the population. Among the wealthiest 20 per cent only 11 per cent of black and ethnic minority people are represented, compared with 22 per cent of the white population (Hills, 1995; Rowntree Foundation, 1995). Thus it would appear that some governments, whilst making a public commitment to combat racism, are simultaneously pursuing economic policies the effect of which is to increase social inequalities and the conditions in which racism flourishes. Whilst it would be naive to suggest that tensions such as this can be resolved through education alone, such tensions do need to be addressed in the human rights education of teachers.

Ethnic tensions and the threat to democracy

In many societies, and particularly in newly emergent democracies, inter-ethnic tensions pose a serious threat to future stability, as people begin to experience new political freedoms but find their opportunities to participate constrained by harsh economic realities. In the Horn of Africa famine and a scarcity of basic resources has often exacerbated ethnic divisions, as in the development of clan warfare over pasture and wells (de Waal, 1992). The Ethiopian government, rather than attempt to play down ethnic divisions in a country of 55 million people, where some eighty languages are spoken, has adopted a policy of federalism, acknowledging and building upon people's sense of ethnic identity. It has established nine regional authorities with considerable powers and responsibilities, including those of taxation and the determination of development policies. Nevertheless, this may simply move the problem from central government to the regional level. The development of a national identity which is inclusive of a range of cultures and ethnic groups may be easier to achieve in a small country, like neighbouring Eritrea. Eritrea also has a multicultural and multiethnic composition but since independence has promoted a common Eritrean identity and purpose while at the same time acknowledging cultural diversity. Education has a major role to play in the establishment of a new democratic culture. Harber (1994) argues that if democratic political institutions are to be sustained in Africa then schools will need to educate for ethnic tolerance and mutual respect, recognising that such an education will require not only direct consideration of such issues within the curriculum but also changes in classroom and whole-school organisation. (Examples of such initiatives, both curricular and organisational, are discussed in the final section of this chapter.)

In Europe, a number of recently independent countries are experiencing ethnic tensions which challenge the process of democratisation and which often arise from past injustices, exacerbated by current difficulties as economies adapt to free-market conditions. In recently-independent Latvia, teacher educators initially saw the role of citizenship education as supporting the establishment of distinct ethnic identities, rather than acting as an integrative force. Their perspectives changed as they worked in partnership with colleagues from Denmark and Britain in a European Union-funded TEMPUS project to develop a new programme of teacher education which would complement constitutional reform. It became clear that teaching and learning materials for democratic citizenship need to acknowledge the past and present complexities of Latvian citizenship and identity, and to explore inequalities, rights and responsibilities; for example, the differing experiences of women and men in Latvian society. An initial reluctance to discuss issues of human rights within the working group appeared to stem from the complex issue of the rights of the Russian minority. Nevertheless, a number of project participants were keen to examine gender issues, in the context of rights and inequalities. This, then, was the starting point for discussions that led into broader human rights questions and a critical examination of power relations, rights and responsibilities (Clough et al., 1996). Where an issue proves to be too politically sensitive or emotionally charged to be tackled directly, a human rights framework, with its inherently holistic view, based on the indivisibility of rights, permits even the most sensitive issues to be considered within an agreed value system.

In a number of Western European countries, membership of neo-fascist movements is strengthening. Historically, Sweden has been noted for its tolerant approach towards immigrants and its acceptance of refugees. Yet in 1995 Stockholm police estimated that the number of skinheads in the city, openly promoting xenophobic attitudes, had risen from around 200 to 1000. It is largely pupils in their early to mid-teens who are joining their ranks and this is posing a problem for a number of high schools:

> Teenage pupils wearing neo-Nazi paraphernalia, often with armbands and racist symbols, are a familiar sight in classrooms. The absence of dress codes and Sweden's liberal laws enshrining the constitutional freedom of expression mean teachers are powerless to intervene. (McIvor, 1996)

In the mid-1990s Sweden has experienced the effects of economic restructuring, following a period of near full employment and a broad recognition of the value of migrant labour during the 1980s. Right-wing nationalist views began to be reflected in a new skinhead subculture of

'White Power' music, which uses racist imagery and draws on Norse mythology. In a well-publicised case, one school principal tried to prevent the open display of neo-Nazi sympathies by buying new clothes for a group of pupils who took advantage of the absence of a school dress code and Sweden's liberal laws and constitution, guaranteeing freedom of expression. Initially, the principal was judged by the National Schools Board to have breached the pupils' integrity. National legislation securing freedom of expression needs to impose limitations which restrict the exercise of this right out of respect for the rights of others or the protection of public order. Such limitations can be found in international legislation, such as in UNCRC article 13 and the European Convention, article 10. In the Swedish case, limitations on freedom of expression were eventually acknowledged and pupils can no longer express neo-Nazi sympathies through their dress in school. Schools can and should take their cue directly from the international instruments, for example, UDHR article 30, and ban the public display of intimidatory signs and paraphernalia which deny others the security to which they are entitled.

A Stockholm teacher, Lasse Navarro, explains developing racist attitudes and behaviour as part of a disillusionment with conventional politics:

> Democracy does not have the same attraction as it did. Youngsters no longer feel it has all the solutions. The economic crisis has made them look for scapegoats. (McIvor, 1996)

The expression of this type of nationalism and xenophobia is not peculiar to Sweden; similar tendencies have been observed in Britain, France, Germany and elsewhere, and they are not exclusive to the young. In those states which were former colonial powers, such as Britain or France, such attitudes may be reinforced by feelings of national superiority which can be traced back to the days of empire. The importance of education-in-action skills to achieve change by democratic means is reinforced. A disillusionment with politics is a threat to democracy itself and therefore to human rights.

Barriers facing ethnic minorities in claiming the right to education

Educational initiatives designed to confront racism, xenophobia, anti-semitism and intolerance often focus on changing the attitudes of individuals and groups from the majority population but neglect structural and institutional racism. The ways in which structural and institutional racism in schooling may prevent the full participation of people from ethnic minority communities within education and the labour market have been well documented (for example, Blair and Arnot, 1993; Brennan and McGeevor, 1990; Eggleston *et al.*, 1986; Mirza, 1992). Klein (1993) outlines debates and developments in the field of multicultural education and identifies a number of key issues in education for 'race' equality in England, for example policy implementation, management and organisational issues, curriculum, assessment and achievement, which should prove invaluable to both new and experienced teachers wishing to develop their own understanding and practice. Nevertheless, the discrimination and disadvantage faced by ethnic minorities within the education system is rarely presented as a human rights issue. This section will briefly address the right to education and consider some of the structural and institutional barriers which prevent the full participation of minorities in exercising this right.

The right to education is enshrined in the Universal Declaration of Human Rights, article 26, and reaffirmed in a number of international human rights texts, including the UN Convention on the Rights of the Child (UNCRC), article 28. Schools have been found to discriminate against children from ethnic minority groups, contravening article 28 of UNCRC which affirms children's rights to education 'on the basis of equal opportunity'. An investigation by the Commission for Racial Equality into secondary school admissions policy in an English education authority found that policies can very easily be indirectly discriminatory, unless positive measures are taken to ensure that they meet principles of equality and legal requirements. For example, the report found that one written admissions policy stated three criteria: having a sibling at the school, living nearby, and reasons provided by parents for wanting a place. In practice admissions depended on the written application from parents and the number of reasons given. This worked against Asian families because they were unaware of the informal criteria for admission and because, in families where the first language is not English, it is more difficult to produce a written application (CRE, 1992). The policy of granting preference to siblings can also discriminate in an indirect way by securing access for communities established in an area but effectively denying it to newly-arrived groups (CRE, 1993).

Schools which operate inflexible policies on dress codes or uniforms may also discriminate against particular cultural or religious groups if these policies include certain rules which are unacceptable to these groups. A notorious example is the French case where Muslim girls were denied access to school because they choose to wear the *hijab* or headscarf, which was judged inappropriate in a secular school system which theoretically prevents pupils from wearing religious symbols or clothing. In practice this is not a rule which is vigorously enforced, and a pupil is unlikely to be denied access to school for wearing, say, a Christian cross. There is evidence that some young Muslim women are choosing to wear the *hijab* as an expression of their religious identity (Altschull, 1995; Gaspard and Khosrokhavar, 1995) and such a rule not only denies them their right to education under article 28 of UNCRC but also might be challenged under article 13, freedom of expression. However, this case, taken together with the Swedish case of the Nazi insignia in schools, demonstrates both the strength and the limitations of a human rights approach. On the one hand we wish to promote freedom of expression and of religion. Against this is the need to provide security for the students and teachers and to permit schools to concentrate on their main task of educating all. Teachers need to work with young people, their parents and the community to resolve conflicts which may limit access to education and equal opportunity. Such conflicts of rights provide excellent case studies for discussion with teachers in training. Ultimately, however, their resolution may require the intervention of the courts.

Girls and women may find the right to education undermined by a number of inter-related factors including the problems of stereotyping, sexual harassment by fellow students and teachers, and traditional attitudes prevalent in many communities. Those from minority communities may experience these in different ways: for example, racist taunts are often overlain with sexual references when applied to ethnic minority women and girls and there have been various reports of female Muslim college students being taunted and harassed by members of the extremist group Hizb ut Tahrir for failing to conform to strict Islamic dress codes (Hugill, 1995; Ward, 1996).

The issue of the disproportionate exclusion of African-Caribbean boys from schools in England is another example of institutional discrimination through which students from a particular ethnic group are being denied the right to education. One explanation for the recent rise in the number of pupil exclusions is the competitive context in which schools are now working, with inspectors' reports open to the public and individual schools' examination performances being published in league tables (NUT, 1992). There is a tendency among some UK teachers to perceive African-Caribbean boys as more troublesome. Research is urgently needed to establish whether there is any relationship between high exclusion rates for particular groups of pupils and other factors, such as diagnosis of special educational needs and the ways in which schools

58

develop and implement policies on racial harassment.

The decision in 1995 by the Department for Education and Employment (DfEE) to effectively end the collection of ethnically-based statistics may work to restrict the full participation of black and ethnic minority pupils in education. Past failure to collect reliable statistics has led the DfEE to abandon this task, which makes it impossible to check on the involvement, achievements and progress of black and ethnic minority pupils on a national scale. While there is a on-going need to put pressure on central government to address these issues, individual schools and LEAs can, of course, continue to collect statistics and monitor what is happening, ensure that services meet the needs of ethnic minority students, avoid indirect discrimination and address inequalities within their provision (Runnymede Trust, 1996).

Initiatives in education for human rights, tolerance and racial equality

Levels of commitment to democracy and human rights are likely to be influenced by a number of socio-economic factors which need to be addressed within any education programme. Ethnic tensions, and levels of racism and xenophobia may be affected by prevailing economic circumstances. While human rights education has an important part to play in promoting tolerance and racial justice, it is even more critical where social and economic conditions lead to feelings of resentment, injustice and exclusion among young people from majority communities. Young people need opportunities to explore the complex factors which can undermine societal tolerance, acceptance of diversity and democratic pluralism. This section surveys initiatives from a variety of societies to challenge racism, xenophobia and tolerance.

Education programmes which seek to promote inclusive concepts of citizenship and national identity need to acknowledge past as well as present realities if they are to be effective (Osler, 1994b). The founders of the Council of Europe recognised in 1949 how history teaching had been misused to promote feelings of national antagonism and cultural and racial superiority. Describing the aims of recent initiatives to support the teaching of history, Maitland Stobart, of the Council of Europe, notes how migrant and other minority communities, such as Gypsies, are threatened by violence in the present resurgence of racism, xenophobia and anti-semitism. Recognising that 'history teaching can be an important, even explosive force in the New Europe – a force for good or evil', he advocates a type of history which will emphasise 'the positive mutual influences between countries, religions and ideas'. He is clear about the urgency of such an approach in the current economic and political climate:

> In all European countries, economic change and restructuring have been accompanied by unemployment, marginalisation and exclusion which threaten the cohesion of our societies. In the present, volatile Europe there is a new sensitivity about national and ethnic identity: a complex concept which covers language, religion and a shared sense of history. (Stobart, 1995)

The approach to history developed by the Council of Europe in collaboration with historians, history teachers and teacher educators is to be welcomed as a way of avoiding nationalistic approaches to history which promote exclusive concepts of citizenship and national identity. A critical understanding of the past can support young people in developing tolerance, recognising shared human values and practising mutual respect.

Non-governmental organisations (NGOs) have a key role to play in supporting civil society, and have begun to flourish both in developing countries and in the former Communist countries of Eastern Europe. Participation in international NGOs has grown fastest in Africa, where the share of country membership has doubled over the last thirty years, and in Asia (CGG, 1995: 33). NGOs have been prominent in advancing respect for human rights, and one way in which they have had a significant impact on education is through the production of teaching and learning materials. This section will consider examples of such materials from North America, Africa and Europe.

North America

One organisation which has developed training programmes and materials for teachers designed to promote intercultural understanding and to challenge racial and other forms of intolerance is the Southern Poverty Law Center (SPLC) of Montgomery, Alabama in the United States. It is an interesting example of fruitful collaboration between lawyers and educators concerned with education in human rights. SPLC was established in 1971 as a civil rights law centre to fight for the rights of the poor by means of legal precedents. It is a non-profit making organisation funded through donations. In 1991, alarmed at the significant rise in 'hate crimes' being committed by young people, SPLC established the Teaching Tolerance project. The aim of the project is 'to make sure that every classroom in America is equipped with tools to help young people learn to live together in harmony'. Accordingly, it publishes a bi-annual teachers' magazine, *Teaching Tolerance,* and a range of high-quality practical resources for schools. These materials are distributed free of charge, upon written request, to educators in schools and higher education and to civic and religious organisations nation-wide. The magazine claims a circulation of 500,000 and aims to provide a national forum for teachers concerned to teach justice and equality.

In 1995 the Teaching Tolerance project produced a teaching pack, *The Shadow of Hate*, which surveys the history of intolerance in America. The pack consists of a video, a teacher's guide and a textbook. While the video provides a historical overview of intolerance, the textbook develops the themes of racial, ethnic and religious intolerance and presents the stories of groups and individuals who have suffered and resisted discrimination. Through these case studies it is possible to examine a number of themes, such as women's perspectives, youth perspectives, the experience of immigrants and that of specific minorities, or to study specific types of intolerance, such as religious discrimination or homophobia.

One chapter recounts the story of Charlie Howard, a young gay man who was killed by three other young men in a small town in New Hampshire in 1984. Students are first invited to consider how intolerance towards homosexuals limited the opportunities available to Howard. They are then asked why they think his attackers felt compelled to assault him and to consider the role that peer pressure might have played in the attack. Discussion and written assignments invite students to examine their own feelings and to consider why it is sometimes difficult to take a moral stand. Data presented in 1986 to the US House Judiciary Subcommittee on Criminal Justice indicates that gays and lesbians are the most frequent victims of 'hate crimes', being four times more likely to be victims of violence than persons in the general population. Students are informed that anti-gay offences are aimed not just at their individual victims but at the communities to which those individuals belong (Carnes, 1995).

These materials raise the issue of gay and lesbian rights as part of a broader struggle for human rights and greater tolerance and democracy. This is critical within a society where right-wing moral lobbyists appear to have gained considerable influence, including control over a number of school boards. In New Hampshire a teacher was recently sacked by her school board for asking her pupils to read E. M. Forster's novel *Maurice*. Penny Culliton, the teacher concerned, was keen that her students should see a relatively positive depiction of a homosexual character. She argued:

> I've seen what it's like for gay youth who see only a negative portrayal of themselves in society and in what we read, and there's just a wall of silence there for them. (Marcus, 1995)

The Shadow of Hate demonstrates that intolerance and violence shown to gays and lesbians is effectively a threat to the human rights of others, and amounts to an attack on democracy itself. Examples drawn from American history from the mid-seventeenth century to the present day demonstrate the need for the on-going struggle for human rights:

> This is the story of some Americans who were hated by others simply for who they were, what they looked like or what they believed. Their experiences remind us that our democracy is still a work in progress. (SPLC, 1995)

Africa

In Ethiopia, the military defeat of Mengistu in 1991 brought to an end a long period of civil war, an exodus of over a million refugees and the internal displacement of millions more. During the seventeen years of the Mengistu regime there were gross human rights violations, over 100,000 people became political prisoners, and tens of thousands were tortured, extra-judicially executed or 'disappeared'. Ethiopia is one of a number of newly emerging democracies which are investing in new education programmes to promote human rights and development (Osler, 1996a). In Addis Ababa a number of new NGOs have begun to contribute to the process of developing a new culture of human rights. One such organisation, the Action Professionals' Association for the People (APAP), has developed a valuable human rights' trainers handbook, *The Bells of Freedom*, for use in non-formal education (APAP, 1996).

These materials have been developed for use with women's groups, urban unemployed adults, street children, prostitutes and other marginalised people. Although designed for non-formal educational settings, much of the material is equally appropriate to teachers, teacher educators or school students and can be adapted for use in a range of cultural contexts to raise awareness of rights and enable participants to make links between human rights issues in Ethiopia and in their own cultures and communities.

The handbook notes that The African Charter on Human and Peoples' Rights (ACHPR, 1981) sets an innovative standard in human rights education, placing responsibility on states not only to promote education in human rights but to ensure that such education is *effective*. Signatory states

> shall have the duty to promote and ensure through teaching, education and publication, the respect for the rights and freedoms contained in the present Charter and to *see to it that these freedoms and rights as well as corresponding obligations and duties are understood.* (APAP, 1996, quoting article 25, ACHPR: emphasis added)

Through a series of structured exercises the handbook encourages participants in training to make links between their everyday concerns and human rights values. The aim is that participants will share new knowledge and skills with others, thus empowering whole communities. Each exercise includes relevant articles from international instruments and the Ethiopian constitution, and there is a particular emphasis on the human rights of women, with over a third of the activities directly addressing their concerns. Sensitive and controversial issues, such as the role of the police in a democracy, arranged marriages, and the traditional practice of female genital mutilation are not avoided. The material makes good use of case studies and is likely to appeal to people with a strong love of stories. It includes the real-life stories of African human rights heroes and heroines, such as the Kenyan Wangari Maathai and the South African Albie Sachs. *The Bells of Freedom* goes some way to answering the question of how to approach human rights education with people who have experienced or are experiencing gross violations of their rights.

One criticism of the Ethiopian materials might be that they do not give sufficient attention to issues of ethnic identity or discrimination by ethnicity. It is difficult to find a balance between raising human rights values that are pertinent to participants' lives and raising those which they may be less willing to discuss. Nevertheless, the materials do attempt to confront prejudice and discrimination more broadly. In another exercise, participants are invited to reflect on their attitudes to a range of groups who are marginalised within Ethiopian society. These include:

• women
• refugees and displaced persons
• people with a different language or accent
• street vendors
• people who beg on the streets and scavenge for rubbish.

One of the case studies shown is reproduced here as Box 4.1. The following international and Ethiopian legislation is offered as a framework for the exercise:

• Universal Declaration of Human Rights: article 23
• Convention on the Elimination of All Forms of Discrimination Against Women (CEDAW): article 11 (employment) and article 14 (rural women)
• Ethiopian Federal Democratic Constitution (EFDC): Article 25: 1. Women have the right to equality with men in the enjoyment and protection of rights provided for by this Constitution. ... 3. In recognition of the history of inequality and discrimination suffered by women in Ethiopia, women are entitled to remedial and affirmative measures. The purpose of such measures shall be to enable women to compete and participate on the basis of equality with men in politics, economic and

social life, and to gain access to opportunities and positions in public and private institutions. (EFDC, Articles 1 and 3)

The exercise examines the gender division of labour in Ethiopian rural areas and participants' values regarding male and female roles, since international law, traditionally understood, does not reach all problems of private discrimination. Participants are thus encouraged to look at the position in terms of culture as well as in terms of laws. They are divided into two groups, one to argue that the division of labour is fair, and the other to argue against this and to suggest changes which will redress the balance. Individuals are allocated to groups without choice and may thus have to argue a position they do not agree with. Each group is given time to prepare their case. The groups sit opposite each other. At the end of the exercise people may cross over to the side they wish to support, or a third group may form who are undecided. The exercise concludes with each person who has moved explaining why they have changed their position and what they might do differently in the future as a result of the exercise.

This rural Ethiopian family lives in a farm on the outskirts of a village without electricity, telephone, or piped water. The village has an Orthodox church, bar, mud-walled tea house, medical dispensary, and three small shops. It is located on a dirt road which connects to a major highway leading to the capital city of Addis Ababa, ninety kilometres away. Farming has become a barely adequate source of income; the soil has deteriorated owing to erosion and the family's plot of land is too small to earn enough money to pay for the children's school expenses, local taxes, clothing, and assorted household expenses. The husband occasionally goes to the city in search of wage-paying employment in a factory, but he has never found more than occasional odd jobs. When he makes these trips he is unable to give sufficient time to the cash crop production that is his source of farm income. The wife maintains and works the land. She has assumed many farming and marketing responsibilities. As he is gone for short periods each month, she spends more time than her husband growing vegetables to sell in the local market to generate some household income. Her family and household responsibilities have increased substantially because of the husband's occasional trips to the city. The job of raising eight children and providing for their daily needs falls almost exclusively on her.

Box 4.1 Equality for rural working women: an Ethiopian case study

64

Wife's work	Husband's work
Farm-related responsibilities (throughout week) Ploughs and prepares soil with hoe Plants, weeds and harvests small cash crop: e.g. beans, maize, and food crops for family Pounds, grinds, sieves, sorts crops for family use/sale Carries cash crop and food not needed for family consumption to local market. Sells at market (one day a week) Oversees children who herd the few goats/cattle	*Farm-related responsibilities (when not travelling)* Fells trees, clears bush, and prepares soil on new plots of land (with use of rented tractor) Harvests and makes decisions on use of farm land, i.e. cash crops to be grown Establishes priorities and guidelines for farming activities Arranges for sale of cash crop, if beyond village
Household/family responsibilities (throughout week) Gives birth to children (average of 8 per family) Prepares meals for family/husband's food to take to city Washes and dresses young children Assists older children to prepare for school Cares for youngest children during day (carrying baby on back), with assistance of eldest daughter Keeps house and family compound clean Oversees and disciplines children Washes and mends clothes for family Deals with emergencies, e.g. illness, accidents Collects firewood (1–2 mile walk every other day) Fetches water (1–2 mile walk every other day)	*Household/family responsibilities (when not travelling)* Socialises with children and wife Repairs house, other buildings, fences etc. Contributes part of income for children's school expenses, house repair, clothes, and perhaps food *Community responsibilities* Socialises with men at local tea house or bar Attends church with family *Average working day:* 8 hours *Income* Wages: urban employment Sales: 'cash crop' sold by wife in market goat or cattle sold in market
Community responsibilities (throughout week) Socialises with women while selling in the market and gathering wood Volunteers labour to self-help project (0.5 day per week) e.g. collecting stones, making bricks for primary school or health clinic construction Assists other women with chores at times of illness/accident Meets with local women to plan formation of women's co-operative to obtain own income Attends church with family *Average working day:* 15–16 hours *Income* Wages: none Sales: 'excess' family food sold in market	

Box 4.1: continued

Europe

The Council of Europe Youth Campaign *All different, All equal* was established in response to the 1993 Vienna Declaration to mobilise public opinion in favour of a more tolerant society, based on the dignity of all its members, and to challenge racism, xenophobia, anti-semitism and intolerance. Acknowledging the complexity of changing people's attitudes and effectively confronting racism and intolerance in society, the campaign has sought to exploit the potential of peer education. The Council of Europe has published a manual, *Domino* (Rothemund, 1995), which explains peer group education and provides examples of good practice from a number of countries. It includes an evaluation of a project whereby peer group education was introduced by an NGO into the formal education system, to support teachers and students in upper secondary schools. *Domino* contains a number of structured activities for exploring issues related to racism, intolerance and peer pressure. These activities draw on participants' creativity and imagination to explore feelings in an area which is inevitably emotionally charged. They include a planning exercise for those wishing to develop peer group education in a variety of educational settings, both formal and informal.

Peer group education has very significant potential in confronting racism and tolerance amongst the young, as recognised by Norwegian Prime Minister Gro Harlem Brundtland in 1993:

> Young people often speak to other young people with more credibility and effect than others. There will be different views among the young about various aspects of immigration and refugee policies. The point is not to agree on everything, but on the essentials needed to protect the most vulnerable groups. If youth speaks to youth and for youth in schools, clubs and the media, taking a clear distance against racism and intolerance, then the days of xenophobic sub-cultures will be numbered, which is precisely what we would like to see happen. It is our young people who carry all our hopes for the future. They are the coming generations within which civility, tolerance and dignity will continue to guide countries and peoples. (Brundtland, quoted in Rothemund, 1995)

Rothemund (1995) suggests there are three broad approaches to peer education and learning:

- *peer group education in formal educational settings:* initiated by teachers, the aim is ultimately to pass the responsibility for the programme on to students. The teacher moves from initiator to facilitator and consultant. This approach is likely to include student paired work, student leadership and advocacy, and the opening up of formal educational settings to a wider public. An example is the *Peace-maker Project* in Offenbach, Germany. Offenbach has the highest migrant population in Germany – one in three residents do not have German citizenship. In the context of increased racism and the electoral successes of the extreme-right Republican party, the town council asked the Youth Office to develop a programme against violence, racism, anti-semitism and right-wing extremism. A conflict resolution and 'violence prevention' programme has been introduced into Offenbach schools. Teachers and students are taught mediation techniques which can be applied when, for example, two students quarrel. Other objectives are the development of an infrastructure for tolerance and human rights education and the setting up of a local network and information service for schools and youth centres.

• *peer group education in informal educational settings*, for example in youth organisations and youth and social work, where adults in such programmes make a 'step-by-step retreat'. Peer group education programmes, existing alongside other more structured programmes, have the potential to reach a wider public than 'organisation members'. Examples include the National Coalition Building Institute's programme in England to train young people aged fifteen to twenty-one in prejudice reduction and conflict resolution. The aims of the project are to welcome and understand diversity; establish participants' pride in their own identities; enable them to make effective interventions; and train others in prejudice reduction methods.

• *peer group education initiated by young people*, grass roots initiatives: one example is the *Stop Volden* or *Stop the Violence* movement in Denmark initiated by five young people in Copenhagen after one of their friends was seriously injured in a stabbing incident. The campaign was targeted at young people aged twelve to twenty-five in urban areas across the country and the aim was to convince them that violence is not a solution to problems. The project works through youth clubs, primary schools, high schools, music festivals and concerts. It began with a concert attended by 1,500 people in 1993, at which they were invited to join the movement by sending special postcards. The movement was eventually extended to parents and those who work with young people, such as teachers, youth workers and the police. The movement believes that to fight violence, racism, anti-semitism and drug abuse it is necessary to understand the social conditions which provoke it, including the search to establish an identity on the part of those who are expressing violence. The members of the movement are invited into schools, but avoid preparing set talks. They rely on humour, and draw on their personal experiences, inviting others to consider why they act violently. They explain their effectiveness largely in terms of their closeness in age to the people with whom they are working.

The advantages of peer group education in confronting racism and intolerance, as identified in the Council of Europe Youth Campaign, may be summarised as follows:

- it builds upon the leadership potential of individuals and relies on in-group values, both of which are important during adolescence;
- each individual builds on his or her own experience of discrimination: racism and xenophobia reflect existing power structures, the powerful discriminating against the powerless. Powerlessness and not having your legitimate wishes taken seriously is a common experience of childhood;
- young people can be empowered to take action and form leadership. These positive feelings make it possible to overcome personal feelings of mistreatment or exclusion which may find expression in racism, xenophobia and intolerance;
- individual and group feelings are strengthened through solidarity and such shared feelings open the way to welcoming diversity;
- new group values and positive standards are established for the group; racist and intolerant behaviour is often the result of group pressure to conform;
- a snowball effect can be created among a wider group; just as racism and xenophobia can have a contagious effect and poison the atmosphere, so peer group education can be shared and form a counter-movement;
- it helps to keep ideals alive and to recognise them as a shared bond and force for changing the world;
- success motivates and leads to further successful action;
- self-confident youth challenge the adults' world and may challenge structural or institutional racism; for example, in youth organisations which are reluctant to start anti-racist programmes they may challenge racist attitudes, power structures and ethnic disparities within the system;
- they have the potential to challenge racism within the home environment of youth as young people adopt new values.

If peer group education, as a means of challenging racism, xenophobia and intolerance, is to have a significant impact on the formal education system, it requires a radical reassessment of the role of the teacher. It is a good example of a change in the organisation of learning as much as in the content of learning. Student teachers, in particular, will benefit from considering its potential and being trained in its techniques.

Summary

This chapter has considered a number of challenges facing educators seeking to confront racism, xenophobia, anti-semitism and intolerance and prepare their students for democratic participation in a multicultural context. It has reviewed a variety of initiatives from around the world, focusing on the work of NGOs and on that of the Council of Europe. It would appear that some of the most creative and imaginative work in confronting racism and intolerance has been achieved through NGOs; their resources, teaching and learning materials have much to offer both schools and teacher education. The work of a multilateral agency such as the Council of Europe is a work of influence. At government level the Council constantly prompts and reminds ministers of their commitment to human rights and to combating anti-democratic activity such as racism and xenophobia. It is able to give moral support and international networking facilities to teachers, youth workers and others working to combat racism. As teacher educators we have a dual responsibility to develop ways of confronting racism and intolerance both through an appropriate curriculum and teaching methods and through a process of awareness-raising which secures justice and the equal rights of minorities to education.

5   Education for citizenship and democracy

Introduction

As we saw in Chapter 2, understandings of children's rights have developed over the past twenty-five years. Whereas there was formerly a call for the liberation of children, there is now an acknowledgement, expressed in the United Nations Convention of the Rights of the Child, that children and young people are citizens with certain citizenship rights. Schooling is thus about educating citizens who are entitled to help shape their present as well as the future. Education is inevitably an instrumental process, providing access to knowledge, skills and qualifications for future life. It is also a process of cultural transmission, linking the past to the present and the future. The encounter with this cultural heritage may strongly influence the way young people integrate into society.

Education for citizenship is also education for democracy. In January 1996 the Parliamentary Assembly of the Council of Europe adopted a Recommendation on a European strategy for children which makes this point well:

> Children are citizens of the society of today and tomorrow. Society has a long-term responsibility to support children and has to acknowledge the rights of the family in the interest of the child. Responding to children's rights, interests and needs must be a political priority. The Assembly is convinced that respect for children's rights and greater equality between children and adults will help preserve the pact between generations and will contribute towards democracy. (Jeleff, 1996: 106)

Democracy is concerned with issues of equality, of participation and of representation. It also implies a commitment to openness, transparency and accountability (Wright, 1994). This agenda can be addressed through the formal curriculum, but it also requires supportive structures which are fundamentally different from those based on hierarchical authority. What is more, education for citizenship is where education and politics meet overtly. Teachers may find this very uncomfortable.

For these reasons there is a degree of ambivalence about education for citizenship and democracy. Students, parents, teachers and politicians all find it easy to criticise education for citizenship as it is currently practised. On the other hand there is considerable rhetorical support for this aspect of education. Work with students, teachers, heads, parents and education officials has convinced us that much effective citizenship education does occur where there is a clear framework, institutional support and appropriate pedagogy. Attention needs to be given both to the formal curriculum and to the structures and ethos of the school. That part of the school curriculum used to be known as 'hidden', but the democratic principle of transparency suggests that it should be made explicit.

Democracy is an ideal and therefore even the most democratic societies can aspire to greater achievements. As Held (1995) puts it:

> The distinctive feature of democracy is, in our judgement, not only a particular set of procedures (important though this is) but also the pursuit of democratic values involving the extension of participation in the democratic process.

One essential purpose of the education of citizens is thus the opportunity to discuss, explore, live, understand and apply democratic values and, in particular, human rights.

Preparation for teaching basic skills and subject specialisms dominates the curriculum of initial teacher education. The contribution of all teachers to the education of citizens receives low priority, as is reflected in the small amount of time devoted to it. All of us need to acquire the confidence to challenge unjust structures, whether in school or university, and prepare ourselves to deal with climates of intimidation or cultures of prejudice. As we saw in Chapter 4 there are ways in which we can prepare teachers for encounters with prejudice and intolerance. Through teacher education we can also encourage democratic practices and help to provide a stimulus to transform schools into real societies of citizens. We give examples in Chapter 9. In this chapter we evaluate two models of citizenship education based on human rights principles, examine some criticisms of current practice, and consider the implications of applying democratic principles to educational institutions.

Models of education for citizenship and democracy

Many models for education for citizenship have been proposed and many approaches have been described (for example, Baglin Jones and Jones, 1992; Mougniotte, 1994; Oliver and Heater, 1994; Roche, 1993; Rowe, 1992). There is in the mid-1990s a particular surge of interest in citizenship education with a European or global dimension (Bell, 1994; Osler *et al.*,

1996; Rovan, 1993; Steiner, 1996). Education for citizenship is concerned with both the personal development of students and the political and social development of society at local, national and international levels. On a personal level, citizenship education is about integration into society. It is about overcoming structural barriers to equality; challenging racism and sexism in institutions, for instance. It is also about developing personal commitment to the promotion of equality and social justice in schools and in the wider society. On a political and social level it is about creating a social order that will help provide security without the need for repression. It is about protecting democracy from anti-democratic forces such as organised racism and xenophobia. It is about promoting democracy and human rights as the basis of the good society.

The distinction between the political and institutional as opposed to the personal and cultural is made explicit in a model of citizenship proposed by Richardson (1996: see Box 5.1). He identifies four main strands or dimensions:

- status, rights and obligations;
- social inclusion and active participation;
- sentiment and sense of identity;
- political literacy and skill.

He suggests that the first two are structural and political, in that they determine the context in which education for citizenship occurs. The other two are more personal and cultural.

	Structural/political	*Cultural/personal*
Minimal	Rights	Identity
Maximal	Inclusion	Competence

Source: Richardson, 1996

Box 5.1 Four components of citizenship

The model implies that rights and a sense of identity are the necessary minimum for citizenship. The French sociologist Alain Touraine appears to agree:

> The autonomous personality (*sujet personnel*) is made up of freedom and identity. Freedom cannot be at the expense of identity. It is for this reason that families have an essential role in forming a sense of democracy. (Touraine, 1994: our translation)

In Box 5.1 the minimalist line expresses in shorthand the components of citizenship that derive on the one hand from the public or social sphere (rights, including freedoms) and on the other hand from the personal or private sphere (identity). School is a place where the specific values and culture of the family meet the more general values of the public sphere. Schools aim to socialise children, that is to facilitate their entry into and participation in the public sphere of institutions and, broadly speaking, of politics. The segment labelled 'rights' stands for the knowledge and experiences provided by the school which enable children to understand the social structures, rules and obligations within which context they can be creative. Rights belong to everyone and the first lesson of socialisation is that no individual's rights are more important than any other's. Reciprocity of respect for rights is the basis of society.

Whereas 'rights' is the shorthand for public ethical principles, 'identity' is based on private or personal ethical principles and a cultural background or inheritance. Civic education is about public principles. Moral education is about personal decisions. Education for citizenship combines these. Whereas in some circumstances it may be helpful to distinguish between public and private spheres, in many cases exactly the same principles apply. Indeed, as the principles of human rights are universal, they apply to the private sphere as much as to the public. However, whereas freedom of conscience and religion is a human right, whether to worship and in what tradition is a personal moral decision. The issue of social exclusion can be discussed and considered from a public and human rights perspective. The decision whether to give money to a beggar is a personal and a moral one.

Citizenship and a vision for society

Both Touraine and Richardson acknowledge that freedom, rights and identity are the essential attributes of citizens, but citizenship itself is more than an entitlement to rights. It is a means to an end, and that end requires struggle, organisation and pressure. It also requires a vision. At the height of the Second World War, A. E. Morgan wrote a book entitled *Young Citizen* in which he set out the basis for education for a democratic future.

> Education is simply the process devised to provide the environment and nurture which enable the young to develop. The nature and extent of education are an expression of the ideals and beliefs which the adult generation holds in regard to life. What we hold life to be is the basis for our educational practice. How we train the young, what we want youth to become is a reflection of our conception of the purpose of life. (Morgan, 1943)

Morgan expresses the belief that education is an environment and a vision. Schooling is to be based on 'our conception of the purpose of life'. Whereas we are fully in agreement with this part of Morgan's statement, in many parts of the world the place of young people in society has evolved. Young citizens are now entitled to participate in discussion and decisions about the purpose of life and the purposes of education. In a democratic society the transmission of values allows for these values and beliefs to be scrutinised and critically examined. Education for citizenship is about participation in shaping the future. This requires the opportunity to understand clearly the principles which underlie current visions of society and the institutions that underpin it.

In 1943 it was essential to produce a vision of a future world society which could be set against one based on a racial hierarchy and blind obedience to a totalitarian state. This alternative vision is set out in the Charter of the United Nations (see Chapter 1). It proposes the ideal of a democratic society based on justice and peace and free from fear and want; a community of citizens. Democratic nations which are parties to human rights instruments are explicitly committed to this ideal. However, democratic nations allow the free expression of non-democratic views of society. Conservative forms of religious morality and ethnic or racial supremacy both still find powerful expression linked to nationalism, for example. Since in a democratic society such views may freely circulate, education for democratic citizenship is essential if young people are to understand the choices implied by any vision or ideology.

Inclusion

Citizens who are able to claim the essential attributes of rights and identity have a chance of achieving a society corresponding to the vision of social justice, creativity and personal and social fulfilment expressed in the Universal Declaration of Human Rights. The alternative is oppression, division and probably violence. Possessing rights and a sense of identity, citizens can collectively work to achieve the good society. Richardson identifies the qualities of such a society as

> not just the absence of discrimination but, rather, the lively presence of many opportunities and spaces for citizens and residents to take part in the cultural, economic and political affairs of the community. (Richardson, 1996: 6)

Since the good society, like democracy, is an ideal and since the world changes, the goal is never entirely attained. To strive for it is, in a sense, maximalist.

The notion of inclusion is, however, problematic. What if the so-called democratic community refuses to acknowledge the rights of certain citizens to participate? What if, in spite of their personal qualities and strenuous efforts, female citizens, poor citizens, citizens with disabilities and citizens from minority communities are denied access to power and responsibility? The democratic community has to be based on reciprocity. The community collectively has obligations to its citizens, for if it denies access to participation in all areas of its life, how can it sustain itself as a democratic community? There are signs that many mature democracies have reached the situation where large sections of the population are alienated from the political process. A non-democratic state can always resort to repression to control its citizens or subjects. What Schnapper (1994) calls 'a community of citizens' can only sustain itself by making conscious and continuing efforts to extend its democracy. Education for citizenship is both about personal involvement in the community and about ensuring that the community remains democratic.

Complex and increasingly globalised societies require highly educated citizens. Understanding society so as to be able to participate and be an actor rather than a passive subject requires an understanding of political processes on the one hand, and skills of expression on the other. This knowledge and these skills combine to give the competence that is essential for full participation in society. If inclusion summarises the notion of the good community of citizens, competence describes the aim of their education.

Components of citizenship education

We have expanded Richardson's model to indicate the implications for the education of citizens (Box 5.2). In order to enjoy rights, citizens must know about them, and so human rights education is an essential minimum. However, rights do not exist in a vacuum, they become real when exercised in the context of democracy, social justice and a lively civil society. Examples of human rights education in action are given throughout this book.

Identities are explored in Chapter 10. We note that there is a double dimension to the notion of identity. On the one hand identity is the result of a series of choices based on oppositions. Our identities are constituted from feelings of 'us' or 'not us'. We identify with certain groups to which we feel we belong, such as family, profession, nationality, social class or culture. We distinguish ourselves from those groups with whom we do not wish to identify. To that extent the constitution of identity is based on a tension between 'us' and 'not us' which we refer to in the chart as 'either/ or'.

	Structural/political	Cultural/personal
Minimal	**Rights** ● knowledge of rights ● democracy ● absence of discrimination ● civil society, e.g. NGOs	**Identities** ● either/or (tension) ● both/and (hybridity)
	implies: **human rights education**	implies: **feelings and choices**
Maximal	**Inclusion** ● basic income ● security: physical, social, psychological ● active participation	**Competence** ● political literacy ● participation skills ● skills to effect change, e.g. language, advocacy, mobilisation
	implies: **the good society/school as the model**	implies: **action skills and training**

Box 5.2 Components of citizenship education

However, education is essentially a process whereby we are enabled to acquire additional identities and identify with wider communities. Human rights education, with its emphasis on essential humanity and equality of rights, enables us to develop these cumulative identities through a process which we refer to as the consciousness of 'both/and'. We can be part of an exclusive linguistic, cultural or religious group and part of a more inclusive entity, such as a democratic nation. We can be Catalan and Spanish, Jewish and French, Muslim and Yorkshire, any of these and European. This hybridity is the norm and the reason why attempts to align ethnic identity and the nation-state inevitably result in appalling human rights abuses including 'ethnic cleansing' and genocide.

The maximal segments involve those competences required for democratic participation, which we explore in Chapter 2, and a vision of the good society, which we develop later in this chapter. Before we do, we examine the difficulties of attempting to put in place human rights education without including individual feelings and choices. Learning about rights requires recognition of the personal, cultural and moral choices open to learners.

The minimalist approach: France and Britain

Richardson's model suggests two basic minimum requirements for citizenship. These are a knowledge of human rights and the opportunity to develop a feeling of identity. Knowledge of human rights is, indeed, a minimum requirement for citizens. Learning about human rights is therefore a minimum requirement for citizenship education. However, learning about human rights is not just a cognitive process. Civic education programmes based on diagrams in textbooks and lists of rights have been singularly unsuccessful. Such an approach to learning about human rights is still widespread in France, in spite of other very creative government-funded projects and many local examples of good practice.

In a study based on the Rhône-Alpes region of France, Roche (1993) quotes the parents of a young teenage girl:

As parents we became concerned with civic education through our daughter, who had this subject in primary school. We have to admit that neither she nor we ourselves found the experience particularly interesting or even instructive. After a brief reference to the 1789 *Declaration of the Rights of Man* there was a detailed study of the organisational structure of the three levels of local government, which is so far from her own interests that it is particularly boring and irrelevant for someone of her age. Moreover, since she has been in secondary school, this subject has not reappeared. This leads us to wonder about the usefulness of the subject and why it is confined to younger pupils. (our translation)

In a polemical best-seller attacking the inadequacies of formal education in France, de Closets (1996) is particularly scathing about civic education textbooks:

In my sample of text-books, all the teams of writers bar one ... covered page after page with theoretical, abstract, formalised, institutional, jargon-ridden quantities of knowledge, without a hint of original research. They included, because it is the pedagogical fashion, and not one I would quarrel with, various 'documents' designed to 'lend authenticity', without noticing that these documents, extracts from official and legal texts, are even more abstract and off-putting for young readers than the stuffy prose of the textbook itself and will only be of any interest to the teachers. For the writing teams, they have done their job if the content sticks faithfully to the National Curriculum. If the pupils don't understand, it is their own fault. (our translation)

In Britain, too, much that goes under the heading of education for citizenship is low status, poorly organised, unpopular with students and teachers and ineffective. It is sometimes asserted that young children are not capable of dealing with complex issues and that they are unable to understand political concepts, but from her research into the political understanding of primary school children Stevens (1982) concluded:

> the indications are that children between the ages of seven and eleven are capable not only of acquiring information, but of using it intelligently, that is, to further their own enquiries and understanding.
>
> ... the fact that some children at nine were able to, and motivated to, argue for social and political alternatives has some further implications for education that are concerned with what might be described as the 'citizen' attitude ... an attitude that approaches society and its problems in a spirit of participation.

She notes that young children are able to identify with 'ours' in relation to country, government, debts, money and problems, and sees their political learning as closely related to an adoption of a social identity. She argues strongly for political education that will enable children to develop peaceful solutions to conflict, enable them to understand the media and provide them with knowledge, skills and values which enable them to interpret the world, and for public debate on what that political education should include.

In spite of this reassurance that education for citizenship including a political dimension is possible, the results at the end of formal school education in Britain are extremely disappointing. A review of research by the Economic and Social Science Research Council on sixteen- to eighteen-year-olds conducted over a five-year period concluded that the majority were politically illiterate and that

> ... Stemming from such political ignorance is the overt racism which the research projects commonly reveal to be endemic among white youth in Britain. Political ignorance and racism are hardly the hallmarks of a healthy multiracial democracy. (McGurk, 1987: 6)

A major British study, published in the early 1990s after the introduction of a National Curriculum, is highly critical of the education system's failure to prepare young people to participate in political life, particularly its failure to meet the needs of those who may be in other ways educationally disadvantaged:

> Perhaps the most disturbing aspect of our findings was the political apathy and the incoherence of much of the political opinion that our respondents expressed. Those who leave for the ostensibly adult world of the workplace are not only the most politically alienated but also likely to be the most politically impotent. Clearly, for a democracy to have any meaning, it must be accessible to and understood by all its citizens. Even the act of voting was rejected by 15% of our 18 year olds. It seems that the pre-16 school curriculum and education policy generally have been neglectful in this respect. Educational institutions offer numerous opportunities for enabling young people to gain understanding of and to exercise political responsibility at the classroom, school and community level.

The curriculum, too, can be made more relevant and meaningful to young people by creating space in it for them to engage continually with current events. Most other European countries recognise the importance of such education for citizenship. The national curriculum in England and Wales needs to recognise it too. (Banks *et al.*, 1992: 187)

A survey commissioned by the charity Barnados and carried out in 1994 found that 59 per cent of young British people aged between twelve and nineteen had little or no interest in politics and only one-fifth supported a political party. Poverty, crime and 'race' issues were among their main concerns, with nearly four-fifths believing that reducing poverty would reduce crime. A significant number had little faith in the criminal justice system, with two-thirds believing that a poor person was more likely than a rich person to be found guilty of a crime they did not commit. Over 40 per cent believed a black person was similarly more likely than a white person to be convicted of a crime of which they were innocent. Twenty-eight per cent admitted to some degree of racial prejudice (Roberts and Sachdev, 1996). Clearly there is simultaneously evidence that young people have an interest in issues of citizenship and a suggestion that schools rarely offer significant opportunities to explore these concerns.

Fear of politics in schools

While young people express little interest in traditional politics, issues about which they express concern are clearly key political and citizenship issues. The challenge for schools is to build upon this concern and support them in developing skills which will enable them to address these issues effectively. However, teachers need to be both prepared for this role and supported in it. A French headteacher, quoted by Roche, tries to explain why education involving political questions is so difficult:

We certainly feel that the government wants us to do it and that it is on the parents' agenda. As a school we welcome this concern, but it worries us! That is why civic education is often formal, descriptive and theoretical. The teachers teach to the syllabus and they fulfil their legal obligations with minimum effort, without taking risks. The pupils soon get the message. At best they find the teaching useful but boring; at worst they find putting civic education into practice risky. (Roche, 1993) (our translation)

As we noted, citizenship education is where education and politics meet, and teachers find this a risky area. How can teachers gain the confidence to raise issues of human rights and democracy with their students? The answer lies in teacher education and in enabling teachers to understand that they are responsible to an international community as well as a national authority. The dangers for the future stability of society are increased when an absence of education for citizenship at a time of economic restructuring leads to a rejection of human rights and democracy.

Roche identifies some further reasons for the lack of results in the French formal human rights education programme. These include:

- lack of time or a feeling that the time is better spent on the traditional subjects of history and geography, with which civic education is explicitly linked;
- the fact that it is not an examined subject;
- the fact that there is, as yet, little progress in France in thinking about schools as communities.

Schools as communities of citizens

Schnapper (1994) theorises about the nation. She posits as the ideal, but existing, form what she calls the 'democratic nation'. A nation is made up of stable political institutions and territory. A democratic nation is what she calls 'a community of citizens' linked by their participation in the democratic institutions of the nation. The citizens, in a democratic nation, legitimise the state, which in turn provides the security and institutional structures within which society operates. Citizens of the democratic nation have a certain affective link to the nation. The nation is essentially a transcendent structure of political institutions within which a number and variety of ethnic and other groups may exist and flourish. As Schnapper puts it:

> Every democratic nation is different for historical reasons. But in every case it has been characterised by a tension between the desire for the formal and abstract rationale of citizenship, this being legal and political, and the need which exists within each society to build social links between citizens. This can only ever be communitarian or ethnic, that is to say direct and emotional. (Schnapper, 1994: our translation)

As we noted in the model in Box 5.2 above, rights are 'formal and abstract', whereas 'identities' are 'direct and emotional'.

> This tension is at the heart of the very idea of the democratic nation. Nationhood is dialectically positioned between the civic and the ethnic, an attempt to go beyond, to transcend the ethnic by the civic or an attempt to wrest away from the ethnic via the civic. (ibid.)

The democratic nation is an abstract framework within which real social relationships can be managed. It depends on a shared understanding of and acceptance of the basic values on which the democratic nation is constructed. As a minimum these are expressed in the formulations of human rights and national constitutions. These formulations need to be sufficiently general for individuals to be able to be creative and express themselves and for groups not to feel their essential identity threatened. On the other hand they need to be sufficiently robust to withstand attacks by non-democratic ideologies seeking to change the balance of the political structures in their favour.

Schnapper goes on to argue that schools are potentially models for the democratic nation. Her argument is in the tradition of Dewey (1909) who maintained:

> There cannot be two sets of ethical principles, one for life in the school, and the other for life outside the school. As conduct is one, so also the principles of conduct are one. The tendency to discuss the morals of the school as if the school were an institution by itself is highly unfortunate.

For Schnapper:

> The school is not just for transmitting a national ideology and a common historical memory through the curriculum. On a deeper level, like the political nation, the school forms a constructed space in which students, like citizens, are treated equally, irrespective of their family or social background. It is a place, both literally and as a concept, which is constructed in opposition to the real and existing inequalities of society and which stands out against the forces of discrimination found in civil society. The concept of the school is, like the concept of citizenship, impersonal and formal. By understanding the idea of school as community, children will learn to understand and feel included in the political nation.

Thus, following Dewey, Schnapper proposes school as a model of the good society. Schools are places where it is theoretically possible to operate a community based on social justice and human rights. If this model can be achieved within the microcosm of the school, then it should be possible to apply it to the complexities of wider society. We look at some examples of this in Chapter 7. Here we will look at some principles that can help make schools into examples of the good society.

Democratic schools

A democratic school is one that is accountable and where the structures are transparent. Schools in the public sector will be accountable to the government or local authority which provides the funding, to the parents who entrust their children to them and to the children themselves. This implies that the pupils, parents and the community understand the aims of the school and that these aims are made explicit. It also implies that all members of the school community have been involved in defining and approving these aims. The principle of transparency does not admit of a hidden curriculum. The project Developing Schools for Democracy in Europe addressed the question of how schools as organisations can embrace social difference and concluded:

> The policy and practice of inclusion involves becoming comprehensive not only in systems and structures but in attitudes and approach. Schools have to make explicit their values and their impact on social relations and structures, so that the hidden curriculum is not so hidden. They can then help develop self-esteem, self-respect and knowledge of others. (DSDE, 1993)

An education authority in London produced a policy on inclusiveness which it distributed to parents, in the spirit of transparency. It includes a section entitled 'The Right to a Supportive School Environment', which states:

> All children have the right to a supportive school environment which:
> - is physically safe
> - creates a sense of security and identity
> - encourages personal, social and academic activity
> - has sufficient human and classroom resources
> - promotes the active participation of parents in the education of their children at school and at home
> - maintains active links with the community at large.
>
> (London Borough of Ealing, 1991)

School communities express and make explicit their values in various ways, including through the example given by teachers and other school staff; the regular rituals and procedures of the school; literature created for different purposes such as school prospectuses or magazines; the use of display; the attention given to communal spaces. All these areas are opportunities for educating about human rights and democracy. Many schools in the UK now have one or more statements of policy which are public documents. Box 5.3 is the equal opportunities policy written by the staff of a primary school in Oxfordshire following a series of meetings involving teaching and non-teaching staff, parents, governors and external advisers.

Participants at the CIFEDHOP human rights summer school in 1993 produced a useful check-list of those features of school life that help a democratic climate and those which can hinder democracy in schools. It is included as Box 5.4.

Definition
We believe in the principles of Human Rights as the basis of our approach to Equal Opportunities. Equal Opportunities is about everyone in the school community having a right to equal access and participation in all aspects of school life, regardless of race, gender, disability, religion, national or social origin.

Aims
We shall aim to achieve

- an entitlement to equal access and participation in all aspects of school life for every child.
- a recognition and valuing of the diversity of cultures, languages, religions, opinions and beliefs in society.
- an atmosphere of open questioning, discussion and countering all forms of stereotyping, prejudice and discrimination, and positive action to enable every child to raise her/his self-esteem, expectations and achievement.

Guidelines
Curriculum
We ensure that all children experience every area of the curriculum and that appropriate provision is made, taking account of cultural and social background, abilities and interests. This includes providing for children whose families, at times, are unable to support them in their learning (e.g. literacy skills).

We consider the potential of a broad multicultural dimension in every area of the curriculum and include it in our schemes of work.

In our choice of resources we try to avoid stereotyping and bias of any kind and to positively reflect a wide range of peoples, cultures and human achievements.

Hidden curriculum
We make every effort to create an atmosphere of mutual respect and trust between child and child: staff and children: staff and parents.

We try to be aware of the 'messages' we may be giving in the language we use (e.g. headteacher, lunchtime supervisor), in the images and displays around the school and in the choice of visitors/speakers invited to the school.

We monitor playground use so that all children can be catered for and no single group is dominant.

Box 5.3 A school equal opportunities statement

Classroom organisation and management

We make every effort to provide equal access for all children to all activities e.g. computers, woodwork, play corner.

We monitor the criteria (gender, cultural, social, ability) used for grouping children.

We are aware of the balance of time and attention we give to all children so that their needs are met. We remember to make time for the undemanding child.

We try to ensure that classroom tasks are not allocated on the basis of gender.

Parents and the community

We try to increase parental involvement by improving communication on a formal and informal basis (e.g. by translating communications as appropriate) and by offering meetings at a variety of times with creche facilities whenever possible.

We actively encourage all parents, regardless of gender and background, to become involved in school activities, in the school association and in our governing body.

Staffing

We ensure that the school's recruitment, selection and promotion procedures are based on good equal opportunities practice, in accordance with the County's Equal Opportunities in Employment Policy.

We regularly review the professional development of all staff within the school.

We are aware of the importance of positive role models both in terms of gender and ethnic origin.

Assessment and achievement

We maintain consistently high expectations of all groups of children and ensure that there is no discrimination in assessment procedures. To help us in this we have developed a whole-school marking policy.

We provide appropriate support for children during assessment (e.g. bilingual learners).

Monitoring and review

We will evaluate our policy regularly and update the areas for action.

Date agreed . . . . .Headteacher . . . .

Date for review . . . .

Box 5.3 continued

A Ways in which schools promote democracy and help students

- good communication
- actively learning to live together
- appropriate supervision
- include a moral/ethical/social element in education
- provide multi-cultural and global perspectives within the curriculum
- include teachers from minority groups
- provide individual opportunities to develop talent
- establish school councils which include pupils, parents, teachers and non-teaching staff
- establish parent–teacher associations
- develop a school newspaper to promote effective communication and pupils' communication skills
- students organise activities
- develop community and international links
- school's democratic values are made explicit to students and parents
- all, including students, have equal access to information
- democratic behaviour is rewarded
- there is no discrimination by gender or group (e.g. minority)

B Ways in which schools are undemocratic and work against students

- authoritarian school
- authoritarian teachers
- pupils' views ignored
- poor communication
- marks and grades are seen as all-important
- no support/expectation to attend school (drop-outs)
- over-strict rules undermine creativity
- unclear system of control
- pupils experience stigma (e.g. through teacher attitudes)
- rote learning restricts creativity
- biased system (e.g. by social class, ethnicity, gender)
- school reflects unsympathetic socio-political aspects of society
- excessive financial control from without (e.g. from the state)
- syllabus imposes time constraints
- lack of choice/'compulsory' extra-curricular activities

Source:Osler and Starkey, 1994

Box 5.4 Democracy in schools

Richardson's model reminds us that citizenship education requires formal knowledge of human rights, a felt sense of identity and the action skills to claim a place in society. In short it is based on thinking, feeling and doing. This triangle is the basis for a further useful model derived by a group of teachers meeting at a Council of Europe symposium in Portugal (Starkey, 1987). It is based on the premise that learning occurs best where there is a combination of the cognitive, the affective and the active or conative (see Figure 5.1).

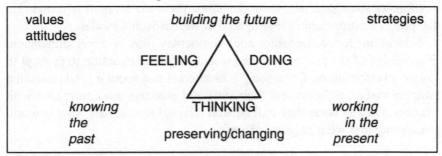

Figure 5.1 Human rights curriculum triangle

For young people to learn about human rights they must experience them and believe in them as well as know about them. This triangle is at the heart of all successful programmes of citizenship education. The cognitive is, of course, the traditional basis of education, namely by the transmission of knowledge via textbooks and lectures. The affective is stimulated by literature, by art, by songs and by stories, also by the creation of posters, artefacts, plays and music. Action implies working to discover more about society at first hand through personal investigation and involvement.

A human rights curriculum has a further triad, the past, the present and the future. Any view of society or of the world is helpfully informed by knowledge of the past. In the case of human rights it is important to know of societies which have or had basic values other than human rights. It is also important to know of the struggles for human rights. A curriculum based on human rights is also one looking to a world of justice and peace, which is a world that does not yet exist. The curriculum must therefore look to the future. Since active learning is effective learning it is important also to act in the present or on the present, leaving the shelter of the classroom and engaging with the wider world.

Summary

As we have implied, the citizenship curriculum deals explicitly with values and attitudes. It attempts to overcome prejudice and exclusion and encourage support for the values underlying human rights instruments. Furthermore since the goal of education is building the world of justice and peace (in the words of the Universal Declaration), this part of the curriculum introduces young people to means and strategies for achieving this. In particular they need to learn a variety of methods and mechanisms for resolving conflicts without resort to violence. This includes a knowledge of political and legal systems and the experience and the confidence to engage with them. Together, these skills and this knowledge become the competences highlighted in Richardson's model.

Education for citizenship and democracy has a time dimension. Knowledge of the past and of the present may lead to action to attempt to create a better future. Citizenship education is not about a fundamentalist utopian vision. Schools and their staff and students are confronted with choices. On any issue they will be well advised to consider what is worth preserving and what requires changing.

6 Teachers' and student teachers' understandings of human rights, citizenship and identities

Introduction

Teachers' perceptions of their own and their pupils' identities are likely to have a direct impact on the way they handle human rights and citizenship issues, both in the design and development of the formal curriculum and through teacher–pupil relationships. Despite this, student teachers are rarely encouraged to examine or reflect on their own identities or biographies as part of their preparation for teaching. This chapter examines teachers' and student teachers' understandings of human rights, citizenship and identities, relating these both to their formal teacher education and to their experiences of teaching. It draws on three separate studies of teachers and student teachers. The first focuses on a group of white British students following a primary initial teacher education course; the second examines the changing perceptions of a broad range of European students who chose to spend part of their higher education studying in another European country; and the third explores the personal and professional identities of British teachers from black and ethnic minority communities.

Human rights education in practice: student teachers' views

A group of students training to be primary school teachers at a British college were introduced to human rights as part of their subject studies in French during the first year of their four-year course. These student teachers had about five hours of class contact time in which they were introduced to human rights, starting with the French Revolution. They went on to undertake a personal research project for which they were required to make formal reference to human rights texts. All this was integrated into their main subject course. For a full account of the aims and content of the course and the methods used see Starkey (1996). While all the students responded positively to this introduction to human rights they nevertheless reported that this was the first time within their formal education that such an opportunity had been provided. A number observed that an explicit examination of human rights values was important to them as future teachers and that they would find ways of introducing human rights values with their pupils:

> I think we as future teachers need to be aware and pass on the values of human rights. It has been interesting to link the various topics covered to the wider issue of human rights.

> My depth of knowledge and understanding has been widely extended through this course. I believe it is important and useful for future teachers to understand what basic rights each human being should be given in order for them to be able to highlight how various problems around the world violate these rights.

The second student is expressing a concern for world justice and acknowledging how human rights help to make sense of the world. 'Problems around the world' are defined in terms of their effect on individuals and their entitlements to 'basic rights'. Such an understanding may not help to identify the causes of problems, nor even their solution. It does help to form judgements about right and wrong. To 'violate these rights' is clearly wrong. In an increasingly complex world, it is important that new teachers are supported in developing the capacity to make such judgements. They need to be able to distinguish right from wrong and to help their pupils to do so. A knowledge of human rights is particularly useful in this regard.

Just as a knowledge of human rights helps teachers to make judgements about issues and problems in the wider world, it also helps them to make such judgements about their own classrooms. As another student expressed it, 'I think it is very important to teach that everyone is equal in the classroom situation. I had never seen the principles written down on paper before.' This student had a previous instinctive belief about the equality of human beings and the responsibility of the teacher to ensure justice in her class. The beliefs may have been based on religious conviction, on humanism, on a political viewpoint, on a non-articulated feeling stemming from her own education or from pragmatism. In any event, seeing 'the principles written down on paper' came as a revelation. Here are principles that can be shown to children, their parents and fellow teachers. These are principles that have the sanction of the international community and yet also have a potential impact on a classroom. These principles are therefore a reference point, a point of common ground. They are based on the essential similarity of human beings, on their equal entitlement to rights in a society and a world where difference is so often stressed and claimed as a strong value.

We would argue that a human rights values framework can be used to explore issues of equality and inequality in the world and in the classroom without undermining the identity of individual pupils in a class. Too often teachers seeking to promote social justice have found that certain approaches promote guilt or resentment among students who may perceive that they are being labelled as the oppressor group. The Burnage Report, published after an Asian student was murdered in a Manchester school playground by a white fellow student, warned against moralistic anti-racism which allowed white students to feel neglected and held at fault for racism within society yet failed to tackle a school climate in which ethnic minority students were harassed. The authors urged schools and teachers not to abandon their anti-racist practices and policies but to re-appraise them to ensure that they are achieving the goal of social justice:

> It is because we consider the task of combating racism to be such a critical part of the function of schooling and education that we condemn symbolic, moral and doctrinaire anti-racism. We urge care, rigour and caution in the formulating and implementing of such policies because we consider the struggle against racism and racial injustice to be an essential element in the struggle for social justice which we see as the ultimate goal of education. (Macdonald *et al.*, 1989: xxiii)

A human rights values framework, which acknowledges that each individual student is entitled to equal respect, and does not seek to promote a hierarchy of oppressions, may support teachers and their students in examining inequality. Working within an agreed framework of values, students from various cultures and traditions can examine historical and present-day events without developing a sense of personal rejection, an undermining of self-identity or feelings of guilt, all of which may be unhelpful in achieving social justice 'as an ultimate goal of education'. On the contrary, a human rights values framework may support teachers and pupils in challenging injustice and allow them to make links between the various injustices, oppressions and violations of rights within their immediate environment and to set these within a broader international context. What other worldview can put on the same footing people from a range of cultural, political and religious backgrounds, be inclusive of those who have direct experience of injustice and those who may not, and do so in a way that is threatening to none?

The students who were introduced to human rights through their initial teacher education course drew the conclusion that if they had not had the opportunity to learn about human rights during their school education, then the education system itself was at fault. One assumed the lack of human rights education to be a peculiarly British phenomenon:

> I feel it is essential that children are taught about human rights and I feel that the British education system fails badly in this respect. The French are far more aware than the British.

It is undoubtedly the case that a discourse of human rights is more prevalent in France than in Britain and that references to human rights occur regularly in the French National Curriculum but not in the English National Curriculum. What for one student is an indictment of the British education system, possibly on moral or ethical grounds, is for another student an indictment in terms of denying a proper education and therefore being at a competitive disadvantage in essential knowledge for life:

> It made me think that British children and students are maybe being disadvantaged by not being given this information sooner.

This instrumental argument, that the denial of information on human rights denies the rights themselves, is picked up in a more altruistic vein by another student:

> More people throughout Europe and even worldwide should automatically be taught about human rights so less people are exploited as more people are made aware of their rights and [it is] then more difficult for them to be ignored.

This student notes that knowledge of human rights is the first step to respect for them. In other words a right, as a strong claim with moral and legal force, only exists if the claimant of the right is aware of it. It follows that, to a certain extent, knowledge of human rights and respect for human rights are inseparable. The first step to a world of 'freedom, justice and peace', in the words of the Universal Declaration of Human Rights of 1948, is to spread the knowledge of human rights.

Why is it, then, that these student teachers were able to go through their education without seeing human rights principles in writing? Partly, it must be supposed, that the teachers who taught them had not had the opportunity to learn about human rights and so were not in a position to teach about them. This vicious circle can be broken by the training of teachers, not only those in initial training but those in service. There is no moral or legal impediment to this happening. After all, governments across the world have committed themselves to respect human rights and to enable their citizens to learn about them. The lack of human rights education is more a question of priorities. Surprisingly, access to knowledge of human rights rarely figures as an entitlement in the curriculum and in those countries where it does, it is likely to figure in a less prestigious part of the curriculum.

European citizenship and study abroad

Within educational research and teacher education, questions of identity are often associated with ethnic minorities; the identities of majority individuals and communities are less likely to be examined. One danger of this approach is that members of majority communities are thus encouraged to perceive their own cultural identities as 'normal', with those of minorities as deviating from this norm. Study in another country can encourage individuals, including those from majority communities, to re-assess their own identities as they come into contact with alternative ways of living. The experience of study abroad and the 'outsider' perspective which this may provide is unlikely to compare with that of racial discrimination and inequality which people from minority communities experience, at home, in their own countries. Nevertheless, for some students from relatively privileged backgrounds, it may offer rich new insights into their own cultures and identities.

Education for citizenship and human rights across Europe was re-emphasised by the 1988 Resolution of the Council of Ministers of Education which reaffirmed their commitment to a programme designed to

strengthen in young people a sense of European identity and make clear to them the value of European civilisation and the foundations on which the European peoples intend to base their development today, that is in particular the safeguarding of the principles of democracy, social justice and respect for human rights. (Council of Ministers, 1988)

Within Europe there is a developing rhetoric concerning European identity and European citizenship, while at the same time some national politicians are re-emphasising the importance of national identity and citizenship. It is expected that one means by which young people may experience the central theme of the 'European dimension' in education, namely learning 'the principles of democracy, social justice and respect for human rights', is through study abroad. The second case study is of student teachers who were studying in another European country, or who had recently returned from a period of study abroad. They were invited to reflect on their own identities and in particular on their own understandings of national and European citizenship. A total of thirty-seven students from seven countries studying at two colleges, one Danish and the other English, took part. Both colleges specialise in teacher education and all but two of the students had firm plans to become teachers. Data was collected by means of tape-recorded individual and group interviews, questionnaires and class discussion. The research focused on students' reasons for studying abroad and the impact they expected this study to have on their future work as teachers; what they felt they had learned about the culture and life of the host country; understandings of national and European citizenship; and how the school curriculum might support education for European citizenship. Each of these issues is explored in some detail elsewhere (Osler, 1996b). We focus here on their developing understandings of national and European citizenship and the impact of this understanding on the student teachers' own identities.

Students' feelings about their national citizenship varied a great deal. Many expressed a strong emotional attachment to their home country and defined their national citizenship in terms of personal identity, a shared culture and a sense of belonging, rather than as a legal status:

> I respect my country. To be a citizen is an emotional feeling, it's not so concrete. I also see the bad sides of our country. I know our culture, our habits in Finland. When you can respect your own culture you can also try to learn and understand other cultures. (Finnish woman)

> Citizenship is to have French culture, to speak French and to talk objectively about my country; to see its successes and failures. European citizenship is part of a mixing of cultures and to have more than one country. (French woman)

> I think citizenship is mainly linked to a common culture you share with other people. For example the same festivities, way of education, food even. (Belgian woman)

In the first of these statements there is the belief that self-assurance and self-respect are preliminary steps towards understanding and tolerance of others. While many students recognise it as important to be able to stand back from their own cultures and countries and to look critically at them, they nevertheless have a monolithic understanding of national culture. The tendency is to assume that there is only one way, for example, to be French. Most students acknowledge the multicultural nature of Europe, but few appear to recognise that their own countries are also, in effect, multicultural. A number refer to the importance of a common language, but overlook the existence of ethnic and linguistic minorities within nation-states. Yet within Europe there are forty-eight European language groups representing 30 million people; 17.5 million European citizens who are migrants from former colonies or the descendants of such migrants and a further 15 million residents who have the status of foreigners (Perotti, 1991).

Three students, each from ethnic or linguistic minority communities, do not make links between their national citizenship status and sense of personal identity, and to a greater or lesser extent wish to distance themselves from their legal national citizenship. One is a French woman of Algerian descent who defines herself as a Muslim and who confided that only since she had been living in Denmark did she feel that anyone else saw her as French. She argued that she had never been perceived by others as French in France, nor in England where she had also spent a period studying. Two other students emphasised another identity, rather than their legal national status: one is a Catalan woman, the other a French man who identified with the region of Brittany. Both these students acknowledge their European citizenship, although each qualifies this in different ways:

> Coming from Brittany means having a mother tongue shared by a million people, a sense of humour, songs, emotions, the weight of words. Yes, I'm European while keeping our cultural identity and hoping Germany won't lead the European Community. (French man – Brittany)

> I'm very, very happy to belong to Catalonia and to be a Catalan citizen. I'm proud to be Catalan because I love the culture, costumes, language, and especially our history. Catalan is not the same as Spanish. I know I'm a European citizen but I think it's important to look at all cultures, not only Europe. (Catalan woman)

These students recognise that identity is multi-dimensional. It is not a question of choosing to be either Catalan or European; it is possible to be both Catalan and European, as it is to be Muslim and European, or Muslim, French and European, even in a context where others may find it difficult to accept such self-definition. Nevertheless, others' unwillingness genuinely to accept and include an individual as a full citizen may lead that citizen to lose a real sense of belonging, so that citizenship becomes little more than legal status.

The experience of living abroad and observing, and to a limited extent participating, in another culture caused many students to look critically at their own values and cultures. Some felt they had to serve as ambassadors of their home countries, educating others about their way of life, and this was particularly true of those from smaller countries who discovered that other students knew little or nothing about their homelands:

> When we go abroad people don't know much about Denmark because we are only 5 million people. Then I feel it is very important for me to show people that I am Danish and our country exists. (Danish woman)

Living abroad gave many students a new sense of pride in their national identity:

> When abroad I sometimes feel proud when people know famous French singers, actors, writers, though I am not at all nationalist. Apart from that, being French does not mean anything to me. But I think about the people whose nationality is devalued. It must be really difficult to cope. (French woman)

With the important exception of those who are members of minority communities or who express a strong allegiance to a regional identity, students from a variety of countries across Western Europe highlighted what were for them common aspects of national citizenship and identity: a sense of belonging, shared values, a pride in shared customs and often a similar pride in a shared language. Additionally, some French students also acknowledged the impact of a shared history and gave some emphasis to the legal and political aspects of citizenship:

> Being French means belonging to a community, having shared values and having a responsibility as a French person to take part, for example in elections, and having a responsibility to defend my values. (French woman)

The students found it much more difficult to establish any consensus on the meaning of European citizenship or identity. Most were in agreement with the student who responded: 'I think nationality still predominates in most people's minds over European citizenship' (French woman). About three-quarters of the students see themselves as European citizens but some qualify this, explaining that this depends on the particular circumstance. That a substantial minority feel ambivalent or negative about identifying themselves as European reflects in many cases the political controversy within their countries concerning membership of the European Union. The research took place in 1995 shortly after a referendum in Sweden which had found a small majority in favour of joining the EU, and three of the four Swedish students in the research group had voted against their country's membership, arguing that European citizenship was an exclusive concept which detracted from a sense of global responsibility. All four were concerned about 'fortress Europe' closing its borders against outsiders.

For many students European citizenship simply means the personal right to travel freely within Europe, for the purposes of work or study. The experience of study abroad had caused a number to re-define themselves as European citizens:

Before I didn't see myself as a European citizen, but since I'm here [in England] it's very different. I met people from France, Finland, Spain, and I feel at home with them. (Belgian woman)

For others, travel beyond Europe and contact with people from other parts of the world led them to define themselves as European:

I didn't feel myself a real European citizen until I travelled, for instance to Arabic countries or the US. Again the contrast with a different culture made me realise that I belonged to Europe. (Belgian woman)

When I travel outside Europe and meet other Europeans, I often feel that we've got a lot in common. Our cultures are closely linked, and our values and norms are very different than those of Americans or Asians. I have often experienced that I have more in common with other Europeans than with most Danes. (Danish man)

Again, students seem to overlook the fact that within the various European states there are citizens whose identities and cultural heritage stem from other parts of the world and other continents, in particular from Africa and Asia. It is possible that many of these students fail to acknowledge the multicultural nature of their own societies because they lack the experience of intercultural contact at home; it is only through travel that some Danes, for example, come into close contact with cultures other than their own. At home, such contact, where it exists, may be through working with children from ethnic minority communities. Many future teachers would appear to lack any substantial contact with adults from such communities. The ethnic make-up of most teacher education institutions remains predominantly or exclusively from the majority ethnic group.

Some students believe that European citizenship is currently little more than an ideal which might be exploited for good, but many are vague about the values behind this ideal. Others feel it represents a sense of European superiority towards other parts of the world. The Council of Europe's 1983 Recommendation on European awareness in secondary schools stressed that education programmes

should encourage all young Europeans to see themselves not only as citizens of their own regions and countries, but also as citizens of Europe and the wider world. (Council of Europe, 1983)

In order to effectively challenge notions of European superiority and develop a clear understanding of global interdependence it is essential that concepts of citizenship and citizenship education incorporate a global perspective (Osler, 1994b). Without such a perspective there is a danger that old notions of national superiority common to citizenship education in the past may be simply replaced by the promotion of a new European identity built on similar beliefs of exclusivity and superiority. There is a real danger in failing to define the values on which the new European vision is based. As O'Shaughnessy warns:

> We must be wary of the danger of replacing an old narrow nationalism with a new, respectable 'European nationalism'. We must not allow ourselves to be agents of a vision of Europe that is seen solely in terms of a white Graeco-Roman and Christian heritage – a vision that excludes minorities and which denies both age-old contact with other parts of the globe and a true understanding of the complex, interdependent nature of the contemporary world. (O'Shaughnessy, 1994: 91)

A minority of students in this sample believe that there are no shared European values but simply common economic interests. While the European Ministers of Education stress 'the safeguarding of the principles of democracy, social justice and respect for human rights' as the 'foundations' of European identity and development, this is not echoed in the consciousness of many of the students. The notable exceptions are students from Sweden and Denmark. They argue that these principles must be explicit in school systems, and in teacher education, especially in terms of teaching methodology and in the principles underlying relationships between teachers and their students:

> For European citizenship we need to teach our democratic system and that men and women are equal through society. We need to teach for freedom and peace. (Swedish man)

> We need to teach children democracy through democratic teaching and democratic education. (Danish woman)

> The education system must be based on freedom, democracy and responsibility. And we must all work for human rights all over the world. Training teachers in Europe should draw on the good aspects of each national system, whether you are studying in Denmark, the UK or any other European country. (Danish woman)

The experience of study abroad in another European country has enabled these future teachers to reflect on their personal identities, both national and European, and to examine critically their own attitudes and values. While for some this has confirmed their national identities, others have adopted a new European identity alongside existing identities. The experience of living and studying abroad has allowed a number of them to stand back from their own cultures and societies and to assess their strengths and weaknesses. It has not necessarily challenged those from majority communities to recognise the pluralist and multicultural nature of individual states or to re-define national identity and citizenship in a more inclusive way. It would seem that it is largely those students who have had direct teaching and experience of human rights and democratic values within their own schooling who identify these as being at the heart of the European ideal.

Ethnic minority teachers, citizenship and identity

The third case study focuses on the personal and professional identities of a group of black and ethnic minority teachers in Britain, drawing on the life histories of twenty-six individuals, ten of whom are in senior management positions within the education service. As each teacher presents the narrative of their education and work they discuss the expectations placed upon on them, by their students, colleagues and the wider community, which help shape their identity as teachers, and more particularly as black teachers. A fuller account of this process and political and ethical issues relating to this research can be found elsewhere (Osler, 1995; 1997 forthcoming) but here we focus on the ways in which the teachers' identities are formed and re-formed as a result of their work experiences. We consider how this development of teacher identities might inform our understanding of ways in which teachers might support pupils in making choices about their own identities as part of education for human rights and citizenship.

The development and shaping of personal identities through a process of choice may be seen as one of the key purposes of education. Nevertheless, this choice may be subject to a number of external restrictions. While in an ideal situation identities are formed through choice, identity can also be imposed from the outside. Labelling theory may inform our understanding of the ways in which children from black and ethnic minorities perceive their cultural identities to be negatively judged in schools. Low teacher expectations of such children or assumptions about their behaviour will be communicated to them, often in unintentional ways, and this is likely to influence subsequent behaviour and achievement. As a number of studies show (for example, Eggleston *et al.*, 1986; Macdonald *et al.*, 1989; Gillborn, 1990), overt racial prejudice remains a problem which is likely to affect the educational chances of many black children in Britain. Children, faced with this situation, and with racist attitudes and behaviours in the wider community, may react by denying aspects of themselves, their families and their cultural identity. Teachers have reported how some black children draw themselves as white and others deny that they are bilingual; parents have similarly commented on children's reluctance to acknowledge themselves as black or their sudden refusal to speak their home language once they have started school. While such developments have been explained in terms of low self-image (Milner, 1975), this explanation is inadequate because it seeks to focus the problem on the child who has been labelled, rather than on the teacher, the labeller. This may help explain why relatively little attention has been given to teacher education and training in this area.

It is in this context that we examine the experiences of black and ethnic minority teachers. Nineteen of the twenty-six in the sample had experienced all or part of their own schooling in Britain. Within their narratives of their own schooling were many examples of racism, both overt and covert, and many also reflected on the issue of teachers' attitudes and expectations of black and ethnic minority children. A number called for direct teaching about issues of power and justice (including issues of 'race'); their experience confirmed that some kind of political education was necessary. They did not argue explicitly for human rights education but nevertheless saw social justice as a central goal. They also recognised that many teachers were ill-equipped to provide such an education.

The teachers in this study were invited to participate as black people, and none of them questioned or challenged this at the outset. Modood (1992) has argued that during the 1980s anti-racist professionals imposed the term 'black' upon people from South Asian communities, with no consideration for the principle of ethnic self-definition. In this study, the term 'black' was generally acknowledged by each of the participants, despite their varied histories, languages, religions and cultures, as one which might be applied to them as people of African, Asian or Caribbean descent, and as a shorthand way of acknowledging some shared experiences within the socio-political context of Britain today. Nevertheless, the understandings which individuals attached to it, and the degree to which they accepted the term as a way of identifying or describing themselves, varied considerably, and were elaborated as each recounted their story. One theme running through each account is each individual's professional development and their changing understanding of what it means to them, at various points in their career, to be a teacher.

A parallel theme is the development of a political identity, what one woman refers to as 'my development as a black person'. One identity does not rule out other identities. This individual sometimes talks of her experiences and identity as a Muslim, particularly as a Muslim woman. At other times she refers to the experience of growing up bilingual in Britain. At different times she stresses her role as a mother. At others she discusses what it means to her to have a management role in the education service. Although sometimes these roles and identities appear conflicting and contradictory, they are not exclusive of each other. It is not a question of either/or but of both/and.

It would seem that for these teachers the black identity which they adopt is largely a question of political choice. Yet a number provide examples of the ways in which some black children, and adults, expect them to behave as black people, conforming to a particular stereotype or model. There is an element of imposition in the expectations of others. This found expression in the case of a number of women within the study as a fixed expectation of how they should dress. One African-Caribbean man recounted how some of his African-Caribbean pupils found it hard to accept him as black. He did not conform to their expectations of blackness, because of his middle-class British accent and personal interests. In the criticism or taunt that a black teacher is 'acting white' there is often the implication that the individual is denying the existence of racism, and rejecting their own culture and identity. In the case of black teachers seeking to work in the interests of all their students, but particularly conscious of the racial discrimination which many black students are encountering, such criticism may be hurtful as well as frustrating. Some black teachers may find themselves facing such external impositions of identity in addition to structural and interpersonal racism. People from black and ethnic minority communities are in such cases experiencing an imposition from the expectations of others from within the black and ethnic minority communities, yet they may still not be fully accepted as part of the national community. Just as the French student of Algerian descent reported that people in France and England did not accept her as French, there is no guarantee that a black British teacher (with or without a British accent) will always be recognised as British by all members of the majority (white) national community.

The experiences of teachers in this study indicate that many white senior managers see black teachers primarily as classroom teachers rather than in positions of leadership (Osler, 1994c). The position of black teachers within the management structures of a school or their invisibility gives out messages to all children about the importance of black teachers.

A vivid example of this was offered by a primary school teacher who, on her arrival at a new school, was asked by a Muslim boy whether she was a Muslim. When told that she was, he then enquired if Muslims could become teachers. In such environments black teachers may need to struggle to assert their basic citizenship rights. Whether or not schools have planned for citizenship education they are actively engaged in it; they legitimate particular knowledge and constructions of knowledge. Black teachers, as teachers, are participating in this process and this may lead to tension between professional and political aspects of identity.

In Britain the political right has attacked anti-racism, and portrayed it at one level as a distraction from the acquisition of basic skills and at another level as a dangerous tendency which threatens British values and undermines British culture. Black teachers, working within such a context, are in a particularly vulnerable position. If they draw attention to issues of injustice or challenge racism within the school or curriculum they may be identified, at best, as outsiders who do not share the dominant values. At worst they may be judged as trouble-makers, lacking professional judgement. Regardless of their particular skills they may be seen as experts on black culture or 'professional ethnics' (Bangar and McDermott, 1989; Blair and Maylor, 1993). In these circumstances the school may be seen to impose a pre-determined identity upon them.

People from black and ethnic minority communities remain under-represented in teaching. The need for more black teachers is often expressed in terms of role-models for all pupils or mentors for black students. We recognise the need for more black and ethnic minority teachers and would argue that people from these communities need to be found at all levels in the education service and not only as classroom teachers. However, there is sometimes a lack of clarity in the arguments put forward for black and ethnic minority mentors to support black students. At the moment there are insufficient numbers to permit each student from black and ethnic minority communities to have the choice of a black mentor. While community schemes – like those which have placed volunteer black men in schools as role-models and mentors, to support the development of black boys judged to be crisis or in danger of exclusion – clearly have an important role to play, there are considerations other than 'race' or ethnicity which need to be addressed in the development of mentoring schemes.

A significant number of the teachers and senior education managers in this study reported that they had been supported in their career by a mentor, who was sometimes, but not always, another black person. It was generally recognised as important for black teachers to network with other black people, regardless of whether they were enjoying the support of a mentor. This in itself provided support when dealing with racism. A mentor needs to be confident in their own identity before they can support others. Mentoring requires the development of certain values, skills and attitudes, including, in particular, listening skills and empathy. As we recognise that individuals may develop multiple identities, and that the ability to make choices about identities is one of the purposes of education, so we also recognise that hybridity is the norm rather than the exception. An individual who is experiencing the effects of racism may wish to turn to another person who has had this experience and hopefully acquired the skills, knowledge and attitudes to be able to support another in this situation, in other words, another black person. In other contexts It may not be critical that someone is mentored by another person of the same ethnic group. First, to assume that black people can only be the mentors of other black people is to re-cast them as professional ethnics and to ignore the range of skills and experiences which they will have which will extend beyond that of racism. Secondly, to decide that a white manager or teacher is unable to offer support to employees or students from black and ethnic minority groups is to reduce the responsibility of the individual and the institution for its black and ethnic minority employees or students. Also it is to ignore the complexity of identities and the role of ethnicity as only one aspect of identity. It may be critical, for example, not that a Scottish-Nigerian student is mentored by someone of identical heritage, but that the individual knows that their mentor accepts them for who they are and does not regard their heritage as exotic or peculiar.

Only those who are self-confident in their own identity can celebrate hybridity. Individuals and communities who are oppressed by racism may be in danger of losing their self-confidence. Black people are not mere victims of racism with no identity or consciousness. The teachers in this study demonstrate that it is possible to accept a black political identity (within the specific context of Britain today) while at the same time maintaining a number of other identities including those of culture, language, religion, role as teacher, employment status as manager and membership of an educational community. While black people's experience is much more than racism, many of these teachers have found strength in a black political identity which has not undermined other aspects of their background or culture. The imposition of identity from outside is one of the hazards of their daily lives, but not something which is accepted without challenge. This case study reminds us that teacher development is not only dependent on training but is strongly influenced and shaped by teachers' professional and personal contexts and biographies (Nias, 1989). It highlights the importance of listening to individuals and of the recognition of both individuals and groups within a human rights framework.

Summary

As these case studies demonstrate, there are close links between teacher identities and the experience of human rights and citizenship. Teachers are unlikely to be able to work effectively towards human rights and social justice in schools without basic knowledge of human rights principles. Such knowledge provides them with a starting point for teaching about justice and equality without undermining the identities of their students. If, as we have argued, supporting children and young people in making choices about their own identities is an important function of education for social justice and an important aspect of teachers' work, then those student teachers who have studied abroad might be judged to be better prepared for their future role as teachers, having had the opportunity to reconsider their own identities as a consequence of their period abroad. Similarly, the case study of black teachers demonstrates that they are likely to have a good understanding of human rights issues and identities through their own lived experience. While some teachers may arrive at this understanding through their own experiences, this cannot be guaranteed for all. Where teachers are able to apply their knowledge of human rights principles to their own experience and that of their students, they are likely to be most effective. An understanding of human rights as a set of guiding principles which can inform schooling has to be explicit. A planned opportunity for student teachers to study and apply human rights values is therefore critical. Such an opportunity, together with study and reflection on their own biographies and identities as part of their initial teacher education, will ensure they are equipped to support their own students in promoting social justice and making informed choices about their identities.

Part 3. Human rights and the curriculum

7   *Curriculum development in teacher education*

Introduction

This chapter describes and evaluates a curriculum development project involving twenty-two university departments of education in thirteen European countries. The project, funded by the European Commission under its ERASMUS programme, was designed to enable teacher educators to learn from each other's experiences of human rights education. Both authors were involved at all stages of the project. Although few participants had experience of working in a transnational project, within three years a Europe-wide network of staff and student exchanges had been set up and a new teaching module was devised and available to each of the participating universities.

The construction of Europe as a peaceful social, cultural and political entity was first identified as a desirable and a realisable goal in the immediate aftermath of World War II. The founding of the Council of Europe in 1949 provided a structure within which this development could progress. The European Economic Community (EEC), with a system of international law to regulate social and economic affairs, was set up under the Treaty of Rome in 1957. In many ways the two European bodies have developed in parallel, both expanding and extending their influence, the Council of Europe working at a fully pan-European level, whilst the European Union expands more slowly.

Educational programmes are an essential complement to political agreements, as we noted in Chapter 1. Both European organisations are based on a vision and any vision of democratic European development requires informed citizens. A human rights education programme is required to help citizens uphold the standards set in the European Convention on Human Rights and enable them to understand the political and economic developments at European level which have an impact on their lives. European Community education policy, as we noted in

Chapter 6, promotes 'the safeguarding of the principles of democracy, social justice and respect for human rights' (Council of Ministers, 1988).

From the earliest days of the EEC new courses about Europe were created in each of the member states but such courses had difficulty in getting established. Cross-curricular courses tend to be undervalued and in fact European studies courses were generally only offered to students as an alternative to the classic university-orientated curriculum. As well as the structural problem of finding curriculum space for a European dimension, there was a conceptual and a pedagogical difficulty. The conceptual difficulty concerned the key objectives of the course. What is there to say about Europe to young people? One answer was to focus on the diversity of Europe's inhabitants, its languages and colourful folkloric customs. Such a presentation of Europe is in many respects inadequate. An understanding of Europe requires a vision of unity as well as one of diversity (Shennan, 1991).

The appropriate unifying concept for Europe is not to do with fast-changing political structures, it is to do with a system of shared values which underpin the political developments. These values are 'the principles of democracy, social justice and respect for human rights'. The Resolution effectively invites a new approach to promoting a European dimension in the curriculum with a focus on shared values rather than difference. The pedagogical challenge is how to translate this perspective into relevant and useful learning experiences. Logically, the development of a European perspective requires a European curriculum development project, and so a network of teacher educators from thirteen states in Western Europe was set up to respond to this challenge.

An ERASMUS curriculum development project

The ERASMUS programme of the European Commission supports universities in developing a European dimension to their work, particularly through the exchange of students and staff and collaboration in curriculum development. In October 1991 there was an opportunity to bid for funds from the European Commission for an ERASMUS curriculum development programme. As a first step a letter was sent to named colleagues in universities in Belgium, Denmark, France, Germany, Italy, Spain, Sweden and Switzerland and eight UK institutions. The contacts were made through the Association for Teacher Education in Europe (ATEE), the International Peace Education Network, the World Studies Trust, an educational trust promoting curriculum development, and the Education in Human Rights Network. The letter invited participation in a bid for a project to develop a European dimension within teacher education. The project would explore and promote common European values as expressed in the Council of Ministers' Resolution, namely 'democracy, social justice and respect for human rights'.

The project was introduced as a plan to create a network of teacher education institutions committed to education for citizenship in a European context, including responsibility to society and to the environment. The invitation to participate in the project made specific reference to pedagogy, affirming that European citizenship 'will not be learnt purely through the study of text books. Active and cooperative learning involving all sections of the local community is required.'

One assumption underlying the project is that teachers in training should themselves be able to feel at home in many communities and recognise the importance for young people of establishing confident identities. In a sense Europeans are already citizens of a nation, of a continent and of the world. Some teachers in training also have family roots outside Europe and it is certain that they will have pupils from many geographical, ethnic, cultural and religious backgrounds. Teachers are responsible for transmitting values. They need to be in a position to help their students be supportive of pluralist democracy and human rights, enjoy cultural diversity and be conscious of their responsibilities to the planet and to all those who live on it. This implies that they should themselves share these values.

The project had four broad aims:

- To ensure that new entrants to the profession are equipped to encourage a global and intercultural perspective in all their teaching and contribute to 'the safeguarding of the principles of democracy, social justice and respect for human rights';
- To identify, support and describe current good practice in education for citizenship and global responsibility in teacher training, specifically evaluating ways in which it is currently included as part of accredited teacher education courses, both cross-curricular and within subjects;
- To create course modules and materials, which, when translated and adapted to local circumstances, can be used in teacher training courses throughout Europe;
- To promote exchanges of students and staff as well as materials.

The proposed outcomes were the translation of materials and handbooks and the collaborative development of teacher education modules and joint courses involving exchanges of staff, students and materials from different countries. It was intended that, within participating institutions, the involvement in a European project would be regarded as prestigious, and that education for citizenship and global responsibility would acquire enhanced credibility and status.

Project aims

Funding was obtained through ERASMUS and the network became an Inter-university Co-operation Programme (ICP). The first meeting was convened in London in September 1992. It was held at the same time as the World Studies Conference, providing an opportunity to meet a larger group of British teachers and educationalists and to attend workshops demonstrating active pedagogy and a global perspective.

Twenty lecturers from sixteen universities in Belgium, Denmark, France, Spain, Sweden, Switzerland and the UK made up the initial project team. The working languages were English and French, interpretation being provided by members of the group throughout the meeting. The project group met for four days, including the Conference. Five sessions were used to launch the project by helping participants get to know each other and identify both shared values and potential points of divergence.

The programme of the meeting was structured to give as much opportunity as possible for personal interaction. The first session was crucial to the future success of the project, as it would set the tone for future professional relationships. Meetings of academics are often characterised by formality and a strong sense of hierarchy. This project needed to create a sense of team work amongst colleagues with eight different mother tongues, the majority of whom were required to communicate in a foreign language.

The first session was therefore both formal, in introducing the project and setting the meeting in the context of the three-year curriculum development programme, and informal, to enable participants to get to know one another. In a speech of welcome and introduction the project co-ordinator referred to the origins of this project, particularly the work of the Council of Europe in human rights education and intercultural education, the experience of the World Studies Trust, and the Association of Teacher Education in Europe. He indicated that the meeting itself was structured so that participants would get to know one another in a personal and a professional sense. They would share and negotiate meanings and have an opportunity to consider and experience several pedagogical activities. They would also be asked to think about their own personal contribution to the project and plan for future collaboration.

The objectives of the project were restated:

- to explore what the European values of democracy, social justice, and respect for human rights, proclaimed at Maastricht and in many other EC meetings, mean for education;
- to situate these values within a sense of global responsibility;
- to ensure that these values are addressed in initial teacher education in Europe;
- to develop some common approaches and materials for helping future teachers learn about, understand and apply these values.

The strategy for the project over the three years was then outlined. Each participant was asked in the first year to identify an area of the curriculum at their university where they could introduce or develop the European and global dimension. They each committed themselves to work with students in a way that would enable them to engage with the project aims. They agreed to share experience, ideas and materials and help to clarify the educational implications of the values of democracy, social justice, and respect for human rights through a series of meetings and through news-letters. As well as this individual activity, thought was given to developing common materials and, if possible, a common module. Participants agreed to develop a European and global dimension by, for instance, making this element a more important feature of their course, by creating a new course or by persuading colleagues to join the work of the project.

From the outset participants knew that they would have the opportunity to undertake some teaching at each other's universities and that the project would cover the costs of their travel and subsistence. Arrangements would also be made for students to move between universities on an exchange basis for a period of study of three months or more. This, too, would be funded by the European Commission.

Team building

At the outset of the project it was crucial for members to get to know each other. Rather than engage in formal meetings, the time was used for activities designed to enable an exchange of information at both a cognitive and an affective level. Thus the initial ice-breaker was a game based on finding out personal information relevant to human rights and democracy using a simple questionnaire and involving brief exchanges between all those in the room. Within the room colleagues had to discover, for instance, who had recently voted, who had experienced discrimination, and who knew the date of the Universal Declaration of

Human Rights. Following this whole-group activity, small groups were arranged and participants explained the origin and meaning of their name, and then each made a time-line representing graphically their (metaphorical) journey to the meeting.

The next formal session introduced the concept of human rights and allowed participants, working in international groups of three, to clarify their understanding of the key terms *democracy*, *social justice*, *global responsibility* and *respect for human rights*. Each group was given a drawing, from *The Human Rights Album* (Council of Europe, 1992), illustrating in abstract form one or more human rights. Each person also had a copy of the Universal Declaration of Human Rights. We identified the articles illustrated and cut out and stuck the articles on the picture. For most of the participants, this was their first opportunity to examine closely the Universal Declaration. This proved to be a significant moment and project members expressed a desire to look closely at other human rights texts.

Participants next worked to identify the key knowledge, skills, attitudes and outcomes associated with each of the four key terms in the project's title (democracy, social justice, global responsibility and respect for human rights). These were displayed on posters and the results examined for similarities and areas of difference or disagreement. This activity revealed a need for further exploration of meanings. In particular, democracy proved to be a concept of which there are many possible interpretations and which revealed considerable differences of opinion.

The ice-breaking activities started dialogues about personal background, experience and values. The next task was to start to understand the diversity of professional situations represented in the project. Project members again worked in small groups and each colleague explained in detail about the opportunities in their university for teaching about democratic and human rights values. Whenever there was a technical term associated with a national education system, this was noted and defined on a flip chart.

After about one hour, two groups were formed to identify and discuss common features and problems. These included, predictably, the lack of time devoted to this area and its low status compared to so-called basic subjects. Further common constraints were the lack of flexibility because of strict regulations about the content of initial teacher training and an overloaded curriculum, causing prioritisation in favour of the so-called basic subjects.

A number of people identified organisational constraints on their work. For instance, where many tutors are involved in teaching a major course, good co-ordination and briefing of all those involved in delivering a course is essential. Pressures of time and the involvement of part-time tutors on course teams sometimes mean that the shared understanding of a course is superficial. This is compounded in the case of values education and intercultural education, which may be perceived by colleagues and students to be threatening.

Each participant agreed to complete a chart with targets for the next six months. Common lines of action included reporting on the meeting to colleagues including managers, discussions about modifications to courses and attempting to re-define the content of current courses. Communication between project participants would be maintained through further meetings and by the compilation and circulation of a newsletter, a task taken on by a group member. There were sufficient funds available to plan for two meetings in 1993 hosted by partner universities in Spain and Portugal. It was also agreed to expand the project to include universities from countries not yet represented.

In spite of the sense of common purpose achieved, many questions remained. In particular there was a concern to clarify further the meanings of the terms in the project title: democracy, social justice, global responsibility and respect for human rights. It was understood that this process of clarification would develop through teaching and curriculum development. The negotiation of meanings cannot be isolated from the task of constructing joint programmes.

Interestingly, the concept that appeared to provoke the greatest controversy was that of Europe. Most of the participants were committed to a global perspective in education. For them the so-called European values identified are, in fact, universal values. This raised questions about the precise nature of European identity. At this stage some participants found it difficult to see themselves as Europeans rather than citizens of a nation or of the world.

After one relatively brief meeting there were, not surprisingly, a number of concerns over the possible final outcomes of a three-year project. The situations represented seemed so diverse: graduate and undergraduate programmes; teacher training and non-vocational educational studies; and a wide range of curriculum specialisms including history, geography, modern languages, psychology, sociology and pedagogics. The target of producing a module, or alternatively a handbook of strategies and teaching approaches, seemed remote.

The second phase

Project members met again in April 1993. The purpose of this meeting was for participants to acquire a more detailed knowledge of each other's work and develop a common understanding of education for democracy and human rights. We hoped for a transfer of ideas as participants identified approaches, materials and organisational frameworks from other universities that could be adapted to their own situation.

The sharing of information continued to be the basic need at this stage. Each participant prepared a poster illustrating a successful activity or course linked to the theme of the project. Time was allowed for detailed questions. Working groups then identified the knowledge, attitudes and activities required to structure learning about European citizenship, democracy, social justice and equality, global responsibility and human rights. They went on to consider possible opportunities for developing these in teacher education courses and in work with schools.

We were able to refine our understanding of a number of terms, particularly the concepts of Europe, citizenship and European citizenship. In Europe, the political and institutional frameworks are constantly changing. Europe is not a fixed entity but an idea, defined in various ways and including different numbers of states according to the geographical or institutional definition used. As well as an idea, Europe appeared to us to be an ideal, constantly being re-created but unlikely ever to be fully realised. We felt that the creation of a European community and awareness was perhaps an intermediate step on the way to creating a world community.

Citizenship (see also Chapters 5 and 6) means belonging to a community and accepting its fundamental framework of laws and values. Democratic citizenship involves belonging to a political community, through the right to vote, and a civil community governed by law. Some citizens, including young people and foreigners, may belong only to the civil community, but they are still subject to the same laws and are equal before the law and equal in their rights. Schools are civil communities also governed by rules and a legal framework. Within the school each individual, whatever their role, has an equal right to security and dignity. The structures and values of the school can ensure that this is, in fact, the case. The same tensions and difficulties about the realisation of this ideal school community are found in society at large.

European citizenship is a sense of belonging to a civil community based on shared ideals. Since 1945, whenever democratic European leaders have come together to make treaties (for example the European Convention on Human Rights 1950 or the 1992 Maastricht Treaty), they refer to the shared values of 'social justice, democracy and respect for human rights and the rule of law'. European rhetoric stresses the ideal of human rights. In reality racism and inequalities are prevalent in all

European societies. A crucial role for education is to help transform societies so that they correspond more closely to the rhetoric. A starting point for this process is to inform young people and teachers about respect for human rights.

A joint module

The third meeting of the project team was held in September 1993 to coincide with the annual meeting of the Association for Teacher Education in Europe. Several new members joined the project, coming from Germany, Greece, Ireland, the Netherlands and Portugal. Apart from the practical details of arranging teaching staff exchanges and planning student exchanges for the following academic year, the main outcome was the production of a joint module (see Box 7.1). Given the wide diversity of institutions, the module is drafted in very general terms. It nonetheless gives an agreed framework within which partners developed and refined their courses.

In the course of the 1993/94 academic year the newly developed curriculum was implemented in each participating institution. In each case the focus and the type of course is different, but the courses can be grouped according to six main types.

Five universities, two in France and three in the UK, have courses or elements of courses specifically called civic or citizenship education. In France all trainee primary school teachers receive a twelve- to fifteen-hour module on civic education. In the UK the provision ranges from a single session of about three hours exploring the cross-curricular theme of citizenship with trainee teachers to a thirty-hour course for experienced teachers. A subset of this provision is media studies, which provides valuable tools for understanding the press and television. The French and Irish universities include this.

Courses for future teachers of history and geography also provide opportunities for exploring citizenship and a European dimension. In France civic education is automatically entrusted to humanities specialists. In other countries these subjects provide the greatest scope. The Spanish partners created a forty-hour course on Europe with a particular focus on migration. The Belgian university specialises in comparative history through a study of textbooks from several countries. Two of the UK universities have a major PGCE course in history or history and social studies. In the 180 hours available there is room for consideration of democracy, social justice and issues of equality. Other major courses where space was found include psychology in Denmark, philosophy in Ireland and modern languages in the UK.

Developed by the participants in ERASMUS Curriculum Development ICP UK-93-2180/05: 'Education for citizenship in a new Europe: learning democracy, social justice, global responsibility and respect for human rights' at their meetings in London, Barcelona and Lisbon September 1992 to September 1993. The module is included within teacher education courses in all participating universities.

Participants
From undergraduate to masters students as required.

Desired learning outcomes – students should be able to:
● apply their subject specialism to investigations related to the general theme of education for European and global citizenship;
● express informed opinions in defining and discussing issues of human rights, global responsibility, citizenship and social justice;
● adopt and make constructive use of awareness of self and how their cultural background has influenced their own values and attitudes;
● recognise the significance of different learning and teaching styles to the promotion of children's understanding in this field;
● work constructively with others (students, staff, parents, community representatives) on an investigation or project.

Key themes – include:
● an exploration of the variety of legal and institutional conceptions of human rights and of their personal implications;
● an awareness that humanity operates in dynamic historical, economic, environmental and spiritual contexts which link past and future;
● understanding the importance of individual participation in a pluricultural democracy;
● an affirmation of the achievements of humanity in realising the ideals of equality and justice.

Pedagogy
● to be consistent with the desired learning outcomes;
● to involve active and critical participation in a programme in which lectures, workshops, active research, directed readings and seminar presentations play a significant role.

Assessment
To be decided by participating and validating institutions.

Box 7.1 Joint module

Another opportunity is to be found in courses looking at international and intercultural issues. The Swiss partner has a course on migration and education. In Sweden the two universities in the project reflected their ministry's concern for internationalisation of the curriculum. One course is entitled 'Education for International Understanding', a second 'Cross-Cultural Perspectives'. One of the Swedish universities had already developed a full-semester course on 'Teaching in Multicultural Institutions'. This course was designed as an international course, with ERASMUS students specifically invited to participate. Such courses may also include a North/South or development education dimension and this is found in the Dutch and Swedish courses. Another approach is through peace education and this is reflected strongly in the work in Germany, Greece and Italy. Both the German and the Italian partners organised international residential courses out of term time. The Greek partner arranged a university-wide cross-curricular programme of open lectures, involving specialists from all faculties contributing to a series on the theme of 'Contemporary World Problems and the Scientist's Responsibility'.

Courses based on schools in context provide further opportunities. 'Personal and Social Development in the Secondary School' is an interdisciplinary masters course in Portugal. The UK has courses with titles such as 'Issues in the Comprehensive School' or 'Educational and Professional Studies'. 'Human Rights Education and the Role of the School' is an in-service course in France.

The impact of the course on students, be they trainee teachers, education specialists or practising teachers, is greatly increased when there is the encouragement or even the obligation to undertake a substantial research project. Amongst projects submitted to course members were studies entitled: Human rights education; Intercultural and human rights education in schools; Do teachers know about children's rights?; How might the teaching of citizenship contribute to education for equality and human rights?; Education for equality, tolerance and human rights in Kenyan primary schools; The implications of the UN Convention on the Rights of the Child on teaching and learning in Japanese schools. As the latter two studies indicate, education courses in European universities, particularly at higher degree level, are likely to recruit a broad international intake.

Evaluation of the project

Although much was achieved in the first two years of the project, it was not until the third year that the first students were exchanged between partner universities. It was at this stage too that experiments from the preceding two years could be consolidated in the light of evaluation and experience. The prospect of the exchange of students provided a new agenda for the project's meetings as it became essential to understand in detail the nature of the courses offered, the assessment requirements and arrangements for school experience. The project group met for a fourth time in Oxford in September 1994 and the group had its final official meeting in Berlin a year later. This meeting changed in nature, as participants had expressed the wish to experience a more academic occasion to demonstrate and disseminate their research interests. The meeting was consequently convened as a symposium, with each member presenting a formal paper, circulated in advance, and comments from nominated discussants. The support of the Council of Europe enabled the project group to invite participants from Russia, Lithuania, Latvia, Romania, the Czech Republic, Poland, and Slovenia who also presented papers. This helped to broaden the definition of Europe and to expand the mental maps of some project members. A selection of the contributions was edited and published (Osler *et al.*, 1996).

It was perhaps relatively easy for project members to demonstrate that the project had had an impact on their courses. This only involved adapting what is, after all, a universal theme to courses within their national context. A more difficult objective was for teaching and pedagogical approaches to be shared internationally. There is evidence from the summative evaluation questionnaire that some such transfer did take place. This Dutch colleague acknowledges the impact of both the meetings of the project and the teaching visits to his university by project members:

> Workshops and visits have taught me how to teach human rights in teacher training. I am experimenting with new forms of teaching and gain encouragement to continue.

This is echoed by the German member:

> The various conferences run by the project were the highlight of the project life. They fostered the whole purpose of the project very much. The teaching mobility gave me many new ideas about content and methods of teaching.

The real test, however, is the impact that the project makes on students. Certainly there is evidence that they appreciate studying human rights: 'Students are very interested in human rights questions. Several chose to do research in this area' reports the colleague from Switzerland. One UK partner uses more coercive methods: 'As part of continuous assessment towards their final degree, all students must write a 3000-word essay demonstrating their understanding of these issues'.

Perhaps the most surprising conclusions come in the attitudes towards and the understanding of Europe. This was one of the problematic questions at the outset, with partners having reservations about the appropriateness of this concept for education. The project did change the perceptions of some participants, such as this British colleague:

> My visits to teacher training institutions in Spain, Portugal, Holland, Denmark and Germany have provided me with a valuable and unique opportunity to appreciate the role of teacher education within a European context. The issues and experiences of freedom, democracy, dictatorship, socialism and capitalism have become real. I have gained a wealth of knowledge about education in other European countries in discussion and workshops. The issues of balance between academic and pedagogical studies, the advantages and disadvantages of a national curriculum, the place of civics and teaching for democracy, and the different ways in which teachers are trained have been explained and demonstrated. This has helped me to evaluate my role as teacher educator from a much wider perspective. My concept of Europe has definitely changed as a result of my involvement in this project. It now includes a greater commitment to the values of democracy, human rights and social justice which the countries of Europe have suffered and fought for.

The two Spanish colleagues viewed their changes in attitude with a geographical eye. As one expressed it:

> The project enabled me to get to know some other countries, but particularly the colleagues who work there. As an educator I now think of Europe as a common space, a crossroads of cultures and peoples and I see diversity as an enrichment and not a problem. The project got me thinking about my own citizenship and the absurdity of frontiers, always ephemeral and politically defined, but capable of creating serious psychological and social barriers. I am sure that this awareness will be reflected in my teaching.

The affective dimension of the project also seems to have been decisive in creating a changed perspective:

> The contact with professionals from European countries has been very important. I see them as European, without the need for any further qualification. I now have colleagues and friends in almost all European countries.

One partner candidly admits his previously national prejudice: 'I've got more humbled, i.e. our [national] way of doing things is not always the best.' On the other hand a colleague from the UK warns of the dangers of national identity being equated with a presupposition of a common experience:

There are perhaps more differences within national groups than between them. Sometimes other participants from England have assumed you share a point of view, have the same experience as them of British politics or education just because you are from the same country. There are many ways of being Danish, Spanish or British.

The project attempted to promote a holistic approach to introducing shared values. It was perhaps the sum of the activities that started to create an impact at institutional level. This would appear to be the case in Spain:

> The project had a real impact because we created a module of forty hours on Europe in the Faculty of Education which is compulsory for all early years and primary teachers. The module has identical objectives to those we worked on in the project. We specially prepared teaching materials including maps and other materials to encourage thinking about the themes with the students. The exchange of students has been a very great success and it is extremely important because there has not been a tradition of exchanges in Spain within teacher training. In general the idea of Europe has become a regular part of teacher training in our Faculty. The project has helped to introduce a sense of Europe in the life of the Faculty: the visits of colleagues of the project, our visits to other European institutions, the meeting of our group in our Faculty and the students' mobility have all contributed to it.

Interestingly the impact in the university in Ireland, which joined the project only in the second year, was also at this interdisciplinary level:

> It has greatly encouraged inter-departmental co-operation and has made an important contribution to the cultivation of the European dimension at the College.

When asked to comment on obstacles to their participation in the project and difficulties, almost all partners mentioned their regret that their linguistic skills were inadequate. On the other hand the project acted as a catalyst for several members to take steps to improve their foreign language communication skills. At least one member embarked on a structured French course, whilst others made determined efforts to communicate in English to the extent that their new-found competence and confidence was clearly apparent by the final meeting.

Summary

One of the speakers at the conference which formed part of the first meeting, Bruce Gill, Chief Inspector for Education for the London Borough of Lambeth, raised the issue of the gap between the rhetoric of democracy as defined in official publications on citizenship and a reality in which real powers of decision-making are being removed from people locally and taken to the centre. The debate on education for citizenship and democracy has, he maintained, ignored the power situated in financial institutions and in the control of public spending, much of which has the effect of disempowering ordinary people and particularly minorities. He raised the question as to whether democracy was now merely a myth that enabled real power to be exercised without accountability to the public.

This challenge and the subsequent debate remained a live issue throughout the project. Developing democracy so that it is able to challenge the abuses to human rights brought about by financial forces may determine if democracy survives the twenty-first century. Transnational corporations, IMF structural adjustment programmes or European programmes for economic convergence may produce insecurity, unemployment and political apathy or extremism. That said, the challenge is to make democracy more effective, and so its possibilities, limitations and structures must be understood. Education for 'citizenship, social justice, global responsibility and respect for human rights' is an essential, if minimal, requirement for the future of a stable and democratic Europe. The experience of this project suggests that such education is most effective if based on an international and multidisciplinary team.

8 Human rights and the professional development of teachers

Introduction

Human rights education is an essential part of preparation for participation in a pluralistic democracy. Moreover, the powerful legal framework of the European Convention on Human Rights itself depends on an educated and supportive public opinion. This chapter considers a number of issues relating to human rights education courses for teachers and others working within the education service, drawing on our experiences of leading workshops and seminars in Britain and internationally. We begin by focusing on the structure, organisation and content of two short courses with which we are involved, both of which run annually as summer schools, one in Geneva and the second in the UK. We then discuss some issues related to the development of an accredited advanced course in human rights education at the University of Birmingham. Each course seeks to explore the relationship between moral and legal aspects of human rights teaching. The Council of Europe Recommendation *Teaching and Learning about Human Rights in Schools* (see Appendix 3) identifies three broad dimensions of human rights education, namely skills, knowledge, and feelings. We argue that this latter affective dimension, as well as facts and pedagogy, is critical to successful teacher education in human rights.

Human rights provide an ethical and moral framework for living in community, whether this be a class, a school, a village, a city, a nation-state, a continent or the global village itself (Best, 1982; Starkey, 1992). Human rights are about the importance of individual human dignity, equality of rights and reciprocal responsibility for ensuring the rights of others are respected. Unlike religiously grounded ethical traditions, which are often passed on by parents and reinforced by formal religious structures independently of schools, human rights as an ethical tradition has scarcely had time to become embedded in the community. The

Universal Declaration of Human Rights was proclaimed scarcely two generations ago and even teachers may not be familiar with its content. Yet in most countries schools are likely to be the most important agency for transmitting information on human rights and in demonstrating, through their structures, their practices and their global outlook, what a commitment to human rights means.

Effective human rights education requires committed and skilled teachers. However, while many teachers have a commitment to human rights principles such as justice and equality, and are skilled in the art of socialising children and young adults, very few have any training or education in human rights law. They may act on ethical principles that accord entirely with human rights. It is quite possible, however, that they remain unaware of the strong legal as well as moral authority that international human rights instruments provide. To take but one example, the United Nations Convention on the Rights of the Child, in its article 29, commits those states that have ratified it, and that is most of the countries of the world, to directing education towards 'the development of respect for human rights and fundamental freedoms and for the principles enshrined in the Charter of the United Nations'. This undertaking by governments implies that teachers should know what is meant by 'human rights and fundamental freedoms' and, indeed, that they are familiar with the content of the Charter of the United Nations. Our experience is that few teachers would claim to be confident in the first area and that to find someone with even a passing knowledge of the UN Charter is very rare indeed. By illustration, a pack of material for personal and social education (Thompson *et al.*, 1993) which includes a section on 'rights and responsibilities' quotes as authority for its position the 1959 UN Declaration of the Rights of the Child. The authors of the material, experienced educators, specialists in social education, were apparently unaware of the existence of the 1989 Convention on the Rights of the Child which effectively superseded the declaration (see Chapter 2).

The development of short courses in human rights

In 1983 the International Training Centre on Human Rights and Peace Teaching (CIFEDHOP), a non-governmental organisation based in Geneva, set out to remedy the lack of teachers' knowledge of what is meant by human rights (Prindezis and Prémont, 1994). It established an annual summer school, lasting one week, which draws on the combined expertise of lawyers and educators to present a human rights education programme for teachers and others involved in formal education. The

CIFEDHOP course is international, drawing participants from a wide range of countries. In 1995 fifty-four countries were represented, including twenty-seven states from within Europe. The African delegates came from Algeria, Burundi, Cameroon, Chad, Madagascar, Niger, Senegal, Tanzania and Tunisia. Additionally there were participants from countries in North and South America and from Asia. The course membership is now about half European, but can claim to be global. Questions relating to human rights and North–South development can therefore be discussed drawing on the direct experience of participants. The course enjoys the active support and sponsorship of the Council of Europe, which makes available a number of bursaries for participants from member states. Being based in Geneva the course also benefits from the proximity of the United Nations and the availability of experts from UN agencies and from numerous non-governmental human rights organisations. In its early years the course was confined to French-speaking participants, but 1988 saw its expansion to include an English-speaking course and since 1991 there has been a Spanish-speaking section as well. Each of the three language sections follows a broadly similar programme with the three sections coming together for common meals, visits, social activities and formal opening and closing sessions. A typical outline programme of the English-speaking section is shown as Box 8.1. We have been responsible for developing the English-speaking section of the course and for promoting team teaching across the three language sections.

A UK course on similar lines was held for the first time in 1993. It was sponsored by the Citizenship Foundation, a London-based educational charity with close links to the legal profession, the Education in Human Rights Network, and the Human Rights Centre of the University of Essex. In its first year it was largely aimed at UK teachers and educators, with just a few overseas participants. Nevertheless, it has attracted a number of overseas teachers, some funded through Council of Europe bursaries, others being students who are based in Britain. Each year the venue has changed to attract teachers from different regions, with the fourth 1996 summer school taking place in Derry, Northern Ireland. Both courses are designed to provide teachers with legal knowledge about human rights, and an opportunity to explore appropriate methodologies for effective teaching and learning about human rights in schools.

```
┌─────────────────────────────────────────────────────────────────┐
```

**11th Training Session on Human Rights and Peace Teaching
for Teachers of Primary, Secondary and Vocational Schools**

Geneva, July 5–10, 1993

Main Theme: HUMAN RIGHTS – DEMOCRACY – DEVELOPMENT

PROGRAMME for the English Speaking Section

Sunday 4 July
15.00–17.30*	Registration at Château de Bossey
17.30	**Meeting of the English Speaking Group**
18.15*	Dinner
19.30–21.00*	**Presentation of participants**

Monday 5 July
8.15*	Breakfast
9.00–9.30*	**Welcome**
	– Guy-Olivier Segond President of CIFEDHOP
	– Jacques Muhlethaler Founding President of EIP and CIFEDHOP
9.30–9.45*	**Presentation of CIFEDHOP's activities and projects**
	– Monique Prindezis (Switzerland) Interim Director of CIFEDHOP
9.45–10.00*	**Presentation of the World Association for School as an Instrument of Peace – EIP activities and projects**
	– Pierre Adossama (Togo) Vice-President of EIP
10.00–10.30*	Coffee break
10.30–12.15*	**Human rights, freedom and democracy** (Round table)
	– Guy Haarscher (Belgium)
	– Rabea Naciri (Morocco) Mohamed V University, Rabat
	– Adama Dieng (Senegal) Secretary General, International Commission of Jurists, Geneva
12.15*	Lunch
14.00–17.30	**Teaching and learning about the Universal Declaration of Human Rights** (workshop)
17.30–18.15*	Welcome drink offered by EIP
18.15*	Dinner

Tuesday 6 July
8.15*	Breakfast
9.00–10.00	**Human rights terms and concepts** (Lecture)
10.00–10.30	Coffee break
10.30–12.00	**What do we mean by democracy at school?** (Workshop)
12.15*	Lunch
14.00–16.00	**Workshops:**
	1 Drama; 2 Non-violent conflict resolutions; 3 Working with photos
16.00–16.30*	Coffee break
16.30–18.00	**Presentations by members of the group**
18.15	Dinner
20.00*	**Demonstration of teaching materials brought by participants**

Box 8.1 CIFEDHOP programme

122

```
Wednesday 7 July
8.15*            Breakfast
8.30*            Bus leaves Château for the United Nations Office in Geneva (UNOG)
9.00–10.30*      United Nations Visit
10.45–12.30*     Visit to the Museum of the International Committee of the Red Cross
Lunch and afternoon Free

Thursday 8 July
8.15*            Breakfast
9.00–10.00       Minorities and human rights (Lecture)
10.00–10.30*     Coffee break
10.30–12.00      Protection of minorities and human rights (Lecture)
                 – Rachel Brett (United Kingdom) Quakers United Nations Office, Geneva
12.15*           Lunch
14.00–16.00      Intercultural simulation
                 – Arnaldo Cecchini (Italy) University of Venice
16.00–16.30*     Coffee break
16.30–18.00      Presentations by members of the group
18.15*           Dinner

Friday 9 July
8.15*            Breakfast
9.00–10.00       Human rights, democracy and development (Lecture)
10.00–10.30*     Coffee break
11.00–12.00      Development and children's rights (Lecture)
                 – Nigel Cantwell (United Kingdom) Defence for Children International,
                   Geneva
12.15*           Lunch
14.00–16.00      Human rights projects (Workshop)
16.00–16.30*     Coffee break
16.30–18.00      Reporting back:
                 Feedback from the group
                 Questionnaire on the session
18.15*           Dinner
20.00*           Participants' party


                          Closing session

Saturday 10 July
9.00–9.30*       Breakfast
9.30–10.30       Feedback from the evaluation of the session
                 Conclusion and future projects
10.30–11.30*     Distribution of certificates
                 Distribution of list of participants' addresses
                 Closing address
                 Farewell drink offered by CIFEDHOP
12.15*           Lunch

*Common to all linguistic sections
```

Box 8.1 continued

The importance of a legal perspective

Since 1978, the Council of Europe has been actively supporting human rights education. Its work on education and human rights is discussed in more detail in Chapter 3. The educational principles on which the Council's human rights education programme have been based draw on important contributions from Heater and Lister from the UK and Audigier and Best from France. These have been developed by hundreds of teachers meeting in seminars across Europe. The work has been summarised by Shafer (1987), Starkey (1991b) and Starkey and Tibbitts (forthcoming). Lister (1984) provided the framework for the development of a human rights curriculum. He identified three essential aims: 'a compound of knowledge, procedural values and skills'. The procedural values are essentially 'fair treatment' and 'due process'; in other words, elements closely identified with a judicial process.

The Council of Europe's view of human rights education is encapsulated in a Recommendation *Teaching and Learning about Human Rights in Schools* adopted in May 1985 by the Committee of Ministers of the Member States (printed in full as Appendix 3), which lists the skills and knowledge expected within a programme of human rights education, drawing attention to the relationship between moral and legal knowledge. Such knowledge should include 'the main categories of human rights, duties, obligations and responsibilities' and 'the main international declarations and conventions on human rights'.

Audigier and Lagelée (1992) also stress the importance of teachers having a basic understanding of law:

> Indeed, to base civics on human rights and make its aim a critical knowledge of the rules of social life implies that it will have a substantial legal element. It is not a question of training young people to be legal experts, but rather of enabling them to develop and think about and act on their relationships with others. The legal dimension is not only concerned with knowledge of the great international instruments but also with the everyday life of the school. Both are based on the same moral principles.

In Britain law has never been incorporated into the school curricula in a systematic way. In an attempt to remedy this, the Law Society funded the Law in Education Project which produced, in the late 1980s, classroom materials for eleven- to fourteen-year-olds and fourteen- to sixteen-year-olds. In 1989 this project was incorporated into the Citizenship Foundation, which runs a broad range of participatory projects for young people, designed to increase their understanding of legal, political and social systems. The official guidance on citizenship education which accompanied the first version of the National Curriculum made specific reference to human rights, the citizen and the law:

> The duties, responsibilities and rights of citizenship are defined within a framework of national and international law. They include such basic human rights as freedom of speech, belief and expression, freedom of association, freedom from discrimination on grounds of race or sex, the right to a fair trial and to the due processes of law (NCC, 1990).

The courses we will now describe all incorporate a legal perspective and seek to provide teachers and educationalists with a basic knowledge of human rights law and its relevance to their professional lives.

Ensuring an affective dimension

While a legal perspective is important it is not sufficient to guarantee effective education in human rights. Lister (1984) also stresses the importance of the affective dimension:

> Human Rights engage not just the intellect but also the emotions, and the sense of fairness, on which Human Rights are based, is intuitive and is strongly *felt* by children. There is need to give concrete and *affective* support for learning, and Human Rights Education cannot limit itself to the *cognitive* domain.

Heater (1984) also supports this emphasis:

> We should be seeking to engender feelings of humaneness in our pupils. Feelings of cruelty, retribution and aggression ill-suit an exponent of human rights. The quality of caring is to be nourished.

He points out that common classroom interactions demonstrate an intuitive understanding of human rights concepts. A child saying, 'That's not fair!' understands something of justice. 'You're picking on her!' suggests an understanding of discrimination and a feeling for equality, for example.

The Council of Europe Recommendation on human rights education also, importantly, stresses the affective dimension, as in:

> The emphasis in teaching and learning about human rights should be positive. Pupils may be led to feelings of powerlessness and discouragement when faced with many examples of violation and negation of human rights. Instances of progress and success should be used.

and

> The study of human rights in schools should lead to an understanding of, and sympathy for, the concepts of justice, equality, peace, dignity, rights and

democracy. Such understanding should be both cognitive and based on experience and feelings. Schools should, thus, provide opportunities for pupils to experience affective involvement in human rights and to express their feelings through drama, art, music, creative writing and audio-visual media. (Council of Europe, 1985)

Effective human rights education requires the combining of legal perspectives and an affective dimension. This is important in the education not only of children but of adults as well.

The CIFEDHOP teacher education programme

Each year the seven-day Geneva CIFEDHOP course follows a broad theme. In 1993, immediately following the World Conference on Human Rights in Vienna, it appropriately took as its theme 'Human rights, democracy, development'. In 1995 the course was entitled: 'Teaching and learning about human rights: new challenges and approaches'. The programme always consists of a mixture of key-note lectures, from a number of internationally respected experts in human rights law or human rights campaigning, and active workshop sessions. Participants acquire some legal knowledge and understanding and consider how they may most effectively combine this knowledge with appropriate pedagogical skills and translate it into classroom practice, for their students or other teachers.

At the annual summer school we attach considerable importance to learning processes, drawing on a model developed by Richardson (1979). We construct the course in three phases, namely establishing the climate, enquiry and synthesis. In the first phase we aim to provide both security and challenge. The second phase includes study and experience, and the third and final stage leaves participants with principles on which they can act and which give them the basis to develop their own plans.

Phase one: security and challenge

The challenge provided to participants at the outset of such a course is all too evident. For the majority it is their first experience of Switzerland and for some their first journey outside their home country. Almost all will be working in a foreign language and with an international group of fellow students with many different experiences and varied responsibilities and positions in their own organisations. The school teachers and representatives of non-governmental organisations are perhaps less intimidated by the participatory style of the course than some of the headteachers, advisers, inspectors, university lecturers and civil servants who may be more used to formal communications. The shared expertise of such a group is inevitably rich, and we build into the programme opportunities for participants to make brief presentations on an aspect of their own work in human rights education. Although all participants are pleased to share their experience, the drafting of the presentation is, for many, a significant linguistic challenge.

Security is a question of calming fears and anxieties and helping participants to feel at ease on the course. The first meeting of the course takes place in French, English or Spanish language groups and the content is simply getting to know the names and identities of the participants. Rather than asking participants to introduce themselves to the group, a possibly daunting task when operating in a foreign language and with strangers, course members introduce themselves to their neighbour and, once warmed up in this private rehearsal, they introduce the neighbour to the group.

By the end of the initial session everyone knows at least one other participant quite well. It is followed by a common meal, with possibilities for further conversation and a chance to appreciate the size of the course, which for reasons of space is limited to about 120 people. After supper the whole course meets outside in an open space for further 'getting to know you' and ice-breaking activities. The instructions for each activity are repeated in the official languages of the course and everyone's linguistic resources are thoroughly stretched as they try to communicate with other course members. The programme includes a conversation wheel, where participants face each other in concentric circles and converse briefly before moving on to the next person. This is followed by a bilingual 'Globingo'-type activity (Pike and Selby, 1988) involving a questionnaire requiring simple answers from a number of different people. The session ends with a huge graffiti wall on which participants write, this time in their own language, their wishes and proposals for peace and human rights in the world.

Phase two: study and experience

The main body of the course consists of lectures and workshops organised in three language groups. The French-speaking group tends to have over sixty participants, the English-speaking group about forty and the Spanish around twenty. Each group has its permanent legal expert who provides the basic information on human rights terms and concepts and on current debates. For instance, in 1993 our expert, Reynaldo Ty from the College of Political Science and Philosophy, Quezon City, Philippines, brought us first-hand news of the World Conference on Human Rights in Vienna with its debates on development and human rights. His continued presence as a member of the group is an important commitment. He experiences and participates in all the activities on an equal basis and he is constantly available as a point of reference. Participants can also question him informally at meal and leisure times. At the UK-based Education in Human Rights Network summer school Kevin Boyle of the Human Rights Centre at the University of Essex has played a similar role.

Both courses place a strong emphasis on legal awareness. Happily our experience is that human rights experts, such as professors of law, politics or international relations, are well aware of the importance of education in the promotion and protection of human rights. We have had no difficulty in persuading eminent academics and advocates to contribute to our sessions. Indeed, in many cases they provide considerable support. The crucial element is to make the legal knowledge accessible to teachers. Lawyers are often skilled at expressing themselves clearly, and transmitting information. For the information to be received, accepted and internalised, however, there are other requirements. The climate of the course must be such as to enable the legal experts to be perceived as equal partners in the process of enquiry. They come as expert witnesses, bringing specialist knowledge and experience, but they must be helped to acknowledge the experience and needs of the course members. Their contribution to the course must be carefully structured, and this is where pedagogical skills are essential. The most effective way of involving legal experts is for them to participate as fully as possible in the life of the course. If accessibility, in all senses, is the first requirement of the legal education, the second is for the course members to use this knowledge actively. This is what the workshops are for.

Workshop sessions are designed so that participants work co-operatively. The need to support each other and find a common means of communication encourages a sense of interdependence and commonality of experience with people of different cultural backgrounds and political histories. Working with others in this way also involves a direct personal investment and hopefully a sense of collective achievement. In this way a strong affective dimension is built into the course.

Workshops need to combine the use of the existing knowledge and experience of the participants with an opportunity to work with new concepts. For example, in one workshop on the 1993 course when we addressed the issues of human rights and development, participants were invited to choose three photographs which illustrated development issues from a set which had been pinned up around the room. Working in groups of four, with members from different backgrounds, they identified the development issues raised and made links with similar issues in their own localities and countries. A collective list was compiled with the whole group. In the third phase of the workshop, groups identified the human rights issues which may arise when such development issues are tackled; specifically they were asked which articles of the Universal Declaration might be relevant to the situation portrayed. The use of photographs as stimulus material on this occasion meant that everyone started on an equal footing, regardless of their linguistic background. The situations did not require complicated or wordy explanations. By focusing on the text of the Universal Declaration, course members familiarised themselves with its content and started to explore its applications and possibly its limitations.

Participants were not initially told where the photographs were from, although they were in fact from the *New Journeys* pack (McFarlane and Osler, 1991) and were all taken in Kenya and Tanzania. Czech and Romanian participants, working with photographs of rural landscapes, were surprised to discover that a scene which looked so familiar was in fact in East Africa, and this activity not only helped establish that different regions may share similar development and human rights issues but also served to break down preconceived ideas about distant places and people. The emphasis, throughout, is on similarities and the universal nature of human rights issues. On the other hand, participants found out that they often had different priorities for development. In fact, the development and human rights agenda in one region was often dependent on policy decisions made in another place. In short, the sense of interdependence and co-operation established in the group was also experienced and required at a global level. Indeed, such co-operation is essential for the maintenance of human rights. Issues arose concerning conflicts of rights, and the group recognised that rights may be in tension; this enabled participants to explore the principle of reciprocity, drawing on examples from their own varied experience.

Another workshop considers the meaning of democracy in a school context. We provide a sequence of individual and small-group activities in which participants clarify their individual understandings of democracy as an abstract or ideal concept, then share and develop these, applying them to the schools they know. Participants produce a list of the ways in which schools can promote democracy and the ways in which they can undermine the process. The list from 1993 is reproduced in Chapter 5 as Box 5.4. The relationship between human rights education and democratic values such as justice, equality and co-operation was made explicit by the participants, as were some of the skills and attitudes needed to guarantee human rights and democracy.

Other workshops focus on human rights and the experiences of particular groups. One way of encouraging teachers to consider the needs and rights of a minority group is to engage in role play. Drawing on materials developed by the Minority Rights Group (van der Gaag and Gerlach, 1985), we ask small groups of participants each to put themselves in the position of a minority community, without knowing precisely who they are supposed to be. The groups are given a set of cards which tell them about 'their' group's past and present achievements and culture. Each group responds by expressing their feelings about themselves and recording these on a poster-sized sheet of paper. Generally, group members feel a sense of pride and strong sense of group solidarity. Each group then receives a second set of cards which outline the injustices which the group has encountered from the authorities and the majority community, covering such issues as misrepresentation in the media and access to services such as health, education, and medical care. Again each group is asked to concentrate on the feelings they experience as a result of this discrimination. Some group members feel anger, others hopelessness and despair. Again the feelings are recorded. In the third phase of the role play participants are asked to respond to these injustices. Reactions vary: some group members may wish to seek out allies beyond the community and enlist their support in challenging discrimination, devising short-term and long-term plans which they hope will give them access to power and the ability to improve their situation. Others opt for non-violent direct action, through public protest and civil disobedience. Occasionally some group members advocate violence as the only response to societal indifference to their rights. They do not trust outsiders and are unwilling to engage in dialogue as a means of redressing grievances. The role play is debriefed by focusing on the relationship between the participants' feelings and their various strategies for change. Comparisons are then made between their responses and those of actual minority groups. Finally, participants are told that they were, in fact, Gypsies. Within Europe, Gypsies and travellers continue to encounter prejudice and widespread discrimination. One way in which the activity can be extended is for teachers to consider strategies for ensuring equality for these minorities within their own schools and classrooms.

In a simple exercise about refugees, participants are told they have ten minutes to leave their homes, possibly never to return, and are asked to make decisions about what they will take and what they will leave behind. Refugees all have one thing in common: their rights are not being respected in their home country. The activity can be developed to explore how refugees apply for asylum, who 'qualifies' as a refugee and public attitudes towards them. We have found that material produced by the

Refugee Council (Rutter, 1996) for use with fourteen- to eighteen-year-olds is also a very rich resource for use with teachers. Role play and simulation games do not have to be complex in order to be effective. The majority of workshop exercises which we use can be adapted for use with children and young people in schools.

Phase three: principles and plans

In a sense the whole course is about principles. However, it is at the end of the course that participants can review the curriculum they have been offered and extract those ideas that will enable them to structure similar learning experiences in their own context. Each day of the course, members complete an evaluation questionnaire, which is one aid to reflection. At the end of each session or each day the leaders also draw out the main principles on which the session has been constructed. Attention is always given to understanding the process as well as the content.

We end the course with a sequence called 'Projects for human rights education'. By this time participants have got to know one another and they work in small groups according to specific interest (for example, teacher training or work with the community through a non-governmental organisation). They plan their future work in human rights education and explore ways in which others on the course can assist them. Each group or individual reports back to the whole group, who become witnesses to a statement of intent. These plans for the future provide a positive and inspiring final formal activity. A further refinement requires participants to write a postcard to themselves stating three or four lines of action. The organisers collect the postcards and post them to participants two or three months after the course. This postcard, arriving unexpectedly, may provide the satisfaction of knowing undertakings have been kept, or alternatively provide a timely nudge to the conscience.

The close of the CIFEDHOP course is designed to reinforce group solidarity and friendship: there is a party, the presentation of certificates of attendance and the writing of personal messages of appreciation and support to the other group members. Each participant is given a postcard stuck to a sheet of paper on which their name is clearly written. Each sheet is circulated around the group and everyone leaves on it a positive and encouraging message for the owner.

A short course on human rights education: the UK summer school

The example of the CIFEDHOP summer school in Geneva inspired a group in the UK to stage a national course in 1993. A committee was formed comprising representatives of a university department of international law, an educational foundation for the promotion of law education in schools, Amnesty International and two university departments of education. This organising group benefited from the expertise of human rights lawyers, human rights campaigners and educationalists working with schools and teachers. This is the same range of expertise as the successful CIFEDHOP formula.

Organising a residential course is inevitably a costly undertaking, and the committee had to work hard to find some small grants to cover some of the initial costs. Mostly, however, organisations and individuals contributed from their own resources in order that the project might be achieved. It appears to be the case that the initiative and putting on the first course is the major and most significant achievement. The sequence of annual courses has continued. That said, the organisers recognised that a three-day course would both stretch their resources to the limit and probably be the maximum period that teachers would be able to attend. This shorter course has a slightly different dynamic from one lasting a week.

Box 8.2 shows the programme of the 1994 summer school, the second of the series. It ran from Friday morning until Sunday lunch. Teachers attended on one schoolday and two days of their weekend. Total numbers were about sixty including the speakers and workshop leaders. These were volunteers who offered their services without payment and attended as much of the course as they wished.

The three-stage model used on the week-long course has to be telescoped in the three-day version. The first phase, establishing a climate of security and challenge, is provided in so-called home groups. Each participant is allocated to a group with an experienced leader. The home groups are intended to provide a friendly and supportive atmosphere in which participants can share their own experience, and also raise questions or concerns about the course or about human rights issues. The leaders ensure that each member is introduced and has opportunities to speak. The home groups meet at the beginning of the course and then on each of the other two days.

Enquiry, study and experience are provided by the three lectures and workshops. Two of the lectures were given by international law specialists, the third by a headteacher with substantial experience of implementing human rights principles in school. The workshops were given by NGO workers engaged in human rights education, and teacher educators. They were grouped under headings: curriculum issues, policy and pastoral issues and wider issues. The wider issues involved international case studies.

132

Programme of Events

'Human Rights in the School'

Friday, 1 July

10.00 am	Registration and coffee	11.00 am	**Plenary Lecture 2**
11.00 am	Welcome and Introduction		*What every teacher needs to*
11.30 am	**Home Groups 1**		*know: the Universal Declaration*
	What do we understand by		*of Human Rights and the*
	'human rights and the		*European Convention on*
	school?'		*Human Rights*
1.00 pm	Lunch	12.00 noon	**Home Groups**
2.00 pm	**Plenary Lecture 1**		*Implementing human rights in*
	Human rights and the		*schools*
	school: the implications of	1.00 pm	Lunch
	the United Nations	2.00 pm	Free time. Bookstall. Displays
	Convention on the Rights of	3.30 pm	Tea
	the Child	4.00 pm	**Workshops 3 – Wider Issues**
3.30 pm	Tea		*Human rights and world*
4.00 pm	**Workshops 1 – Curriculum Issues**		*citizenship*
	Human rights education and the		*Rhetoric and reality: human*
	primary school		*rights education in*
	Human rights and the		*Commonwealth countries*
	citizenship curriculum		*Children working for peace: case*
	Approaches to human rights		*studies from Northern Ireland,*
	education in secondary school		*Sri Lanka and Liberia*
	Human rights and religious		*Central and Eastern Europe:*
	education		*thinking afresh about human*
	Teaching about human rights		*rights*
	through literature		*Teaching about refugees*
6.30 pm	Supper	6.30 pm	Supper
8.00 pm	**Council of Europe video**	8.00 pm	**Presentations by course**
	'Human Rights'		**members**

Saturday, 2 July

Sunday, 3 July

9.00 am	**Workshops 2 – Policy and**	9.30 am	**Home Groups 3**
	Pastoral Issues		*Projects and plans*
	Non-violent conflict resolution in	10.30 am	Coffee
	schools	11.00 am	**Plenary Lecture 3**
	Developing a school policy on		*Human rights and the school*
	behaviour on bullying	12.30 pm	Light lunch. Conference ends
	Developing a school equal		
	opportunities policy		
	Reluctant attenders, children		
	with special needs, and the right		
	to education		
10.30 am	Coffee		

Box 8.2 UK Summer School 1994

The third stage of the course, synthesis, principles and plans, took place in the home group where participants planned and presented their personal intentions concerning human rights education. This was followed by a final inspirational lecture by the headteacher which gave course members specific ideas for implementing change to promote democracy and a human rights ethos in schools.

The three-day course was built around a three-by-three grid: three home group sessions, three workshops and three lectures. Even in such a short course it is important to build in some free time, and there was such an opportunity on the second afternoon. A further element was a bookstall, provided by a local specialist bookseller, and offering the opportunity to purchase the latest resources.

Reflections on the courses

Legal and moral knowledge

At the UK summer school one difficulty we have encountered in addressing the legal dimension of human rights education is UK teachers' lack of familiarity with the legal frameworks which support moral obligations and responsibilities. Teachers have little experience or understanding of the ways in which human rights legal instruments might support their goals in education for human rights. This was well illustrated during a workshop on the first day of the first 1993 summer school when teachers were encouraged in a workshop to familiarise themselves with the Universal Declaration of Human Rights. They had previously listened to lectures by human rights lawyers and were then introduced to the Universal Declaration in a way which actively engaged them in exploring its content. Once in a workshop setting where they could readily express their views, a small number queried the value of the exercise as they did not perceive it to be of direct benefit in school. The study of the Universal Declaration in the abstract, without focusing on a specific context or situation, is not necessarily an inspirational or engaging experience.

Yet a similar workshop on the rights of the child, run later in the course, was judged by many of the same people to be valuable. The second workshop did more than familiarise participants with the legal instrument; it discussed the ways in which children better understand the rights of the child by relating the Convention to their other work in school. The Universal Declaration and the Convention on the Rights of the Child are not just abstract statements, they have to be applied to contexts including the context of the school. They have both legal and moral implications and on reflection it would seem appropriate to make explicit the relationship between the legal and moral aspects of human rights. Nevertheless, it is interesting to note that in the UK, which lacks a written constitution, teachers should find it difficult to see the relationship between legal and moral frameworks whereas in other political contexts such things are taken as understood.

Human rights education and democratic teaching methodologies

Although we wish to build upon participants' existing skills and interests, neither course hands over responsibility for the course to the group. We adopt a democratic style of working where participants have maximum influence over the detailed carrying-out of tasks, including deciding exactly how the task is tackled. However, as course leaders we take the responsibility of devising and sequencing the activities and setting these within a pre-determined framework. We adopt an approach which provides opportunities for student-led activities, and small-group activities which permit maximum participation and encourage co-operation, toleration and decision-making. We try to make explicit the reasons for our choice of teaching methodologies, stressing our belief that education for human rights and democracy cannot take place in a teaching context that is undemocratic or does not respect the human rights of both students and teachers.

For longer courses, other models may be appropriate; for instance Harber and Meighan (1986) discuss democratic practices in teacher education and indicate that there is likely to be a correspondence between the values underpinning a teacher education course and the values which students subsequently adopt in their own teaching. Together with their students they adopted 'democratic learning co-operatives' where students and tutors drew up a contract to promote group responsibility for their work. Choice of course organisation was left to the students who worked together over a year. This approach is routinely adopted in teacher education colleges in Denmark. The Geneva course, however, lasts only for seven days and the UK course for three. It is not realistic or appropriate to structure such a short course along this type of model. Within the short course, we wish to cover a pre-determined programme within a limited time. A totally open-ended, participant-centred course, with an international and intercultural group of students who have not met or worked together before, would risk being dominated by the more confident and articulate students or by those who are most fluent in the course language and so, in fact, be undemocratic. Our structure provides first a framework within which all have access to information, and second the opportunity to participate in activities which help to clarify, interpret and apply this information.

Human rights education and personal experience

It is important within any course on human rights education that participants should not only address the legal dimension (knowledge) and teaching methodologies or skills but that they should also have the opportunity to experience human rights in a positive way. In other words, the course should incorporate the affective dimension as well as those of knowledge and skills. We have provided some examples of how personal experiences and feelings can be incorporated in our discussion of teaching methodologies. In many ways it might be argued that feelings and experiences of human rights should be the starting point since education in human rights with pre-school children and in the first years of schooling is necessarily going to begin with the experiences of the child and be concerned with values.

The educational experience of living and experiencing human rights clearly does not need to be confined to schools. This experience should be incorporated at all levels, including within teacher education. Human rights issues are invariably ones to which people respond on an emotional as well as on an intellectual level, and this needs to be borne in mind in the planning of courses.

An accredited course in human rights education: University of Birmingham

Background to the course

The School of Education at the University of Birmingham offers a course in 'Human Rights and Equality in Education' at MEd, BPhil and diploma levels. The course is open to teachers and others in related professions, and students are normally expected to have a minimum of two years professional experience. The course lasts one year for full-time students, but many local teachers also follow the programme on a part-time basis over a longer time span. All students follow the same basic programme of study regardless of the qualification they are working towards. Students studying for different qualifications are assessed at different levels. Study generally involves independent research for a project or dissertation as well as participation in taught courses. Transfer between qualifications is possible. The course is modular, and some students elect to study for the shorter Advanced Certificate in Education (three modules) which can be completed over a period of twelve weeks full-time. Students specialising in other fields, for example education management, curriculum studies or special education, can elect to follow a module in human rights education. Individual modules are generally also available to local teachers, education professionals and others, for example school governors, who may wish to follow them as a short course without accreditation. Modules are run in the day-time and evenings in alternate years, to ensure access for local teachers studying on a part-time basis. Nevertheless, even when particular modules have been scheduled in the day-time they have attracted a significant number of local teachers who have negotiated their participation with their school or college.

The module 'Human Rights, Citizenship and the Environment' was first introduced in 1992 when it was linked with existing modules entitled '"Race" and Education Today', 'School Management Policy and Gender' and 'Personal Skills for Women and Men in Educational Management' to form a new programme of study: 'Equal Opportunities in Education'. More recently a module in bilingualism has been added to the programme. The name of the programme of study was changed in 1994 to 'Human Rights and Equality in Education' to reflect the increased emphasis placed on the legal and moral aspects of human rights, on children's rights and on issues of citizenship and democracy within the course. We felt that the term *rights* rather than *opportunities* more accurately reflected our understanding of equality and justice in education. While some writers use the terms interchangeably, we wish to stress the notion of entitlement and to acknowledge that human rights are increasingly the benchmark by which governments are recognising each other and deciding on co-operation or aid (Osler and Davies, 1994). Moreover, the course was starting to attract students internationally and the term 'human rights education' has a broader international currency.

A qualification in 'Human Rights and Equality in Education' generally means not only that students will have acquired some familiarity with international human rights legislation and had the opportunity to apply it to their own professional context, as during the summer schools, but that they will also have specialised in a particular area, such as women's human rights in education, children's rights, human rights and development education, or 'race', ethnicity and rights, and will have completed a number of written assignments and undertaken a research project in the field. There are limited opportunities to acquire an advanced qualification in human rights education in the UK, and the only other courses we are currently aware of are based at the University of London, at the Institute of Education and at Birkbeck College.

The students

The 'Human Rights and Equality in Education' programme attracts students from a wide range of contexts and specialisms, including teachers in primary, secondary and further education, headteachers, advisory teachers, school inspectors, NGO workers, and ministry of education personnel, for example those responsible for women's education and areas such as health education and family planning education. About half the students are local people. Of the rest, a few students are from other parts of Europe, North America and the Caribbean but most are from countries in Africa and Asia, with recent students coming from Botswana, the Gambia, Kenya, Tanzania, Hong Kong, Taiwan, and Japan. They are sometimes joined on the course by visiting scholars and research students who are working in related fields, such as peace education or religious education. It can be seen that the students are themselves a very rich resource within the programme, and over the twelve-week period of an individual module they have the opportunity to work co-operatively together, sharing not only their wide range of professional expertise but also their varied experiences of political systems, cultures and human rights.

Course development

The courses have developed over the years in response to student needs and as a result of two concurrent projects. During 1994–95 the module 'Human Rights Education, Citizenship and the Environment' was linked to a curriculum development project developed in partnership with a local NGO, to explore ways of teaching about local human rights and development issues in the upper secondary school and in further and adult education settings. Seven local teachers and lecturers took part in the module as part of this project. The project is discussed elsewhere (Osler, 1996d) but it is interesting to note that the production of teaching materials and their trialing by teachers in local schools had an unintended impact on a number of overseas module participants who developed and adapted the ideas of their UK colleagues. Some of them subsequently developed materials and ideas for teaching about local human rights issues in their own communities and presented these as part of their course assessment. From the outset the EC-funded project 'Education for Citizenship in a New Europe' (see Chapter 7) has also enriched the development of the human rights education module at Birmingham, permitting staff exchanges with other European countries and an opportunity to reflect, discuss and research issues of European citizenship and identity with student teachers and teacher education colleagues across Europe.

Assessment

One significant difference between an accredited course in human rights education and the short courses discussed earlier in the chapter is the need for assessment. Registered students are assessed by written assignments, which they are required to produce at the end of each module. Our aim is to ensure not only that the assignment tests a student's knowledge and understanding of key human rights concepts and their ability to apply this knowledge to their own professional context but that, where possible, it should also inform the understanding of other students and have some practical benefit to the individual student in their professional context, whether this be an education office in Tanzania, an NGO in Japan or a classroom in the West Midlands. Each assignment is individually agreed with the tutor and consequently the pieces of work are very varied. Some recent examples of assignment titles are:

- Empowerment, citizenship and human rights: a case study of adult learners in the inner city
- How might the teaching of gender issues in a Hong Kong primary school contribute to education for equality and human rights?
- Teaching for human rights through English literature: a curriculum review
- The implications of the Convention on the Rights of the Child for Japanese schools
- Human rights, children's rights and the development of a behavioural policy in one school.

An outline programme is presented at the beginning of the course and students invited to identify themes which they wish to see developed, added or changed. They quickly recognise that they have much to learn from each other and readily agree to a student-led seminar in the second half of the semester, when each individual presents an aspect of human rights education from their own perspective, usually in preparation for the written assignment. Overseas students are often invited into the schools and classrooms of the local teachers on the module and this generally leads to interesting comparisons and debate. A spirit of co-operation and friendship is established early on and students benefit from the questions, criticisms and suggestions which are made by their peers. Past students, who have developed human rights initiatives in their own workplace, have returned to the course to share their experience with current students.

Research in human rights education

Students studying at MEd and BPhil levels also prepare a dissertation, based on a piece of original research. Local students normally carry out their research in their own or neighbouring institutions and have open to them a wide choice of research methods. Their main limitations are time and resources. For the vast majority of overseas students the most appropriate and useful location for their research is their home country and community. Since few are in a position to finance a return trip home, this research must be carried out at a distance, and students tend to rely on colleagues, friends, and family to act as informal research assistants. This often limits the range of research tools they are able to use. For example, interviews, even when appropriate, are usually impossible, and the normal difficulties of using, say, questionnaires are further complicated, particularly in countries where communications are poor. Nevertheless, they tend to be resourceful, and valuable pieces of original work have been completed.

Women's human rights have formed an important focus of students' work. Friedman (1995) analyses the processes leading up to the 1993 World Conference in Vienna which ensured that women's human rights activists and advocates were able to promote their issues successfully at both the NGO forum and the official meeting. Through the Global Tribunal on Violations of Women's Human Rights and through the recommendations made by women's rights groups they were able to ensure that many of their concerns such as abuse within the family, war crimes against women, violations against women's bodily integrity, socio-economic human rights abuses, and political participation and persecution were addressed in *The Vienna Declaration and Programme of Action*. They were able to demonstrate to the Conference that it is inadequate that existing human rights mechanisms merely be extended to women. Women's rights need to be understood as human rights. First, gender-based abuses must be recognised as human rights abuses, and secondly, this understanding must lead to the transformation of prevailing concepts of human rights. Traditionally there has been an artificial divide between crimes by state actors and those by non-state actors. Human rights work has focused on state-sanctioned or state-condoned oppression, that is, abuses which take place in the public sphere. Women's human rights violations have mostly taken place in the private sphere, and so have not been covered by international legislation.

A number of overseas students on the course are employed in posts specifically to promote women's rights and gender equality in their home environments, and these students, often funded by the British Council, have been keen to explore those human rights issues which have a particular impact on women's lives and may in some cases be literally issues of life and death. Consequently, students' research projects have addressed such issues as women's reproductive health or the conflicts between international legislation and customary law and practice which serve to restrict women's access to education.

Amongst local students, research projects at MEd level have included action research projects which have adopted a human rights framework, such as bilingual students' access to the curriculum or the issue of bullying at school. For example, one primary school headteacher set out to reduce discriminatory behaviour among children and thus develop an environment where each child's right to achieve their potential was guaranteed. Children addressed the problem of bullying and devised effective strategies for countering it. In the process children have become active in decision-making and have been helped 'to consider the rights of others and to take a shared responsibility for their future' (Thorne, 1996). The headteacher sees this as an important step in involving children in democratic processes and in developing the school as a human rights community.

There is an established tradition of research students at the University and a number of students are investigating themes on issues of justice and equality in education; for example, there is a research group looking at various aspects of African Caribbean education in Britain. MPhil/ PhD students have recently started to adopt an explicit human rights framework for their research. A female history teacher in a boys' secondary school explored issues related to masculine cultures and bullying through action research, introducing teaching and learning about the UN Convention on the Rights of the Child. A primary school teacher investigated the potential of human rights education for the wider school community, to involve pupils, teachers and parents.

The setting up of an accredited course in human rights education has been a demanding but immensely rewarding experience. Students share and benefit from each other's personal and professional experience and they also make direct contributions to human rights education through the projects they undertake and by adding to the literature as they write about them. Short courses can only ever be introductory. Longer courses, such as this, including a research element, enable human rights education to develop.

Summary

We try in our courses to introduce legal, moral and affective dimensions of human rights. The course structure is important, as is the quality of the legal information. However, the unique element of these courses is that we make the human rights element explicit in the conduct and the process of the course. Each member is treated with respect, individual dignity is always a concern, the humanity of course members and their affective as well as their intellectual needs are acknowledged. The courses are focused on the future, on projects and action to be taken in communities all over the world. The courses are continually being revised and developed to meet students' needs. Each new group of students informs our own understanding of the issues and the accredited courses, in particular, permit students to apply their learning to their professional work through research and reflection. All will be strengthened by a greater awareness of the legal and moral basis of human rights as essential and universal values.

9 Human rights and the school curriculum

International human rights agreements provide us with a values framework which can form the basis of school management and organisation, pedagogy and curriculum. We have seen how a human rights approach places emphasis on inclusion and on student participation and expression. The challenge facing teachers is to develop schools which reflect this emphasis and particularly to develop a curriculum which acknowledges that students' right to education can most effectively be achieved when the teaching methods are also based on human rights principles. In this chapter we begin by examining structured approaches to learning democracy based on the ideas of Freinet. We focus on ways in which students can experience democracy in action and examine curriculum strategies, such as project work, which are able to promote student participation. In previous chapters we make reference to a wide range of curriculum materials which address human rights issues and which can be used to promote knowledge, skills, and experience of human rights. Here we review further materials which might support the development of human rights education and encourage participative citizenship. We conclude with an attempt to define some pedagogic principles based on human rights.

The Freinet movement

The legacy of the French educator Célestin Freinet (1896–1966) is a child-centred pedagogy, active learning approaches, formal co-operative structures at class and school level, pupils' publications, class and school exchanges and an international perspective. Two influential educational movements in France, the *Office Central de la Coopération à l'Ecole* (OCCE) founded in 1928 and the *Institut Coopératif de l'Ecole Moderne – Pédagogie Freinet* (ICEM), founded in 1947, refer specifically to their origins in the work of Freinet. Both organisations promote international links, the ICEM since 1957 through the international federation, the

FINEM, whose members are drawn from Europe, Francophone Africa and Latin America. The publishing arm of ICEM, PEMF, provides a wide range of classroom material used by teachers who are not necessarily members of the movement. The journal of the OCCE, *Animation et Education*, has a circulation of 50,000. Both organisations focus on human rights and children's rights as basic values for their educational work.

The statutes of the OCCE define co-operative education as:

> An active approach to civic, moral and intellectual education aiming to develop the spirit of mutual help and solidarity, to stimulate initiatives towards collective efforts, to give a feeling for and commitment to taking responsibility and thereby enable learning freedom, democracy and human rights. (OCCE, 1986: our translation)

Legrand identifies three central aspects of the Freinet tradition:

- the organisation of school life based on individual and collective responsibility;
- acquiring knowledge through personal research and through co-operation in research, also in confronting one's conclusions with those of others;
- engaging the school with its surrounding community, educating citizens. (Legrand, 1996: 8: our translation)

Freinet was an influential practitioner of new forms of education rather than a theoretician. He was brought up in rural south-east France. He trained as a primary school teacher, but was sent to the war front in 1917, where he received a serious chest injury. He returned to his class in 1920 questioning the role of an education system based on hierarchy and a blind obedience to the authority of the teacher. His damaged lungs made sustained periods of speaking painful, so he experimented with new approaches to learning, less reliant on teacher talk. In addition, the purchase and installation of portable printing equipment in the class allowed children to make their own reading material and publish a class newspaper and selections of children's writing. It also enabled the class to correspond with another, hundreds of kilometres distant, which led to the development of class exchanges (Peyronie, 1994: 212).

Freinet's pedagogy is child-centred in that children are given great responsibility for their own learning. One of his innovations was the use of workcards providing tasks and exercises which can be corrected by pupils themselves referring to an answer card rather than the teacher. Another was the use of personal weekly workplans or contracts agreed with each child. He also encouraged children to follow their own lines of research and gave them opportunities to suggest class investigations or projects. His class would regularly leave the school building to study and observe animal and plant life in the locality, the children themselves being encouraged to initiate investigations and discussions. This direct contact with the local environment, whether natural or social, is still very much a feature of the Freinet tradition. In a collective book entitled *History Everywhere, Geography the Whole Time*, secondary school teachers suggest that space and time, the essence of geography and history, are present in any situation.

> When curiosity is sparked off by contact with real life, young people ask questions about their environment and feel a need to understand, to know how the different parts of their surroundings inter-relate. They formulate hypotheses which they try to check on the spot, they work on real-life situations which they personally experience and which enable them to develop more abstract generalisations. ...These pupils no longer put up with their environment as fixed and unchangeable; they realise that, like the organisation of their class, the space in which they live can be modified, that nothing is permanent. (ICEM – Pédagogie Freinet, 1984: 39: our translation)

As this quotation suggests, the child in Freinet pedagogy is not only an individual learner but part of a group, the class. Children's freedom of action and expression are exercised within the limits necessary to protect the freedoms of the others. To quote Freinet himself:

> It is through work and life itself that the child should come to feel and achieve freedom. Freedom is not the starting point. Freedom is the result of the new co-operative organisation of the work of the class. (ICEM – Pédagogie Freinet, 1984: 71: our translation)

Co-operative classes

In fact the organisation of a class co-operative was a response to the poverty-stricken rural milieu. A small contribution from each child's family, used collectively for the good of the class, could enable each child to have the basic learning materials. Participation in visits and outings could be extended to even the poorest children if the class collectively raised funds. This has become a tradition of the Freinet movement.

A co-operative class or school is a way of organising school life for its members, but it is also a mechanism for enabling enhanced learning experiences based on visits, projects or productions. The co-operative is a semi-legal structure with its own resources. In fact the word co-operative links directly to the international Co-operative Movement and in this sense is considered part of the social economy:

> The school co-operative should be considered as an enterprise. Not in the sense

that it makes a contribution to the national economy, but as an organisation which, having as its object the creation of joint projects, sets up a programme of work, a contract, produces accounts and is dependent on the sound management of its material and financial resources. (OCCE, 1986: our translation)

In keeping with the spirit of co-operation and democracy, the decision to form a class co-operative is a collective one, though usually at the suggestion of the class teacher. Once agreed, the co-operative requires officers and funds. The teacher helps, suggests and observes but rarely controls. The designation of officers is an introduction to democracy. Typically of the global approach of Freinet teachers it is also an opportunity for integrating other areas of the curriculum, such as maths. As one teacher describes it:

It is vital to ask their opinion about the various ways in which people are appointed: drawing lots, teacher's choice, choice of the 'best', examination, rotation or votes. The pros and cons of each option were expounded. A consensus was reached that appointment should be by vote. (Fortunately, as how else could any particular method be selected?)

- Who must be elected?   – definition of responsibilities or duties
- Who must do the electing?   – electoral list
- How and where should voting   – voting equipment
  take place?
- When should elections take place? – type of poll; mathematical
                                         calculations

It is important for all these procedures to be specified before the election (written rules) and that the right to vote is granted by the teacher, that boys and girls have equal voting rights, that religion and nationality are not asked before this right is granted. The count is supervised by the teacher. (Sabourin, 1994)

Once constituted, the class co-operative needs to produce a project and formulate its rules. In the words of another teacher:

We have to find collective ways of working which enable us to take decisions, preferably by consensus, about the programme of work, the organisation of time and of the classroom, the rules of this micro-society and the assessment and evaluation of our work. Of course freedom of expression is essential, but obviously the freedom of each is limited by the freedom of the others, the group attempting to regulate the expression of this individual freedom within the class. (Giroit and Poslaniec, 1985: 92: our translation)

The children may formulate their rules in writing, but in any case good communications are the key:

Every morning, in my class, ...we begin with a short meeting during which pupils can bring what they want and talk about anything. It is often during this meeting that we hit on the research topics that we will investigate over the following days and weeks. Some bring in books, articles, documents that they speak about briefly. Others bring their own writing or drawing or creative work. Several tell about things that have happened.

At the end of the week we have a more formal meeting to evaluate the week, to agree the following week's programme (which can be adjusted each morning) and to note and try to resolve any problems that have arisen. (ibid.)

Such meetings do not necessarily need a record, but decisions about project work requiring the raising of funds may need to be more formal. Such formal meetings are conducted by the elected officers, chair, secretary and treasurer. Children from the middle years of the primary school are initiated into these formal roles. One of the first tasks of a co-operative is to agree the 'contract for the life of the class', in other words the rules by which the class will live. The drawing up of the contract may well use as a starting point the contract of the previous year, or of another class, but it will be amended to suit the particular conditions of the new group. Here are some extracts from the contract of a class of eight- and nine-year-olds (our translation):

I respect what others are saying

I take care of things in the class whether they are the school's, my classmates' or my own.

I behave sensibly: people can trust me and give me responsibility.

If I don't understand, I tell someone.

I never make fun of others for whatever reason.

I have the right to disagree with the teachers and to tell them so politely.

I write helpful suggestions politely and put them in the suggestions box.

The teachers agree not to raise their voices, to keep to the timetable and do everything agreed by the class, never to punish without the agreement of the class, to do their utmost to ensure everyone achieves.

If I don't respect this contract, the group can pardon me or decide on a punishment. These decisions are taken after a discussion and a vote if necessary.

The class teacher comments that the advantage of the contract is to make explicit what is too often hidden. The contract, which may seem like a list of detailed rules, expresses the essential values on which the life of the class is based, and in particular the idea that freedom is not about lack of regulation, but comes from an understanding of rights and responsibilities (Aubertin, 1996: 18).

Projects and curriculum integration

Typically a co-operative class will run one major project in a school year. This might be a few days exploring a region on bicycles, a dramatic performance, a class exchange involving a visit abroad and receiving guests, a visit to a nature reserve involving a boat trip. In other words, the class agrees to undertake something beyond the usual curriculum, but in which all are involved. Once the project is decided, funds have to be raised. Parental contributions may certainly help, but the children themselves are expected to make an effort too. One classic fund raising approach is to sell cakes to other pupils during break or lunch times, another is to make and sell calendars at the end of the year. The major project is an integrated learning experience involving all parts of the curriculum. It is a democratic form of learning in that the participants have real choices and themselves make all major decisions:

> The members must be given time to discuss plans. Their first task was to organise a school trip. The officers of the co-operative would be in charge of collecting parental permissions and financial contributions, solving any difficulties, and then preparing the visits. A meeting of the whole co-operative organised ways in which the visit could be put to use. Alone or working in groups, pupils chose the topic, particular moment or incident to report on. All presentations were programmed and contracts were prepared. (Sabourin, 1994)

A co-operative project, whether a major one involving fund raising or a more routine exploration of a theme, is carefully structured. The ICEM working group of history and geography teachers suggested that a project has ten distinct phases, as outlined below.

1 Choosing the subject. Making up the project team.
2 Preliminary search for sources of information, including library. Keeping a list of sources.
3 Sharing the tasks in the light of individual strengths and need for support.
4 Understanding and assimilating the information.
5 Deciding on how the information is to be presented (avoid reading out a text).
6 Making a plan for the presentation.
7 Drawing up deadlines working back from the date of presentation.
8 The presentation (including, possibly, posters, other visuals, handouts, video, musical or dramatic elements).
9 Questions and discussions with the class and the teacher.

10 Evaluation. A mark, awarded on criteria. Feedback. What the team feel went well and what could be improved. Communicating results beyond the school (e.g. to partner schools, newspapers).

The working group describes the project as an iceberg, largely hidden from view. There is a visible product, the presentation of the conclusions, but this is the final stage of a lengthy sequence. The work of preparation in the first seven stages determines the quality of the outcome. The results of the project are always presented to the group. In other words each project team is accountable to the other members of the class and is prepared to discuss its findings. The evaluation of the project will include suggestions from the class teacher, but also reflections by the members of the project team themselves to help them with their next project.

A Swedish teacher, who engaged in a project on environment and development with a class of twelve- and thirteen-year-olds, developed a set of aims which reflect her concern to develop a pedagogy which is sensitive and responsive to students' needs. She wanted her students to:

work from their own ideas and interests;

work in an interdisciplinary way and through research;

meet the community outside the walls of the school and connect with professionals from different areas within school;

develop an interest and knowledge about their native place and environment;

gain self-confidence in asking their own questions;

become conscious of the fact that they could affect the situation in their own village;

extend their interest to the global situation through knowledge about the local situation;

see if and how our little village is dependent on the rest of the world, but also has an impact on the world;

take responsibility for their own work by picking out problems and solving them within given frameworks of aims, equipment, skills and time;

follow through a project from beginning to end, giving them the joy of creativity, pride and self-esteem. (Thyr, 1994: 154–5).

She observes:

If you follow the students' interests and questions, they are carrying you in the work. If you are following your own questions, and do not listen to the students, you have to carry them. (Thyr, 1994: 165)

The project aims to promote a responsive pedagogy, and encourage the development of skills for democratic participation. In encouraging the students to develop their own interests the teacher does not withdraw but offers a clear framework and guidance. The interests of the children in this project led them to investigate various aspects of local history and to study local industry. They became interested in a local military camp and began to examine aspects of the global arms trade. Teachers sometimes express concern that such student-led investigations may lead to children wishing to campaign and engage in action in their communities. It is at this point that some people question whether taking action is an appropriate part of education. Certain forms of action, such as the clearing of litter from the school or local environment, may not provoke controversy, but what if children's concerns lead them to oppose the actions of the local council, business interests or even government policy? For example, groups of children and whole schools have become involved in campaigns to prevent the deportation of a classmate, and there are published materials produced illustrating the efforts of young children engaged in one such campaign (Hasbudak and Simons, 1986).

Projects are potentially one of the most powerful educational tools for learning about and experiencing issues of democracy and human rights. However, it is also important to be realistic and note that the outcomes may be unpredictable and variable in quality. Projects require a flexibility in the use of time and in particular the availability of blocks of time. The Austrian Ministry of Education issued detailed guidelines for teachers embarking on project work (see below) which suggest that this is no easy option for teachers. Indeed, managing project work involves managing many complex relationships and calls for insight and tact on the part of the teacher.

Features of project work

Targeting the interests of participants

The theme must be chosen primarily to reflect the interests of students and teachers. The choice depends not only on the content but also on the proposed activity. In many cases, the activity (e.g. shooting a film) may be the key reason for deciding, while the contents may not become interesting until the activity is fully under way.

Self-organisation and self-responsibility

The objective, manner and method of learning are selected jointly. Teachers and students collect all necessary information and develop a schedule. It is an explicit goal of project work for the students to learn planning strategies and resource management and to develop ways and means of imparting acquired knowledge and skills.

Targeted Planning

For project work to be beneficial it is absolutely necessary to reach a consensus on the objectives and goals of the project. Similarly, participants must discuss, plan and decide on the type of activities proposed, the forms of work to be pursued, the time schedule available and the assigning of responsibilities.

Interdisciplinary

Project work focuses on a theme, a problem, which is to be discussed and solved by means of various disciplines. The method aims to help the students to learn networked thinking and integrated approaches.

Social learning

By joining in to pursue a project and aiming to achieve a specified goal, students need to try out new forms of communication in order to learn with and from each other. Interaction, co-operation and communication, conflict resolution strategies, co-ordination between groups, coping with criticism, assessment and supervision etc. need to be learned. Social and objective goals are of equal value.

External effect

Project work aims to affect realities inside and outside school. In this way, the school ceases to be an island and starts to participate actively in designing the social environment.

Teachers' roles

Assistance in structuring planning and decision-making processes; creating awareness of group dynamics; providing feedback.

Integration of many senses

A major quality of project work is its sensible combination of physical and intellectual work and its inclusion of as many senses as possible.

Results

Project work is characterised by a clear conclusion. All participants are given an opportunity to present their results to each other and, if possible, to a wider public. The decisive factor in selecting the type of conclusion must be to award recognition and a critical review to the students and to ensure that the results of the project can be communicated. The project documentation acts as a foundation for the concluding project feedback stage and starting point for further project work. Therefore it must furnish information on all key stages of the work process and personal experience of the project members. (Federal Ministry of Education and Arts, 1992)

Curriculum materials to support participation

In a curriculum project designed to explore the meaning of human rights and citizenship through a locally focused study, a teachers' group worked together to produce materials for a handbook, *Learning to Participate* (Osler, 1996c), which takes the UN Convention on the Rights of the Child (UNCRC) as its framework. It is designed for use by teachers working in upper secondary schools or further education colleges. The details of the project design and methodology are described elsewhere (Osler, 1996d). Here we focus on education as a right and examine how teachers might explore this right with young people using these curriculum materials as a starting point. The materials aim to encourage a critical examination of the processes of schooling and encourage young people to reflect on their own education. A study of the right to education may allow students to consider its potential as a means for challenging inequality and injustice and empowering them to become participative citizens.

Learning to Participate draws on newspaper cuttings and articles which raise questions about the nature of schooling. The issues raised include anti-racism, the stereotyping of minorities, curriculum content, academic standards, peer pressures, pupil exclusions and students' civil rights. Activities draw on the UNCRC and invite students to consider school organisation, curriculum, admission policies, staffing policies and the physical environment of an ideal school. Most of the activities require group work and co-operation between students. Students are given 'controversial' statements about education which they are asked to sort, prioritise, and where appropriate, re-draft. Facts and figures about school exclusions are presented, and teachers and students asked to consider case studies within a human rights framework. The aspects of schooling covered are among those which attract considerable public debate and it is likely that in many cases there will not be a consensus among students or between students and teacher. Similarly, some of the issues may be perceived as overtly political in nature. Nevertheless, if teachers use a human rights framework as their starting point and avoid imposing their ideas on their students they should be able to refute confidently any allegations of political bias. The planning and development of this work requires careful thought and reflection. By understanding some of the issues and current debates in education and contributing to them, students may be enabled to take the first steps towards effecting change and creating more democratic classrooms. Through the process of learning, students will acquire a range of skills which will enable them to take on the role of active citizens. Teachers who engage in such debates with their students are working towards the development of a more responsive pedagogy.

Another set of materials designed to prepare young people for active citizenship has been developed by Oxford Development Education Centre. A booklet, *Power Points*, one of a series of four, has as its subtitle 'How to take action on issues you care about'. It defines citizenship as 'active participation in social and political structures based on a sound knowledge of an individual's rights and responsibilities' (Norris, 1993). Accordingly, the pack aims to support the study of 'democracy in action' by a series of activities designed to equip students with the skills and knowledge needed to engage in citizenship.

The first exercises focus on confidence building, using assertiveness training techniques. The assumption is that students often feel powerless, and need to learn how to use their personal power effectively and develop skills in assertive behaviour through role play. These exercises are followed by an introduction to campaigning, where students develop new skills through

- personal and group-based research;
- inviting speakers with particular skills: e.g. campaigners, marketing experts;
- developing their communication skills;
- planning their own campaign;
- learning about successful campaign groups and techniques from other parts of the world.

The material explicitly links with the campaigning activities of non-governmental organisations (NGOs). For instance it provides a number of examples of campaigning materials, particularly leaflets, and asks the students to classify the types of action according to whether the focus is lobbying government, supporting a political party or creating a new one, consumer action such as boycotts, demonstrating, fund raising, public education or culture and entertainment. Any single campaign may demonstrate more than one type of action.

The other materials in the series study issues of trade, transport and car manufacturing. The second pack looks at the clothing and textile trade and the links between the clothing industry in India and in Britain. Questions of wages and working conditions are raised, as are international trade agreements or restrictions. There are role play exercises in which students may be asked to identify with free trade supporters, trade unionists or a group campaigning for promoting the products of companies with good employment practice and conditions of work.

Assessment of project work

One interesting feature of the materials is that they seek to build in assessment of students' work. Often education for human rights and citizenship is placed in a less prestigious part of the curriculum, and it is considered inappropriate for it to be assessed. The status of work which is not assessed is often further devalued by students themselves. *Power Points* suggests that there is a place for both student and teacher assessment of work and provides a set of assessment objectives for each unit. For the unit on democracy these are:

Knowledge

Roles and relationships in a democratic society, in particular: the nature of co-operation and competition between individuals and groups. The nature and basis of duties, responsibilities and rights, in particular: fairness, justice and moral responsibility.

Preparation

1 Study skills
 - defining the task, setting targets, devising strategies, formulating questions, acquiring knowledge, identifying bias
2 Communication skills
 - selecting appropriate methods, applying them effectively
3 Personal and social skills
 - listening, giving and accepting constructive criticism

Application

1 Problem-solving skills
 - recognising and defining a problem, making choices and decisions in the light of available information, using acquired knowledge and skills
2 Evaluation
 - making and justifying comments and drawing conclusions on planning and application. (Norris, 1993)

Pedagogic principles derived from human rights

We examine the relevance of the UN Convention on the Rights of the Child to schools in Chapter 2, and argue that the principle of participation running through the Convention requires schools to re-assess their structures, organisation and management. The Convention also has wide-ranging implications for classroom organisation, curriculum and pedagogy. Our understanding of pedagogy is likely to be closely related to a range of personal and cultural beliefs about the way children learn, what may be understood by individual intelligence, the subject matter, and our particular students. These beliefs, whether culturally-based or related to our own biographies as teachers and learners, may or may not be challenged by the formal processes of teacher education. The rights enacted in the Convention suggest a number of principles, which we should apply to the processes of teaching and learning:

Pedagogic principles	Article(s) of the UNCRC
dignity	preamble, 28
security	19, 23, 29
participation	12, 13, 14, 15, 31
identity	7, 8, 16
inclusivity	preamble, 2, 23, 28, 29, 31
freedom	12, 14, 15
access to information	13, 17
privacy	16

Dignity and security

The student's right to dignity implies a relationship between teacher and student which avoids abuse of power on the part of the teacher, including the avoidance of sarcasm. In this relationship the teacher's own right to dignity should not be forgotten. Teachers need to establish, with their students, a classroom atmosphere in which name-calling and mockery are unacceptable. It is the teacher's responsibility to ensure that those who are most vulnerable are protected from bullying and have the opportunity to learn in a secure environment.

Participation

The principle of participation which runs through the Convention has a particular application in the classroom, and an appropriate pedagogy will be responsive to the needs of individual students and to the group as a whole. Students should be given opportunities to exercise choice and responsibility in decisions which affect them at classroom level, for example in the planning and organisation of their own work. It is noteworthy that approaches based on choice, responsibility and negotiation which are regularly developed with very young children are often abandoned as they grow older. It is, of course, the case that interdisciplinarity and a certain flexibility is built into the primary curriculum in the sense that the same teacher is likely to be responsible for several if not all areas of the curriculum. Although limitations on the choices open to older students are frequently explained in terms of curriculum constraints and subject specialisation, they may also be closely related to teacher beliefs about the extent of children's autonomy and teacher control.

Identity and inclusivity

The preservation and development of identity, including the recognition of the multiple identities which the individual may adopt is, as we argue in

Chapter 6, a key right within education, yet one which is perhaps the most easily violated. Teachers need to ensure that they meet certain basic requirements, such as correct use and pronunciation of the child's name. Respect for individual children, their cultures and families is critical. This requires us to value diversity in the classroom and to recognise that diversity and hybridity are essential characteristics of all human communities. It means seeing children's characteristics, whether cultural, emotional, or physical, as attributes to be built upon, rather than deficiencies. Education systems, schools, and classrooms which deny or marginalise diversity are likely to discriminate against those who do not match the presupposed norm. Children whose social and cultural backgrounds are different from those of their teachers, and those with learning difficulties or disabilities, are particularly disadvantaged in such systems.

Freedom

Pedagogy needs to permit maximum freedom of expression and conscience. The exercise of the rights of freedom of expression, freedom of conscience and religion, and freedom of association and peaceful assembly all require a range of skills which need to be developed in the classroom. The right of children to have their opinion taken into account in decisions made about them similarly requires a pedagogy which promotes skills of expression and decision-making. Teaching and learning need to be based on student–teacher dialogue. It assumes a model of learning and development in which the learner will often be the person best suited to identifying her or his own needs. The model assumes that the teacher is continually developing his or her own teaching skills and is also open to learn from the students. Freedom of expression will have certain limitations, as we have seen, in order to protect the freedoms, security and dignity of others.

Access to information

The exercise of the right of freedom of expression is at least partially dependent on access to information and ideas, including information from the mass media and from a diversity of national and international sources. Teachers have a responsibility to ensure that the child not only has skills of reading and writing to gain access to information but is able to interpret visual images critically, in newspapers, video and other media. Skills involved in the development of visual literacy include questioning, recognition of bias and discrimination and those skills associated with the design and production of visual materials, for example a photo sequence or video. An appropriate pedagogy will permit students to identify issues about which they wish to learn more, analyse the mass media, encourage creativity, imagination, criticism and scepticism, and arrive at their own judgements. The selection and range of sources of information in the classroom is usually determined by teachers, within the confines of available resources. While the teacher is responsible for ensuring that the child is protected from materials injurious to his or her well-being, there is also an obligation to develop a pedagogy whereby children have access to information on a need-to-know basis and are encouraged to identify and express their needs.

Privacy

The right to privacy which is jealously guarded by so many adults is as often disregarded when we are dealing with children, in the context of the school, the staffroom and the classroom. Pedagogy should respect the child's right to privacy, with regard to family and home, and schools need safeguards, in the form of guidelines, to protect the child's reputation when sharing information about individuals. While recognising that we often ask personal questions of children in order to build upon their own experiences, cultures and identities, as teachers we need to remember that there exists a power relationship between teacher and student which may sometimes cause children to reveal more than they might wish to do. The teacher should consider the context, and avoid situations where children may be asked to reveal personal information in public, as for example in a whole-class discussion. If the principle of the child's best interests is consistently applied as a primary consideration, this should not prevent teachers seeking information designed to protect a child judged to be vulnerable in some way.

Summary

The co-operative education movements provide many lively examples of formalised learning in the spirit of human rights. Classes and schools operating within these structures may be considered as examples of Schnapper's idealised democratic communities of citizens mentioned in Chapter 5. Human rights instruments can also help us to elaborate pedagogical principles by which the implementation of the school curriculum can become an education of democratically-minded citizens.

We would argue that if children's research and investigation genuinely leads them towards action, if teachers are confident that they are not imposing their own political viewpoints on their students, and if students are not denying or violating the human rights of others through their action, then such action can form a valuable part of education for democratic participation. The key question is rather whether students have the knowledge and skills to take action on the issues that they care about and whether their education has provided them with opportunities to acquire such knowledge and skills.

10 *Looking to the future*

Introduction

Throughout this book we maintain that education for human rights is likely to be based on thinking, feeling and doing. This is the basis for our model of a curriculum for human rights or citizenship education proposed in Chapter 5 (Figure 5.1, p.85). We contended that students need to know about the past, look to the future and act in the present. In this concluding chapter we return to this model and provide illustrations of how it can be applied. In so doing we underline several of the key ideas running through the book and suggest how these may be implemented in initial or in-service education to support the development of human rights principles in schools.

We learn about human rights by thinking, feeling and doing. As teachers and educationalists we are by definition concerned with the future, and we need to know about the past in order to prepare the future. Constructing or even trying to influence the future entails acting in the present. But why should we attempt to intervene? Why should we not leave the future to evolve as it happens?

The answers to these questions are of two orders. There is a cognitive response and an affective one; one based on thinking and one on feeling. The cognitive response looks at the past and notes that democratic societies are less likely to be provocative or to incite war. As Bonanate (1995: 42) points out, democratic states tend to peace; conversely and simultaneously peace is a condition that encourages democracy. Given that the casualties of modern warfare are usually the most vulnerable civilians, namely children, teachers will logically favour peace and democracy. We will not, in most circumstances, help to prepare a future that puts at risk children and their families. Where teachers have been prepared to accept war as an option it is when they have perceived the identity of themselves and their community to be threatened. However, as we noted in Chapter 1, a commitment to human rights enables communities to coexist within a common political framework. We maintain that a rational teacher will support education for human rights and democracy because it is in the interest of children.

Reason is not always a sufficient motivation to any sort of action, particularly actions that may require effort and where results will not necessarily bring short-term rewards or recognition. In reality a commitment to human rights in education often comes from feelings. Human rights educators, like active democratic citizens, act on intrinsic motivation (Crewe, 1996). We support the rights of others out of a belief that it is right to do so, out of a sense of conscience. Such altruism stems from our upbringing or education. We learn from our families, our peer group, our social or religious community or our school that it is important to respect the rights and the dignity of others. Not to do so is an affront to our sense of identity and worth.

An inclination to support human rights thus comes from *knowing* about rights and their status and origins on the one hand and from *feeling* that such support is an expression of identity and human worth on the other. Education in human rights must itself have an affective dimension. This affective dimension finds expression in action. Action will, in turn, reinforce both the cognitive and the affective aspects of this education.

Two key concepts: equality and dignity

An important strand running through this book concerns equality. This concern has, as we will see, a long history. A feeling for equality and a commitment to it are, we have argued, essential to preserve democracy. Democracy can only survive by ensuring that all those in the polity feel equally included in it and that their rights are respected. Equality is not an absolute, however. Equality without liberty is likely to mean very little. Dignity needs to be guaranteed equally for all. Equality, freedoms and dignity are thus key concepts in a discourse of human rights.

The universal validity of human rights was proclaimed by the founders of the United States of America in their Declaration of Independence of 1776 in the celebrated second paragraph:

> We hold these truths to be self-evident, that all men are created equal; that they are endowed by their Creator with certain unalienable rights; that among these are life, liberty and the pursuit of happiness.

Hancock, Jefferson and the other fifty-four signatories affirm the essential, in their view God-given, equality of human beings with respect to their fundamental rights, notably the right to life itself and to freedom.

The rights were not, at this stage, defined, nor indeed were they in practice extended to all. The principle of human equality is nonetheless enunciated.

The French Declaration of the Rights of Man and Citizen of 1789 starts with the same assertion, namely 'Men are born and remain free and equal in rights'. The principle is identical, namely that the status of human being confers equality of rights. Of course, Olympe de Gouges famously proclaimed her Declaration of the Rights of Women and Citizens to point out some of the considerable limitations of the implementation of the first declaration. However, this fundamental principle of equality of rights and equality before the law was proclaimed as a principle which underlies all subsequent human rights texts, whether declarations with moral force, or conventions with legal force.

The concept of equality of rights has developed in scope considerably since the eighteenth century. Since 1948 it has become truly universal as a fundamental principle that makes any discrimination on the basis of ethnic or religious origin unacceptable. Article 14 of the European Convention on Human Rights (1953) further extended the definition:

> The enjoyment of the rights and freedoms set forth in this Convention shall be secured without discrimination on any ground such as sex, race, colour, language, religion, political or other opinion, national or social origin, association with a national minority, property, birth or other status.

The more recently adopted Quebec Charter of Human Rights and Freedoms (1982) outlaws discrimination on fourteen separate grounds:

> All persons have a right to full and equal recognition and exercise of their human rights and freedoms, without distinction, exclusion or preference based on race, colour, sex, pregnancy, sexual orientation, civil status, age except as provided by law, religion, political convictions, language, ethnic or national origin, social condition, a handicap or the use of any means to palliate a handicap.
>
> Discrimination exists where such a distinction, exclusion or preference has the effect of nullifying or impairing such rights. (Leduc and de Massy, 1989)

The list from 1982 is longer than the European list dating from the 1950s and recognises questions of gender and sexuality as areas where discrimination contrary to the spirit of human rights occurs. The principle of equality has not changed. Social circumstances have changed as has the understanding of situations and conditions to which the concept of equality of rights may be applied. Evolution and development of human rights is largely a question of new applications. Education, as this book testifies, is an area where human rights principles can helpfully be applied. This process has only begun very recently. For instance, policies for equal opportunities, whether addressing the specific interests of women or ethnic minorities or students with special needs, can all be seen as essentially human rights policies. It is only recently that such policies have been united, conceptually, within the framework of human rights.

Respect for dignity is also a particularly important concept for educators and one introduced into international human rights texts in the Universal Declaration of Human Rights in 1948. The preamble to the Universal Declaration starts with the words 'Whereas recognition of the inherent dignity and the equal and inalienable rights of all members of the human family is the foundation of freedom, justice and peace in the world ...' The importance of the notion of human dignity is given even greater prominence in the European Parliament's declaration of fundamental rights and freedoms presented by the outgoing Parliament to its successor in 1989. The first article of the declaration states: 'Human dignity shall be inviolable.' This comes even before the right to life. Dignity is a right which 'all members of the human family' possess equally. It is a right that can only be fully realised where there is liberty. Equality of rights is also equality of dignity.

An audit of human rights

We have argued that preparing the future entails acting in the present. Before starting to act, however, one sensible preliminary is to undertake an audit of the present situation. A good starting point is to examine statements of rights and ask questions to ascertain whether they are currently being implemented in the institution being examined.

The basic principles proposed by the Commission for Global Governance and quoted in Chapter 1 provide one possible starting point. All the suggestions are based on human rights considerations, although not all are yet formulated as rights within international law. One advantage of this particular starting point is the emphasis on rights and responsibilities. Responsibilities are usually implicit in human rights texts, and an acceptance of responsibilities is the basis of any living in community. We have noted in Chapter 9 that schools and educational institutions are potentially models of communities of citizens. We will list the proposed rights and provide a commentary and key questions for each.

The Commission for Global Governance indicates as its core proposal rights to the following.

A secure life

The institution is responsible for the security of its members. This may mean applying measures that limit freedoms. Some areas, for instance balconies or ponds, may be put out of bounds. Security is both physical and psychological. In either case it is a question of feeling safe. Aggressive behaviour, whether by staff or pupils, causes feelings of insecurity.

What measures does the school take to ensure all its members feel secure? Are there mechanisms for noting feelings of insecurity? How do members voice their concerns? What procedures are in place to take action when staff or students report insecurity?

Equitable treatment

In order to judge the equity of treatment, schools need to monitor both results, achievements, and groupings and also punishments or exclusions. These should be examined by gender, social background and ethnic group, at least, as these are known areas of concern.

How precisely will equity be measured? Which are the most important areas to monitor? How might resources be reallocated to promote equal outcomes?

An opportunity to earn a fair living and provide for their own welfare

The instrumental value of education is overriding. Education is the basis for future employment prospects. Pupils have the right to achieve capability in core skills and knowledge and a range of competencies that will facilitate social and economic inclusion.

Does every pupil leave the school with the basis for lifelong learning and prepared for either further education or training or employment? What action is taken to ensure that the future choices of individuals or groups are not restricted?

The definition and preservation of their differences through peaceful means

This right allows for the development of a confident sense of identity and the capacity to take on new identities. It implies a pluralistic model of national and local culture and the respect of the cultures and identities of others, provided these do not espouse forms that are inimical to human rights.

Is the school a place of intercultural sharing or is there an imposed and monolithic model of what constitutes culture and identity?

How precisely are the different backgrounds and cultural traditions of pupils and staff recognised and celebrated?

How can we as teachers be responsive to each child's individual culture and identity?

Participation in governance at all levels

This is a question both for staff and for pupils and their parents. In many countries school councils and year councils including pupils are a statutory requirement. In France there have been noteworthy schemes for training class delegates (Jourdan and Gisbert, 1990; Jourdan, 1993). Participation is more likely to be perceived as worthwhile and genuine if the decisions concern the allocation of real resources. This implies that the committee, council or co-operative has some funds to spend. The co-operatives described in Chapter 7 operate on this principle.

Does the school have formalised pupil participation? What priority is given to ensuring the efficacy of structures?

Does the system for electing delegates ensure equal chances for all pupils without discrimination? How can this be achieved?

What resources are allocated by the decision of pupils?

Free and fair petition for redress of gross injustices

We noted in Chapter 2 the five-stage model of investigation, resolution, restitution, sanction and communication proposed by Cunningham. It is to be hoped that schools will avoid gross injustices by formalising their procedures and by applying standards that are as high as those acceptable in other judicial systems. Children, as well as adults, have the right to equality before the law.

If a member of the school staff or a pupil or parent feels that an injustice has been done, are the steps for an appeal made widely known? Are they used?

Equal access to information

The curriculum should be accessible to all, and pupils presented with a range of viewpoints and ideas. This may be a question of whether some parts of the curriculum are, in practice, reserved for certain types of student. There is a distinct tendency in the UK for science subjects to be taken by boys and languages by girls, for example. This comes after apparently free choices. Cultural forces or peer pressure, for instance, may effectively reduce the access of boys to languages. It is also known that in the UK African-Caribbean boys are over-represented amongst those excluded from school altogether and thus being denied access to education.

How does the school guarantee that all pupils have access to the curriculum? Do pupils have access to a range of viewpoints, cultures and ideas?

Are there, in the school, areas of the curriculum that are, in practice, reserved for or dominated by a particular group of pupils? Is there a mechanism of unjustified discrimination at work in such cases and, if so, how will this be addressed?

Equal access to global commons

At school level the commons are those facilities available to all pupils, such as gymnasium and sports facilities, the library, the dining room, toilets and common rooms. It is known that in some schools pupils feel intimidated into not using the toilets, either because of their unpleasant and unhygienic state, their lack of privacy or their monopolisation by groups who threaten the vulnerable.

How does the school manage to ensure equality of access to common facilities? Does it monitor the usage of the facilities to see whether all sections of the school population make use of them? What steps will be taken if monitoring reveals unequal access?

What arrangements exist to ensure physical access to buildings and classrooms for those with disabilities?

An audit of responsibilities

The list of universal responsibilities drawn up by the Commission for Global Governance can also usefully be applied to schools and universities. The starting point is that people share a responsibility to do the following.

Contribute to the common good

This active obligation to work to further the aims of the community supposes that the aims are made known and that they are shared, that is that each member of the community feels ownership of the goals of the institution. The aims will need to be re-visited periodically to take into account changing circumstances and changing cohorts of students, and to enable new members of the community to contribute to the process of reformulation. There are many ways in which institutions can initiate their members and retain their loyalty to the common purpose. In some cases this will include an identification of institutional goals in some form of shared acknowledgement of symbols. Provided that the ceremonies or rituals are based on human rights principles, it can be expected that all members of the school will be able to support the aims expressed. All activity in the school should then be directed to achieving the aims and thus contribute to the common good. However, ceremonial expression of common loyalties needs to be matched by real opportunities for sharing in the benefits provided by the institution.

Consider the impact of their actions on the security and welfare of others

This obligation follows from the previous one. When many people interact in close physical proximity, as in schools, these considerations are particularly important. Although individuals have the responsibility to be considerate, the institution is greatly helped when approved practices and procedures are formalised. For instance, something as simple as keeping to the left on stairs or not running in corridors will contribute greatly to security and welfare.

Promote equity, including gender equity

In view of the right to equitable treatment, the institution is obligated to have policies that help to ensure equity. At the same time individuals have the responsibility to do their best to promote the policies. At a minimum that implies that both staff and students are familiar with equal opportunities issues and the policies that derive from them.

Protect the interests of future generations by pursuing sustainable development and safeguarding the global commons

All members of the institution will be committed to preserving its assets and protecting communal facilities. They will also have an education that helps them acquire a global perspective and an understanding of the concept of sustainable development.

Preserve humanity's cultural and intellectual heritage

Traditionally this has been a major function of schools and universities. The reference is to the heritage of humanity rather than of single nations or regions. This implies a broadly based curriculum again with a global perspective.

Be active participants in governance

Institutions are obligated to provide structures for participation. Individuals have a responsibility to be involved. Involvement can take many forms, and at its most basic may simply imply voting for a representative.

Work to eliminate corruption

Most schools are financed with public funds and those ultimately responsible for the institution must be accountable for the use of those funds. Democracy implies transparency in the use of resources, and any use of the funds for purposes incompatible with the goals of the institution may be considered corrupt. All members of the institution, staff and students, should be aware of the possibility of corruption and know what steps are open to them if corruption is suspected. As with issues of security, measures of prevention should be in place. It is likely that work to eliminate corruption will be collective, perhaps involving unions or associations of parents, for example.

Acting in the present

As we noted in Chapter 7, it is possible for schools and their pupils to interact with the world beyond the school as part of the formal curriculum when they are engaged in project work. In France schools can bid for extra funds for undertaking projects. Grants may be awarded to projects which are interdisciplinary, involve several staff, have specific links with external agencies such as businesses, local authorities or NGOs, and are put forward by and supported by the school as a whole.

Several primary schools in France have, for example, linked up with their local radio station and have a contract to provide a weekly item lasting three to five minutes (OCCE, 1996: 32). Often the item is recorded during a class discussion of a topic. The teacher records the discussion and edits the highlights down from about half an hour to three minutes, then takes the tape to the radio studio. One class participated in a charity project, selling stamps to raise money to help victims of tuberculosis. They prepared their weekly radio programme by doing research on the disease and reporting on the disease, its importance and the action they had taken. Another class sets out to meet and record interviews with local people, for instance, the oldest inhabitant of a nearby home or a farmer. Such projects give the pupils both a sense of responsibility and a feeling of being part of the local community.

In secondary schools such projects very often take human rights themes as their starting point. At a secondary school in Strasbourg, the school librarian co-ordinated a project on 'Tolerance and Human Rights' where the students published a newspaper, and made their own collections of materials on subjects such as slavery in classical times, working children, apartheid, colonisation, Gypsies, religious wars, Gandhi and Martin Luther King. The co-ordinator concluded:

> One of the most notable outcomes is the clear improvement in the behaviour of the students. They started feeling more positive about themselves and gained a sense of identity. They took an interest in current events. They got absorbed in their research and learnt a great deal. Most of all they viewed the news more critically. However perhaps the greatest achievement of this project is the improvement in writing skills. In the first year of the project only 11% of the pupils involved wanted to write articles or captions, but by the third year it was up to 48%. (CRDP, 1989: our translation)

A group of five secondary schools in Hampshire in the UK and a similar number in Baden-Wurttenburg in Germany came together in a joint project designed to address issues of racism and xenophobia in a European context. Students exchanged information and messages by e-mail and decided collectively to celebrate International Human Rights Day (10 December), each school organising its own programme. Activities included an all-night vigil including drama, music and a teach-in on human rights, workshops for younger pupils organised by older ones, participation in the schools by speakers, story tellers and dance groups, a letter-writing campaign and the launch of jointly developed curriculum materials. Schools asked for faxes of support to be sent and they received such letters from MPs, MEPs, embassy officials and a minister of education (Massey, 1995: 42).

Creating networks

Given the importance of human rights education for the future of Europe and the world, those actively committed to it have every incentive to pool their efforts and co-ordinate their activity. In the UK a group of educationalists who had been impressed by the work of the Council of Europe, and wished to see it developed and disseminated, set up the Education in Human Rights Network.

The Network was set up in January 1987 to enable and encourage communication between people working in a variety of educational settings who recognise and wish to build upon the work of the Council of Europe and of many non-governmental organisations in promoting an awareness and an understanding of human rights.

The Network has a Steering Committee, with open membership, which meets in London in June and December. Organisations regularly attending include Amnesty GB, the British Institute of Human Rights, the Centre for Global Education, the Citizenship Foundation, the Council for Education in World Citizenship, the Human Rights Centre University of Essex, the Islamic Rights Movement, the Minority Rights Group, Quaker Peace and Service, the Refugee Council, UNICEF and the Women's International League for Peace and Freedom.

The Network helped to set up the education project which produced educational material for primary schools entitled *Our World, Our Rights* (Brown, 1996). It also promotes an annual summer school, and a termly newsletter. In 1988 it adopted the following statement of aims.

1 To promote an understanding of human rights and responsibilities as fundamental values in a pluralist democracy and for the world community. To encourage knowledge of both the protection of human rights and abuses of human rights in the UK, in Europe and in other area. ~f the world. To affirm the importance of human rights as basic values in education, at work and in society.

2 To ensure that the spirit and the contents of the Universal Declaration of Human Rights, the European Convention for the Protection of Human Rights and Fundamental Freedoms, and other major rights documents are known to teachers and to young people in schools.

3 To help to implement in the UK the Recommendation R(85)7 of the Committee of Ministers of the Council of Europe 'On teaching and learning about human rights in schools'. The resolution states notably:

'Throughout their school career, all young people should learn about human rights as part of their preparation for life in a pluralist democracy';

'Schools are communities which can, and should, be an example of respect for the dignity of the individual and for difference, for tolerance, and for equality of opportunity';

'Concepts associated with human rights can, and should, be acquired from an early stage';

'The emphasis in teaching and learning about human rights should be positive';

'The study of human rights in schools should lead to an understanding of, and sympathy for, the concepts of justice, equality, freedom, peace, dignity, rights and democracy.'

4. To work through education to combat racism and sexism and make an educational contribution to the ending of discrimination on any ground such as sex, race, colour, language, religion, political or other opinion, national or social origin, association with a national minority, property, birth, age, disability or sexual orientation.

5 To help develop good practice and strategies in education which will further the aims above.

6 To establish and maintain links with projects and networks in Europe and elsewhere and to publish a termly bulletin to facilitate this.

The Education in Human Rights Network was launched following an open meeting attended by some sixty individuals and representatives of groups. A steering committee was elected which set about organising a large-scale celebration of the fortieth anniversary of the Universal Declaration of Human Rights. This took the form of a human rights education forum and fair. The fair included stalls and exhibitions from some eighty organisations which identified with human rights issues. The forum consisted of a number of workshops, illustrating human rights education in a variety of contexts, both formal and informal.

Setting up and implementing the project gave the Network an identity and a sense of direction and purpose. The committee went on to raise funds to undertake a curriculum development project, the results of which were published by Amnesty International (Brown, 1996). This material, devised by a group of primary school teachers working with the Centre for Global Education in York, enables teachers to explore human rights issues with their pupils through game-like activities, role plays, stories, guided fantasy and project work. Amongst the other achievements of this Network are the setting up and continuing existence over a number of years of a newsletter and a series of summer schools, as described in Chapter 8.

A network is essentially a light and therefore low-cost structure for sharing and disseminating information. The Education in Human Rights Network has no official legal status. It is held together by a co-ordinator who takes the responsibility for convening meetings and circulating minutes. Members of a network are representatives of organisations sharing a common interest. Sharing enables synergy. Any member may take an initiative and request support from other network members. It can also help to avoid duplication of effort. Most of the costs can be borne by the member organisations themselves so that central costs are low.

In order to get established, networks require an initial meeting and an agreement amongst the partners to work together. This will probably involve the drafting and agreement of a statement of aims. The initial meeting can be convened by an organisation with the standing and resources to advertise and host it.

The activities of a network are determined by the members. They are likely to include:

- regular, but not necessarily frequent, meetings
- a newsletter or news exchange system (e.g. the minutes of meetings or an Internet electronic bulletin board or conference)
- projects under the aegis of the network.

Tasks involved in the maintenance of the network and its activities may be undertaken as required, possibly on a rota basis, by a member organisation on behalf of the others.

Ideally a network for human rights education would involve representatives of partners from education and from civil society such as local education authorities; schools; teacher unions; teacher education institutions; educational research institutions; curriculum development projects concerned with citizenship; ministry representatives and/or inspectors; parents; pupils or students; local/regional/national government; law and politics faculties and research institutes; the police; employers; NGOs concerned with the protection and promotion of the rights of children, minorities, women, refugees etc.; churches and religious groups; trusts and foundations interested in funding projects.

Teacher education and human rights: the pedagogical challenge

Evidence is starting to emerge from the UK that the idea of community is not well understood and increasingly rarely experienced by the public at large. Crewe reports that, taking – as a measure of civic engagement in communities – activities such as membership of voluntary organisations including churches, attendance at public meetings, contacts with neighbours: 'Nearly one third of British respondents do not engage in any of these activities and only one out of ten engage at least occasionally in most of them' (Crewe, 1996).

It would appear that the feeling for community and for citizenship may be declining. If this is the case, a feeling of support for human rights principles in the sense of universally applicable rights and responsibilities may be threatened. It could be that the more frequently felt relationship is the contractual one of consumer and supplier. However, such a relationship is inevitably uneven, as those with greater purchasing power have greater choice and those with few resources may be largely denied participation in communal activities.

In these circumstances, enabling people to experience the positive and supportive feeling of working and living in community becomes a vital role for schools. A feeling of being part of a democratic community of citizens is an experience that every child can have if schools are committed to providing it. Without this experience at a young age, it is now apparently possible to go through life without ever feeling part of a community of citizens.

This is the pedagogical challenge, to enable young people to experience a community based on human rights principles and to understand the basis of those principles. Not everybody, certainly not every pupil in school nor every student training to become a teacher, is immediately attracted by international declarations of human rights. The minimal pedagogical task is to make the basic texts known and accessible to all. We know that conventional methods of informing young people about human rights, for instance a civic education class based on a textbook and diagrams, are not by themselves effective methods. Schools that use only these approaches will not succeed in giving the majority of their students a global vision and an understanding of human rights. That is why we have been involved in developing approaches to human rights education that are likely to engage pupils and teachers.

Human rights are made known in two ways in schools: first by opportunities to learn about human rights in a formal and structured way; second by the ethos and the climate of the school expressed in public documents making specific reference to human rights. The formal teaching approaches need to be combined with an active approach to learning. Project work involving contacts with the world beyond the school is an important element. Creative work involving writing, artistic expression and research is also a key pedagogical strategy. Opportunities for formally assessing work on human rights issues can add to motivation and suggest a seriousness of purpose.

To achieve this, schools need a flexible use of time and a creative approach to assessment. Ideally team work involving several staff and others from within and beyond the school will be made possible.

Many schools across Europe have achieved such an effective approach to enabling a global perspective, including global values, to be transmitted. Many others still have a long way to go. We are not advocating a radical restructuring of schools. We wish to encourage schools and teachers to consider global ethical principles and promote a global vision through a curriculum provided in a variety of ways with a flexible use of time, space and resources.

Many educators have spoken about bringing the world into the school. We are also proposing the reverse. Schools are very special communities. They are communities based on explicit ethical principles. Within the school the principles of equity and respect for human dignity are particularly valued. For many children, school is the one place where they are secure and where they are valued. Schools at their best are idealised microcosms of society and of the world. A significant challenge is to develop this model and see our schools as vehicles for conveying concepts of democracy and human rights to society at large. In this way we may attempt to make our communities and the wider world reflect more adequately the values and the global perspectives that we already practise in our schools.

Appendix 1

The United Nations Universal Declaration of Human Rights

Whereas recognition of the inherent dignity and of the equal and inalienable rights of all members of the human family is the foundation of freedom, justice and peace in the world.

Whereas disregard and contempt for human rights have resulted in barbarous acts which have outraged the conscience of mankind, and the advent of a world in which human beings shall enjoy freedom of speech and belief and freedom from any fear and want has been proclaimed as the highest aspiration of the common people.

Whereas it is essential, if a man is not to be compelled to have recourse. as a last resort, to rebellion against tyranny and oppression, that human rights should be protected by the rule of law.

Whereas it is essential to promote the development of friendly relations between nations,

Whereas the peoples of the United Nations have in the Charter reaffirmed their faith in fundamental human rights, in the dignity and worth of the human person and in the equal rights of men and women and have determined to promote social progress and better standards of life in larger freedom.

Whereas Member States have pledged themselves to achieve, in cooperation with the United Nations, the promotion of universal respect for and observance of human rights and fundamental freedoms,

Whereas a common understanding of these rights and freedoms is of the greatest importance for the full realization of this pledge.

Now, Therefore,
THE GENERAL ASSEMBLY
proclaims

THIS UNIVERSAL DECLARATION OF HUMAN RIGHTS as a common standard of achievement for all peoples and all nations, to the end that every individual and every organ of society, keeping this Declaration constantly in mind, shall strive by teaching and education to promote respect for these rights and freedoms and by progressive measures, national and international, to secure their universal and effective recognition and observance, both among the peoples of Member States themselves and among the peoples of territories under their jurisdiction.

Article 1. All human beings are born free and equal in dignity and rights. They are endowed with reason and conscience and should act towards one another in a spirit of brotherhood.

Article 2. Everyone is entitled to all the rights and freedoms set forth in this Declaration, without distinction of any kind, such as race, colour, sex, language, religion, political or other opinion. national or social origin. property, birth or other status.

Furthermore, no distinction shall be made on the basis of the political, jurisdictional or international status of the country or territory to which a person belongs, whether it be independent, trust, non-self-governing or under any other limitation of sovereignty.

Article 3. Everyone has the right to life, liberty and security of person.

Article 4. No one shall be held in slavery or servitude; slavery and the slave trade shall be prohibited in all their forms.

Article 5. No one shall be subjected to torture or to cruel, inhuman or degrading treatment or punishment.

Article 6. Everyone has the right to recognition everywhere as a person before the law.

Article 7. All are equal before the law and are entitled without any discrimination to equal protection of the law. All are entitled to equal protection against any discrimination in violation of this Declaration and against any incitement to such discrimination.

Article 8. Everyone has the right to an effective remedy by the competent national tribunals for acts violating the fundamental rights granted him by the constitution or by law.

Article 9. No one shall be subjected to arbitrary arrest, detention or exile.

Article 10. Everyone is entitled in full equality to a fair and public hearing by an independent and impartial tribunal, in the determination of his rights and obligations and of any criminal charge against him.

Article 11. (1) Everyone charged with a penal offence has the right to be presumed innocent until proved guilty according to law in a public trial at which he has had all the guarantees necessary for his defence.

(2) No one shall be held guilty of any penal offence on account of any act or omission which did not constitute a penal offence. under national or international law, at the time when it was committed. Nor shall a heavier penalty be imposed than the one that was applicable at the time the penal offence was committed.

Article 12. No one shall be subjected to arbitrary interference with his privacy, family. home or correspondence, nor to attacks upon his honour and reputation. Everyone has the right to the protection of the law against such interference or attacks.

Article 13. (1) Everyone has the right to freedom of movement and residence within the borders of each state.

(2) Everyone has the right to leave any country, including his own, and to return to his country.

Article 14. (1) Everyone has the right to seek and to enjoy in other countries asylum from persecution.

(2) This right may not be invoked in the case of prosecutions genuinely arising from non-political

174

crimes or from acts contrary to the purposes and principles of the United Nations.

Article 15. (1) Everyone has the right to a nationality.

(2) No one shall be arbitrarily deprived of his nationality nor denied the right to change his nationality.

Article 16. (1) Men and women of full age, without any limitation due to race, nationality or religion, have the right to marry and to found a family. They are entitled to equal rights as to marriage, during marriage and at its dissolution.

(2) Marriage shall be entered into only with the free and full consent of the intending spouses.

(3) The family is the natural and fundamental group unit of society and is entitled to protection by society and the State.

Article 17. (1) Everyone has the right to own property alone as well as in association with others.

(2) No one shall be arbitrarily deprived of his property.

Article 18. Everyone has the right to freedom of thought, conscience and religion; this right includes freedom to change his religion or belief, and freedom. either alone or in community with others and in public or private, to manifest his religion or belief in teaching, practice, worship and observance.

Article 19. Everyone has the right to freedom of opinion and expression: this right includes freedom to hold opinions without interference and to seek, receive and impart information and ideas through any media and regardless of frontiers.

Article 20. (1) Everyone has the right to freedom of peaceful assembly and association.

(2) No one may be compelled to belong to an association.

Article 21. (1) Everyone has the right to take part in the government of his country, directly or through freely chosen representatives.

(2) Everyone has the right of equal access to public service in his country.

(3) The will of the people shall be the basis of the authority of government; this will shall be expressed in periodic and genuine elections which shall be by universal and equal suffrage and shall be held by secret vote or by equivalent free voting procedures.

Article 22. Everyone, as a member of society, has the right to social security and is entitled to realization. through national effort and international cooperation and in accordance with the organization and resources of each State, of the economic, social and cultural rights indispensable for his dignity and the free development of his personality.

Article 23. (1) Everyone has the right to work, to free choice of employment, to just and favourable conditions of work and to protection against unemployment.

(2) Everyone, without any discrimination, has the right to equal pay for equal work.

(3) Everyone who works has the right to just and favourable remuneration ensuring for himself and his family an existence worthy of human dignity, and supplemented, if necessary, by other means of social protection.

(4) Everyone has the right to form and to join trade unions for the protection of his interest.

Article 24. Everyone has the right to rest and leisure. including reasonable limitation of working hours and periodic holidays with pay.

Article 25. (1) Everyone has the right to a standard of living adequate for the health and well-being of himself and of his family, including food. clothing, housing and medical care and necessary social services, and the right to security in the event of unemployment, sickness, disability, widowhood, old age or other lack of livelihood in circumstances beyond his control.

(2) Motherhood and childhood are entitled to special care and assistance. All children. whether born in or out of wedlock, shall enjoy the same social protection.

Article 26. (1) Everyone has the right to education. Education shall be free, at least in the elementary and fundamental stages. Elementary education shall be compulsory. Technical and professional education shall be made generally available and higher education shall be equally accessible to all on the basis of merit.

(2) Education shall be directed to the full development of the human personality and to the strengthening of respect for human rights and fundamental freedoms. It shall promote understanding, tolerance and friendship among all nations, racial or religious groups. and shall further the activities of the United Nations for the maintenance of peace.

(3) Parents have a prior right to choose the kind of education that shall be given to their children.

Article 27. (1) Everyone has the right freely to participate in the cultural life of the community. to enjoy the arts and to share in scientific advancement and its benefits.

(2) Everyone has the right to the protection of the moral and material interests resulting from any scientific, literary or artistic production of which he is the author.

Article 28. Everyone is entitled to a social and international order in which the rights and freedoms set forth in this Declaration can be fully realized.

Article 29. (1) Everyone has duties to the community in which alone the free and full development of his personality is possible.

(2) In the exercise of his rights and freedoms, everyone shall be subject only to such limitations as are determined by law solely for the purpose of securing due recognition and respect for the rights and freedoms of others and of meeting the just requirements of morality, public order and the general welfare in a democratic society.

(3) These rights and freedoms may in no case be exercised contrary to the purposes and principles of the United Nations.

Article 30. Nothing in this Declaration may be interpreted as implying for any State, group or person any right to engage in any activity or to perform any act aimed at the destruction of any of the rights and freedoms set forth herein.

10th December 1948

Appendix 2

Summary of the UN Convention on the Rights of the Child

Adopted by the General Assembly of the United Nations on 20 November 1989

Unofficial summary of main provisions

PREAMBLE

The preamble recalls the basic principles of the United Nations and specific provisions of certain relevant human rights treaties and proclamations; reaffirms the fact that children, because of their vulnerability, need special care and protection; and places special emphasis on the primary caring and protective responsibility of the family, the need for legal and other protection of the child before and after birth, the importance of respect for the cultural values of the child's community, and the vital role of international co-operation in achieving the realization of children's rights.

Article 1
Definition of a child
All persons under 18, unless by law majority is attained at an earlier age.

Article 2
Non-discrimination
The principle that all rights apply to all children without exception, and the state's obligation to protect children from any form of discrimination. The state must not violate any right, and must take positive action to promote them all.

Article 3
Best interests of the child
All actions concerning the child should take full account of his or her best interests. The state is to provide adequate care when parents or others responsible fail to do so.

Article 4
Implementation of rights
The state's obligation to translate the rights in the Convention into reality.

Article 5
Parental guidance and the child's evolving capacities
The state's duty to respect the rights and responsibilities of parents and the wider family to provide guidance appropriate to the child's evolving capacities.

Article 6
Survival and development
The inherent right to life, and the state's obligation to ensure the child's survival and development.

Article 7
Name and nationality
The right to have a name from birth and to be granted a nationality.

Article 8
Preservation of identity
The state's obligation to protect and, if necessary, re-establish the basic aspects of a child's identity (name, nationality and family ties).

Article 9
Separation from parents
The child's right to live with his/her parents unless this is deemed incompatible with his/her best interests; the right to maintain contact with both parents if separated from one or both; the duties of states in cases where such separation results from state action.

Article 10
Family reunification
The right of children and their parents to leave any country and to enter their own in order to be reunited or to maintain the child–parent relationship.

Article 11
Illicit transfer and non-return
The state's obligation to try to prevent and remedy the kidnapping or retention of children abroad by a parent or third party.

Article 12
The child's opinion
The child's right to express an opinion, and to have that opinion taken into account, in any matter or procedure affecting the child.

Article 13
Freedom of expression
The child's right to obtain and make known information, and to express his or her views, unless this would violate the rights of others.

Article 14
Freedom of thought, conscience and religion
The child's right to freedom of thought, conscience and religion, subject to appropriate parental guidance and national law.

Article 15
Freedom of association
The right of children to meet with others and to join or set up associations, unless the fact of doing so violates the rights of others.

Article 16
Protection of privacy
The right to protection from interference with privacy, family, home and correspondence, and from libel/slander.

Article 17
Access to appropriate information
The role of the media in disseminating information to children that is consistent with moral well-being and knowledge and understanding among peoples, and respects the child's cultural background. The state is to take measures to encourage this and to protect children from harmful materials.

Article 18
Parental responsibilities
The principle that both parents have joint primary responsibility for bringing up their children, and that the state should support them in this task.

Article 19
Protection from abuse and neglect
The state's obligation to protect children from all forms of maltreatment perpetrated by parents or others responsible for their care, and to undertake preventive and treatment programmes in this regard.

Article 20
Protection of children without families
The state's obligation to provide special protection for children deprived of their family environment and to ensure that appropriate alternative family care or institutional placement is made available to them, taking into account the child's cultural background.

Article 21
Adoption
In countries where adoption is recognised and/or allowed, it shall only be carried out in the best interests of the child, with all necessary safeguards for a given child and authorisation by the competent authorities.

Article 22
Refugee children
Special protection to be granted to children who are refugees or seeking refugee status, and the state's obligation to co-operate with competent organisations providing such protection and assistance.

Article 23
Children with disabilities
The right of disabled children to special care, education and training designed to help them to achieve the greatest possible self-reliance and to lead a full and active life in society.

Article 24
Health and health services
The right to the highest level of health possible and to access to health and medical services, with special emphasis on primary and preventative health care, public health education and the diminution of infant mortality. The state's obligation to work towards the abolition of harmful traditional practices. Emphasis is laid on the need for international co-operation to ensure this right.

Article 25
Periodic review of placement
The right of children placed by the state for reasons of care, protection or treatment to have all aspects of that placement evaluated regularly.

Article 26
Social security
The right of children to benefit from social security.

Article 27
Standard of living
The right of children to benefit from an adequate standard of living, the primary responsibility of parents to provide this, and the state's duty to ensure that this

responsibility is first fulfillable and then fulfilled, where necessary through the recovery of maintenance.

Article 28
Education

1. *States parties recognise the right of the child to education and, with a view to achieving this right progressively and on the basis of equal opportunity, they shall, in particular:*

   (a) *make primary education compulsory and available free to all;*

   (b) *encourage the development of different forms of secondary education, including general and vocational education, make them available and accessible to every child, and take appropriate measures such as the introduction of free education and offering financial assistance in case of need;*

   (c) *make higher education accessible to all on the basis of capacity by every appropriate means;*

   (d) *make educational and vocational information and guidance available and accessible to all children;*

   (e) *take measures to encourage regular attendance at schools and the reduction of drop-out rates.*

2. *States parties shall take all appropriate measures to ensure that school discipline is administered in a manner consistent with the child's human dignity and in conformity with the present Convention.*

3. *States parties shall promote and encourage international co-operation in matters relating to education, in particular with a view to contributing to the elimination of ignorance and illiteracy throughout the world and facilitating access to scientific and technical knowledge and modern teaching methods. In this regard, particular account shall be taken of the needs of developing countries.*

Article 29
Aims of education

1. *States parties agree that the education of the child shall be directed to:*

   (a) *the development of the child's personality, talents and mental and physical abilities to their fullest potential;*

   (b) *the development of respect for human rights and fundamental freedoms, and for the principles enshrined in the Charter of the United Nations;*

   (c) *the development of respect for the child's parents, his or her own cultural identity, language and values, for the national values of the country in which the child is living, the country from which he or she may originate, and for civilisations different from his or her own;*

   (d) *the preparation of the child for responsible life in a free society, in the spirit of understanding, peace, tolerance, equality of sexes, and friendship among all peoples, ethnic, national and religious groups and persons of indigenous origin;*

   (e) *the development of respect for the natural environment.*

2. *No part of this article or article 28 shall be construed so as to interfere with the liberty of individuals and bodies to establish and direct educational institutions, subject always to the observance of the principles set forth in paragraph 1 of this article and to the requirements that the education given in such institutions shall conform to such minimum standards as may be laid down by the state.*

Article 30
Children of minorities or indigenous populations
The right of children of minority communities and indigenous populations to enjoy their own culture and to practise their own religion and language.

Article 31
Leisure, recreation and cultural activities
The right of children to leisure, play and participation in cultural and artistic activities.

Article 32
Child labour
The state's obligation to protect children from engaging in work that constitutes a threat to their health, education or development, to set minimum ages for employment, and to regulate conditions of employment.

Article 33
Drug abuse
The child's right to protection from the use of narcotic and psychotropic drugs and from being involved in their production or distribution.

Article 34
Sexual exploitation
The child's right to protection from sexual exploitation and abuse, including prostitution and involvement in pornography.

Article 35
Sale, trafficking and abduction
The state's obligation to make every effort to prevent the sale or trafficking in and abduction of children.

Article 36
Other forms of exploitation
The child's right to protection from all other forms of exploitation not covered in articles 32, 33, 34 and 35.

Article 37
Torture and deprivation of liberty
The prohibition of torture, cruel treatment or punishment, capital punishment, life imprisonment, and unlawful arrest or deprivation of liberty. The principles of appropriate treatment, separation from detained adults, contact with family and access to legal and other assistance.

Article 38
Armed conflicts
The obligation of states to respect and ensure respect for humanitarian law as it applies to children. The principle that no child under fifteen take a direct part in hostilities or be recruited into the armed forces, and that all children affected by armed conflict benefit from protection and care.

Article 39
Rehabilitative care
The state's obligation to ensure that child victims of armed conflicts, torture, neglect, maltreatment or exploitation receive appropriate treatment for their recovery and social re-integration.

Article 40

Administration of juvenile justice

The right of children alleged or recognised as having committed an offence to have respect for their human rights and, in particular, to benefit from all aspects of the due process of law, including legal or other assistance in preparing and presenting their defence. The principle that recourse to judicial proceedings and institutional placements should be provided wherever possible and appropriate.

Article 41

Respect for existing standards

The principle that, if any standards set in national law or other applicable international instruments are higher than those of this Convention, it is the higher standard that applies.

Article 42

Implementation and entry into force

The provisions of articles 42–54 notably foresee:

(i)   *the state's obligation to make the rights contained in this Convention widely known to both adults and children.*

(ii)   *the setting up of a Committee on the Rights of the Child composed of ten experts, which will consider reports that states parties to the Convention are to submit two years after ratification and every five years thereafter. The Convention enters into force – and the Committee would therefore be set up – once twenty countries have ratified it.*

(iii)   *States parties are to make their reports widely available to the general public.*

(iv)   *The Committee may propose that special studies be undertaken on specific issues relating to the rights of the child, and may make its evaluations known to each state party concerned as well as the UN General Assembly.*

(v)   *In order to 'foster the effective implementation of the Convention and to encourage international co-operation', the specialised agencies of the UN (such as the ILO, WHO and UNESCO) and UNICEF would be able to attend the meetings of the Committee. Together with any other body recognized as 'competent', including NGOs in consultative status with the UN and UN organisations such as the UNHCR, they can submit pertinent information to the Committee and be asked to advise on the optimal implementation of the Convention.*

Appendix 3

Recommendation R(85)7

COUNCIL OF EUROPE
COMMITTEE OF MINISTERS

RECOMMENDATION No. R (85) 7

**OF THE COMMITTEE OF MINISTERS TO MEMBER STATES
ON TEACHING AND LEARNING ABOUT HUMAN RIGHTS IN SCHOOLS**

*(Adopted by the Committee of Ministers on 14 May 1985
at the 385th meeting of the Ministers' Deputies)*

The Committee of Ministers, under the terms of Article 15.*b* of the Statute of the Council of Europe,

Considering that the aim of the Council of Europe is to achieve a greater unity between its members for the purpose of safeguarding and realising the ideals and principles which are their common heritage;

Reaffirming the human rights undertakings embodied in the United Nations' Universal Declaration of Human Rights, the Convention for the Protection of Human Rights and Fundamental Freedoms and the European Social Charter;

Having regard to the commitments to human rights education made by member states at international and European conferences in the last decade;

Recalling:

– its own Resolution (78) 41 on 'The teaching of human rights',

– its Declaration on 'Intolerance: a threat to democracy' of 14 May 1981,

– its Recommendation No. R (83) 13 on 'The role of the secondary school in preparing young people for life';

Noting Recommendation 963 (1983) of the Consultative Assembly of the Council of Europe on 'Cultural and educational means of reducing violence';

Conscious of the need to reaffirm democratic values in the face of:

– intolerance, acts of violence and terrorism;

– the re-emergence of the public expression of racist and xenophobic attitudes;

– the disillusionment of many young people in Europe, who are affected by the economic recession and aware of the continuing poverty and inequality in the world;

Believing, therefore, that, throughout their school career, all young people should learn about human rights as part of their preparation for life in a pluralistic democracy;

Convinced that schools are communities which can, and should, be an example of respect for the dignity of the individual and for difference. for tolerance, and for equality of opportunity,

I. Recommends that the governments of member states, having regard to their national education systems and to the legislative basis for them:

a. encourage teaching and learning about human rights in schools in line with the suggestions contained in the appendix hereto;

b. draw the attention of persons and bodies concerned with school education to the text of this recommendation;

II. Instructs the Secretary General to transmit this recommendation to the governments of those states party to the European Cultural Convention which are not members of the Council of Europe.

Appendix to Recommendation No. R(85)7

Suggestions for teaching and learning about human rights in schools

1. *Human rights in the school curriculum*

1.1. The understanding and experience of human rights is an important element of the preparation of all young people for life in a democratic and pluralistic society. It is part of social and political education, and it involves intercultural and international understanding.

1.2. Concepts associated with human rights can, and should, be acquired from an early stage. For example, the non-violent resolution of conflict and respect for other people can already be experienced within the life of a pre-school or primary class.

1.3. Opportunities to introduce young people to more abstract notions of human rights, such as those involving an understanding of philosophical, political and legal concepts, will occur in the secondary school, in particular in such subjects as history, geography, social studies, moral and religious education, language and literature, current affairs and economics.

1.4. Human rights inevitably involve the domain of politics. Teaching about human rights should, therefore, always have international agreements and covenants as a point of reference, and teachers should take care to avoid imposing their personal convictions on their pupils and involving them in ideological struggles.

2. *Skills*

The skills associated with understanding and supporting human rights include:

    i. *intellectual skills*, in particular:

– skills associated with written and oral expression, including the ability to listen and discuss, and to defend one's opinions;

– skills involving judgment, such as:

    – the collection and examination of material from various sources, including the mass media, and the ability to analyse it and to arrive at fair and balanced conclusions;

    – the identification of bias, prejudice, stereotypes and discrimination;

    ii. social skills, in particular:

– recognising and accepting differences;

– establishing positive and non-oppressive personal relationships;

– resolving conflict in a non-violent way;

– taking responsibility;

– participating in decisions;

– understanding the use of the mechanisms for the protection of human rights at local, regional, European and world levels.

3. *Knowledge to be acquired in the study of human rights*

3.1. The study of human rights in schools will be approached in different ways according to the age and circumstances of the pupil and the particular situations of schools and education systems. Topics to be covered in learning about human rights could include:

    i.   the main categories of human rights, duties, obligations and responsibilities;

ii. the various forms of injustice, inequality and discrimination, including sexism and racism;

iii. people, movements and key events, both successes and failures, in the historical and continuing struggle for human rights;

iv. the main international declarations and conventions on human rights, such as the Universal Declaration of Human Rights and the Convention for the Protection of Human Rights and Fundamental Freedoms.

3.2. The emphasis in teaching and learning about human rights should be positive. Pupils may be led to feelings of powerlessness and discouragement when confronted with many examples of violation and negations of human rights. Instances of progress and success should be used.

3.3. The study of human rights in schools should lead to an understanding of, and sympathy for, the concepts of justice, equality, freedom, peace, dignity, rights and democracy. Such understanding should be both cognitive and based on experience and feelings. Schools should, thus, provide opportunities for pupils to experience affective involvement in human rights and to express their feelings through drama, art, music, creative writing and audiovisual media.

4. *The climate of the school*

4.1. Democracy is best learned in a democratic setting where participation is encouraged, where views can be expressed openly and discussed, where there is freedom of expression for pupils and teachers, and where there is fairness and justice. An appropriate climate is, therefore, an essential complement to effective learning about human rights.

4.2. Schools should encourage participation in their activities by parents and other members of the community. It may well be appropriate for schools to work with non-governmental organisations which can provide information, case-studies and first-hand experience of successful campaigns for human rights and dignity.

4.3. Schools and teachers should attempt to be positive towards all their pupils, and recognise that all of their achievements are important– whether they be academic, artistic, musical, sporting or practical.

5. *Teacher training*

5.1. The initial training of teachers should prepare them for their future contribution to teaching about human rights in their schools. For example, future teachers should:

i. be encouraged to take an interest in national and world affairs;

ii. have the chance of studying or working in a foreign country or a different environment:

iii. be taught to identify and combat all forms of discrimination in schools and society and be encouraged to confront and overcome their own prejudices.

5.2. Future and practising teachers should be encouraged to familiarise themselves with

i. the main international declarations and conventions on human rights;

ii. the working and achievements of the international organisations which deal with the protection and promotion of human rights, for example through visits and study tours.

5.3. All teachers need, and should be given the opportunity, to update their knowledge and to learn new methods through in-service training. This could include the study of good practice in teaching about human rights, as well as the development of appropriate methods and materials.

6. *International/Human Rights Day*

Schools and teacher training establishments should be encouraged to observe International Human Rights Day (10 December).

Bibliography

Abdallah-Pretceille, M. (1988) *Human Rights Education in Pre-Primary Schools*. Donaueschingen seminar No 40. Strasbourg: Council of Europe. (DECS/EGT (88)31.)

African Charter on Human and Peoples' Rights (ACHPR) (1981) adopted at the 18th Conference of Heads of State and Government, Organisation of African Unity, Nairobi, 27 June.

APAP (1996) *Bells of Freedom*. Addis Ababa: Action Professionals' Association for the People.

Agi, M. (1979) *René Cassin fantassin des Droits de l'Homme*. Paris: Plon.

Altschull, E. (1995) *Le Voile contre l'Ecole*. Paris: Seuil.

Archard, D. (1993) *Children, Rights and Childhood*. London: Routledge.

Aubertin, J.-P. (1996) Le contrat de vie du groupe-classe, *Animation et Education*, 131. Paris: Office Central de la Co-opération à l'Ecole.

Audigier, F. and Lagelée, G. (1992) *Civic education: teaching about society, passing on values*. Donaueschingen seminar No 57. Strasbourg: Council of Europe. (DECS/SE/BS Donau (92)3.)

Baglin Jones, E. and Jones, N. (eds) (1992) *Education for Citizenship*. London: Kogan Page.

Bangar, S. and McDermott, J. (1989) Black women speak, in H. de Lyon and F. W. Migniuolo (eds) *Women Teachers: issues and experiences*. Milton Keynes: Open University Press.

Banks, M., Bates, I., Breakwell, G., Bynner, J. and Emler, N. (1991) *Careers and Identities*. Milton Keynes: Open University Press.

Batelaan, P. (1994) *Education and Tolerance in Multi-cultural Groups*. Donaueschingen seminar No 63. Strasbourg: Council of Europe. (DECS/SE/BS Donau (94)3.)

Bell, G. H. (1994) (ed.) *Educating European Citizens*. London: David Fulton.

Berque, J. (1991) *New Minority Groups in the Citadel of Europe*. Strasbourg: Council of Europe.

Best, F. (1982) Les droits de l'homme: une éducation morale et civique pour notre temps, in Centre Nationale de Documentation Pédagogique, *Pour une éducation aux droits de l'homme: Références Documentaires No. 30*. (2nd edition 1989.)

Best, F. (1990) *The Sciences, Ethics, Human Rights and Education*. Donaueschingen seminar No 48. Strasbourg: Council of Europe. (DECS/EGT (90)23.)

Best, F. (1991) Human rights education and teacher training, in H. Starkey (ed.) *The Challenge of Human Rights Education*. London: Cassell.

Best, F. (1992) *Human Rights Education*. Strasbourg: Council for Cultural Co-operation.

Birzea, C. (1995) *Strategies for Interculturally-oriented Civics Teaching at Primary and Secondary Level*, Timisoara, Romania, December 1994. Strasbourg: Council of Europe. (DECS/SE/DHRM (95)3.)

Blair, M. and Arnot, M. (1993) Black and anti-racist perspectives on the national curriculum and government education policy, in A. King and M. Reiss (eds) *The Multicultural Dimension of the National Curriculum*. London: Falmer.

Blair, M. and Maylor, U. (1993) Issues and concerns for black women teachers in training, in I. Siraj-Blatchford (ed.) *'Race', Gender and the Education of Teachers*. Buckingham: Open University Press.

Bonanate, L. (1995) Peace or Democracy?, in D. Archibugi and D. Held (eds) *Cosmopolitan Democracy*. Cambridge: Polity.

Brennan, J. and McGeevor, P. (1990) *Ethnic Minorities and the Graduate Labour Market*. London: Commission for Racial Equality.

Brown, M. (1996) *Our World, Our Rights*. London: Amnesty International.

Brownlie, I. (1971) *Basic Documents on Human Rights*. Oxford: Oxford University Press.

Cantwell, N. (1992) The Origins, Development and Significance of the United Nations Convention on the Rights of the Child, in S. Detrick (ed.) *The United Nations Convention on the Rights of the Child: a Guide to the 'Travaux Préparatoires'*. Dordrecht: Martinus Nijhoff.

Carnes, J. (1995) *Us and Them*. Montgomery, Alabama: Teaching Tolerance Project, Southern Poverty Law Center.

Carpentier, J. (ed.) (forthcoming) *The Development of Human Rights in Europe: an anthology of texts*. Strasbourg: Council of Europe.

Cassese, A. (1990) *Human Rights in a Changing World*. Cambridge: Polity.

Clough, N., Menter, I. and Tarr, J. (1996) Developing citizenship education programmes in Latvia, in A. Osler, H.-F. Rathenow and H. Starkey (eds) *Teaching for Citizenship in Europe*. Stoke-on-Trent: Trentham.

Commission for Racial Equality (1992) *Secondary School Admissions: a report of a formal investigation into Hertfordshire County Council*. London: CRE.

Commission for Racial Equality (1993) *Draft Circular on Admissions Arrangements*. London: CRE.

Commission on Global Governance (1995) *Our Global Neighbourhood*. Oxford: Oxford University Press.

Council of Europe (1983) *Recommendation No. R(83)4 of the Committee of Ministers to Member States Concerning the Promotion of an Awareness of Europe in Secondary Schools*. Strasbourg: Council of Europe.

Council of Europe (1985): see Appendix 3.

Council of Europe (1992) *The Human Rights Album*. Strasbourg: Council of Europe.

Council of Europe (1993) *Vienna Declaration*, 9 October. Strasbourg: Council of Europe.

186

Council of Europe (1994) *Resolution on Education for Democracy, Human Rights & Tolerance.* Standing Conference of European Ministers of Education, 18th session, Madrid, March.

Council of Europe (1995) (video) *Stand up NOW for Human Rights!* Dramatic Productions for Council of Europe.

Council of Ministers (1988) *Resolution of the Council and of the Ministers of Education Meeting Within the Council on the European Dimension in Education 24 May (88/C177/02). European Community.* Re-printed in M. Shannon (1991) *Teaching About Europe.* London: Cassell.

Covell, K. and Howe, R. B. (1995) Variations in support for children's rights among Canadian youth, *International Journal of Children's Rights,* 3, 2, pp. 189–96.

CRDP (1989) *Connaissance et Rencontre des Cultures à L'Ecole.* Paris: Centre Régionale de Documentation Pédagogique.

Crewe, I. (1996) *Citizenship and Civic Education.* Paper presented to seminar of the Citizenship Foundation, Royal Society of Arts, London, 21 May.

Crick, B. and Porter, A. (eds) (1978) *Political Education and Political Literacy.* London: Longman.

Croall, J. (1996) Beating the law of averages, *Times Educational Supplement,* 18 March.

Cunningham, J. (1991) The Human Rights Secondary School, in H. Starkey (ed.) *The Challenge of Human Rights Education.* London: Cassell.

Dadsi, D. (1994) *Particularismes et Universalisme: la problématique des identités.* CDCC Seminar, 'Democracy Human Rights and Minorities', Klingenthal, France, June 1994. Strasbourg: Council of Europe. (DECS/SE/DHRM (94)10.)

Davey, A. G. (1986) Learning to be Prejudiced, *Multicultural Teaching,* 4, 3, pp.13–15.

de Closets, F. (1996) *Le Bonheur d'Apprendre: et comment on l'assassine.* Paris: Seuil.

de Waal, A. (1992) Howitzer culture, *New Internationalist,* 238, pp. 26–7.

Delrot, J. (1991) *The Nationalities Question – from Versailles to the Present Day.* European teachers' seminar, Esneux, Belgium. Strasbourg: Council of Europe. (DECS/SE/BS/Sem (91)2.)

Demel, K. (1995) *History and Identity.* European teachers' seminar, Vienna, Austria, May 1995. Strasbourg: Council of Europe. (DECS/SE/BS/Sem (95)10.)

Department of Education and Science (1985) *Education for All: the report of the Committee of Enquiry into the education of children from ethnic minority groups.* The Swann Report. London: HMSO, Cmnd 9453.

Dewey, J. (1909) *Moral Principles in Education.* Boston: Houghton Mifflin.

Docking, J. (1990) *Primary Schools and Parents.* London: Hodder and Stoughton.

Doek, J. (1992) The Current Status of the United Nations Convention on the Rights of the Child, in S. Detrick (ed.) *The United Nations Convention on the*

Rights of the Child: a guide to the 'Travaux Préparatoires'. Dordrecht: Martinus Nijhoff.

DSDE (1993) *The Training & Development of Teachers Interim Consultative Documents*. Oxford: Oxford University Department of Educational Studies.

Duparc, C. (1993) *The European Community and Human Rights*. Luxembourg: European Communities.

Eggleston, J., Dunn, D. K. and Anjai, M. (1986) *Education for Some: the educational and vocational experiences of 15–18 year old members of minority ethnic groups*. Stoke-on-Trent: Trentham.

Etzioni, A. (1995) *The Spirit of Community*. London: Fontana.

Federal Ministry of Education and Arts (1992) *Grundsatzerlass zum Projektunterricht* (English version). Vienna: BM für Unterricht und Kunst.

Féron, J. (1987) *Les Droits de l'Homme*. Paris: Hachette.

Ferry, L. and Renaut, A. (1988) *La Pensée 68*. Paris: Gallimard.

Fogelman, K. (1994) *Education for Democratic Citizenship in Europe – new challenges for secondary education*. Amsterdam: Swets & Zeitlinger.

Fogelman, K. (1995) *Citizenship Education*. European teachers' course, Uppsala, Sweden, November 1994. Strasbourg: Council of Europe. (DECS/SE/BS/Sem (95)1.)

Freeman, M. (1988) Taking children's rights seriously, *Children and Society*, 4, pp. 299–319.

Freeman, M. (1992) Introduction: Rights, Ideology and Children, in M. Freeman and P. Veerman (eds) *The Ideologies of Children's Rights*. Dordrecht: Martinus Nijhoff.

Freeman, M. (1993) Laws, conventions and rights, *Children and Society*, 7, 1, pp. 37–48.

Freidman, E. (1995) Women's human rights: the emergence of a movement, in J. Peters and A. Wolper (eds) *Women's Rights, Human Rights: international feminist perspectives*. London: Routledge.

Gallagher, C. (1996) *History Teaching and the Promotion of Democratic Values and Tolerance*. Strasbourg: Council of Europe. (CC-ED/HIST (96)1.)

Gallagher, C. and Cross, C. (1990) Children Act 1989: an introduction, *Maladjustment and Therapeutic Education*, 8, 3, pp. 122–9.

Galtung, J. (1994) *Human Rights in Another Key*. Cambridge: Polity.

Gaspard, F. and Khosrokhavar, F. (1995) *Le Foulard et la République*. Paris: La Découverte.

Georgescu, D. (1994) *Strategies for Interculturally-Oriented Civics Teaching at Primary and Secondary Level: report of the experimental phase*. Strasbourg: Council of Europe. (DECS/SE/DHRM (94)11.)

Ghosh, R. and Attieh, A. (1987) The right to education free from discrimination: the cases of India and Saudi Arabia, in N. Bernstein Tarrow (ed.) *Human Rights and Education*. Oxford: Pergamon.

Gillborn, D. (1990) *'Race', Ethnicity and Education: teaching and learning in multiethnic schools*. London: Unwin Hyman.

Giroit, A. and Poslaniec, C. (1985) *Une Journée à l'Ecole Freinet*. Paris: Retz.

188

Gomien, D. (1991) *Short Guide to The European Convention on Human Rights*. Strasbourg: Council of Europe Press.

Gray, J. (1995) *Enlightenment's Wake*. London: Routledge.

Hall, J. (ed.) (1971) *Children's Rights: Towards the Liberation of the Child*. London: Elek.

Halliday, F. (1995) *Islam and the Myth of Confrontation: religion and politics in the Middle East*. London: I. B. Tauris

Hannam, D. (1995) Democratising Secondary Schools, in C. Harber (ed.) *Developing Democratic Education*. Ticknell: Education Now.

Hansen, S. and Jensen, J. (1971) *The Little Red Schoolbook*. London: Stage 1.

Harber, C. (1994) Ethnicity and education for democracy in sub-Saharan Africa, *International Journal of Educational Development*, 14, 3, pp. 255–64.

Harber, C. and Meighan, R. (1986) Democratic method in teacher training for political education, *Teaching Politics*, 15, 2, pp.179–87.

Hart, R. (1992) *Children's Participation; from tokenism to citizenship*. Innocenti Essays No. 4. Florence: UNICEF/International Child Development Centre.

Hart, S. N. (1991) From property to person status: historical perspective on children's rights, *American Psychologist*, 46, 1, pp. 53–9.

Hasbudak, Z. and Simons, B. (1986) *Zeynep: that really happened to me*. London: ALTARF.

Heater, D. (1984) *Human Rights Education in Schools: concepts, attitudes and skills*. Strasbourg: Council of Europe. (DECS/EGT (84)26.)

Held, D. (1995) Democracy and the New International Order, in D. Archibugi and D. Held (eds) *Cosmopolitan Democracy*. Cambridge: Polity.

Henaire, J. (1995) *Education in Human Rights and Peace: issues and guidelines for teaching*. 13th International Training Session on human rights and peace teaching, Geneva, Switzerland, July 1995. Strasbourg: Council of Europe. (DECS/SE/BS/Sem (95)14.)

Hills, J. (1995) *Inquiry into Income and Wealth, volume 2: a summary of the evidence*. York: Joseph Rowntree Foundation.

Hodgson, K. and Whalley, G. (1992) Spotlight on children, *Education*, 24 January.

Holub, R. C. (1991) *Jürgen Habermas: critic in the public sphere*. London: Routledge.

Hughes, M. (1989) The child as a learner: The contrasting views of developmental psychology and early education, in C. Desforges (ed.) *Early Childhood Education*. Edinburgh: Scottish Academic Press.

Hugill, B. (1995) Young Muslim zealots target British schoolgirls, *The Observer*, 5 February.

Human Rights Directorate (1992) *Intercultural Learning for Human Rights*. Seminar held in Klagenfurt, Austria, October 1991. Strasbourg: Council of Europe Press.

Illich, I. (1971) *Deschooling Society*. Harmondsworth: Penguin.

ICEM – pédagogie Freinet (1984) *Histoire Partout, Géographie Tout le Temps*. Paris: Syros.

Jeleff, S. (1996) *The Child As Citizen*. Strasbourg: Council of Europe.

Johnson, D. (1992) Cultural and Regional Pluralism in the Drafting of the UN Convention on the Rights of the Child, in M. Freeman and P. Veerman (eds) *The Ideologies of Children's Rights*. Dordrecht: Martinus Nijhoff.

Jourdan, P. (1993) *Délégué Flash*. Grenoble: CRDP.

Jourdan, P. and Gisbert, R. (1990) *Lycée – les Délégués d'Elèves: Méthodologie d'une Formation*. Grenoble: CRDP.

Klein, G. (1993) *Education Towards Race Equality*. London: Cassell.

Lang, S. (1991) *Teaching about European History and Society in the 1990s*. European teachers' seminar, Tuusula, Finland. Strasbourg: Council of Europe. (DECS/SE/BS/Sem (91)4.)

Lansdown, G. and Newell, P. (eds) (1994) *UK Agenda for Children*. London: Children's Rights Development Unit.

Laszlo, E. (ed.) (1993) *The Multi-Cultural Planet*. Oxford: Oneworld.

Laqueur, W. and Rubin, B. (1979) *The Human Rights Reader*. New York: Meridien.

Law, C. (1994) *In-Service Teacher Training Seminar on Human Rights Education*. Tyumen, Russian Federation, April 1994. Strasbourg: Council of Europe. (DECS/DBE/1994/01.)

Law, C. and Rendel, M. (1992) *Human Rights Materials in British Schools*. Strasbourg: Council of Europe. (DECS/SE (92)1.)

Leduc, C. and de Massy, P. (1989) *Sharing a better life together through human rights*. Québec: Modulo.

Legrand, L. (1996) Dans la mouvance de Freinet, *Animation et Education*, No. 131. Paris: Office Central de la Co-opération à l'Ecole.

Lindsay, M. (1990) The Children Act 1989: a consideration of the implications for children's rights, *Maladjustment and Therapeutic Education*, 8, 3, pp. 167–73.

Lister, I. (1974) *Deschooling*. Cambridge: Cambridge University Press.

Lister, I. (1981) *Human Rights Education in the Secondary School*. European teachers' seminar, Bergen, Norway, August 1981. Strasbourg: Council of Europe. (DECS/EGT (81) 71.)

Lister, I. (1984) *Teaching and Learning about Human Rights*. Strasbourg: Council of Europe. (DECS/EGT (84)27.)

London Borough of Ealing (1991) *In Ealing Every Child is Given Space to Grow*. London: London Borough of Ealing.

Lorenz, W. (1996) *New Style Workshop on Ethnic Minorities, Language Teaching and In-service Training: an intercultural exchange of experiences and developments*. Graz, Austria, November 1995. Strasbourg: Council of Europe. (DECS/SE/BS/Sem(96)1.)

Louis, R. (1993) *The Intercultural Dimension as an Essential Factor for Secondary Education Reform*. Timisoara, Romania, May 1993. Strasbourg: Council of Europe. (DECS/SE/Sec (93)19.)

Lyseight-Jones, P. (1985) *Human Rights Education in Primary Schools*. Donaueschingen seminar No 28. Strasbourg: Council of Europe. (DECS/EGT (85)46.)

Macdonald, I., Bhavnani, R., Khan, L. and John, G. (1989) *Murder in the Playground: the report of the Macdonald inquiry into racism and racial violence in Manchester schools*. London: Longsight.

McFarlane, C. and Osler, A. (1991) *New Journeys: teaching about other places, learning from Kenya and Tanzania*. Birmingham: Development Education Centre.

McGurk, H. (1987) (ed.) *What Next*? London: Economic and Social Research Council.

McIvor, G. (1996) Sweden's jackboot Vikings, *The Observer*, 21 January.

Marcus, J. (1995) Forster novel costs a teacher her job, *Times Educational Supplement*, 20 October.

Mariet, F. (1980) *The Teaching of Human Rights*. Donaueschingen seminar No 8. Strasbourg: Council of Europe. (DECS/EGT (80)50.)

Massey, I. (1995) Education against racism and xenophobia in Europe, *Multicultural Teaching*, 14, 1, pp. 42–7.

Milner, D. (1975) *Children and Race*. Harmondsworth: Penguin.

Mirza, H. (1992) *Young, Female and Black*. London: Routledge.

Modood, T. (1992) *Not Easy Being British: colour, culture and citizenship*. Stoke-on-Trent: Runnymede Trust and Trentham Books.

Moore, M. (1987) *Bullying in Schools*. European teachers' seminar, Stavanger, Norway, August 1987. Strasbourg: Council of Europe. (DECS/EGT (88)5.)

Morgan, A. E. (1943) *Young Citizen*. Harmondsworth: Penguin Books.

Mougniotte, A. (1994) *Eduquer à la Démocratie*. Paris: CERF.

National Curriculum Council (1990) *Education for Citizenship: curriculum guidance 8*. York: NCC.

National Union of Teachers (1992) *NUT Survey on Pupil Exclusions: information from LEAs*. London: NUT.

Newell, P. (1991) *The UN Convention and Children's Rights in the UK*. London: National Children's Bureau.

Newell, P. (1993) Too Young to be Kept in Chains, *Times Educational Supplement*, 1 January.

Nias, J. (1989) *Primary Teachers Talking: a study of teaching as work*. London: Routledge.

Norris, A. (1993) *The Power Pack: unit 1, power points*. Oxford: Oxford Development Education Centre.

OCCE (1986) *Qu'est-ce que l'OCCE?* Paris: Office Central de la Co-opération à l'Ecole.

OCCE (1996) *Animation et Education*, 131, Paris: Office Central de la Co-opération à l'Ecole.

O'Keeffe, D. (ed.) (1986) *The Wayward Curriculum: a cause for parents' concern*? London: Social Affairs Unit.

Oliver, D. and Heater, D. (1994) *The Foundations of Citizenship*. Hemel Hempstead: Harvester Wheatsheaf.

Oscarsson, V. (1996) Pupils' views of the future, in A. Osler, H.-F. Rathenow and H. Starkey (eds) *Teaching for Citizenship in Europe*. Stoke-on-Trent: Trentham.

O'Shaughnessy, M. (1994) Development education and the teaching of modern languages, in A. Osler (ed.) *Development Education: global perspectives in the curriculum.* London: Cassell.

Osler, A. (1994a) *Development Education: global perspectives in the curriculum.* London: Cassell.

Osler, A. (1994b) Education for development: redefining citizenship in a pluralist society, in A. Osler (ed.) *Development Education: global perspectives in the curriculum..* London: Cassell.

Osler, A. (1994c) 'The flavour of the moment'? Bilingual teachers' experiences of teaching and learning, in A. Blackledge (ed.) *Teaching Bilingual Children.* Stoke-on-Trent: Trentham.

Osler, A. (1995) *The Education, Lives and Careers of Black Teachers in Britain.* University of Birmingham: unpublished PhD thesis.

Osler, A. (1996a) Education for human rights and development in Ethiopia, in J. Lynch, C. Mogdill and S. Mogdill (eds) *Education and Development: tradition and innovation.*, vol. 7. London: Cassell.

Osler, A. (1996b) European Citizenship and Study Abroad: student teachers' experiences and identities, paper presented to conference: Education for Citizenship in a New Europe, Goethe Foundation, Klingenthal, France.

Osler, A. (1996c) *Learning to Participate: human rights citizenship and development in the local community.* Birmingham: Development Education Centre.

Osler, A. (1996d) Urban protest, citizenship and human rights: curriculum responses to local issues, in A. Osler, H.-F. Rathenow and H. Starkey (eds) *Teaching for Citizenship in Europe.* Stoke-on Trent: Trentham.

Osler, A. (1997, forthcoming) Black Teachers and Citizenship: researching differing identities, *Teachers and Teaching, 3.*

Osler, A. and Davies, L. (1994) Teacher education and equal rights. Editorial. *Educational Review*, Special Issue 26, 46, 2, p.107.

Osler, A. and Hussain, Z. (1995) Parental choice and schooling: some factors influencing Muslim mothers' decisions about the education of their daughters, *Cambridge Journal of Education*, 25, 3, pp. 327–47.

Osler, A., Rathenow, H.-F., and Starkey, H. (eds) (1996) *Teaching for Citizenship in Europe.* Stoke-on-Trent: Trentham.

Osler, A. and Starkey, H. (1994) Fundamental Issues in Teacher Education for Human Rights: a European perspective, *Journal of Moral Education*, 23, 3, pp.349–59.

Palley, C. (1991) *The United Kingdom and Human Rights.* London: Stevens.

Pearse, S. (1987) *Human Rights Education in a Global Perspective.* European teachers' seminar, Are, Sweden, August 1987. Strasbourg: Council of Europe. (DECS/EGT (87) 59.)

Perotti, A. (1991) *Action to Combat Intolerance and Xenophobia in the Activities of the Council of Europe's Council for Cultural Co-operation 1969–1989.* Strasbourg: Council of Europe.

Peyronie, H. (1994) Célestin Freinet, in J. Houssaye (ed.) *Quinze Pédagogues.* Paris: Armand Colin.

Prindezis, M. and Prémont, D. (1994) Teacher education and training for teachers of human rights, in M. Galton and B. Moon (eds) *Handbook of Teacher Training in Europe*. London: David Fulton.

Pike, G. and Selby, D. (1988) *Global Teacher, Global Learner*. London: Hodder and Stoughton.

Pyke, N. (1993) Able-bodied only, please, *Times Educational Supplement*, 23 July.

Ray, D. (1994) *Education for Human Rights*. Paris: UNESCO.

Richardson, R. (1979) The life-cycle of a course, in World Studies Project, *Learning for Change in World Society*. London: One World Trust (revised edition).

Richardson, R. (1995) National identity; debates summer 1995, *The Runnymede Bulletin*, 288, September, pp. 2–3.

Richardson, R. (1996) The terrestrial teacher, in M. Steiner (ed.) *Developing the Global Teacher*. Stoke-on-Trent: Trentham.

Roberts, H. and Sachdev, D. (1996) *Young People's Social Attitudes*. Ilford: Barnados.

Roche, G. (1993) *L'Apprenti-Citoyen*. Paris: ESF Editeur.

Rodham, H. (1973) Children under the law, *Harvard Educational Review*, 43, pp. 487–514.

Rodway, S. (1993) Children's rights: children's needs. Is there a conflict? *Therapeutic Care and Education*, 2, 2, pp. 375–91.

Rosengren, B. (1984) *Social Development and Social Education for Young Children*. European teachers' seminar, Reykjavik, Iceland, August 1983. Strasbourg: Council of Europe. (DECS/EGT (84)103.)

Rothemund, A. (1995) *Domino: a manual to use peer group education as a means to fight racism, xenophobia, anti-semitism and intolerance*. Strasbourg: Council of Europe, Youth Directorate.

Rovan, J. (1993) *Citoyen d'Europe*. Paris: Laffont.

Rowe, D. (1992) The citizen and the law, in E. Baglin Jones and N. Jones (eds) *Education for Citizenship*. London: Kogan Page.

Rowe, D. (1993) *Citizenship Education in Secondary Education*. Donaueschingen seminar No 60. Strasbourg: Council of Europe. (DECS/SE/BS Donau (93)2.)

Rowntree Foundation (1995) *Inquiry into Income and Wealth: volume 1*. York: Joseph Rowntree Foundation.

Runnymede Trust (1993) *Equality Assurance in Schools*. Stoke-on-Trent: Trentham.

Runnymede Trust (1996) *The Multi-Ethnic Good Society: vision and reality*. London: Runnymede Trust.

Rutter, J. (1996) *Refugees: we left because we had to*. London: Refugee Council.

Sabourin, E. (1994) Case Study, in D. Georgescu, *Final Report of the Experimental Phase of the Pilot Project No. 1 of Strategies for Interculturally-Oriented Civics Teaching at Primary and Secondary Level*. Strasbourg: Council of Europe. (DECS/SE/DHRM (94)11.)

Schnapper, D. (1994) *La Communauté des Citoyens*. Paris: Gallimard.

Scruton, R., Ellis-Jones, A. and O'Keeffe, D. (1985) *Education and Indoctrination*. Harrow: Education Research Centre.

Selle-Hosbach, K. (1986) *Human Rights Education and the Teaching of Social, Civic and Political Education*. Donaueschingen seminar No 34. Strasbourg: Council of Europe. DECS/EGT(86.)

Serageldin, I. (1994) Our Common Humanity. European Association for International Education Newsletter 1994, pp.3–10.

Shafer, S. (1987) Human rights education in schools, in N. Bernstein-Tarrow (ed.) *Human Rights and Education*. Oxford: Pergamon.

Shennan, M. (1991) *Teaching about Europe*. London: Cassell.

Sone, K. (1993) A ritual of suffering, *Times Educational Supplement*, 22 January.

Speaker's Commission on Citizenship (1990) *Encouraging Citizenship*. London: HMSO.

SPLC (1995) *The Shadow of Hate*. Montgomery, Alabama. Teaching Tolerance Project, Southern Poverty Law Center.

Starkey, H. (1984) *Human Rights Education in Schools in Western Europe*. Vienna, May 1983. Strasbourg: Council of Europe. (DECS/EGT(84)25.)

Starkey, H. (1985) *Teaching and Learning about Human Rights in Schools*. European teachers' seminar, Livry-Gargan, France, May 1984. Strasbourg: Council of Europe. (DECS/EGT(85).)

Starkey, H.(1986) *Teaching and Learning about Human Rights in the Compulsory School*. European teachers' seminar, Birkerød, Denmark, October 1985. Strasbourg: Council of Europe. (DECS/EGT (86)91.)

Starkey, H. (1987) *Teaching and Learning about Human Rights in Secondary Schools*. European teachers' seminar, Carcavelos, Portugal, December 1986. Strasbourg: Council of Europe. (DECS/EGT (87)20.)

Starkey, H. (1991a) *Socialisation of School Children and their Education for Democratic Values and Human Rights*. Amsterdam: Swets & Zeitlinger.

Starkey, H. (1991b) *The Challenge of Human Rights Education*. London: Cassell.

Starkey, H. (1992) Back to basic values: education for justice and peace in the world, *Journal of Moral Education*, 21, 3, pp.185–92.

Starkey, H. (1996) Intercultural education through foreign language learning: a human rights approach, in A. Osler, H.-F. Rathenow and H. Starkey (eds) *Teaching for Citizenship in Europe*. Stoke-on-Trent: Trentham.

Starkey, H. and Tibbitts, F. (forthcoming) *Human Rights Education in Schools*. Strasbourg: Council of Europe.

Steiner, M. (ed.) (1996) *Developing the Global Teacher*. Stoke-on-Trent: Trentham.

Steiner-Khamsi, G. (1993) *Education, Migration, Minorities*. Seminar on Education: structures, policies and strategies. Strasbourg, December 1993. Strasbourg: Council of Europe. (CE.ED/CSCE (93)11.)

Stevens, O. (1982) *Children Talking Politics*. Oxford: Martin Robertson.

Stobart, M. (1992) *Speech delivered at Moscow seminar*. Council of Europe internal document .

194

Stobart, M. (1995) The New Europe in practice, *Times Educational Supplement*, 10 November.

Thompson, M. *et al.* (1993) *The Co-op PSE Handbook*. Manchester: CWS.

Thorne, S. (1996) Children's rights and the listening school: an approach to counter bullying among primary school pupils, in A. Osler, H.-F. Rathenow and H. Starkey (eds) *Teaching for Citizenship in Europe*. Stoke-on-Trent: Trentham.

Thorpe, T. (1996) *Young Citizen's Passport*. London: Citizenship Foundation.

Thyr, M. (1994) Environment and development: a cross-curricular project in a Swedish school, in A. Osler (Ed.) *Development Education: global perspectives in the curriculum*. London: Cassell.

Touraine, A. (1994) *Qu'est-ce que c'est la Démocratie?* Paris: Fayard.

Trant, A. (1995) *Education for Mutual Understanding in an International Context*. European teachers' seminar, Belfast, Northern Ireland, November 1994. Strasbourg: Council of Europe. (DECS/SE/BS/Sem (95)3).

United Nations High Commissioner for Refugees (1994) *Human Rights: the new consensus*. London: Regency Press (Humanity).

van der Gaag, N. and Gerlach, L. (1985) *Profile on Prejudice*. London: Minority Rights Group.

Verhellen, E. (1989) A strategy for a fully fledged position of children in our society, in E. Verhellen and F. Spieeshchaert (eds) *Ombudswork for Children*. Leuven: ACCO.

Walker, J. (1989) *Violence and Conflict Resolution in Schools*. Strasbourg: Council of Europe. (DECS/EGT (89)24.)

Wallace, W. (1996) The tougher side of village life, *Times Educational Supplement*, 8 March.

Ward, W. (1996) Inquiry into Muslim extremists in colleges, *Times Educational Supplement*, 1 March.

Watts, J. (1977) *The Countesthorpe Experience*. London: Allen and Unwin.

World Commission on Culture and Development (1996) *Our Creative Diversity*, 2nd edition. Paris: UNESCO/London: HMSO.

Wright, T. (1994) *Citizens and Subjects*. London: Routledge.

Zhou Nan-Zhao (1994) Educational Rights: perspectives and practices in China, in D. Ray (ed.) *Education for Human Rights*. Paris: UNESCO.

Index

access 24
  to global commons 164
  to information 154, 155–6,163–4
accredited course 135–40
action 85,158–9,164–7
Action Professionals' Association for the People (APAP) 61–4
action research projects 140
admissions policies 56
affective dimension 85, 124–5, 135, 158–9
Africa 61–4
African Charter on Human and Peoples' Rights (ACHPR) (1981) 61
African Charter on the Rights and Welfare of the Child (1990) 19
All different, all equal campaign 47, 52, 65–8
America, North 59–61
anti-semitism 51–3
assessment 138, 152–3, 171
audit of human rights 161–4
audit of responsibilities 164–6
Austrian Ministry of Education 149–50

Bells of Freedom, The 61–4
'best interests of the child' principle 21–2
Birmingham University course 135–40
black teachers 97–102
Britain *see* United Kingdom
Burnage Report 89

campaigning 152
Cassin, René 3, 4
Central and Eastern Europe 46
Children Act (1989) 22
children's rights 16–33
Children's Rights Development Unit 23
child's opinion 22–3
China 8–9
CIFEDHOP (International Training Centre on Human Rights and Peace Teaching) 43
  teacher education programme 119–20, 121–2, 125–30

citizenship 110, 111, 170–1
  education for 69–86
  European 91–7, 110–11
  students'/teachers' understandings of 87–102
Citizenship Foundation 120, 123
class co-operatives 144–6
cognitive dimension 85, 158–9
Commission on Global Governance (CGG) 9, 10–11, 52, 161–6
common good 164–5
commons, global 164, 165
communication 31
communities of citizens 79–80, 170–1
conflicts/disputes 29–31, 163
contracts (for classes) 146
co-operative classes 144–6
corporal punishment 38
corruption 166
Council for Cultural Co-operation (CDCC) 35
Council of Europe 5–6,13,14,103
  history teaching 58–9
  and human rights education 6, 34–47
  Recommendation R(85)7 27, 40–1, 118, 123, 124–5, 181–3
  response to racism/xenophobia 51–2
  Youth Campaign 47, 52, 65–8
Covell, K. 50
culture, respect for 162–3
Cunningham, J. 29–31
curriculum, school 142–57
curriculum development 103–17
curriculum integration 147–50
curriculum triangle 85

Declaration of the Rights of the Child (1924) 16
Declaration of the Rights of Women and Citizens 160
democracy 13–14,96,116–17
  education for 69–86
    multicultural societies 48–51
  ethnic tensions and threat to 53–5
  peace and 158–9
Democracy, Human Rights and Minorities project 46
democratic nation 79–80

democratic schools 80–5, 128
democratic teaching methodologies 134–5
Denmark 66–7
Developing Schools for Democracy in Europe (DSDE) project 81
development 128, 165
dignity 24, 154, 159–61
Directorate of Education, Culture and Sport 40
disabilities, children with 25, 26–7
division of labour 63–4
Domino 65
dress codes 56–7

Ealing, London Borough of 81
education, right to 36–9, 55–8, 162
'Education for Citizenship in a New Europe' project 103–17, 137–8
Education for Democratic Citizenship project 47
Education in Human Rights Network 167–9
education legislation 21–6
enlightenment, democracy and 13–14
Enlightenment Project 2, 11–12
equality 88–90, 159–61
equity 162,165
ERASMUS curriculum development project 103–17,137–8
Eritrea 53
ethic, global 9–11
Ethiopia 53, 61–4
ethnic minorities 49, 55–8
ethnic minority teachers 97–102
ethnic tensions 53–5
Europe 65–8
   concept of 109, 110, 115–16
European citizenship 91–7, 110–11
European Convention on the Exercise of Children's Rights (1996) 19
European Convention on Human Rights and Fundamental Freedoms
   (1953) 5–6, 35–6, 47, 160
European Court of Human Rights 35, 36–9
European Cultural Convention (1954) 35
European Union 6, 103–4
European Youth Centre 46–7
exclusion rates 57–8
expectations 99

experience, personal 135

female circumcision 28–9
France 76–8
  Declaration of the Rights of Man and Citizen (1789) 160
freedom 154, 155
Freeman, M. 21–2
Freinet movement 142–4

Germany 66
global commons 164,165
globalisation 9–11

Habermas, J. 13–14
Hart, R. 32, 33
Hart, S.N. 17–18
'hate crimes' 59–61
heritage, preservation of 165
history teaching 58–9
Howe, R.B. 50
Human Rights Album 43–5
human rights school 26–31

identity 154, 154–5, 162–3
  citizenship education 71–2, 74–5, 76
  teachers'/students' understandings 87–102
inclusion/inclusivity 71, 73–4, 75, 154, 154–5
India 7
information, access to 154, 155–6, 163–4
injustices, redress of 29–31, 163
Institut Coopératif de l'Ecole Moderne (ICEM) 142–3
institutional racism 55–8
intolerance, challenging 48–68
investigation 29–30
Iran 7
Islamic Declarations of Human Rights 8

justice 88–90
  school 29–31, 163

knowledge of human rights 71–2, 74, 75, 76, 90

labelling theory 97–8
labour, division of 63–4
Latvia 54
Law in Education Project 123
Learning to Participate 150–1
legal perspective 28–9, 123–4, 127, 133–4
legislation, education 21–6
Little Red Schoolbook, The 16–17

mentors 100–1
minimalist citizenship education 71, 75, 76–8
minority groups 49, 129
    see also ethnic minorities
moral perspective 28–9, 133–4

National Coalition Building Institute 66
nationalism, right-wing 54–5
networks 167–70
Newell, P. 22–3
non-governmental organizations (NGOs) 43, 59–64, 68
North America 59–61

Offenbach, Germany 66
Office Central de la Coopération à l'Ecole (OCCE) 142–3
ombudsperson for children 21–2

parents 28,49
participation 154,163,165–6
    children's rights 24, 27–8, 32, 33
    citizenship education 71, 73–4, 75
    supportive materials 150–2
Peacemaker Project 66
pedagogic principles 153–6
peer group education 65–8
personal experience 135
personality 25
politics 77–9
post-modernism 11–14
poverty 52–3

Power Points 151–2, 153
privacy 154,156
professional development 118–41
projects 147–50, 152–3, 166–7

Quebec Charter of Human Rights and Freedoms (1982) 160

racism 97–102
  challenging 48–68
refugees 24–5,129–30
René Cassin Institute 43
research 139–40
research workers 42
resolution 30
respect for human rights 25
responsibilities 161
  audit of 164–6
restitution 30–1
Richardson, R. 71
role play 129–30

sanctions 31
Schnapper, D. 79–80
school curriculum 142–57
School as an Instrument of Peace 43
schools 171–2
  democracy in 80–5, 128
  human rights school 26–31
security 154, 161–2, 165
sex education 37–8
Shadow of Hate, The 60–1
Southern Poverty Law Center (SPLC) 59–61
Stand Up NOW for Human Rights video 45–6
Stobart, M. 39–40, 58–9
Stop the Violence movement 66–7
structural racism 55–8
student teachers 87–97
study abroad 91–7
sustainable development 165
Sweden 54–5
symposia 42

talents 25
teachers' seminars 42
teachers' understandings 87–102
Teaching Tolerance project 59–61
tolerance, education for 48–51
traditional practices 28–9
Ty, Reynaldo 126–7

United Kingdom 76–8
  Summer School 120, 130–3
United Nations (UN) 13, 14
  Charter (1945) 2,3,73,119
  Committee on the Rights of the Child 19, 20, 23, 26
  Convention on the Rights of the Child
  (UNCRC) (1989) 18–20, 56, 119, 133–4, 175–80
    implementation 16–33
    pedagogic principles 153–6
    tolerance 49, 50
  Declaration of the Rights of the Child (1959) 16, 119
  Universal Declaration of Human Rights (UDHR) (1948) 2, 3–5, 56,
    119, 133–4, 161, 173–4
United States Declaration of Independence (1776) 159–60
universal standards 1–15
universality 6–9
  denial of 11–14

Vienna Declaration (1993) 8, 65, 139
violence, protection from 24
vision for society 72–3

welfare 165
women's rights 139–40
World Summit for Children 19

xenophobia, challenging 48–68

Young Citizen's Passport 17